Industrial Ecology

Industrial Ecology

Towards Closing the Materials Cycle

Robert U. Ayres

Sandoz Professor of Management and the Environment and Director, Center for the Management of Environmental Resources (CMER), INSEAD, France

and

Leslie W. Ayres

CMER, INSEAD, France

With contributions by:
  Paolo Frankl
  Howard Lee
  Paul M. Weaver
  Nichole Wolfgang

Edward Elgar
Cheltenham, UK • Brookfield, US

Published by
Edward Elgar Publishing Limited
8 Lansdown Place
Cheltenham
Glos GL50 2HU
UK

Edward Elgar Publishing Company
Old Post Road
Brookfield
Vermont 05036
US

British Library Cataloguing in Publication Data
Ayres, Robert U. (Robert Underwood), 1932–
    Industrial ecology : towards closing the materials cycle
    1. Environmental economics   2. Factory and trade waste –
    Environmental aspects
    I. Title
    333.7

Library of Congress Cataloguing in Publication Data
Ayres, Robert U.
    Industrial ecology : towards closing the materials cycle / Robert
    U. Ayres [with] Leslie Ayres.
    Includes bibliographical references
    1. Industrial ecology.   I. Ayres, Leslie, 1933–   . II. Title.
    TS161.A97   1996
    658.7–dc20   96–923
                                                                     CIP

ISBN 1 85898 397 5

Printed in Great Britain at the University Press, Cambridge

Contents

Tables

Figures

Abbreviations

3M	3M Corporation
ABS	acrylonitrile-butadiene-styrene
ACN	acrylonitrile
ALCAN	Aluminum Corporation of Canada
ALCOA	Aluminum Corporation of America
ANRED	name of organization
APC	company name
APME	Association of Plastics Manufacturers
APPEAL	Association Professionelle des Producteurs Européens d'Acier
AR	asphalt rubber
ASNAES	company name
AT&T	American Telegraph & Telephone Company
A/C	airconditioning
BASF	Badische Anilin und Soda Fabrik
BCL	Battelle Columbus Laboratories
BDI	Bundesverband der Deutschen Industrie
BHC	benzene hexachloride
BOF	basic oxygen furnace
BP	British Petroleum Corporation
BTU	British thermal unit
BTX	benzene-toluene-xylene
CAFE	composite average fuel economy
CAR	Continuous Ablative Thermolysis Reactor
CCA	copper-chrome-arsenic
CEFIC	industry association of chemical manufacturers
CEN	Chemical and Engineering News
CEPI	Council of European Packaging Industries
CFC	chlorofluorocarbon
CHC	chlorinated hydrocarbon
CIS	former USSR
CMER	Center for the Management of Environmental Resources
CMR	Chemical Marketing Reporter
CNS	central nervous system

CV	commercial vehicle
CVD	chemical vapor deposition
CZ	Czochralski process
DAL	direct acid leach
DAP	diammonium phosphate
DCE	dichloroethylene
DCP	dichloropropane
DDT	dichloro-diphenyl-trichloroethane
DEHP	di (2 ethyl hexyl) phthalate
DES	diethylsybestrol
DFE	design for environment
DMDS	dimethyl disulfide
DMS	dimethyl sulfide
DNA	deoxyribonucleic acid
DOC	United States Department of Commerce
DOE	United States Department of Energy
DOP	t-dioctyl phthalate
DRI	Data Resources Incorporated
EAF	electric arc furnace
EC	European Commission
EDC	ethylene dichloride
EDF	Electricite de France
EER	Elm Energy and Recycling
EGS	electronic grade silicon
EIAJ	Electronic Industries Association of Japan
EIU	Economist Intelligence Unit
ENECHEM	name of organization
ENEL	name of organization
EOP	end-of-pipe
EPA	United States Environmental Protection Agency
EPRI	Electric Power Research Institute
ESP	electrostatic precipitator
EU	European Union
Eurochlor	European Association of Chlorine Producers
EUROSTAT	Statistical Office of the European Union
FDA	United States Food and Drug Administration
FGD	flue-gas-desulfurization
FZ	float-zone process
GCA	company name
GE	General Electric Company
GM	General Motors Corporation
GNP	gross national product

GW	gigawatts
HCFC	hydrochlorofluorocarbon
HCH	hexachlorocyclohexane
HDPE	high density polyethylene
HFC	hydrofluorocarbon
HMDA	hexamethylene diamine
HMDS	hexamethyldisilane
IBA	International Bauxite Association
IBM	International Business Machines Corporation
IC	integrated circuit
ICRI	Industrial Chemistry Research Institute (Warsaw)
IDEA	International Database for Ecoprofile Analysis
IE	industrial ecology
IEA	International Energy Agency
IIASA	International Institute for Applied Systems Analysis
INSEAD	European Institute of Business Administration
ISIC	international standard industrial classification
ITC	United States International Trade Commission
ITT	company name
J	joule
KIST	Korean Institute of Science and Technology
kMT	thousand metric tons
kWh	kilowatt hour
LDPE	low density polyethylene
LES\ETH	Laboratory for Energy Systems, Swiss Federal Institute of Technology
LGA	Landesgewerbenanstalt Bayern
LLDPE	low low density polyethylene
LRL	low-rolling-resistance
LTV	Ling Temco Voight
MAP	mono-ammonium phosphate
MDI	methylene di-isocyanate
MGS	metallurgical grade silicon
MIT	Massachusetts Institute of Technology
MITI	Ministry of International Trade and Industry (Japan)
MMBTU	million British thermal units
MMT	million metric tons
MOS	metal oxide silicon
MRI	Midwest Research Institute
MT	metric tons
MTBE	methyl-tert-butyl ether
MW	megawatts

MWh	megawatt hour
NAE	United States National Academy of Engineering
NAS	United States National Academy of Sciences
NCR	National Cash Register Corporation
NDC	Noyes Data Corporation
Ng/J	grams of nitrogen per joule
nicad	nickel-cadmium
NMAB	National Materials Advisory Board
OE	original equipment
OECD	Organization for Economic Cooperation and Development
OEM	original equipment manufacturer
OPEC	Organization of Petroleum Exporting Countries
PAH	polyaromatic hydrocarbon
PAN	peroxy-acyl nitrate
PBT	poly-butylene terephthalate
PC	personal computer
PC	passenger car
PCA	polycarboxylates
PCB	polychlorinated biphenyl
PCDD	polychlorinated dioxin
PCDF	polychlorinated dibenzyl furans
PDAL	pressure digestion-acid leach
PET	polyethylene terephthalate
PG	phospho-gypsum
PP	polypropylene
PPP	pollution prevention pays
PREGYPAN	process
PROSYNCHEM	company name
PS	polystyrene
PV	photovoltaic
PVC	polyvinyl chloride
PWMI	European Center for Plastics in the Environment
PYGAS	pyrolysis gas
PYREG	pyrolysis of recycled gas streams
RCA	Radio Corporation of America
RCRA	'superfund'
RDF	refuse-derived fuel
RE	replacement equipment
RMA	United Kingdom Retread Manufacturers Association
RUMAC	rubber modified asphalt concrete
R&D	research and development
SAN	styrene-acrylonitrile

SERI	Solar Energy Research Institute
SESSI	Service des Statistiques Industrielles
SGS	solar grade silicon
SIA	Semiconductor Industries Association
SIC	Standard Industrial Classification
SLI	starting-lighting-ignition
SNG	synthetic natural gas
SRF	solvent refined coal
SRI	Stanford Research Institute
STPP	sodium tripolyphosphate
SX-EW	solvent extraction-electro-winning
TBA	tert-butyl alcohol
TCA	1,1,1-trichloroethane
TCE	trichloroethylene
TCPP	tricresyl phosphate
TCS	trichlorosilane
TDI	toluene di-isocyanate
TECNON	company name
TEL	tetraethyl lead
TFE	tetrafluoroethylene
Tg	teragrams
TNO	technical institute in the Netherlands
tonne	metric ton
TRI	Toxic Release Inventory
TRW	Thomson Ramo Woolrich Corporation
TVA	Tennessee Valley Authority
UBA	name of organization
UF	urea-formaldehyde
UK	United Kingdom
UKRMA	United Kingdom Retread Manufacturers Association
UN	United Nations
UNCTAD	United Nations Commission on Trade and Development
UNSO	United Nations Statistical Office
US	United States
USBM	United States Bureau of Mines
USDA	United States Department of Agriculture
USDOC	United States Department of Commerce
USDOE	United States Department of Energy
USEPA	United States Environmental Protection Agency
USFDA	United States Food and Drug Administration
USITC	United States International Trade Commission
USNAE	United States National Academy of Engineering

USNAS	United States National Academy of Sciences
USSR	Union of Soviet Socialist Republics
UV	ultraviolet
VAT	value added tax
VCM	vinyl chloride monomer
VP	vice president
WEC	World Energy Council
WHO	World Health Organization
WRAP	waste reduction always pays
WRI	World Resources Institute
y	year
yr	year

Acknowledgements

The present book evolved mainly from a study carried out by the Center for Management of Environmental Resources at INSEAD for the European Commission DG XII, Science Research and Development, Directorate C, Industrial and Materials Technologies (Ayres *et al.* 1995). The original title was 'Material Cycle Optimization in the Production of Major Finished Materials'. The study was intended to identify possibilities for reducing material wastes and losses at all stages of the materials life cycle, with special emphasis on identifying research priorities. To make the conclusions and recommendations concrete, the study analyzed 12 specific groups of non-energy materials, including metals (aluminum and gallium; copper, cobalt, arsenic and silver; chromium; zinc and cadmium), chemicals (sulfur-based; phosphates, fluorine and gypsum; nitrogen-based; chlorine-based), finished materials (electronic grade silicon for semiconductors) and several types of wastes (plastic packaging, scrap tires and coal ash). We also noted a variety of interlinkages including input, output, co-product and byproduct relationships. These materials were chosen to illustrate a variety of different engineering/ technological possibilities and approaches.

We are grateful for the support and encouragement of Lellis Braganza, our project officer in DG XII, who urged us to revise the original manuscript into a form suitable for publication and circulation to a wider audience. While the EU supported the greater part of the work and encouraged us to seek publication in book form, it is not responsible for any errors, nor does it necessarily endorse any of the conclusions or policy recommendations. Similarly, we are grateful to the Center for Management of Environmental Resources at INSEAD, for providing the balance of the financial support. However, the conclusions and recommendations are strictly our own.

Additionally, many of the chapters owe a debt to prior studies co-authored by ourselves and several others:

Chapters 4, 5 and 6: Some material in these chapters was adapted from *An Historical Reconstruction of Major Pollutant Levels in the Hudson–Raritan Basin 1800–1980* (Ayres *et al.* 1988).

Chapter 7: Some of the material in these chapters has appeared previously in a 1988 summer study performed at IIASA, *Industrial Metabolism, the*

Environment, and Application of Materials-Balance Principles for Selected Chemicals (Ayres *et al.* 1989) and in *Industrial Metabolism of Sulfur* (Ayres and Norberg-Bohm 1993).

Chapter 9: This chapter was based in part on earlier work by the authors (Ayres *et al.* 1988), and expanded in the course of a 1988 summer study at IIASA (Ayres *et al.* 1989); the latter was updated again in a working paper *Industrial Metabolism of Nitrogen* by the authors together with V. Norberg-Bohm (then at Harvard, now at MIT) (Ayres *et al.* 1993). The global nitrogen disequilibrium problem was first discussed in a 1992 working paper 'Industrial Metabolism and the Grand Nutrient Cycles' by R.U. Ayres, based on a presentation at a summer workshop of the Global Change Institute, Snowmass, Colorado, August 1992. The latter, in turn, led to a collaborative paper 'Industrial Metabolism and the Grand Nutrient Cycles' with R. Socolow and W. Schlesinger, in Socolow *et al.* (eds), *Industrial Ecology and Global Change*, Cambridge University Press (Ayres *et al.* 1994).

Chapter 13: We acknowledge with thanks an earlier student paper (cited several times in the text), based on work by Yves Guelorget and Veronica Jullien, who were then students at the Ecole des Mines, Fontainebleau, masters degree program in environmental management. Their original paper was done for credit as part of their course work. It was subsequently extended and modified in some ways by Paul Weaver of CMER and published jointly with them as a CMER Working Paper, under the title *A Life Cycle Analysis of Automobile Tires in France* (Guelorget *et al.* 1993). The present chapter borrows significantly from that work, though it focuses much more on the recycling issue. Paul Weaver was the primary author. It has been edited for inclusion and further material has been added by RUA.

Chapter 14: We note that some of the material in this chapter has been published previously by us; in particular, we refer to R.U. Ayres, *Coalplex: An Integrated Energy/Resources System Concept*, UNEP Seminar on Environmental Aspects of Technology Assessment, United Nations Organization, Geneva, November/December 1982 (Ayres 1982). Also, R.U. Ayres, *Transboundary Air Pollution: An Opportunity for Innovation*, RAND–EAC Conference 'The Law of the Atmosphere', Delft, Netherlands, May 24–26, 1993 and R.U. Ayres *Industrial Metabolic Systems Integration: The Black Triangle* in 'Sustainability — Where Do We Stand?' International Symposium, Graz, Austria, July 13–14, 1993 (Ayres 1993 and 1993a).

Chapter 15: This chapter is substantially based on a journal article, to appear in *International Journal of Technology Management*. The material was not part of the original EU study.

There are many individuals who have reviewed parts of the manuscript and/or provided data. We thank them for their efforts and emphasize that they are not responsible for any remaining errors or misunderstandings on our part, nor do they necessarily agree with our views. A partial list includes:

Chapter 3: D.A. Kramer and E.D. Sehnke of the Bureau of Mines, US Department of Interior, Washington DC, Prof. D. Altenpohl, formerly VP Technology, Alusuisse, Zurich, Dr. Noel Jarrett, former Director of Smelting Research, ALCOA Technical Center, New Kensington, PA. and Prof. John E. Tilton of the Colorado School of Mines.

Chapter 4: D.L. Edelstein and an anonymous reviewer of the US Bureau of Mines, and Prof. John E. Tilton of the Colorado School of Mines. We received substantial data on arsenic flows in Europe from Stefan Anderberg of IIASA, Laxenburg, Austria.

Chapter 5: Donald Rogich, Director, Office of Mineral Commodities and, especially, John F. Papp, chromium specialist, Bureau of Mines, US Department of Interior, Washington DC and Prof. John E. Tilton of the Colorado School of Mines. We received substantial data on cadmium flows in Europe from Stefan Anderberg of IIASA, Laxenburg, Austria.

Chapter 7: Michael Chadwick and Paul Raskin of the Stockholm Environment Institute.

Chapter 8: David E. Morse, Tom Llewellyn and A. Michael Miller of the US Bureau of Mines provided recent data and cleared up several misconceptions on our part. Philippe Pichat, formerly of ADT, Paris, provided us with important information with regard to current and possible uses of phosphogypsum.

Chapter 10: Donald Rogich, Director, Office of Mineral Commodities and, especially, Dennis Kostick, commodity specialist for salt, Bureau of Mines, US Department of the Interior, Washington D.C. Philippe Feron, Executive Director of Eurochlor also reviewed the chapter and provided us with helpful comments.

Chapter 11: Paolo Frankl, PhD student at the University of Rome, Italy, Howard Lee, PhD, MBA student at INSEAD, Nichole Wolfgang, undergraduate student, Chemical Engineering, Drexel Institute of Technology, Philadelphia, Pennsylvania, US and summer intern at INSEAD.

Chapter 12: Vince Matthews of the European Centre for Plastics in the Environment (PWMI) in Brussels, Fritz Mauerhofer, President of MBT in Zurich, and Robert Williams of the Center for Energy and Environment at Princeton University.

Chapter 14: Noel Jarrett, ALCOA Research Center.

1. Introduction: materials perspective

1.1. BACKGROUND

As a point of departure, we note that every substance extracted from the earth's crust, or harvested from a forest, a fishery or from agriculture, is a potential waste. Not only is it a potential waste, it soon becomes an actual waste in almost all cases, with a delay of a few weeks to a few years at most. The only exceptions worth mentioning are long-lived construction materials. In other words, materials consumed by the industrial economic system do not physically disappear. They are merely transformed to less useful forms.[1] In some cases (as with fuels) they are considerably transformed by combination with atmospheric oxygen. In other cases (such as solvents and packaging materials) they are discarded in more or less the same form as they are used. It follows from this simple relationship between inputs and outputs — a consequence of the law of conservation of mass — that economic growth tends to be accompanied by equivalent growth in waste generation and pollution.

Although quantitatively much of the pollution of our environment consists of combustion products from the use of fossil fuels, fossil fuels, as such, are not considered in this book inasmuch as there is no realistic potential for utilizing those combustion products (mainly CO_2) productively in the economic system. We do, however, consider possibilities for utilizing sulfur and ash (Chapters 7 and 14, respectively).

Apart from fossil fuels, however, enormous quantities of minerals and metal ores are extracted from the earth's crust. Table 1.1 shows world consumption of concentrated (or selected) metal ores and metals.[2] The rate of extraction is increasing rapidly (Figure 1.1).

Annual production (i.e., extraction) of metals in the US is more than 1.5 tonnes per capita (down from a maximum of close to 2 tonnes in the early 1970s. However, the decline merely reflects the fact that the US is increasingly dependent on imported ores or metals. Allowing for ores processed elsewhere, the real US *consumption* level is now more than 2.5 tonnes per capita. Consumption levels in Europe cannot be much less, though figures are harder to find.

Each tonne of refined metal involves the removal and processing of at least 4 tonnes of ore (in the case of aluminum) and up to several thousand tonnes

Table 1.1:   *World production of metal ores 1988 (kMT)*

	Gross weight of ore kMT	Metal content %	Net weight of metal kMT	Mine and mill waste kMT
Aluminum	97 660	37.3	36 400	61 220
Chromium	14 000	32.5	4 207	10 000
Copper	>1 750 000[a]	0.5	8 450	>1 740 000
Gold (1979)	170 000	<0.001	1.19	170 000
Iron	953 000	59.0	564 400	390 000
Lead	101 000[b]	3.33	3 380	98 000
Manganese	30 500	28.0	8 540	22 000
Nickel	80 000[c]	1.0	835	79 000
Platinum group (1979)	30 000	<0.001	0.20	30 000
Uranium (1978)	1 900 000	0.002[d]	36	1 900 000
Zinc	220 000[b]	3.22	7 115	213 000

Notes:
a. Extrapolated from US data for 1978 (0.5% grade ore). For surface mines overburden averages 2.5 tons per ton of ore in addition.
b. Total, including overburden, extrapolated from US data.
c. Based on US Bureau of Mines estimates of the average grade of known reserves. Sulfide ores currently being mined are richer, however.
d. Based on Barney 1980.

Source: UN *Industrial Statistics Yearbook.*

of gangue and overburden, in the case of uranium, platinum group metals or gold. These figures rise over time as the best grades of ore are used first. Thus, other factors remaining equal, energy consumption and costs of exploration, extraction and beneficiation *per unit* would tend to rise over time. Only technological progress could compensate for this trend. The fact that resource prices have, on average, declined over many decades is regarded by resource economists as a strong indication of the power of technology — called forth by free markets — to keep resource scarcity at bay.[3] It must be said that the neo-Malthusian worries about resource scarcity do not appear to be a near-term threat to economic growth, as has been suggested at times in the past.

Other threats are more immediate. The mining, beneficiation and smelting of metal ores is inherently dirty. Even though modern technology permits the capture of most toxic waste pollutants from the process, these materials must still be disposed of somehow. A number of very toxic metals are byproducts of copper, zinc and lead, for instance. These include arsenic, bismuth, cadmium,

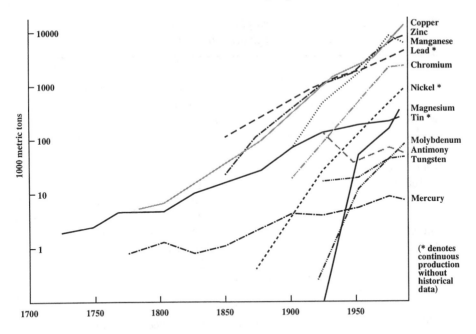

1000 metric tons

Copper
Zinc
Manganese
Lead *

Chromium

Nickel *

Magnesium
Tin *

Molybdenum
Antimony
Tungsten

Mercury

(* denotes continuous production without historical data)

Data Source: Pacyna 1986.

Figure 1.1: *Annual worldwide production of selected metals, 1700–1983*

cobalt, selenium, silver, tellurium and thallium. While many of these metals are recovered for use in other commercial products, the products in question — from pesticides, herbicides, fungicides and wood preservatives to pigments and batteries — are almost entirely dissipated or discarded after use. (Toxic heavy metals are also dispersed into the environment via coal ash, which contains significant quantities of them.) Tables 1.2 and 1.3 show air and water emissions data for a number of heavy metals, in comparison with natural rates of mobilization. While the data are incomplete, it seems clear that anthropogenic sources — at least in Europe — already far exceed natural sources.

It is evident, however, that current levels of emissions are not the whole story. Large quantities of toxic substances, including chlorinated organic compounds and heavy metals have accumulated in the human environment, the so-called *anthroposphere*. They are dispersed in painted surfaces, under old factory sites, under and adjacent to highways and airports sitting on materials dredged from rivers and harbors, in old (and new) landfill sites, in streambeds, sediments deposited in river deltas, and — most worrisome — in ground water and in topsoil that has been enriched by phosphates or dried sewage sludge. Many of these substances are currently in chemically

Table 1.2:   *Land-based and atmospheric contributions to heavy metals in the waters of the North Sea, circa 1984*

Metal	Land based MT/day	Atmospheric MT/day	Relative contribution (land to atmosphere)
Arsenic	2.20	0.63	3.5
Cadmium	0.68	1.56	0.4
Chromium	18.30	1.83	10.0
Copper	12.90	10.80	1.2
Lead	17.90	8.00	2.2
Mercury	0.18	0.14	1.3
Nickel	11.10	4.30	2.6
Zinc	86.30	19.20	4.5

Source: Pacyna 1986.

Table 1.3:   *Estimated annual global emissions of selected metals to the atmosphere, circa 1980*

Metal	Human activity kMT	Natural activity kMT	Ratio: human to natural
Lead	2000	6	333
Zinc	840	36	23
Copper	260	19	14
Vanadium	210	65	3
Nickel	98	28	4
Chromium	94	58	2
Arsenic	78	21	4
Antimony	38	1	38
Selenium	14	3	5
Cadmium	6	0.3	20

Source: Galloway *et al.* 1982.

immobile and therefore temporarily harmless forms. But increasing environmental acidification (caused by fossil fuel combustion) may mobilize some of these toxic substances in the future.

For this, among other reasons, it is important to begin to close the materials cycles.

1.2. POLLUTION CONTROL

Pollution was actually recognized as a serious problem long ago. Even 'pollution prevention' has a long history. An English monarch attempted to reduce the smoky fog of London by prohibiting the use of coal as a household fuel, as early as the 16th century. (An interesting but impractical 19th-century proposal to reduce urban smoke pollution was to discharge smoke into the sewers rather than into the atmosphere.[4]) However, the initial societal response to problems of pollution has generally been an attempt to redirect or sequester the waste, not to reduce their quantities or transform them into useful substances. This strategy for pollution control has come to be known as 'end-of-pipe' (EOP) treatment.

Incineration of wastes was probably the first example of EOP treatment. Primary sewage treatment (by controlled bacterial action), and the use of filters (bag-houses) and cyclone-type centrifugal separators were early examples. Electrostatic precipitators (ESPs) were introduced — initially for copper smelters, later for electric power plants, steel mills and other metallurgical plants, and incinerators — early this century. The Claus process for removing sulfur from natural gas and refinery gases was also an early success. Other important, more recent examples of end-of-pipe treatment include secondary and tertiary sewage treatment (now being applied to industrial wastewaters as well as municipal sewage), catalytic convertors for motor vehicles and flue-gas desulfurization (FGD). It is fair to say that most expenditure on environmental controls, up to now, has been in this category.[5] Sequestration and disposal of wastes in 'safe' disposal sites is also a kind of EOP treatment. This is the normal route for municipal solid wastes, ashes, FGD sludge, toxic chemicals, radioactive wastes and contaminated soils.

Another basic environmental control strategy is to 'clean up' after a pollution episode that has already occurred. This approach is now termed *remediation*. It applies mainly to toxic waste dumps. In the former case, the idea is to dig up the old wastes — such as leaking drums of toxic chemicals — and re-bury them in safer landfills.

However, none of the traditional approaches to pollution control actually reduces or eliminates the wastes. These approaches attempt to shift the wastes from a place where they can do harm to a place where they are less likely to do so. In some cases they are converted from a dangerously harmful form to a less potentially harmful form or location. Indeed, regulation medium by medium has, in some cases, encouraged the recovery and treatment of wastes from one medium, only to find them reappearing in another. For instance, the burning of solid wastes may generate air pollution. Air pollutants, especially particulates and oxides of nitrogen and sulfur can be (re)deposited on land via rainfall, only to be carried into rivers and streams via surface runoff. Landfills may also leach toxic substances into the ground water. In some cases, these intermedia transfers can generate multiple control costs (for instance, water treatment costs downstream from effluent outfalls) without ever really eliminating the basic problem.

Actually, in many of the foregoing examples of pollution control (except sewage treatment and incineration), the physical quantity of waste materials is not reduced by EOP treatment. Indeed, in several cases (such as FGD and radioactive waste) the volume of the ultimate waste to be disposed of is significantly increased. The only possible way out of this mess (!) is to find ways of using materials more efficiently in the first place i.e. getting more functional 'bang for the buck'.

In this book we adopt two perspectives. The first is the engineering/technological perspective, as exemplified by industrial ecology (IE) and discussed in this chapter. The major focus of IE is to identify opportunities for reducing wastes and pollution in the materials-intensive sectors by exploiting opportunities for using the low-value byproducts (i.e. wastes) of certain processes as raw materials for others. Technical feasibility is the primary criterion for initial consideration.

The IE strategy is also closely related to a number of other currently popular approaches to pollution control, like 'delinking', 'decoupling', 'dematerialization', 'pollution prevention', 'clean technology', 'design for environment (DFE)' and 'eco-efficiency'. This is not the place to describe the differences and similarities between/among them. Suffice it to say that there is a good deal of overlap, but that some of the differences in approach are significant. In particular, there is an emerging controversy with regard to whether IE is (or is not) an impediment to the achievement of truly 'clean technology'. The argument is that to develop profitable markets for wastes could actually result in higher production, and might reduce incentives for discovering and implementing processes generating no wastes at all. One major conclusion of our study is that among the 12 families of materials considered, there are virtually no cases where this problem could plausibly arise.

A complementary perspective is that of resource and environmental economics. Economics is sometimes characterized as the discipline concerned with production and allocation of useful goods and services from 'scarce' resources. To most economists, by long tradition and habit, capital and labor are the only scarce resources usually considered. As noted previously, resource economists have satisfied themselves that, despite growing consumption, scarcity is not yet a serious problem for most extractive mineral and fuel resources *per se*. This is because declining prices, over a period of decades, indicate that technological progress has (more than) kept pace with rising demand, up to now.

But land, fresh water, clean air, benign climate, ecological balance and many — if not all — renewable natural resource flows (e.g. agricultural products, meat, dairy products, fish, wood) can also be characterized as scarce. In some of these cases there are no markets at all, so that market prices do not exist, but in all cases evidence of approaching scarcity are unmistakeable. In some cases — notably clean air, topsoil, ground water, and biodiversity — a significant cause of deterioration is pollution from industrial processes and dissipative consumption of toxic substances. But these resources also provide essential services to man. It is appropriate for economists to consider how the productivity of *all* resources, including environmental resources, can be increased. The problem is becoming urgent.

Thus, another important objective of our study is to identify and analyze current and potential opportunities for increasing resource productivity by using economic and regulatory policy levers e.g. using tax strategies and/or exchangeable permits to change the relative prices of factors of production. The purpose of this would be to induce absolute demand reduction or use substitution and/or to induce emissions reduction by inducing process change, source substitution, re-use and recycling. There are many interesting avenues to pursue, including the broader systems aspects of the problem. However, it is the specific industrial implications, for specific classes of materials, that we want to discuss hereafter.

1.3. STRATEGIES TO INCREASE RESOURCE PRODUCTIVITY

In brief, there are three elements to the long-term materials productivity program. The first is to reduce, and eventually eliminate, inherently dissipative uses of non-biodegradable materials, especially toxic ones (like heavy metals). This involves process change and what has come to be known as 'pollution prevention' via 'clean technology'. The second is to design products for easier disassembly and re-use, and for reduced environmental impact, known as 'design for environment' or DFE. The third is to develop much more efficient technologies for recycling consumption waste materials, so as to eliminate the need to extract 'virgin' materials that only make the problems worse in time.

It is not really necessary to describe in detail how this can be accomplished. It is sufficient to know that it is technically and economically feasible.

(It remains, still, for policy makers to create the appropriate incentives to harness market forces. But this is a separate topic.) Of course, specific 'scenarios' might be helpful in making such a conclusion more credible to doubters. However, this would serve a communications purpose rather than an analytic one.

Returning to the specifics, we note four basic strategies for raising the productivity of material resources. These four generic strategies are:

1. *'Dematerialization'*   More efficient use of a given material for a given function.
2. *Substitution of a scarce or hazardous material by another material*   Again, either technology or policy can drive such a shift.
3. *Repair, re-use, remanufacturing and recycling*   For convenience we refer to this simply as the 'recycling' strategy. Obviously all of these variants tend to reduce the need for virgin materials, and (indirectly) all of the environmental damage and energy consumption associated with the extraction and processing of virgin materials, *including their toxic byproducts.* Aluminum cans, stainless steel automotive components, copper wire and galvanized iron/steel are particularly good examples of candidates for more recycling. Arsenic and cadmium exemplify toxic byproducts that could be reduced thereby.
4. *Waste mining*   Utilization of waste streams from (currently) unreplaceable resources as alternative sources of other needed materials. This strategy simultaneously reducing (i) the environmental damage due to the primary waste stream, (ii) the rate of exhaustion of the second resource, and (iii) the environmental damage due to mining the second resource.

All of the above strategies can be *technology (and economics) driven* or *policy driven*. They are summarized, with examples, in the following 4×2 matrix.

1A *Dematerialization, technology driven* Example: microminiaturization in the electronics industry.	1B *Dematerialization, policy driven* Example: imposition of Composite Average Fuel Economy (CAFE) standards for automobiles in the 1970s (US) led to significant reductions in vehicle weight.
2A *Material substitution, technology driven* Examples: substitution of PVC for cast iron or copper water/sewer	2B *Material substitution, policy driven* Examples: ban on CFCs leading to replacement by HCFCs or HFCs in air

pipe in buildings; substitution of optical fibers (glass) for copper wire for point-to-point telecommunications.

conditioners and refrigerators; ban on tetraethyl lead (TEL) leading to substitution by aromatics and alcohols (e.g. MTBE) as octane enhancers in gasoline.

3A *Recycling, technology driven* Examples: recycling of lead from starting–lighting–ignition (SLI) batteries used in motor vehicles; recovery of catalysts from catalytic convertors.

3B *Recycling, policy driven* Mandatory minimum levels of recycled pulp in paper products, e.g. in Germany; recycling of aluminum cans, Sweden; recovery of mercury from fluorescent lights, Sweden.

4A *Waste 'Mining', technology driven* Flue-gas desulfurization (FGD) for oil and gas refineries with recovery of elemental sulfur; recovery of fluosilicic acid from phosphate rock processing wastes in the US.

4B *Waste 'mining', policy driven* Enforcement of FGD in non-ferrous metal smelters, with recovery of sulfuric acid; enforcement of FGD for electric power plants, with recovery of lime/limestone scrubber waste for use in wallboard production, Denmark.

1.4. THE DEMATERIALIZATION STRATEGY

The classical example of 'dematerialization' is, of course, the electronics industry. Functionality per unit mass has increased spectacularly from the days of vacuum tubes. The transistor performed the same (switching) function as a single vacuum with a tiny fraction of the mass. The integrated circuit continued the trend. The earliest electronic computer (ENIAC at the University of Pennsylvania) filled several rooms. A tiny pocket calculator (already mass produced two decades ago) performed the same functions. Every decade we see similar reductions in mass and increases in performance. Government intervention was not needed to bring this about. On the contrary, the primary driving force seems to have been a 'virtuous circle' of relationships: higher switching speed requires smaller circuit elements, which can be packed more tightly into a given space. Smaller circuit elements dissipate less heat and require less power to operate. Smaller size is cheaper to make. Lower prices encourage more complex designs using more and faster circuit elements, and so on.

Copper wire in power transmission and communication offers a less well-known example. The mass of wire needed to transmit a given amount of electrical energy was repeatedly reduced by raising the transmission voltage. (This was done mainly to cut transmission losses, incidently.) Currently, transmission lines of 600 000 volts, and higher, are routine.

Similarly, the early telegraph and telephone lines used simple twisted copper wires. But increased demand for telephone services forced greater efficiencies in the use of wire. Coaxial cables were the next step in this evolutionary trend towards continuously increasing the number of messages that could be transmitted per unit mass of copper. More recently microwave transmission lines, satellite and optical fibers have continued the trend towards more messages using less mass. Again, government intervention was not needed in this case.

The high price of silver has induced significant progress in the chemistry of photography (film manufacture and developing). This has made it possible to reduce the silver content of a roll of film very significantly in recent decades. (It has also encouraged recycling.)

There are no substitutes for sulfur, phosphorus and nitrogen in agricultural fertilizers. On the contrary, these uses will inevitably grow. Thus, it is important to find ways of utilizing these nutrient elements more efficiently, both to conserve on energy and to minimize disruption of the nutrient cycles. Non-fertilizer uses of phosphates and nitrates (e.g. explosives), particularly, should be minimized for the same reason.

However, in the case of chlorine and its compounds, it is essential to minimize losses to the environment to minimize potential threats to human health, especially from chlorinated organics that may be 'estrogen-like'. The use of chlorinated solvents should be minimized for this reason, and also because of threats to the ozone layer. It is not clear, however, to what extent it may be possible to increase chlorine-use efficiency (i.e. reduce losses) as opposed to finding substitutes.

In the case of tires, the steel-belted radial tire has extended tire life and correspondingly reduced material use. This development, led by Pirelli and Michelin, was technology driven. Further extensions of tire life appear to be technically feasible, but this will probably not occur without government intervention. Incidentally, a strictly enforced speed limit would be a very effective means of extending tire life (and reducing fuel consumption, not to mention accidents), all other factors remaining equal.

The packaging sector contains several examples of dematerialization. For instance, there has been a steady reduction in tin requirements for tinplate (thus keeping tinplate competitive with aluminum) by improving tinplate technology to reduce the thickness of tinplate. A parallel example arises in the case of aluminum cans, which have also been 'dematerialized' significantly by improvements in aluminum rolling and forming technology that permit much thinner aluminum cans than was formerly the case. The same trend has also occurred with respect to plastic bottles, with improvements in forming and other innovations (e.g. multilayering) combining to reduce the weight of material in a typical plastic bottle. To be sure, there is no dematerialization in this last case, unless the plastic bottle is re-used or recycled as often as the glass one. (This is normally the case, but it is possible, at least for PVC and PET.) The proliferation of packaging waste does not appear at first glance to be a case of dematerialization (quite the contrary), but to some extent dematerialization has occurred within the sector. For instance, the use of light polyethylene bags and bottles for milk in place of much heavier glass bottles can be regarded as dematerialization as well as substitution.

1.5.   THE MATERIAL SUBSTITUTION STRATEGY

Aluminum has found many new uses in recent decades, resulting in increased demand for the metal. The most obvious case in point is the substitution of aluminum cans for tinplated steel cans and glass bottles. Aluminum has displaced wood for window frames, which are now almost entirely prefabricated, although PVC is now a major competitor in this application. Aluminum has largely replaced copper and galvanized iron sheet for roofing and siding purposes, and to some extent for exterior drainpipes. (PVC is also a strong competitor in this market.) It has captured at least part of the market for brass 'hardware' fixtures such as doorknobs, hinges and handles. Also, in many cases aluminum, now cheaper than copper, has replaced copper for some kinds of electrical wiring, especially for high-power transmission purposes.

Copper has already lost many of its former markets, and others are being eroded. For instance, copper roofing is no longer used, and copper pipe is being replaced in many cases by PVC. Similarly, copper wire for telephone lines is now being replaced by optical fibers, while some transmission lines have switched to aluminum. Brass is being challenged for many applications, by aluminum as well as plastic, although it is not likely to be replaced completely. Copper chemicals have lost some markets, though copper sulfate continues to be widely used in viniculture, while copper remains important — with arsenic — as a component of copper–chrome–arsenic (CCA) wood preservative chemicals. In fact, this is now the biggest single use of arsenic. Yet the Japanese have found satisfactory substitutes for CCA, which may well be adopted elsewhere. Arsenic has already been replaced (by synthetic organic chemicals) in most of its former pesticide and herbicide applications.

Chromium remains irreplaceable in its major markets, which are corrosion-resistant (stainless) steel, heat-resistant steel alloys, and corrosion-resistant plating and coatings. Markets for high-temperature superalloys also continue to grow, though there is potential competition from ceramics for such applications as turbines and jet engines, if the manufacturing problems can be solved. Nevertheless, other applications of chromium, and chromium chemicals, are substitutable. In particular, alternatives to the use of chromium sulfate in leather tanning are already available and their use should be encouraged.

Zinc's major use is for galvanizing steel, especially in automobile and truck frames and bodies. This practice greatly increases corrosion resistance and has probably extended vehicle life by one or two years — with significant savings in terms of other resources consumed. On the other hand, galvanized iron sheet (e.g. for roofing) has been replaced by aluminum. Zinc castings for the auto industry are gradually being displaced by engineering plastics. There is no obvious substitute for zinc oxide used in the tire industry, or for zinc in batteries.

Metal-based pigments (cadmium, chromium, lead, zinc) have been partly replaced by organic pigments, largely because of concern about toxicity. This trend has proceeded further in the US than in Europe.

Organo-chlorine compounds are increasingly regarded as environmental risks, for several different reasons. Yet no serious attempt has yet been made to ascertain the extent to which alternatives may exist to the use of chlorinated compounds. In fact, substitutions have tended to be in the other direction. For example, PVC has replaced copper pipe in many cases; it has also replaced cast iron pipes. PVC is widely used in France for bottled water (in place of glass). Metal-based pesticides, fungicides and herbicides have also largely been replaced by organic chemicals. At first the substitutes were primarily chlorinated compounds, but as a result of restrictions on persistent chlorinated pesticides (DDT, chlordane, toxaphene, benzene hexachloride, pentachlorophenol, etc.), these have since been replaced by a variety of other more toxic but less persistent types. Similarly, the use of polychlorinated biphenyls (PCBs) as transformer fluids (and some other uses) was stopped almost overnight without major disruption, though the substitutes in some cases are also chlorinated compounds such as benzene trichloride. More recently, the phase-out of chlorine use as a bleach for paper pulp in Europe was accomplished (voluntarily) in less than a decade. The agreed phase-out of CFCs under the Montreal Protocol in favor of HCFCs and HFCs also appears to be on schedule.

In most of these cases, substitutes of comparable effectiveness were found without great difficulty, once the necessity was recognized. Indeed, it could be argued that bans of this sort have been quite useful in stimulating innovation in otherwise mature sectors. Nevertheless, a complete ban on chlorine (as proposed by some environmental organizations) would adversely affect a large number of industries and processes for which straightforward substitutes may not be found easily — or may not even be possible.

Substitution of light materials for heavier ones is especially important in transportation applications, because unnecessary weight imposes severe penalties in terms of fuel consumption. Thus aluminum cans have displaced steel cans and glass bottles, to a large extent, to reduce weight. Similarly, lightweight plastic packaging materials such as polyethylene bags or PET bottles have displaced glass bottles in some cases (e.g. for milk) and paperboard in others. Polystyrene foam has replaced papier maché in many cases for the same reason.

1.6. THE RECYCLING STRATEGY

Recycling is an approach to waste reduction that has been strongly advocated by many environmentalists, although both the economics and the environmental benefits are unclear in many cases. Of course, scrap metals have been collected and recycled since ancient times, but not for pollution-control purposes. The same is true of glass, and to a lesser extent, of tires and paper. In recent times the idea of recycling has been applied more systematically to aluminum beverage cans, paper and some packaging materials. In the case of paper, recycling has been promoted in Europe by legislative mandate. However, recycling also entails waste and pollution and it is not always clear whether recycling actually reduces waste and pollution (as compared, say, to controlled incineration) or increases them. Indeed, life-cycle analyses have suggested that in some cases (e.g. packaging materials) incineration with energy recovery is often environmentally preferable to recycling.

It is not easy to point to a long-term trend in regard to recycling/re-use. Indeed, the increasing complexity of both materials and products has made recycling and re-use more difficult in many cases. For instance, old wool clothes were once routinely collected by rag-merchants and recycled (after a complicated process of washing, unpicking, bleaching, respinning, reweaving and redyeing) into blankets and pea-coats. Today, because of the prevalence of blends of natural and synthetic fibers, recycling of textiles is almost impossible. Much the same problem occurs in many other cases, for instance multilayer packaging (e.g. Tetrapak®). To increase re-use and recycling, it may be necessary to induce manufacturers to sell services, rather than products, and/or to take back products they have previously made.

More recently the idea of recycling has been further refined to distinguish several intermediate stages, e.g.

- *Re-use* of a discarded product, as such, but in a less demanding application. For instance, discarded railroad ties have been extensively re-used as garden walls and stairs. Old bricks, tiles and cobblestones can be re-used. Similarly, some obsolete computer chips have been re-used in electronic games.
- *Repair* of a discarded product, for subsequent re-use. Old clothes and furniture, as well as automobiles, are often repaired to allow further use. (Unfortunately, modern technology and sophisticated composite materials often makes repair more difficult than it was in the past, although products may last longer without repair.)
- *Remanufacture* of a discarded product (such as a pump, engine or tire), replacing worn parts such as bearings, gaskets, piston rings or wearing surfaces but retaining structural components that retain their integrity. The remanufacturing option is gaining in popularity, since it offers a means of upgrading certain components (e.g. of computers, telecommunications equipment or copying machines) without discarding the whole unit.

Re-use, repair and remanufacturing avoid many of the problems of recycling, although re-use and repair are probably declining, partly because products are becoming more complex (making repair difficult), partly because manufacturers would prefer to sell replacements for complete units rather than parts, and partly because the more easily reparable breakdowns are gradually being eliminated by improved design and higher quality.

Remanufacturing is not an important economic activity at present. However, it will probably grow in importance, especially as the shortage of landfill sites induces governments to force original equipment manufacturers (OEMs) to take back old equipment. Remanufactured refrigerators, A/C units, kitchen appliances, cars (or engines), tires, and PCs can offer a good low-priced alternative to new equipment for low-income workers in the rich countries, or they could fill an important economic niche in some of the developing countries. Actually, since remanufacturing will always be more labor intensive than original equipment manufacturing (OEM), it is inherently a suitable activity for border regions such as Mexico, Eastern Europe or North Africa. (As these countries develop, of course, the 'border regions' will shift too.)

In the case of municipal wastes (mostly paper products and containers), recycling is already increasing in importance. Again, the shortage of land for disposal is mainly responsible. More efficient technologies for separating materials will certainly be developed in coming decades. In any case, there is no technical reason why the recycling/re-use rate for most types of materials should not be dramatically increased from the low levels of today. This will happen, eventually, when material prices better reflect the true environmental costs of both extraction and use.

1.7. THE 'WASTE-MINING' STRATEGY

As mentioned earlier, waste mining is the recovery of low-value byproducts and wastes for use as industrial raw materials. In this particular case, economies of scale and what we have called 'economies of integration' are critical. (See the next chapter for a more detailed discussion.) Another major problem is that such sources are often somewhat more difficult, or more costly to exploit than natural sources. However, if the implicit costs arising from environmental damages caused by currently unutilized waste streams could be charged as direct costs to the waste generator, the latter could reduce his or her own costs by offering a subsidy to some user. Some potential examples along these lines, discussed in subsequent chapters, are briefly listed below.

Arsenic recovery from copper mining and smelting, and cadmium recovery from zinc mining and smelting, are both examples of waste mining, since each metal is a minor constituent of the ore of another more important metal. Unfortunately, both of these metals are exceedingly toxic and the objective of public policy should be to minimize both production and dissipative use. Gallium, cobalt, silver and even gold are other examples of waste mining with a long history. All of these metals are already recovered from process wastes, but in some cases significant fractions are lost because further recovery is too expensive, given the current level of market demand. Assuming a fixed level of demand for the 'parent' metal (copper, lead or zinc), the choice is between leaving the unwanted fraction of the minor metal in gangue, slag or dust, or recovering it for use. In the case of gold and silver most of the uses are environmentally harmless, and may as well be encouraged. However in the cases of arsenic and cadmium, many uses, such as pesticides, herbicides, stabilizers for plastic and pigments, are dissipative and should be discouraged or even banned. On the other hand, gallium-arsenide semiconductors and nickel-cadmium batteries are uses that are potentially valuable and recyclable. This whole topic needs further study.

The recovery of elemental sulfur from natural gas and petroleum refineries is probably the classic case of recovering a useful material from a waste.[6] This technology is already far advanced, and now accounts for a significant (and rising) percentage of the world sulfur supply. The recovery of sulfuric acid from copper, zinc and lead smelters is another example, although many smelters outside the industrialized countries have not exploited this opportunity, either because of lax environmental regulations or lack of local demand for sulfuric acid, or both.

Wastes that should be 'mined' for resources, but are not as yet, include lime/limestone FGD scrubber wastes from electric power plants, and phosphate rock-processing wastes, all of which can be converted to synthetic gypsum and used to replace natural gypsum. In the case of phosphate rock processing, it is also feasible to recover fluosilicic acid. This could replace most of the fluorspar (calcium fluoride ore) that is now mined (from which hydrofluoric acid is manufactured).

Another waste that should be more consistently exploited as a resource is coal ash. Given that coal will be a major source of energy in some countries for decades to come, it is important to make the best possible use of the enormous quantities of ash that are produced when coal is burned. This ash can be recovered (as currently) by means of electrostatic precipitators or, in future, from coal pyrolysis or gasification plants. The latter can also recover elemental sulfur. The ash, in turn, can be used as such in a variety of ways, including cement manufacturing.

However, the most attractive potential use of coal ash, in the future, is as a source of metals, including aluminum and ferrosilicon. This would not only reduce a waste-disposal problem, but would also cut down significantly on environmental damage from bauxite mining and processing. There are a number of technological problems involved in the use of ash, but the major obstacle will be resistance from the aluminum companies, especially those with long-term contracts for electric power at below-market rates. Thus, the most promising strategy for encouraging the development of newer technologies for aluminum recovery would be to eliminate subsidies to aluminum companies and — instead — provide ash disposal credits.

In the concluding chapter (Chapter 16) we summarize our major findings in more detail, with respect to both technological and economic aspects.

NOTES(1)

1. Each tonne of fossil fuel burned results in the ultimate release of roughly 3 tonnes of CO_2 to the atmosphere, not to mention significant quantities of sulfur oxides (SO_x) and oxides of nitrogen (NO_x) — the main causes of environmental acidification. Atmospheric carbon dioxide concentration has increased by about 20% since the last century.
2. The quantities of ore removed from the earth are normally much larger, but physical separation techniques leave much of the excess material at the mine, where it is piled up into small mountains, but not put back into the ground. For instance, copper ores mined in the western part of the US contain less than 0.4% copper, whereas concentrates delivered to refineries average 20% copper. Thus, for every tonne of concentrate, at least 50 tonnes of crude ore were dug up and processed (by flotation ponds) at the mine. For 1 tonne of refined copper 250 tonnes of ore are processed. In some cases the quantities of ore processed are much larger. For example, roughly 140 000 tonnes of ore must be processed to yield 1 tonne of platinum group metals.
3. See Barnett and Morse 1962 and Smith 1979.

4. John Evelyn FRS (1661) described the smoke pollution of London and attributed it to the industrial use of channel coal. The proposal to discharge smoke into sewers was made by a Rev. Gibsone in New York and a Mr Spence in England (*Harpers Magazine*, 1872). See Landsberg 1961.
5. One continuing problem is that such expenditures are easy to identify and monitor. It is much harder to determine when expenditures on process change are motivated by environmental concerns *vis-à-vis* process improvement.
6. Natural gas itself was formerly a waste, as was coke oven gas. Both are now very valuable resources.

2. Resource perspective

2.1. RESOURCES AS FACTORS OF PRODUCTION

Economists of the 18th century assumed that agricultural land and labor were the source of all wealth. The importance of capital was recognized only later. Land is now regarded as a type of capital. The special role of exhaustible resources was pointed out by Malthus (land), and again in the 19th century by Jevons (coal). However, the contribution of resource flows to economic growth *per se* is still neglected in much of the theoretical literature on economic growth, which still focuses largely on labor and capital. Present-day economists generally think in terms of production functions. Thus, the total output of the economy F is thought of as a function of three generic 'factors of production', namely labor (L), capital (K), and natural resource flows (R).

Natural resources are of two kinds, renewable and non-renewable. The former can usefully be regarded as a steady or gradually increasing flow.[1] Land is a convenient surrogate for renewable resources such as agricultural products and forest products that are land based. Over the past two centuries the productivity of the land has been increased dramatically — far more than Malthus considered possible — by continuing technological progress. However, this category of resources is not relevant to the present study.

Non-renewable resources (including fossil fuels and minerals) constitute a theoretical problem for quasi-static models, precisely because of their finiteness. Theorists have dealt with the difficulty by envisioning the use of finite resources over an indefinitely long period of time, and asked the question: what is the optimal rate of extraction? The optimal rate of extraction has been taken to be that which would maximize the discounted present value of all future uses. The rate of extraction at a given time, of course, must balance current supply and demand. A hypothetical monopoly supplier can thus adjust demand by adjusting his price. The classic paper, by Hotelling, not only formulated this problem but also solved it for a very simplified case (Hotelling 1931). The Hotelling solution is that the optimal rate of extraction corresponds to a price that rises at the societal discount rate.

A rather large theoretical literature on optimal extraction under more realistic conditions (allowing for competition, discovery, technological change, etc.) has been spawned by the Hotelling theorem. In the 1970s, the 'limits to growth' controversy raised the question of whether economic growth could continue indefinitely given the finiteness of resource stocks. This question led to another burst of theorizing, based on the Hotelling framework.[2] The problem was formulated at that time in terms of the substitution of anthropogenic capital K for natural capital (i.e. exhaustible resources). Needless to say, the problem is only mathematically tractable if one can assume that the two types of capital are completely substitutable, one for the other. Although common sense suggests that they are not, economic theorists (especially Solow) have been very reluctant to give up this assumption. In fact, this problem has largely dominated theoretical resource economics up to now.

On the empirical front, there has been an unproductive controversy over the magnitudes of mineral reserves and rates of exhaustion. Some alarmists have prematurely predicted impending mineral resource crises (e.g. the limits to growth debate in the early 1970s (Meadows *et al.* 1972)). Some conservatives have reacted by asserting that such fears are absolutely groundless because impending shortages are invariably signalled by rising prices which, in turn, automatically call forth investment in technological alternatives. As regards most industrial materials extracted from the earth's crust, so far at least, the latter thesis has generally been confirmed by historical experience (Barnett and Morse 1962; Smith 1979). It appears that resource scarcity has not constituted an effective limit to growth, up to now. Moreover, resource economists do not expect physical resource scarcity to constitute such a problem within the next few decades, at least.[3]

However, economists have been slow to look at the other side of the coin. If lack of resources could conceivably put a brake on economic growth, it must surely follow that the availability of high-quality natural resources at low prices — especially fossil energy — has contributed significantly to past economic growth. This proposition seems eminently reasonable. Yet it has not been tested econometrically, as far as we know. The major econometric work to 'explain' historical growth of aggregate economic output (GNP) in terms of the underlying factors of production was carried out in the late 1950s (Abramovitz 1956; Solow 1956, 1957). The major conclusion of that work was that aggregate growth could not be explained by increases in either labor or capital inputs. The missing ingredient, suggested by Solow and others, was 'technological progress'. Of course, technological progress in the discovery and extraction of fossil fuels and other material resources was doubtless a factor.

2.2.   INCREASING RESOURCE PRODUCTIVITY

Since the 18th century there has been a remarkable acceleration of economic growth. Indeed, it can be said with considerable accuracy that economic growth itself dates from that period, since output (and wealth) per capita scarcely changed from century to century (and actually fell in some centuries) until the 1600s. The period of real growth began then and accelerated particularly since the industrial revolution.[4]

By convention, technological progress has been conventionally subdivided into two components, namely 'labor productivity' and 'capital productivity'. These are, respectively, the ratios of total output to factor input. Productivity growth is thus defined as the rate of change of these ratios. Since the 18th century, the growth of real output (call it F) has been almost entirely due to increasing labor productivity. (Capital productivity has increased only occasionally and for brief periods.) Thus, based on this econometric analysis, the 'engine of growth' appears to have been technological innovation and capital investment in labor-saving technology. Labor productivity thus defined (F/L), has increased enormously (by a factor of several hundred) since the beginning of the 19th century.

Indeed, in most public discussions of economic growth, 'factor productivity' is confused with 'labor productivity'. The latter, in turn, is invariably taken to be attributable to capital investment in 'labor-saving' technology. The capital/labor ratio (K/L) thus becomes a significant explanatory variable.

Unfortunately, energy and other resource flows were not considered explicitly in the seminal econometric work cited above.[5] But it is a fact that resource inputs (R) to production (F) have increased enormously since the 18th century. It is likely that much of the observed economic growth should be attributed to the increased input of natural resources (especially energy) to the economy. Had resource flows (R) been explicitly included as factors of production, it would have been necessary to introduce an additional productivity term to the standard production function representation, namely the productivity of resource inputs, (F/R). Since resource inputs R have increased far more rapidly than labor supply L (in other words the ratio R/L has increased over time) it is fairly obvious that resource productivity (F/R) has not increased nearly as fast as labor productivity (F/L). In fact, it is even possible that resource productivity has fallen.

In principle, if the factors are all independent, aggregate production F can be increased by increasing any of the factors. Thus, it should be possible to increase labor inputs at the same rate as the growth of F, holding labor productivity constant, by increasing the productivity of capital K and energy/material resources R instead. This strategy has not been followed consistently in any country, up to now. On the contrary, most developing countries have regarded cheap capital, cheap energy and cheap materials as 'engines of growth', disregarding the fact that this policy tends to encourage the (excessive) use of capital, energy and materials all of which are scarce and becoming scarcer — as a substitute for labor, which is not scarce. If labor were in short supply, these policies would make sense. However, given that labor is now in surplus supply virtually everywhere, it would make more sense to substitute labor for other inputs, rather than *vice versa*. In brief, encouraging more use of energy-consuming, labor-saving machinery and equipment will simply increase unemployment.

In addition, excessive use of energy and material resources on a finite earth results in excessive wastes, pollution and environmental pressure. Every increment of raw material extracted from the environment is a future waste or pollutant, after a delay of weeks, months, or (in a few cases) years. The production function, which is supposed to be an aggregate measure of social welfare, should reflect this negative aspect of increasing resource use. Moreover, excessive use of materials also means that limited resource stocks will be exhausted faster than need be. (As noted above, there is no immediate threat of resource exhaustion, for most metals and fuels, but high-quality resources are, nevertheless, finite in all cases.)

Conservative business leaders and neoclassical economists are in the habit of arguing that market forces will determine the optimum rate of use of raw materials, and that government intervention is therefore inappropriate. We realize the debate will not be settled soon, but we argue that, on the contrary, most resource prices are too low — in some cases much too low — because of market failures. The most important market failure (or 'externality') in this case is that the indirect social costs of pollution and environmental damage are not paid by the materials extraction and processing industries. If those costs had to be paid by oil and gas companies and mining enterprises, the costs of resources themselves, and of resource-intensive products and services, would be significantly higher.

However, it is not our business here to theorize further about the 'right' prices for resources. We merely point out that, in the absence of a market mechanism that reflects environmental and other concerns, it is not inappropriate for government to intervene. In fact, governments do intervene in markets quite regularly, in a variety of ways, some beneficial, some counterproductive. Policy analysis strives to provide justifications to favor the beneficial interventions over the counterproductive ones.

2.3.   THE ECONOMICS OF 'WIN–WIN'

We turn now to another set of issues in economics, namely: how realistic is it to expect to find opportunities for reducing wastes and pollution (or other externalities) and to do so at a profit? Most economists assume that it is rare and unlikely, for reasons discussed below. However, there is one very funda-mental reason for not taking this skepticism too seriously. The reason for being hopeful is that reducing waste and pollution — or, better yet, turning a waste into a useful product — is that there are actually two distinct opportu-nities for savings. The first is via reduced input costs. The second is via reduced waste-treatment/disposal costs. And the clincher is that cutting un-necessary inputs to any process *automatically* cuts unwanted outputs from that process.

This issue is important, because there has been a public controversy as regards the extent to which pollution prevention through process change can be expected to be profitable in the short-term sense.[6] As evidence often cited, the 3M Company began its in-house program, called 'Pollution Prevention Pays' (PPP), to encourage employees to notice and implement opportunities to reduce energy consumption and pollution and thereby eliminate 'end-of-pipe' costs of pollution control. This program has apparently been extremely successful, both from an environmental protection perspective, and also from an economic standpoint. In fact, between 1975 and 1990, the 3M Company estimates that it saved $537 million in first year costs alone. Dow Chemical Co's similar program, 'Waste Reduction Always Pays' (WRAP) also claims to have achieved substantial economic savings as well as environmental benefits. Many other comparable examples could be mentioned.

On the other hand, there is a lot of skepticism about such claims, especially among economists. The reason is simple. In traditional economic terms the optimal degree of pollution abatement is at the level of abatement Z where the sum of the marginal damage cost D and the marginal abatement cost A is at a minimum. This picture is shown in Figure 2.1. We call it the 'equilib-rium' picture because it assumes that the economy has reached an equilib-rium state, in the sense that all actions have already been taken that could have been taken to reduce pollution emissions at negative or zero cost. Hence the abatement cost curve $A(z)$ is monotonically increasing from zero.

In a recent article in the *Harvard Business Review*, Noah Walley and Bradley Whitehead, of McKinsey and Co., deprecate the win–win rhetoric, as exemplified by the 3M and Dow cases noted above:

> Questioning today's win–win rhetoric is akin to arguing against motherhood and apple pie. After all, the idea that environmental initiatives will systematically increase profitability has tremendous appeal. Unfortunately, this popular idea is

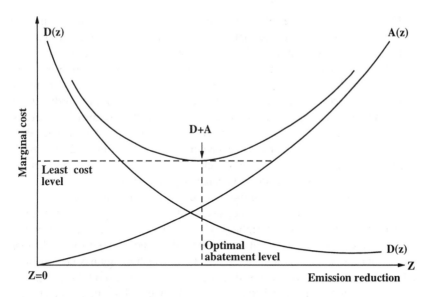

Figure 2.1: Optimal abatement in economic equilibrium

also unrealistic. Responding to environmental challenges has always been a costly and complicated problem for managers. In fact, environmental costs at most companies are skyrocketing, with little economic payback in sight. (Walley and Whitehead 1994)

Later, they say 'in almost all cases, *it is impossible to get something for nothing*' (ibid., p. 47; italics added).

It must be said that most economists tend to assume that the equilibrium picture is valid for many purposes, despite considerable engineering and technological evidence to the contrary. The evidence suggests that win–win opportunities are much more common than they 'should' be in theory: not all actions that could abate emissions at zero or negative cost have been taken (Ayres 1994). At the macroeconomic level, the existence of win–win opportunities corresponds very closely to the phenomenon known as 'freeze-in' of inferior technologies and 'lockout' of superior ones. The general idea is that economies of scale or 'economies of adoption' can freeze in the first comer in a technological competition by raising the barriers against later entrants too high.[7] For example, it is widely agreed that the two early nuclear reactor designs (boiling water and pressurized water) are not particularly good ones and that if a new generation of reactors were to be designed 'from scratch' today, the choice of technology would probably be quite different. Yet the two original designs were standardized and frozen in by the very high cost of designing, building and testing alternatives.

However, by the same token, this implies that it is not safe to assume (as macroeconomists tend to do) that every technology in place is the optimal choice, as if it had been the winner in a Darwinian competition against all possible candidates. In fact, the process of technological evolution is much messier than that. As often as not there are superior 'on the shelf' alternatives that simply never had a chance to get established. If the initial hurdle could be surmounted, the superior alternative(s) might quickly take over. This means the real economy is not always at or very close to an equilibrium state. But, even if the economy were nearly always in equilibrium (Figure 2.1) techno-logical progress (or other exogenous changes, such as upward shifts in re-source prices, or a tax on resources) can change the picture.

The altered situation is more like Figure 2.2, in which there is some room for improvement at zero or even negative cost. This not only pushes the least-cost abatement level to the right (higher Z), but it also brings the actual damage D and the actual cost of abatement A down below their former levels. The important point to note is that the fact that a technology has been widely adopted is not good evidence of its superiority. In fact, a small breach in the barrier — whether financial, legal or simply habitual — that protects the established way of doing things can sometimes be just enough to allow a competitor to establish itself.

In short, exogenous change can create new unrecognized (hence unexploited) economic opportunities.[8] The question that needs deeper study is why firms

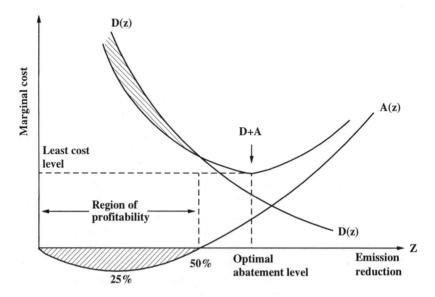

Figure 2.2:   Optimal abatement in economic disequilibrium

do not look harder than they do to find and exploit opportunities in their own economic interests? In any case, there may be some cases where there are potential returns to systems integration that have not been applied in practice up to now. Future changes, e.g. in resource prices, should create even more such opportunities for profitable innovations that increase the productivity of material resources.

In fact, in some cases the adoption of a basic new manufacturing technology can shift the competitive advantage in an industry from the established producer (whether a firm or a nation) to a new entrant. The adoption of new steelmaking technology by the Japanese steel industry (discussed later) illustrates how this can happen. Toyota's *kan ban* (or 'just in time') system gave it a similar lead in automobile manufacturing. In fact, the timely adoption of a basic new technology is, perhaps, the *only* way that such a shift can occur. Nevertheless, profitable opportunities for technological change are neglected by most firms, more often than not. Evidence for this is not hard to find. History is full of examples. The established leaders in an industry are typically the least interested in change. When a basic new technology comes along, it is almost always an outsider or a newcomer that leads the way. The classic example of this phenomenon is the semiconductor business, where Texas Instruments took the initial leadership away from established firms like RCA, GE and Sylvania. Each subsequent technological generation since then has led to another shakeup of the industry, and a new set of leaders has replaced the older ones.

This occurs for a variety of reasons, most of which are tantamount to lack of critical information and knowledge at the decision-making level, arising from internal barriers to information flow. The question that needs deeper study is why firms do not look harder than they do to break down such barriers and find and exploit opportunities that are in their own long-term economic interest. In any case, future changes, e.g. in resource prices and/or waste-disposal costs, should create many more opportunities for profitable innovations that increase the productivity of material resources. Some of them are discussed hereafter.

2.4. ROLE OF GOVERNMENT

There is now a fairly general and robust consensus among policy analysts that the necessary and appropriate role of government is, above all, to create incentives for individuals and firms to do what is good for society as a whole and to refrain from doing what is bad. In other words, it is the role of government to increase the number of win–win opportunities, in the broadest sense.

Thus, one arm of government, the central bank, is now generally viewed as the custodian of macroeconomic policy, through its control over interest rates and the money supply. This mechanism of social control is less onerous and far more efficient than direct price controls, which are the means relied on in less-developed countries, including the 'centrally planned' economies.

In other domains, such as energy policy, transportation policy, materials policy and environment policy, most governments exert influence partly by financing infrastructure (e.g. building roads and airports) and partly through subsidies, quotas, standards, and other regulations. So-called 'industrial policy' is often derided as attempting to 'pick winners' which often turn out to be losers. However, there have been some spectacular successes.

For example, it was the Japanese who first adopted the (then) new basic oxygen furnace (BOF) for steelmaking in the 1950s, although it was a European (Austrian) innovation. This happened because Japan was then in the process of expanding its steel industry rapidly, which meant building new plants, whereas the much larger US steelmakers were then heavily committed to open hearth furnaces. Even so, the top executives of the Japanese steel companies, who knew the open hearth process, were very skeptical of changing from a 'tried and true' technology to one in which they had no experience. (The top executives of European and US steel companies reacted exactly the same way.) The massive industry-wide Japanese adoption of BOF was brought about by a kind of 'palace revolution' of younger engineering executives (who had familiarized themselves with the new technology in unofficial 'skunkworks'), coordinated by technocrats in the Japanese Ministry of International Trade and Industry (MITI).[9] MITI's main role in this case was to act as a monopsonist master licensee, effectively dictating terms to the licensor and sub-licensing to all the Japanese steel firms. (When US, German and other firms negotiated licenses later they were forced to pay much higher royalties, which gave the Japanese a critical advantage.) The success of this tactic, repeated in the case of continuous casting technology, gave Japan a worldwide lead in steel manufacturing which it still retains.[10]

Environmental regulations are typically administered by officials of various kinds — with a variety of administrative and police powers — and ultimately enforced by the courts. It is well known that many of these regulations are inefficient, some are counterproductive or even contradictory. Others are unenforced and some are unenforceable. (The lesson of Prohibition in the US is easily forgotten.) This problem is especially acute in the environmental area, because the number of applicable regulations has multiplied greatly in recent years.

There is a growing backlash against the traditional regulatory approach to pollution abatement, as it has been practiced in recent years, on account of its growing costs and decreasing cost-effectiveness. Indeed, some of the US legislation (notably RCRA and 'superfund') has been extraordinarily costly — resulting in protracted and expensive lawsuits — with little progress to show for it. While no major environmental legislation has yet been 'rolled back', the case against adding to the existing regulatory burden is growing stronger every year.

Yet the regulatory role of government, in the larger sense, remains essential. Only the available tools for regulation may be changing. In the remainder of this chapter we summarize some of the materials/energy/environment policy recommendations that have suggested themselves in the course of our study.

2.5.   EMPLOYMENT AND RESOURCE PRODUCTIVITY

For several hundred years labor productivity has been increased by systematically using machines and fossil energy to displace human labor. Thus, labor productivity has been driven up to a large extent by increasing the consumption of capital and natural resources. Natural resources, on the other hand, have declined in real price terms, encouraging consumption and providing little or no incentive for conservation. While there have been some increases in the efficiency with which fossil fuels are converted into useful work, since the beginning of the industrial revolution, these efficiency gains are swamped by the increased consumption of fossil fuels and other materials extracted from the environment. To state the situation in a nutshell, most economic growth in the past two centuries must be attributed to labor productivity growth.

Currently, Western Europe is being forced to recognize that even economic recovery does not seem to bring with it any growth in employment. Unemployment has been rising on the average, if not quite monotonically, for over twenty years. The social 'safety net' that eases the pain for the unemployed and which undoubtedly has helped prevent any social protest, has become unreasonably costly to those who are still employed. In Western Europe, the direct burden on wages of social security charges amounts to over 50% in most countries and closer to 80% in Germany. In the European Union (EU) central government revenues are overwhelmingly (more than 80%) based on labor or income from labor, while only a small proportion is arguably based on capital or resource consumption. The gasoline tax is the primary example of the latter.[11]

The present situation is that unemployment is becoming an acute social problem in Europe, at least. Moreover, conventional 'jobs' programs, based on Keynesian demand stimulation policies, are no longer feasible because of intolerable government budget deficits. Belgium, Greece, Italy and Spain have literally no room to increase deficit spending. Most other European countries are approaching this point, as is the US. What this may mean, however, is that the most attractive policy option at the national and European levels is to focus on tax reform. The time has come to consider shifting taxes away from labor onto resource consumption and pollution as a means of reducing labor costs and increasing resource costs instead. This policy should have the effect, over time, of stimulating growth through resource productivity gains, rather than through labor productivity gains. In fact, there are indications that this could be a true win–win approach at the macro-level.

Academic economists have argued for many years in favor of using taxes or tradeable permits rather than emission standards or quotas as a more effective and efficient instrument of environmental policy. However, the environmental movement has strongly resisted the tax approach on the moralistic ground that taxation of pollution amounts to a 'license to pollute' that can be purchased by the wealthy but not the poor. The alliance against environmental taxes has long included businessmen, who obsessively oppose taxation of any kind, lawyers who prefer specific regulation to generalized incentives, and public finance economists who have argued that taxes should not be used for 'social engineering'. However, the growing resistance to direct regulation — which appears increasingly unworkable and counterproductive — may have begun to turn the tide.

In November 1993 Jacques Delors, President of the European Commission, presented a 'White Paper'[12] setting forth an agenda for a 'new approach' to economic growth. Given the political process involved in preparing the paper, it is not surprising that much of the emphasis was on new investment in infrastructure such as high-speed railways and high technology, especially 'multimedia' and 'information superhighway'. However, Chapter 10 of the White Paper also suggested something much more radical: a gradual change of the tax system to reduce the excessive burden on labor and to shift the burden, instead, to energy, pollution and traffic congestion. This chapter of the White Paper drew its inspiration partly from two influential books: *Erdpolitik* (von Weizsäcker 1991) and *Ecological Tax Reform: A Policy Proposal for Sustained Development* (von Weizsäcker and Jesinghaus 1992).

A follow-up seminar 'Towards a new approach to development' sponsored by the EU (Directorate XI, Environment, Nuclear Safety and Civil Protection) was held in Brussels, November 24 and 25, 1994. The European Commission circulated a number of papers for discussion, including one on tax reform and sustainable development which presented the results of background work by a number of groups during the year since the original White Paper. The most important new research presented at the conference was a major econometric analysis carried out by economists at Data Resources Incorporated (DRI), together with a number of consultants (DRI *et al.* 1994).

In brief, the study compared three scenarios out to the year 2010. The three were (i) an extrapolation of current economic trends, termed the 'reference' scenario, (ii) a modified scenario, assuming implementation of policies currently under serious consideration (such as the carbon/energy tax) and (iii) a scenario reflecting a range of fiscal and other measures integrated into sectoral policies, including increased energy taxes, charges for water, congestion charges and auction systems to set upper limits on environmental resource use, with all incremental tax increases being recycled as reductions in income or other taxes on labor. Even though the assumed tax adjustments were comparatively minor, the impact was clear and unmistakable: the third 'integrated policy' scenario was both significantly more effective at reducing pollution and more effective at increasing employment — hence overall growth — than either of the other two (DRI *et al.* 1994).

The DRI analysis assumed only modest changes in the structure of the tax system, and the postulated increases were mostly on fossil energy and traffic congestion. In the following, we note a number of other more specific opportunities for using taxes, tariffs and related economic instruments, such as returnable deposits, to cut down on pollution and waste. Such instruments are especially needed to encourage recycling of secondary materials and more efficient use of hitherto wasted materials such as phospho-gypsum and coal ash. We believe that, if an econometric analysis of the aggregate impacts of these measures were done (a difficult task, admittedly), it would confirm the potential for even more startling gains both in terms of environmental quality and in terms of employment and welfare.

2.6. INFORMATION NEEDS FOR ENVIRONMENTAL POLICY ANALYSIS

The need for economic data to support policy analysis — as exemplified by the European Commission studies cited in the foregoing paragraphs — is widely recognized. It is to provide for such needs that census data are collected and national accounts data are compiled and published in internationally comparable form by government statistical offices, and coordinated by the UN Statistical Office. The importance of this activity is not seriously questioned, even though it employs thousands of statisticians and economists, and tens of thousands of clerks and other support personnel, worldwide.

Since energy became a major international priority concern in the mid-1970s, energy statistics (production and consumption, by category) have also been compiled by most countries. Indeed, the International Energy Agency of the OECD was created to coordinate these data on an international basis.

Unfortunately, the need for comparable data covering production, processing and use of other environmentally important materials — especially metals and chemicals — has not yet been adequately recognized. To be sure, the UN Statistical Office compiles and publishes 'Industrial Statistics' on outputs of about 550 major commodities, ranging from agricultural, forest and mineral products, fuels, metals, chemicals and finished industrial goods.

However, while better than nothing, the global coverage is very incomplete, and the categories are far too aggregated for detailed analysis of materials. For instance, fewer than 50 basic chemicals are included (e.g. ammonia, chlorine, ethylene, sulfuric acid) which means that no data are reported for the vast majority of chemicals of environmental concern. Even in the US, where the data on chemicals and minerals are most complete, many important chemicals are produced by fewer than four companies, whence data are suppressed on the grounds that publication might tend to reveal the activities of a private firm. In other words, such data are treated as proprietary and 'confidential', regardless of the possible public interest. In Europe, there are virtually no public sources of data on minerals and chemicals production and use beyond the level of detail found in the UN 'Industrial Statistics'.

The difficulty of obtaining reliable quantitative data on chemicals and minor metals production and use, as well as waste outputs and disposal, is clearly illustrated in a number of the case studies that follow. In many cases, the only sources of data are private consulting firms that charge sizeable fees. Even with the help of such proprietary data bases (whose accuracy cannot be verified) it is effectively impossible to make a complete accounting of environmentally important (and potentially toxic) materials, such as arsenic, cadmium, chromium or chlorine and their compounds.

The EU should undertake a serious program of minerals/metals and chemical statistics collection and compilation in the coming years. Without such data, intelligent policy choices in a number of fields, ranging from taxes to environment, cannot be supported by serious quantitative analysis.

A detailed discussion of the data sources used in the present study is included as Appendix B of this study.

NOTES(2)

1. In this sense, renewable resource flows R are comparable to the labor supply L, which also increases slowly and predictably over the long run.
2. See, for instance, Robert Solow's Richard T. Ely Lecture, 'The Economics of Resources and the Resources of Economics' and references cited therein (Solow 1974).
3. Petroleum may be the exception here. There is a fairly wide consensus, even among petroleum industry geologists, that demand will begin to outrun supply, probably within two or three decades. One of the reasons for this is that world oil prices were forced down (mainly by bribing Saudi Arabia to keep production high, using fancy weapons as bait),

after the 1979–80 Iranian Revolution. This was done partly to punish Iran but mainly as a Cold War strategy for financially weakening the USSR, which was then (and now) dependent on earnings from petroleum exports. Oil prices remain low today because the former USSR is now desperate for cash and the potential Iraqi supply overhangs the market. But, of course, low oil prices have encouraged demand — especially the growth of the world automobile industry. With fast economic growth in SE Asia, and large new discoveries becoming increasingly rare, the era of low oil prices is surely approaching its end.

4. An excellent overview touching on both socioeconomic and technological aspects of the growth problem can be found in Braudel (Braudel 1981).

5. To introduce resource flows is not simple, for two reasons. First, energy and material resources are not normally expressed in comparable units. A ton of iron ore is not equivalent to a ton of coal. Fuels can be equated with each other in terms of heating value (e.g. BTUs or joules). This difficulty can be overcome only by introducing sophisticated thermodynamic measures. Second, some fuels are also an item of final consumption. To be consistent, fuels consumed as intermediates in the production process would have to be broken out and considered separately from fuels used by households. This would be a major statistical effort.

6. This controversy was low level and academic until the publication of a widely quoted article asserting the beneficial impact of regulation on innovation, namely, 'America's Competitiveness Strategy' by Michael Porter of Harvard Business School (Porter 1991).

7. The mechanism has been described and discussed in detail by Brian Arthur (Arthur 1988, 1988a).

8. The dispute on win–win between optimists and skeptics seems to depend mostly on the choice of baseline for comparison. The skeptics' (Walley and Whitehead) view essentially compares the cost of pollution abatement with the cost in a hypothetical unregulated world. The optimistic view, exemplified by 3M, Dow and others, views the world as dynamic and seeks opportunities that will arise in changing and evolving circumstances.

9. The full story of this 'palace revolution' is told in the book *How Japan Innovates* (Lynn 1982).

10. The same method was used for the acquisition of basic integrated circuit technology by Japanese firms (through MITI) in the 1960s.

11. Figures compiled by the statistical office of the European Union (EUROSTAT) for 1992 indicate that taxes of all kinds took 41.28% of European GNP (of which taxes on labor, consumption and capital accounted for 23.44%, 10.86% and 6.98%, respectively); revenues linked in any way to environmental problems added up to 2.65% of GNP, of which taxes on vehicle ownership and fuels accounted for 2.37%. See CEPC 1994.

12. The full title is 'Growth, Competitiveness, Employment — The Challenges and Ways Forward Into the 21st Century', White Paper, European Commission (EC 1994).

3. Alumina, aluminum and gallium

3.1. SUMMARY

Aluminum is an industrially important metal that plays an extremely important part in modern society. Without it there would be no aircraft industry, for instance. It is light, corrosion resistant, and easy to bend, draw, extrude, stamp and form into shapes. It is highly reflective. It is a good thermal and electrical conductor. It is also very easily recycled. There are virtually no environmental problems associated with its use or disposal.

However, the extraction and refining of aluminum are less benign. Aluminum is mainly found in nature in combination with oxygen, as alumina Al_2O_3. The mineral bauxite is the richest source of the oxide alumina. The mining of bauxite is environmentally destructive, for one thing. Bauxite is obtained from open pit mines, from which overburden has been removed, using draglines. The layer of ore is usually rather thin. It follows that relatively large amounts of material are removed in relation to the amount of ore recovered. Some companies have restored former bauxite mines in exemplary fashion, even receiving UN awards. However, regulation tends to be weak or unenforced in many of the less-developed countries where bauxite is mined. Given the mixed record, bauxite mining has been strongly opposed by local residents in some areas (e.g. India).

The processing of bauxite to alumina generates large quantities of caustic waste, called 'red mud', which has proved hard to dispose of, or to utilize. Furthermore, aluminum metal smelting is extremely energy intensive. For this reason alternative processes for extracting aluminum, from different sources and by different technical means, should be considered seriously, even though aluminum and its major source (bauxite) are hardly scarce.

Aluminum has been called 'congealed electricity' because so much electric power is consumed in its production. The energy required to manufacture four aluminum soft drink or beer cans would be equivalent to the energy content of one of those cans filled with motor gasoline. Because of its high energy intensity, aluminum companies have located smelters mainly in areas where long-term contracts for cheap electricity could be obtained — generally at or near the sites of new dams in remote locations. The industry points out that in many cases the aluminum industry provides a reliable base-load without which the hydroelectric project could not have been justified in the first place.

But, while this is true, it is hardly a sufficient justification for very long-term contracts at extremely concessionary prices. Many third-world politicians are willing to negotiate such contracts in exchange for immediate benefits to themselves, but at the expense of future generations of their own people. Meanwhile, the aluminum companies and their customers from the industrialized world benefit from unreasonably low prices, which also encourages frivolous uses (such as beer cans) — together with wasted energy — and discourages technological innovation in the industry. For these reasons, metallic aluminum should not be used in ways that lead to dissipative losses, especially in packaging. To the extent that it is used for beverage cans, it should be recycled far more intensively than it is at present. Recycling requires only about 5–7% of the energy needed for producing virgin aluminum. In fact, the low rate of recycling of aluminum cans in Europe — much lower than in the US — is extremely wasteful (see Chapter 12, Packaging).

Aluminum smelting is also responsible for significant problems of atmospheric fluorine pollution. While largely controllable, it is nevertheless a hazard, especially to workers and local residents if the technology (and its maintenance) are not of the highest standard.

Gallium is a metal that has found economic uses only in recent years, partly because it is never found in pure form or in high-quality ores. It is currently recovered as a byproduct of aluminum refining. Gallium is a 'transition metal' of considerable potential importance because of possible future increases in demand for gallium-arsenide and other semiconductors.

Goals of public policy: reduce environmental damage caused by surface mining; reduce generation of wastes (red mud) from Bayer process; reduce electric power consumption; reduce dependency on petroleum coke; reduce fluoride emissions; increase recycling of aluminum (especially cans) in Europe.

3.2. ALUMINUM, ELECTRICITY AND DEVELOPING COUNTRIES

Aluminum companies argue that they should not be charged with wasting energy on the grounds that most aluminum is smelted with cheap coal or hydroelectric power from remote places where other uses for that energy have not developed. Aluminum companies have even argued that the energy intensiveness of aluminum is an advantage, as an added incentive to develop such energy resources. However, even where 'cheap' energy resources are used, as in Australia, Canada, Brazil, Ghana, Iceland (and formerly in France, Norway, Switzerland and the US) the argument is often deceptive.

In the first place, the long-term contracts that attract aluminum companies are typically much longer than the 'development' argument would justify. In the second place, electric power, regardless of source, is potentially fungible, even though there may be no way to transport the power at the moment the aluminum smelter is first built in a remote place. It can also be transported for very long distances, overland or even under water, by using extremely high voltages, up to 1 million volts. Third, if the local electricity supply is limited by prior appropriation, other kinds of industrialization may be inhibited. In effect, hydroelectric power now used to smelt aluminum could — in many cases — just as well be diverted to other social purposes, creating more jobs for local people.

The aluminum industry has unquestionably promoted hydroelectric (and nuclear) power development. It has not simply followed hydroelectric development that would have occurred anyway. On the contrary, new hydroelectric facilities are often built — as in Brazil, Ghana and Venezuela — with the explicit intention of attracting aluminum smelter investments to follow. The argument is that aluminum smelters provide hydroelectric power suppliers with a predictable 'base load' thus making it possible to exploit power sources that might not otherwise be economical, and facilitating other economic development. For example, Venezuela apparently saw hydropower development as a way of diversifying its energy base away from oil (Altenpohl 1982, p. 9).

The other side of the coin is that some extremely questionable hydroelectric dam projects have been built in a number of remote areas, flooding and otherwise damaging huge areas of virgin forest and tundra. This has been done largely for the special benefit of the aluminum industry. A few examples are worth citing (Young 1992):

1.   The Akosombo dam on the Volta River in Ghana sells three-quarters of its power to an aluminum smelter, at extremely low prices (the world's lowest in the early 1980s); it has done so by flooding 5% of the land area of the country, and accelerated coastal erosion by interfering with the movement of sediments to the Volta estuary. Ghana has received virtually no collateral benefits from the project, not even promised irrigation. It has lost arable land, thanks to the Akosombo project.

2.   The Tucurui dam on the Tocantins River, a tributary of the Amazon, is part of the infamous Carajas Project in Brazil, partially financed by the World Bank. The dam sends one-third of its output, at subsidized prices, to aluminum smelters. The artificial lake behind the dam flooded six towns and two Indian reservations. It left at least 20 000 people homeless. Another Indian Reservation was heavily damaged by the building of power lines and an electrified railroad to carry iron ore (to a blast furnace

fueled by wood!). A Brazilian government report estimated that subsidies account for 60% of the value of exported aluminum.

3. The James Bay project of the utility Hydro Quebec has offered aluminum producers long-term contracts at 0.75 cents per kWh for the first five years and 1.5 cents/kWh thereafter. This project, when complete, will flood an area larger than Lake Erie. It is especially mysterious that the Quebec government should elect to provide heavy subsidies to aluminum smelters, given that all of the power could easily be sold (at market prices) to the power hungry northeastern US. Each job 'created' by these subsidies cost $171 000 in lost revenue.

The nuclear power industry in Britain, France and Germany was also linked (in the 1960s and 1970s) to expansion of the aluminum industry. Nuclear power plants could be justified more readily if there was a ready-made customer waiting for the electric power (Kirchner 1988, cited by Young 1992). When subsidies are withdrawn, the industry usually moves away. This happened in the US when long-term contracts dating back to the 1930s for cheap power from the dams of the Tennessee Valley Authority (TVA) and the Bonneville Power Authority in the Pacific Northwest finally expired a few years ago. ALCOA moved its smelters to Brazil and Australia. In Europe, Alusuisse, which was unsubsidized, has closed all its smelters except one in Norway and one in Iceland, where cheap hydroelectric power is available.

ALCAN, the Canadian company, owned all of its hydroelectric power supply (until the arrival of the James Bay project), either in British Columbia or Quebec. Since the plants were built before 1950 the power was being charged internally at the marginal cost of production. In 1983 this was only 0.3 cents (US) per kWh, one-sixth of the average cost to the world aluminum industry at the time (Brown 1983). By contrast, the price of electricity to US aluminum smelters was 2.6 cents/kWh and Japanese smelters were paying 6 cents/kWh. To be sure, there is some justification for a price differential since it costs more to service many small customers than one large one. However it is hard to believe that the cost differential is anywhere near as great as the price differential.

In summary, the aluminum industry typically secures long-term supply contracts at very low cost when newly available electricity supply exceeds local demand for electricity. Yet, in most cases, these long-term contracts continue long after the electric power surplus is exhausted. Then, either further economic development is inhibited, or new supply — at much higher cost — must be provided by government to replace that which is being used for aluminum production. In Europe, four of the five leading aluminum companies are heavily subsidized. (The exception is Norsk Hydro, which also owns its own power source.) Pechiney receives electricity from the state-owned utility, Electricité de France (EDF) at a rate of 1.5 cents/kWh, compared to other industrial users who pay 6 cents/kWh and residential users who pay 12 cents/kWh. Pechiney apparently gets its electric power at one-half to one-third the actual cost of generation (Nectoux 1991, cited by Young 1992). This electricity could obviously be sold elsewhere in Europe at market rates.

In short, while aluminum smelting operations might conceivably be the 'leading edge' of economic development in some remote regions, in the long run aluminum smelting has been significantly subsidized by other electric power users who arrive on the scene later and are forced to pay higher prices than they should. This is especially true in Europe. Apart from this, there are significant environmental costs associated with extraction and refining primary aluminum. It is argued by the industry that the leading-edge investor is entitled to whatever long-term advantage it can negotiate. If markets were perfect, this argument would be conclusive. However, in practice, large multinational firms often negotiate deals with political leaders of developing countries who are corrupt at worst and have very short time horizons at best. Politicians, elected or not, typically, care little for the interests of future generations.

There is a further downside to the aluminum industry's worldwide quest for cheap (often subsidized) electricity. The very success of this strategy in recent decades has inhibited the industry from investing in new and improved technologies. Indeed, despite its association with technologically advanced sectors such as aerospace, the aluminum industry is still largely locked in to the same technology (notwithstanding marginal improvements) that launched it into the 20th century. True, this is not *per se* a proof of technological backwardness, if the original technology happens to be the best possible one. However, there is some evidence that better (and cheaper) technologies do exist, as we note later.

3.3.   ALUMINA: SOURCES AND PROCESSES

Aluminum is very abundant. It constitutes 8% of the earth's crust (compared to 27.7% for silicon and 5% for iron), but never occurs in pure form. The major commercial ore at present is bauxite, which is largely found in the tropics and relatively near the earth's surface. There are two types of bauxite: karstic and lateritic. The former contains mostly alumina monohydrate ($Al_2O_3 \cdot H_2O$) and the latter contains mostly alumina trihydrate ($Al_2O_3 \cdot 3H_2O$). The lateritic type is the product of weathering under humid tropical conditions, which is why so many bauxite mines are located in the tropics.

Early in the 1970s several major bauxite producers, including Guyana, Surinam and Jamaica, began to nationalize bauxite mining properties. In

1974 the major producers formed a cartel, modelled on OPEC, called the International Bauxite Association (IBA) with headquarters in Kingston, Jamaica. Royalties were increased and bauxite production taxes were imposed by four countries (Jamaica, Haiti, the Dominican Republic and Surinam), providing 80% of US bauxite imports. The prospect of a bauxite shortage, and higher prices, prompted the US Congress to ask the Bureau of Mines to investigate whether alternative sources of aluminum could be extracted at moderate additional cost from aluminum-bearing minerals such as aluminum phosphate rock, alunite,[1] anorthosite, dawsonite (in oil shale), kaolinite (clay), and nepheline[2] (Patterson 1977). A number of minerals and extraction processes were investigated under this program (USBuMines 1975; Peters and Johnson 1974). However, the producer cartel collapsed and prices stabilized before any of the alternative processes were sufficiently developed to attract investment.[3]

The major producers are Australia, Guinea, Jamaica and Brazil, although there are 13 countries with annual production in excess of 1 million metric tons, or MMT. Total world bauxite output in 1991 was 107.92 MMT, barely up from 1988, as shown in Appendix A, Table A.1. Total world production of primary aluminum in 1991 was 19.575 MMT, as compared to 18.495 MMT in 1988.

The biggest producer of bauxite in Western Europe is Greece (2.13 MMT in 1991), followed by France (193 kMT in 1991, down from 1.53 MMT in 1985). Total mine output of bauxite in Western Europe was 2.335 MMT in 1991. In Eastern Europe, Hungary and Yugoslavia are also producers (2.037 MMT and 2.7 MMT, respectively). However, over two-thirds of the bauxite consumed in Western Europe is imported, either from Africa, South America or Australia.

Bauxite is a mixture of aluminum oxide, Al_2O_3 (about 50%) and other oxides, notably Fe_2O_3, SiO_2, TiO_2 and combined water as shown in Table 3.1. It is first reduced to alumina trihydrate ($Al_2O_3 \cdot 3H_2O$), or aluminum hydroxide ($Al_2(OH)_3$) by a chemical process of purification and separation, known generically as the Bayer process. The Bayer process starts with finely ground bauxite, which is mixed with lime (to control phosphorus impurities) and dissolved in a hot solution of caustic soda.[4] This yields a soluble salt: sodium aluminate. Some of the alumina reacts with silica to form insoluble sodium-aluminum-silicate. This constitutes the greatest loss mechanism in the Bayer process, since the caustic soda could be completely recycled if it were not for the sodium combined with the silica. (In other words, the amount of caustic soda required is directly proportional to the silica content of the bauxite.) A variant of the Bayer process for high silica domestic ore — the combination process — was developed in the US, but apparently it has not been significantly applied in Western Europe. The undissolved residue, including iron

Table 3.1: Composition of some typical bauxites, by weight percent

Constituent	Jamaica	Surinam	Guinea	Arkansas	Oregon	Washington	Hawaii
Al_2O_3	49.0	59.8	58.6	40–60	35.0	38.3	25.9
Trihydrate	47–50	59.6	52.7				
Monohydrate	2–9	0.2	5.9				
Fe_2O_3	18.4	2.7	4.1	3–6	31.5	28.7	39.4
SiO_2	0.8	3.8	4.9	1–20	6.7	6.5	4.7
TiO_2	2.4	2.4	2.5	1–3	6.5	4.2	6.7
Other minor	0.7	0.1	0.02				
H_2O, combined	27.5	31.2	29.6				
Loss on ignition				15.35	20.2	21.7	20–26

Source: Hall *et al.* 1975, Appendix B.

38

Table 3.2: *Alumina via the Bayer process: three unit-process descriptions*

A. *Composite process derived from production data*

Utility inputs and outputs			Other uncounted	
Electricity (input)	0.216	MWh	Water, process (input)	na
Heat (input)	15.630	GJ	Water, waste (output)	na

INPUTS (metric tonnes)		OUTPUTS (metric tonnes)	
Bauxite	1.922	Particulates, misc. aluminum	0.013
Limestone (CaCO₃)	0.039	Red mud, sludge	0.969
Caustic soda (NaOH)	0.039	ALUMINA, ANHYDROUS (Al₂O₃)	1.000

INPUTS ACCOUNTED FOR	2.001		OUTPUTS ACCOUNTED FOR	1.982
Source: Authors.		0.019	= Difference = .9% of Inputs	

B. *Process as used in Europe as described in IDEA data base (Lübkert et al. 1991)*

Utility inputs and outputs			Other uncounted	
Electricity (input)	0.364	Mwh	Water, process (input)	na
Heat (input)	9.885	GJ		

INPUTS (metric tonnes)		OUTPUTS (metric tonnes)	
Bauxite	3.378	Particulates, misc. aluminum	0.530
Lime (CaO)	0.050	Red mud, sludge	2.027
Caustic soda (NaOH)	0.113	Water, waste	0.668
Starch	0.015	ALUMINA, ANHYDROUS (Al₂O₃)	1.000

INPUTS ACCOUNTED FOR	3.557		OUTPUTS ACCOUNTED FOR	4.225
Source: IDEA database.		0.668	= Difference = –18.8% of Inputs	

C. *Balanced process (US) described by Battelle*

Utility inputs and outputs		
Electricity (input)	na	na
Heat (input)	na	na

INPUTS (metric tonnes)		OUTPUTS (metric tonnes)	
Water, process	10.539	Red mud, sludge (inc 1.183 water)	1.9634
Bauxite (full wgt-dry=2.225)	2.557	Water, waste	9.516
Limestone	0.073	Stack loss (misc. Al particulates)	0.769
Sodium carbonate	0.075	ALUMINA, ANHYDROUS	
Starch	0.006	(Al₂O₃=99%)	1.000

INPUTS ACCOUNTED FOR	13.249		OUTPUTS ACCOUNTED FOR	13.249
Source: Battelle 1975, p. 150.		0	= Difference = 0.0% of Inputs	

Sources: A. Authors; B. IDEA database; C. Hall *et al.* 1975, p. 150.

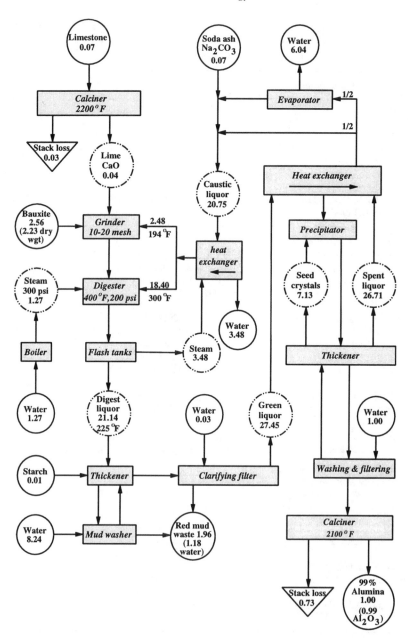

Source: Battelle 1975, p. 150.

Figure 3.1:   *The Bayer process for producing alumina*

and titanium oxides, is thickened, precipitated and filtered out, after which the solution is cooled to precipitate alumina hydrate. The latter is calcined to drive off the water and yield the dehydrated alumina that goes to the smelters.

Approximately 2.2 tonnes of bauxite (dry weight) are needed, on average, to produce 1 tonne of dehydrated alumina (Hall *et al.* 1975). Three cases are described in Table 3.2, differentiated mainly in terms of the quality of the bauxite. With a high-quality bauxite (1.922 tonnes per tonne of alumina) the other chemical inputs are limestone (39 kg) and caustic soda (39 kg) plus water (about 60 kg per tonne of alumina). A lower-quality ore is also illustrated, namely 3.3 tonnes of bauxite per tonne of product. It requires 50.5 kg of lime (or 95 kg of limestone) and 113 kg of caustic soda per tonne of alumina output. However, another alternative is to start from soda ash (74.5 kg) and lime (38.5 kg). In this case, soda ash is reacted with lime to produce caustic soda on site (Hall *et al.* 1975, 'Aluminum' Figure 3, p. 150). This case is illustrated in the flow chart Figure 3.1. There are numerous possible combinations. In fact, every alumina plant is designed for a particular ore (Altenpohl 1982), which makes the industry relatively inflexible.

The Bayer process is quite energy intensive, because of the need to heat the caustic solution, and the various calcination stages. This energy — about 18.8 MMBTU per ton of contained aluminum in 1970 — is supplied by natural gas or other fuels. The alumina refining generates significant process wastes, especially in the mining and alumina production stages. A composite flow chart for primary aluminum production in the US is shown in Figure 3.2.

The waste sludge from the Bayer process is called 'red mud'. The initial solids content of red mud before dewatering normally ranges from 17% to 20%. It contains insoluble oxides of iron, silicon, titanium and other trace metals as well as some aluminum silicate. Alumina may be recovered from the aluminum silicate by heating the red mud with soda ash and limestone, yielding a soluble sodium aluminum oxide and a calcium–silica waste called 'brown mud'. Titanium might also be recoverable from some red muds, but this is not economical at present. In fact, despite a great deal of research over six decades, no significant use has been found for this waste material. A possibility that has received some attention is to use aluminum ore as a source of the semiconductor gallium, which may find significantly greater uses in the future. This is discussed in a later section.

According to the US Bureau of Mines, anywhere from one-third of a tonne to 1 tonne (dry weight) of waste red mud is generated per tonne of alumina produced. However, the second case described in Table 3.2 generates much more waste — over 2 tonnes of red mud per tonne of alumina. The quantity of red mud obviously depends on the quality of the ore. The sludge is corrosive to the skin, because of residues of caustic soda used in the refining process. It is normally accumulated in settling ponds adjacent to the refineries.

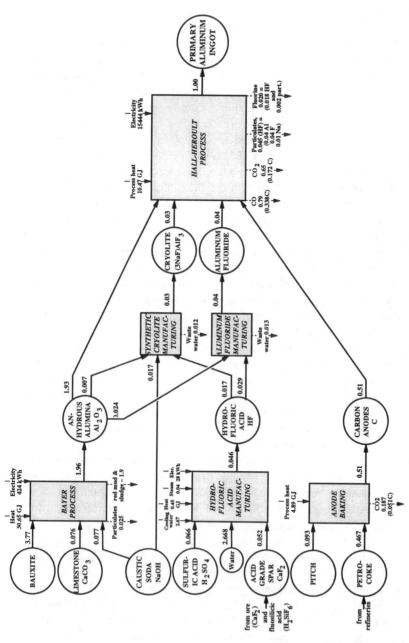

Data Sources: Various, 1970s.

Figure 3.2: *Composite aluminum ingot process*

The caustic liquid can pollute surface or ground water. In dry climates, after some time for drying, the impounded area can be recultivated (though it is not very fertile). However, in tropical regions of high rainfall, impoundment presents significant engineering problems and auxiliary treatment is likely to be needed to prevent groundwater contamination.

Alumina as such is used as an abrasive, as an adsorbent, and for chemical manufacturing, although an overwhelmingly large percentage of the output is currently smelted to produce aluminum metal.

3.4. ALUMINUM SMELTING PROCESSES

The only process used for smelting aluminum today is the so-called Hall–Heroult electrolytic process. The alumina is dissolved in a bath of molten cryolite, which is sodium aluminum fluoride (Na_3AlF_6), plus a small amount of aluminum fluoride, AlF_3. Carbon anodes react with the alumina, generating carbon dioxide and metallic aluminum. Fluorine is also lost at the anode, partly as hydrogen fluoride and partly as fluoride particulates. We have noted that the electrolytic reduction of alumina to aluminum requires significant quantities of electricity — of the order of 15 000 kWh per tonne, at present. It also consumes petroleum coke (for carbon anode production). In terms of energy requirements, the last item amounts to 30 MMBTU per tonne of aluminum. The carbon combines with oxygen from the alumina in a fixed coke/aluminum ratio of 0.42. (We reconsider the carbon source problem later.)

The Hall–Heroult smelting process also consumes aluminum fluoride, to make up for the fluorine lost from the electrolyte at the anodes. The estimated average (untreated) emission rate is 20 kg per tonne of aluminum. (Actually, this is apparently an underestimate, for some smelters, as noted below.) Industry practice in the US in the early 1970s was said to recover about 70% of the fluoride emissions. In 1970 the US Environmental Protection Agency (USEPA) set the standard for control of new potlines at 95.5% or 1.8 kg/tonne of aluminum. Existing smelters were supposed to achieve about 90% control. The losses occur in two forms: gaseous hydrogen fluoride and particulates. The gaseous emissions are considered most hazardous (especially to vegetation, and to animals that consume it) but it can be recovered most easily in wet scrubbers; dry scrubbers are much more efficient (up to 99%) for particulates. The two can be used in combination, but there is some tradeoff involved. Recovered fluorides can be recycled within the refinery, but this leads to a buildup of impurities in the aluminum. Elaborate methods of 'ore management' are then needed to maintain aluminum product purity at the desired (99.9%) level.

European smelters capture and recycle some of their fluorine emissions, but not nearly up to the USEPA standard. The 1991 average makeup AlF_3 consumption for European smelters was 20 kg/tonne, with a range of 15 (Germany) to 26 (Italy) (data from EcoPlan). Estimated requirements for aluminum fluoride in Western Europe are 70 kMT/yr. Details are given in Appendix A, Table A.9. Aluminum fluoride consumes 6.5% of Western European hydrogen fluoride and synthetic cryolite takes an additional 1.3%. Thus, nearly 8% of the fluorine consumed in Western Europe is used in the aluminum industry. (For further discussion of fluorine, see Section 8.4, Sources and uses of fluorine). Since it is not embodied in the product, all of this makeup fluorine is either accumulated in a solid waste of some kind (e.g. water treatment sludge) or dissipated into the environment as air or water pollution.

An alternative to the Hall–Heroult electrolytic cell that promised to reduce electric energy consumption by 30% was (and is) the so-called ALCOA process. Instead of dissolving alumina in cryolite, the general idea is to convert aluminum oxide (alumina) to aluminum chloride by direct chlorination (Hall *et al.* 1975; Altenpohl 1982). Then the aluminum chloride can be dissolved in an electrolyte consisting of sodium and calcium or lithium chlorides. It can then be electrolytically reduced, but at a temperature lower than that needed for the Hall–Heroult process. More important, the bipolar chloride cells can be 'stacked', unlike the Hall cells, thus reducing the voltage requirements and the resistance losses. The process releases chlorine at the carbon anode for recycling. ALCOA had a pilot plant in operation at Palestine, Texas, from 1976 to 1981, but according to a company insider, the process has never been implemented in full-scale operation because of a major strategic change of direction in the company (putting much more emphasis on downstream aluminum products and less on primary production). Nevertheless, it continues to attract interest.

One problem that arose with the early versions of the ALCOA process was that chlorine reacted with the carbon anodes — made from petroleum coke — and generated trace quantities of chlorinated aromatics, such as chlorobenzenes, polychlorobiphenyls (PCBs) and even dioxins (PCDDs) (Jarrett 1982). These would constitute a potential toxic pollution problem. On the other hand, it was believed that the emissions problem could be contained by suitable waste treatment (Jarrett 1994). Also, of course, fluorine emissions would be eliminated automatically. A detailed tradeoff analysis would have to be undertaken, of course, before making any major investment in the new technology.

An interesting possibility that deserves more attention is to use aluminum chloride rather than alumina as a feedstock for the ALCOA process. In principle, aluminum chloride can be obtained from a number of sources, from clay to coal fly ash, by hydrochlorination or direct chlorination. The economics of this combination appear to be potentially favorable. The major difficulty here is that for the ALCOA cell to work, the aluminum chloride must be anhydrous. Unfortunately, aluminum chloride (like calcium chloride) happens to be extremely hygroscopic i.e. 'water loving'. To dehydrate it is a non-trivial (and energy-intensive) technological task. Nevertheless, this possibility is considered further in another section (See Chapter 14, Coal ash).

Recovery of primary aluminum by thermochemical means, not requiring electrolysis, has been considered. Three such processes were described in a 1975 report to the US Bureau of Mines (Hall *et al.* 1975). They are the ALCAN process, the Toth process and the 'monochloride process' of Peacey and Grimshaw. The ALCAN process, as described by Hall *et al.* (ibid.) involves an electric arc furnace to smelt bauxite directly (with coke) yielding an aluminum silicon alloy. This was chlorinated in a reactor, and subsequently decomposed in a high-temperature decomposer. A pilot plant was built, but later shut down because of stress corrosion problems. These were apparently solved, but the plant was never reopened. Details of the process are not available.

The Toth process, as then described, used manganese to reduce aluminum chloride. The details are somewhat complex (Peacey and Davenport 1974). Manganese metal is produced in a blast furnace; it reacts with liquid aluminum chloride (Al_2Cl_6) at moderate temperature and pressure, reducing the aluminum as powder. The aluminum powder is separated by a cyclone from the (liquid) manganese chloride. Unreacted aluminum chloride is evaporated and returned to the purifier. The latter is then oxidized at high temperature, releasing the chlorine which is returned to the aluminum chlorinator. The source of aluminum was to have been calcined clay. Both alumina and silica are chlorinated, but the silicon tetrachloride is recycled to the chlorinator to suppress chlorination of the silica. Chlorinated aluminum is separated from the other chlorination products (iron, sodium, potassium, calcium, etc.) by multiple fractionation and condensation stages. Most of the process steps take place at high temperatures.

The major disadvantages of the Toth process appear to be (i) complexity (ii) the likelihood of corrosion problems at the high temperatures involved (iii) significant losses of chlorine through chlorinated silica, iron and other minor contaminants and (iv) relatively high coke requirements. Three kg of manganese are needed to reduce one kg of aluminum metal, and the reduction of each kg of manganese requires 1.5 kg of coke. Thus the coke requirement alone would be 4.5 kg per kg of Al. Also, blast furnace manganese is not pure. It contains significant quantities of the carbide Mn_7C_3, which would not be as effective a reductant for aluminum chloride. The losses of chlorinated byproducts would constitute a significant problem for environmental control.

The monochloride process mentioned above has been tested on a laboratory scale (Peacey and Davenport 1974). The process is superficially much simpler than that of Toth, though it does not yield pure aluminum, but rather an aluminum silicon alloy (less than 1% Si). In brief, hot Al_2Cl_3 is passed through a bed of calcined bauxite and coke at high temperature. The carbon in the coke combines with the oxygen in the alumina. Everything else combines with chlorine. A variety of gases are formed (as in the Toth process), consisting of CO, $AlCl_2$, $SiCl_2$ and $FeCl_2$. The hot gases are then decomposed by a spray of molten lead. The aluminum chloride is reduced to aluminum, which ends up floating on the lead. Separation is presumably by fractional crystallization. In equilibrium, the aluminum retains a small lead and silicon residue. Further purification is not discussed in the report. Of course, the use of lead suggests a significant environmental risk.

Still another class of thermochemical reduction processes has been analyzed in some detail by ALCOA, under cost-sharing contract to the US Department of Energy (1977–82). This contract was initiated in response to reports of a Japanese plan to undertake national level R&D leading to a pilot plant and a commercial plant. The results of the study suggested that the production of aluminum or aluminum-silicon alloys by means of an oxygen-blown blast furnace would be practical. The output of the blast furnace would be molten Al-Si-Fe. This would be separated into two phases (Al-Si and Fe-Si) in a fractional crystallizer. The Fe-Si fraction (ferrosilicon) is a valuable product with growing markets. The Al-Si fraction would then be electrolytically separated to Si and Al in a membrane cell (Bruno 1982).

The major advantages seen at the time for the process would be that instead of using coke derived from petroleum, the process would directly utilize much cheaper low-grade coal refuse or even shale. It would also eliminate fluoride emissions. The blast furnace process would also cut down on bauxite requirements by substituting domestic clay or fly ash for imported bauxite. Finally, the process would have been considerably less energy intensive than the Hall–Heroult process, namely, 105–133 MMBTU/tonne of aluminum, vs. 192–232 MMBTU, depending on details.

3.5.   CARBON VERSUS INERT ANODES

It was noted above that the Hall–Heroult process requires 0.42 tonnes of petroleum coke per tonne of primary aluminum smelted. There are two established processes for manufacturing carbon anodes. The older is the so-called Soderberg process, consisting of a single carbon anode that is fed continuously into the cell and is baked in place by the heat of the cell. The Soderberg process has been replaced in virtually all modern plants (except a few in developing countries) by the pre-baked type of anode, which pollutes less and has higher electrical efficiency. Pre-baked anodes are made and baked outside the electrolytic cell.

Pre-baked anodes can only be made from petroleum coke made by a special process in which the hydrocarbon feed is preheated and 'flashed' into a cold chamber, depositing carbon granules on every surface. This finely divided carbon is then ground, calcined and mixed with pitch and made into a paste, which is then baked.

Petroleum is not in short supply at present, but a future 'oil crisis' cannot be ruled out. In any case, it would be useful either to find a cheaper source of carbon for anode production or to avoid the use of carbon anodes altogether. There are two attractive possibilities here. The first is to learn how to make carbon anodes with the desired electrical properties from a cheap source of carbon. The second is to learn how to make inert (non-reactive) permanent anodes that are not consumed in the electrolysis process.

The first approach may be nearer to realization. The starting point could be solvent-refined coal (SRC), which would permit removal of ash and sulfur prior to combustion, yielding solid briquettes of 'coke' and a liquid hydrocarbon comparable to crude petroleum. This liquid can be refined like oil. It would seem to follow that petroleum coke could be produced from it by the same process that is now used in oil refineries.

The possibility of developing an inert anode for the Hall–Heroult cell has attracted the attention of researchers for a long time. Unfortunately, while there has been progress, the fundamental problem — corrosion — has not yet been solved. It is rumored that Vittorio de Nora, the Italian inventor of the mercury cell for chlorine electrolysis, has been working on the problem in recent years. Confirmation is entirely lacking, however.

3.6. CONCLUDING REMARKS ON ALUMINUM

Surprisingly, there are a number of promising new technologies for the alumina–aluminum industry. These range from new sources of alumina and petroleum coke to new smelting processes. In most cases some additional research or engineering development is needed, though in some cases — notably the ALCOA process — the remaining technical problems appear to be soluble. The major problem here may be to find the capital to scale up from the pilot scale to the industrial scale.

The fact that these new technologies have not been commercialized, in most cases, does not imply that the processes in question are faulty, though they are still largely untested and some will surely fall by the wayside. Industry spokesmen and neoclassical economists invariably claim that 'if the technology was superior it would be in use today'. Neoclassical economists tend to believe that capital markets, in particular, operate efficiently and therefore rational managers would make such investments if they were economically justifiable. This claim is naive and easily refuted. There are many examples in a variety of industries of admittedly superior technologies that have been, and still are neglected. This may occur for perfectly rational reasons, e.g. because they would require massive new investment and therefore cannot compete with a fully depreciated older plant (see, for example Chapter 10, Chlorine), or for much less rational reasons, such as personal experience (on the part of the managers) with the older technology.

In the aluminum case, of course, the new technologies have not reached the point of being widely accepted as superior. However, neither does their neglect to date prove inferiority. It can be laid to the fact that the relevant industries — notably electric power and primary aluminum –are generally mature, slow growing (or non-growing), oligopolistic, and extremely risk averse. The conditions (OPEC cartel, possible bauxite producers' cartel) that stimulated a number of research projects in the 1970s did not last long enough to see any of the projects to completion. Nevertheless, future crises of a similar kind may occur.

The ALCOA process for aluminum smelting offers a special opportunity — potentially comparable to the BOF case noted in Section 3.4, Aluminum smelting processes — since it is a process that has already been tested at the pilot stage. The tests revealed some potential pollution problems that were thought to be soluble, but the main reason for failure to proceed was a change in the strategic direction of the company, namely, that the firm should take advantage of opportunities to obtain long-term commitments to cheap resources, using tried and true technology, and devote its capital and R&D capabilities to developing high-value aluminum alloys and to manufacture downstream components for the (then booming) aerospace sector.

While ALCOA may not be willing to commit large amounts of capital to building a plant based on a new process (given overcapacity in the industry and slow growth in demand), it might well be interested in a joint venture with a high-cost European firm, or an East European or Asian firm. Should the process be successfully adopted by producers in Russia or China (for instance), the BOF story could repeat itself.

3.7.   GALLIUM SOURCES, USES AND LOSSES

Gallium is a transition metal whose properties make it potentially very valuable for high-speed switching devices and lasers. It is not extraordinarily rare — 15 ppm in the earth's crust, as compared to 16 ppm for lead — but is rarely found in high natural concentrations. It is most conveniently extracted as a trace contaminant in aluminum ores (bauxite), although it is also potentially recoverable from zinc ores, phosphate rock and from coal fly ash.[5] Typical gallium content of bauxites ranges from 30 ppm to 80 ppm. Among the large-scale bauxite producers, Surinam has 80 ppm, India 70 ppm, Australia, Jamaica and China 60 ppm, Brazil and Guyana 50 ppm, Guinea and Venezuela 30 ppm (USBuMines 1992).

There is one small copper–zinc–germanium–gallium–silver deposit in Nevada (Apex) where the gallium content of the ore, as originally graded, is 0.039% (3900 ppm) (USBuMines 1991). The mine has been closed since 1987, however. Even richer germanium–gallium ore — up to 1.85% gallium — has been found in small quantities at Tsumeb, Namibia.

A number of proprietary processes have been developed for extracting the gallium from Bayer process liquors, mostly by electrolysis or electrodeposition. Solvent extraction is also used. Virtually every producer has its own process variant. Major gallium producers or refiners in Europe in the 1980s were Rhone–Poulenc (using feedstock from Pechiney in France), AluSuisse (a refiner), VAW in Germany (which supplies feedstock to Ingal (International Gallium) GMBH in Germany, and Elkem in Norway (Roskill Ga 1990). In 1990 Elkem closed its operation and Rhone–Poulenc shifted its production from France to a new 50 tonne per year plant in Australia, using feedstock from ALCOA; in 1994 Rhone–Poulenc purchased the Ingal facility (Kramer 1994). Sumitomo is apparently also a gallium producer.

Annual worldwide *potential* gallium production capacity, based on existing alumina capacity, exceeds 4000 tonnes/yr (if all bauxite mines were operating at full capacity). On the other hand, *actual* world production capacity in 1993 was estimated to be 145 tonnes, including Rhone–Poulenc's Australian facility, plus 30 tonnes per year capacity in the former USSR, 20 tonnes per year capacity in Germany and 7 tonnes per year capacity in Japan (Kramer 1994). Actual world production in 1993 was only 35 tonnes (ibid.); US consumption was just over 11 tonnes almost entirely for gallium-arsenide and indium-gallium-arsenide semiconductor applications, such as lasers, light emitting diodes, photodetectors and photovoltaic cells and integrated circuits. By comparison, world consumption of electronic grade silicon in 1988 was roughly 750 tonnes; current consumption is somewhat larger (see Chapter 11, Silicon).

A few years ago it was thought that gallium-arsenide-based semiconductor technology was on the point of replacing silicon-based semiconductor technology for integrated circuits, because gallium-arsenide circuit elements are undoubtedly faster. (They are also more radiation resistant, which tends to make them the choice of preference in most military equipment.) As regards integrated circuitry, the expected general substitution did not occur, however, because of continued improvements in silicon technologies. Other applications of gallium-arsenide and indium-gallium-arsenide, for opto-electronic devices, continue to appear promising. A 'day of gallium-arsenide' may yet come. Nevertheless, advances in micro-miniaturization keep reducing the quantity of semiconductor material required per circuit element. Taking this into account, current sources of gallium (from bauxite, zinc ores and coal ash) appear to be ample for the foreseeable future. Thus, a potential need for gallium cannot justify large-scale bauxite mining.

NOTES(3)

1. Alunite is a potassium-aluminum sulfate. It is mined in the Zaglik district of Azerbaijan. Potash (for fertilizer) is a useful byproduct of alumina operations.
2. Some alumina is, or has been, produced in Russia from nepheline syenite, mined in the Kola peninsula, and in Siberia. Nepheline concentrate contains 28–30% alumina. It is processed by sintering with lime, followed by leaching to remove the carbonates, followed by a second lime sinter to yield cement. For each tonne of alumina produced, the nepheline process also yields 9–11 tonnes of Portland cement, 600–800 kg of sodium carbonate (soda ash) and 200–300 kg of potassium carbonate (potash).
3. An interesting possible process for producing sulfur, alumina and portland cement from flue-gas desulfurization (FGD) scrubber waste and kaolin, was proposed by TRW Inc. (Motley and Cosgrove 1978). It is discussed in more detail in connection with Section 7.3, Potential sulfur recovery from coal. Another possible source of alumina is coal fly ash. We discuss this possibility subsequently (Chapter 14, Coal ash). The major advantage of both of these schemes is that they would make bauxite mining essentially unnecessary while simultaneously converting waste materials (FGD scrubber waste and ash) into resources.
4. The production of alumina from bauxite currently consumes 6% of all the caustic soda produced in Europe (see Chapter 10, Chlorine).
5. As a matter of interest, the average gallium content in US coal ash is about 65 ppm. In some coal ashes gallium has been found in concentrations up to 1000 ppm (0.1%) (Roskill Ga 1990). Recovery potential is based largely on the fact that gallium is further concentrated in flue dusts (fly ash). A recovery process for gallium and germanium was developed in the UK by GEC Research Laboratories and Johnson-Matthey & Co. It was operated commercially between 1950 and 1970 (ibid., p. B8). (See Chapter 14, Coal ash for more detail.)

4. Copper, cobalt, silver and arsenic

4.1. SUMMARY

Copper is man's oldest metal (because it was found in workable nuggets) and remains one of the most important industrial metals because of its remarkable malleability, ductility, electrical and thermal conductivity and resistance to corrosion. Its red-orange color is also very attractive. For all of these reasons copper will continue to be used in many applications, especially tubing, pipe and electrical wire, notwithstanding strong competition from aluminum in some of them and glass fibers for others. Cobalt is also a very important industrial metal, particularly as a binder for ultra-hard carbides and an alloying agent for high-temperature resistant superalloys (used in jet engines, for instance) and permanent magnets. Cobalt is so valuable for these properties that it is commonly regarded as a 'critical' metal for modern aerospace technology.

The byproducts of copper are zinc, lead, molybdenum, cobalt, arsenic, selenium, tellurium and silver, as well as sulfur. These metals are often (but not always) found in the same ores, usually as sulfides. However, zinc, lead and molybdenum are primarily found in distinct ore bodies in which copper is a minor constituent, and which are mined for their own sake. (See Chapter 6, Zinc.) This is partly, but less true of silver. Sulfur is a major byproduct, but never a primary product. (See Chapter 7, Sulfur.) Non-ferrous metal mining and smelting has long been a major sulfur dioxide polluter; it is an increasingly important source of sulfur for industry today. According to one source, 1.3 tonnes of sulfur dioxide are generated at the smelter for each tonne of pure primary copper. In the industrialized countries, most of this sulfur is captured, but elsewhere much of it is still emitted to the atmosphere as SO_2 — which becomes acid rain — rather than being recovered for useful purposes.

Moreover, copper ores are low in grade and most copper is mined from large open pit mines requiring large amounts of materials processing (in the US 165 tonnes of inert material per tonne of Cu, exclusive of overburden), at high energy cost, to extract the virgin metal. Copper mining involves more materials displacement than any mining activity except coal mining and uranium mining, with all that this implies for physical damage to the environment.

Arsenic is a byproduct of copper ore mostly used for its extraordinary bio-toxicity (e.g. in herbicides and wood preservatives). The distribution of arsenic in the environment is widespread and worrisome. It moves relatively easily from one environmental medium to another, e.g. from soil to air to water. Arsenical herbicides and pesticides, used in the past, can be taken up by plants, or metabolized by anaerobic bacteria to form methyl arsines which are extremely volatile. Airborne arsenic is a probable cause of cancer. Arsenic has an important potential electronic use (the semiconductor gallium-arsenide), which could conceivably 'soak up' some of the excess potential supply,[1] assuming gallium were also sufficiently available. (This appears to be the case: see Chapter 3, Aluminum).

Silver is used mainly for coinage, jewelry and decorative plating. However, it is still used extensively in photography, although this use is declining because of technological progress in photochemistry and increasing competition by electronic-imaging technologies. It is important that silver be recovered to the maximum feasible extent, however, if only to conserve it for the future. In the first place, silver has extraordinarily valuable physical and chemical properties. Apart from its opto-electric properties, it is the best of all metallic conductors of heat and electricity. Yet it is inherently quite scarce in the earth's crust. Most of it is recovered from copper ore, nowadays. Furthermore, most silver compounds are toxic.

The interdependency illustrated by this group of metals is that of byproduct and co-products. In particular, the only plausible way to reduce the amount of arsenic extracted from the earth's surface, globally, would be to sharply reduce the global mining of high-arsenic ores of copper (and nickel). While direct regulation is the most important factor in the short run, it would be at least marginally helpful, in this regard, to increase the rate of recovery and recycling of copper and cobalt. That would also reduce the new silver supply and encourage greater conservation of silver.

Goals of public policy: reduce dependence on imported raw materials; reduce environmental damage caused by surface mining; reduce environmental harm associated with smelting and refining; reduce energy consumption; reduce production and dissipative uses of toxic metals, especially arsenic; increase recycling of copper and cobalt; increase recovery of sulfur.

4.2. COPPER SOURCES AND REFINING

Copper is relatively scarce in the earth's crust (58 ppm). Nevertheless, in the recent past it was still being found in native form and quite high-grade ores. This is no longer the case. Copper is only found in rather low-grade ores today, though a great many different minerals contain copper. It is now mined

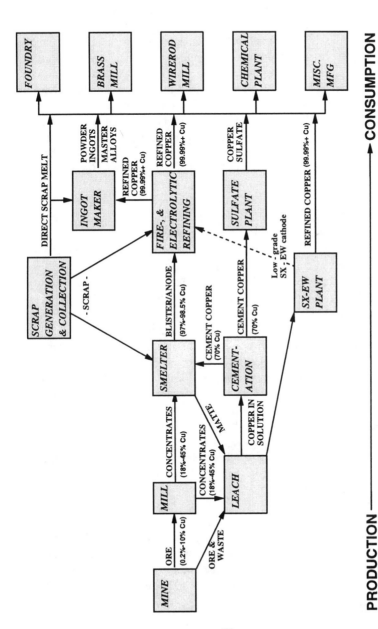

PRODUCTION ──────────► **CONSUMPTION**

Data Source: US Bureau of Mines.

Figure 4.1: Generalized copper flow chart

predominantly from relatively low-grade porphyry (sulfide) ores from large open pit mines. Open pit mines account for 55% of the world output (83% in the US).

US ores now being mined average about 0.5–0.6% Cu, although Chilean ores are about twice as rich and some Zambian/Zairian ores can be up to 5% Cu, though the average is about 1.2%. The main consequence of this fact is that large amounts of inert material must be processed to obtain a small amount of copper, resulting in large energy consumption and large quantities of mine waste. In the US over 500 tonnes of inert material must be moved and over 165 tonnes of ore must be processed to produce a tonne of virgin copper. A generalized flow chart for copper is shown in Figure 4.1.

World mine production in 1989 was 8.89 MMT (Cu content); 1993 production was about the same, 9.3 MMT. Copper is mined in many countries, but the two principal producers in 1993 were Chile (2.02 MMT) and the US (1.77 MMT). These were followed by Canada (750 kMT), the former USSR (800 kMT), Zaire (90 kMT, down sharply from 475 kMT in 1989), Zambia (420 kMT) and Poland (390 kMT). Other European sources are minor, as shown in Appendix A, Table A.2. Output from older Scandinavian mines is declining; newly opened Portuguese mines are increasing output, however.

The 'standard' process starts with ore from an open pit or underground mine. It is processed by crushing and grinding, concentrated by froth flotation, and the concentrate (30% Cu) is then reduced in a primary smelter to a copper sulfide–iron sulfide 'matte' (up to 60% copper). The latter then passes to a 'convertor' in which the sulfur is removed (by oxidation to SO_2) which is later recovered as sulfuric acid. The convertor stage increasingly uses oxygen enrichment — a technology borrowed from the steel industry — and the iron is removed as convertor slag, yielding 'blister copper'. The latter is further 'fire refined' in a furnace to produce anodes for the final electrolytic refining stage. A simplified process-product flow chart for the standard process is shown in Figure 4.2. However, the figure is a composite that does not reflect the full range of technologies and changes now under way. The most active area of technological change is in the smelter technology, which is switching from reverberatory batch furnaces to flash furnaces and continuous smelters.

The most important innovation (since 1968) is known as solvent extraction–electro-winning, or SX–EW technology. Certain ores (so-called 'acid-soluble oxide' ores and chalcocite (CuS_2) ores) are leached with dilute sulfuric acid — a byproduct of conventional smelters — in heaps, pads or even *in situ*. The next step is solvent extraction, using organic solvents. The concentrated copper sulfate then goes directly to an electrolytic cell to produce 'cathode copper', thus bypassing both the smelting and refining steps. The SX–EW process has been under development for a long time, with gradually increasing yields and improvements in product quality, but by 1977 EW

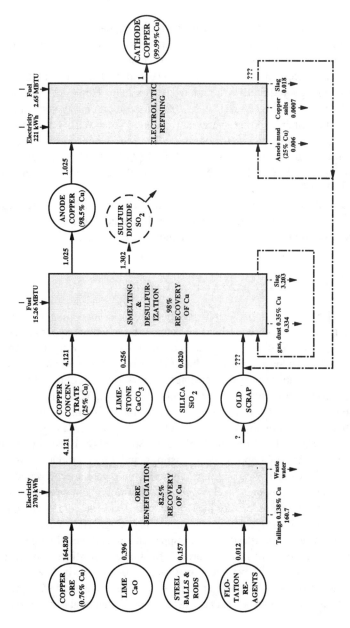

Figure 4.2: The 'standard process' for copper

55

cathode copper was pure enough to go directly to wire-rod plants. US output
from this process was only 32.7 kMT in 1971, but reached 441 kMT in 1991
(27% of US mine production) and is expected to peak at 690 kMT by 1998.
World SX–EW capacity was 1.1 MMT in 1991 and will nearly double by the
year 2000.

Curiously enough, while the new hydro-metallurgical process is economically favorable (and permits exploitation of low-grade ores, including waste
dumps from former mines) it is not an improvement over the standard pyro-
metallurgical process in terms of energy consumption. This is due to the large
amount of energy required to circulate the leachate. However, the energy
used in electro-winning *per se* is only 20% of the total energy consumption
from mine to refinery, so that energy may be used (or saved) at a number of
different points, depending on the ore body. The energy consumed to produce
a tonne of refined copper ranges from 100 GJ (95 MMBTU) for high-grade
ore (1% Cu) to 200 GJ (190 MMBTU) for the lowest-grade ore currently
mined (0.3%) (Forrest and Szekely 1991).

Copper is normally concentrated at the mine and smelted to 'blister' copper nearby, though a few smelters (mainly in Japan and Western Europe) use
imported ores and concentrates. See Appendix A, Table A.2.

4.3.   COPPER USES AND RECYCLING

End-uses of copper are mostly (97%) as metal. Pure refined copper is generally used for wire and wire products and copper tube, while copper alloys —
especially brass (an alloy of copper and zinc) — are or were used for a
variety of other products, such as architectural hardware, clocks and watches,
bearings, coins, batteries, bronze castings, screws, ammunition, automobile
radiators, air-conditioning, heat exchangers, and so on. Wire mill products
accounted for about 51% of copper consumption in 1936 (the earliest available statistics) and only 43.5% in 1940, but since World War II this has risen
steadily to 70% in 1980 and probably over 80% today. By contrast, the
relative importance of copper sheet, castings and brass products has de-
creased sharply. Copper wire and pipe, and brass hardware are recovered and
recycled to a significant degree. But a good deal of metallic copper and brass
is lost in solid wastes, especially junked vehicles, discarded electrical appliances, consumer electronic devices, ammunition casings, and so on.

In recent decades, industrial uses of copper chemicals, including catalysts
(especially in aniline dye manufacturing), fungicides (mostly in vineyards)
and wood preservatives, have been small and growing slowly. The case of
wood preservatives — which also utilize arsenic — is discussed in Chapter 5,
Chromium, and need not be repeated here. Copper chemicals are produced

from copper sulfate (made by sulfuric acid treatment of scrap copper); they amount to less than 3% of total copper consumption, but a much larger fraction of scrap.

Secondary copper refined from old scrap accounts for only about 25% of current consumption in the US (USBuMines 1991). If 'new' scrap (from fabrication processes) is included, the figure is significantly higher, of course. According to industry statistics, consumption of refined copper in the EU in 1992 was 2.956 MMT, copper refined from scrap was 627 kMT (21.2%) while total secondary copper scrap recovery was 787.5 kMT (26.5%) (METAL 1993). The recovery rate for copper has been rising steadily, but it is still surprisingly low. We do not have reliable figures for individual countries in Europe, although West Germany reported 42% copper recycling in 1982 (BDI 1984).

The main reason the recycling rate, measured in terms of scrap as a fraction of total consumption, appears low is that much of the copper is used in long-lived products, such as appliances, vehicles and structures. Thus much of it is tied up for many years in 'inventory'. However, the fundamental problem is that disassembly of vehicles, demolition waste and consumer products to recover electrical wiring buried inside is seldom worthwhile on economic grounds.

Yet there are strong arguments for encouraging more recycling of copper and its alloys (e.g. brass) to the maximum feasible degree, which should certainly be considerably higher than 25% or even 40%. This would reduce the need for mining and smelting of virgin copper, thus cutting down on most of the above sources of emissions, as well as reducing arsenic production at the source. The energy savings are compelling: the energy required to recover copper from scrap varies from 14 to 40 GJ/tonne, depending on the quality of the scrap, as compared to 100–200 GJ/tonne for virgin copper (Forrest and Szekely 1991).

Almost certainly the solution is not technological. That is to say, there is no imaginable machine or chemical process for extracting copper wires efficiently from a crushed automobile body, a washing machine, a TV set, or an electric clock, as now manufactured. Manufacturers, currently, take no responsibility for the ultimate disposal of their products, and they do not design their products for easy recyclability. Yet, in the case of copper, it seems likely that much could be done at the design stage of the manufacturing to facilitate easy removal of copper wiring and copper-bearing components (such as the windings of transformers and motors). In short, the 'Design for Environment' concept could be particularly valuable in terms of increasing the rate of copper recovery.

Even when products are designed to make it possible, disassembly will still be relatively labor intensive compared to original manufacturing. To make it happen — as opposed to making it *possible* — it will be necessary to accomplish either (or both) of the following: (1) to sharply increase the value (i.e. price) of copper *vis-à-vis* labor and (2) to encourage the export of used copper-containing consumer appliances and PCs to low-wage countries where valuable materials can be separated and recovered for use at reasonable cost.

How either of these conditions is to be met is beyond the scope of the present study. However, it may be worth noting that a resource-based taxation system now being discussed in the European Union could be designed to reduce the tax burden on labor by shifting the burden, at least partly, to raw materials, especially non-renewables. It would do so by altering the current price advantage that currently tends to favor virgin over secondary materials. This would increase domestic employment in the high-wage user countries, notably Europe.

4.4.   COPPER IN THE ENVIRONMENT

Copper is mobilized from anthropogenic sources to a much greater extent than by natural processes. Globally, natural processes (dust, volcanism, fires) account for atmospheric emissions of about 6 kMT/yr, compared to 35 kMT/yr by anthropogenic processes, of which by far the largest share (23.6 kMT/yr) was due to copper smelting and refining, while another 8 kMT/yr is attributable to coal combustion (Nriagu 1990). In Europe, another study counted 15.5 kMT of atmospheric copper emissions in 1979, of which half was attributable to copper smelting and refining, and most of the rest was due to fuel (i.e. coal) combustion (Pacyna 1986). Copper mining by acid leaching undoubtedly contributes significantly to water pollution, with a further contribution from tailings dumps and smelter slag heaps. The leaching rate may increase as rainfall becomes more acid.

4.5.   COBALT SOURCES AND USES

Cobalt is mobilized in significant amounts by natural processes. The most cited estimate puts biological extraction processes at 30 kMT/yr, rock weathering at 10 kMT/yr, and fossil fuel (i.e. coal) combustion at 5 kMT/yr (Donaldson 1986). Shedd has modified the Donaldson figures with respect to losses from mining and refining processes. Cobalt recovery varies considerably from mine to mine, and from refinery to refinery, but Shedd estimates an average of 50% taken over all mines and refineries. In this case, for each ton of cobalt produced, another ton is lost in tailings, slag or other products of metallurgical processing (Shedd 1993, p. 3).

Cobalt is usually a byproduct of copper, although it is also found with some nickel ores (in Australia, Brazil, Canada, France and the Philippines) and with platinum (in South Africa). Zaire recently accounted for over half of recent world output: about 25 kMT in 1989, of the world total of about 45 kMT in that year. However, political turmoil has crippled Zairian production. The two largest producers in 1993 were Canada (5738 tonnes) and Zambia (5300 tonnes), followed by Russia (3300 tonnes) and Zaire (2459 tonnes). The world total for 1993 was 22 224 tonnes. Albania was the only active (nickel) mine source in Europe, though production has effectively ceased.

Zaire was formerly the largest cobalt refiner, as well as the largest source of ore, followed by the (former) USSR. However, in 1993 the major refiners were Russia (4000 tonnes), Zambia (3700 tonnes), Canada (2695 tonnes), Norway (2414 tonnes) and Finland (2200 tonnes). The world total for 1993 was only 16 893 tonnes, sharply down from 1989. Some of the Norwegian output is derived from Canadian concentrates. The Finnish refineries obtain concentrates and semi-refined materials from Australia, New Caledonia and Indonesia. There is a nickel-cobalt refinery in France (Le Havre) that produces about 150 tonnes per year from New Caledonian nickel ores.

The largest end-use of cobalt is for high-temperature resistant 'superalloys' (usually with nickel and chromium) notably in jet engines. Of 7065 MT consumed in the US in 1989, 2813 went for this purpose. Consumption for this purpose in 1993 was slightly lower (2614 tonnes). This use had been increasing for several decades, but now appears to have peaked. Cemented carbides for cutting tools accounted for 569 tonnes in 1993. Magnets — mainly AlNiCo and Samarium-Cobalt — accounted for 860 MT in 1989 and 629 tonnes in 1993 (USBuMines 1993).[2] Chemical uses of cobalt included catalysts (935 tonnes in 1993), driers for paint (732 tonnes in 1993), pigments (193 tonnes) and several uses for colorizing and decolorizing ceramics and glass. Some cobalt is consumed for animal feeds. Superalloys and magnets are recoverable. Catalysts, pigments, driers, animal feeds and other chemical uses and carbide-cutting tools are likely to be dissipative. The European consumption pattern is probably similar to the US pattern. Losses from dissipative uses appear to average about 50% of total consumption, or about 10 kMT for the world, which is far less than other sources of cobalt in the environment (Shedd 1993, Table 1).

Cobalt is undoubtedly a 'strategic' mineral, given the small number of producers and the importance of its uses. In the circumstances it is perhaps surprising that the recycling rate is so low. Despite relatively high recent prices, only about 20–25% of US cobalt consumption is recovered from purchased scrap (Shedd 1993). However, unless cobalt turns out to have unexpectedly major environmental impacts, the obvious strategy is to increase the cobalt recovery rate from copper, nickel and/or lead mining.

4.6.   ARSENIC SOURCES, USES AND LOSSES

Arsenic constitutes only about 2 parts per million of the earth's crust (compared to 58 ppm for Cu). It is found in sulfide minerals associated with
copper, zinc, lead and gold ores, but predominantly with copper. About 15%
of all commercial copper, zinc, lead and uranium ores are classed by the
Bureau of Mines as arsenical, with an average Cu/As ratio of 50:1 (in non-
arsenical copper ores the ratio is 500:1). In smelters, arsenic is normally
allowed to remain in the concentrator tailings, since it has a low commercial
value. It is recovered (if at all) at copper smelters[3] in a preliminary roasting/
sublimation stage, where there are also significant losses to slags and flue
dusts, which are typically dumped on land. Flue dusts constitute a major
disposal problem, although methods of converting the contained arsenic to an
insoluble form are under investigation (USBuMines 1989, p. 125).

World mine production of arsenic in 1993 was 47 kMT, down from 57.91
kMT in 1989. Major European producers in 1989 were

	1989	*1991*
	kMT	kMT
Belgium	3.50	3.00
France	7.00	3.00
Germany	0.36	0.36
Portugal	0.18	0.20
Sweden	10.00	2.50
Total	21.04	9.06

In the case of Belgium the arsenic is a byproduct of copper refining, mainly
from Zaire. In the case of France, the arsenic appears to be a byproduct of
nickel-cobalt ore refining, from New Caledonian ore. In the case of Sweden,
the source of the arsenic is a very high arsenic copper ore. Production from
all three countries has declined sharply since 1989. Figures for 1991 were:
Belgium 2.5 kMT; France 3 kMT, Sweden 2.5 kMT. By 1993 Belgian output
was down to 2 kMT and Swedish output was only 0.5 kMT. Declining
demand is the probable explanation.

Arsenic is processed into a number of chemical forms (Figure 4.3). Metallic arsenic (produced only in China) accounts for only 3% of total use. In the
US, 70% of total demand is now for wood preservatives, in the form of
chromated copper arsenate (CCA) (see Figure 4.4.). (This use is discussed
further in Chapter 5, Chromium.) Herbicides and desiccants account for most
of the rest. Sodium arsenite, $NaAsO_2$, is still used as a domestic insecticide.
Arsenic acid, H_3AsO_4, is used as a desiccant for cotton plants (to remove
their leaves prior to mechanical harvesting by cotton strippers). There has

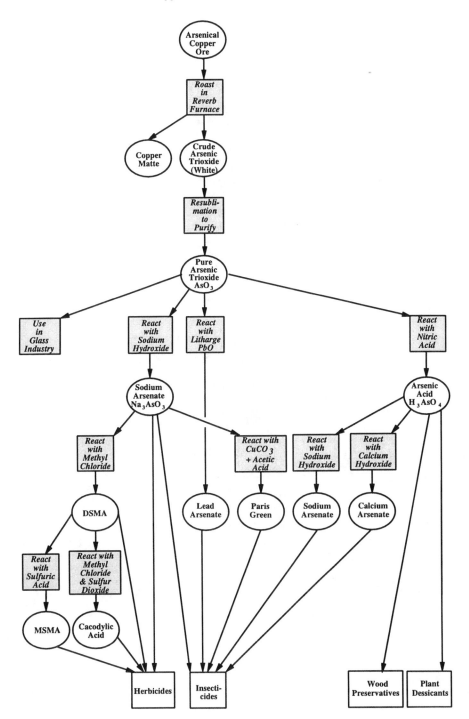

Figure 4.3:   Arsenic process-product flows

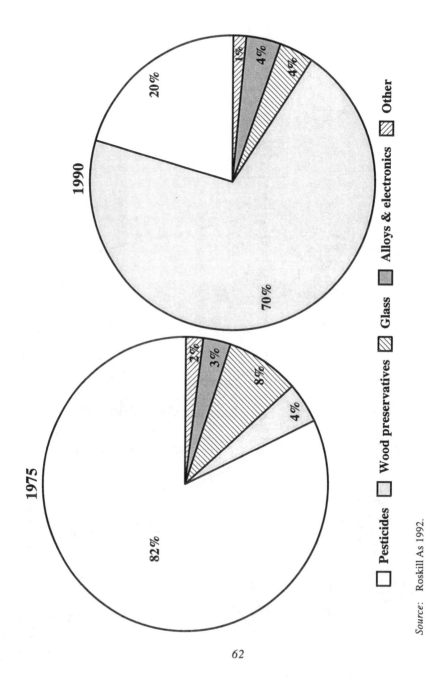

Source: Roskill As 1992.

Figure 4.4: US consumption of arsenic by end-use, 1975 and 1990 (%)

been increasing use since the 1960s. The European consumption pattern is almost certainly similar, except that cotton is not grown in Europe.

Other minor uses of arsenic include: glass and ceramics, where arsenic has long been used as a decolorant and fining agent (~5%); an additive to chicken feed (~1%); treatment of syphilis and African sleeping sickness (~1%); alloying agent for lead in lead-acid batteries (to strengthen posts and grids) and to increase the tensile strength of copper (~3%).

A use that is still extremely small, but which is growing rapidly, is in semiconductor manufacturing: specifically, gallium-arsenide is now used for preference in very fast microprocessors and solid-state laser devices. The manufacturing process itself is a potential source of very toxic arsenic emissions (e.g. arsine) but the long-run problem is likely to arise from the difficulty of recycling electronic devices and their consequent buildup in landfills. However, compared to others, this problem is minor. Moreover, it seems unlikely that electronic uses could ever account for more than a small percentage of global arsenic supply. This use should therefore be encouraged as a way of 'soaking up' arsenic that is otherwise likely to be dissipated in other less benign ways. The environmental impact of arsenic flows is discussed in Section 4.7 below.

4.7. ARSENIC IN THE ENVIRONMENT

Obviously, if arsenic is not recovered from the copper ore during the refining process, it must remain with the tailings or slag, or be lost to the air. Unfortunately, arsenic is rather volatile and any arsenic that enters a furnace is likely to be vaporized. According to another source (referring to the US alone) 9.7 kMT/yr was lost in leach liquor from copper mining, about 5.3 kMT/yr was vaporized in copper smelting, 10.6 kMT/yr was captured as flue dust (and dumped) while 3.7 kMT/yr was incorporated in copper smelter slags (Ayres *et al.* 1988). By contrast fly ash from coal combustion contained 2 kMT/yr of arsenic, of which only 100 tonnes was emitted to the air and the remainder was captured by electrostatic precipitators and dumped on land. (See Figure 4.5.)

More recently, Nriagu has estimated global atmospheric arsenic emissions from metal — mostly copper — mining, smelting and refining at 12.4 kMT/yr, compared to 2.2 kMT/yr from coal combustion, 2 kMT/yr from manufacturing processes and 2.3 kMT/yr from commercial uses, transportation and waste incineration (Nriagu 1990). Evidently atmospheric emissions alone are comparable to consumptive uses. Anthropogenic activities account for 19 kMT compared to 12 kMT for natural processes such as vulcanism and forest fires (ibid.). Within Europe, Pacyna has accounted for 6.5 kMT/yr in airborne

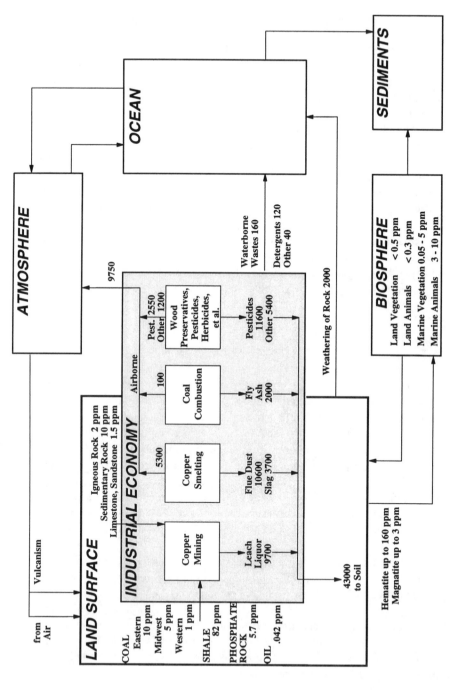

Figure 4.5: Global arsenic cycle, 1980 (metric tonnes)

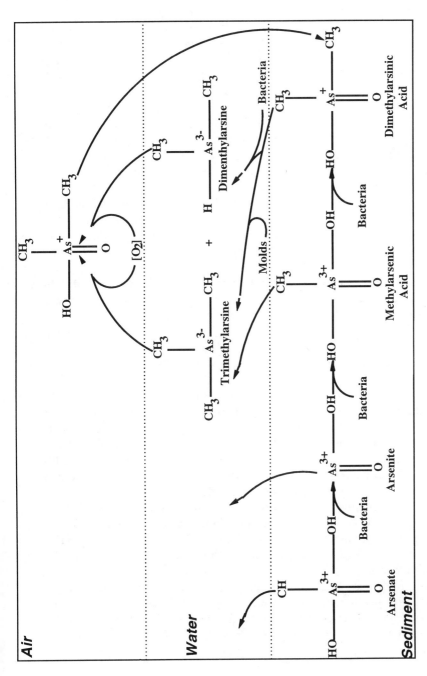

Source: Wood 1974.

Figure 4.6: Biological cycle for arsenic

65

emissions from all anthropogenic sources, of which copper/nickel smelting and refining accounted for 4.5 kMT/yr and other non-ferrous smelting and refining accounted for another 1.2 kMT/yr and fuel combustion the rest (Pacyna 1986). Emissions to the North Sea have also been estimated at 2.2 tonnes/day from rivers as compared to 0.63 tonnes/day from atmospheric deposition, for a land/water ratio of 3.5 (ibid.). The major problem of arsenic in the environment is its inherent mobility.

Arsenic has a comparatively low boiling point, so that it is relatively easily vaporized. Arsenic is also metabolized by some anaerobic bacteria in soils and sediments. These bacteria produce methylated arsenic compounds, some of which are water soluble, others being volatile. As yet there is no authoritative description of the biological 'arsenic cycle', but Figure 4.6 illustrates some of the possible transformations and fluxes.

The point is that once arsenic is released into the environment, it accumulates and moves. It may wash into the sea, but it can also escape back into the atmosphere. There may be mechanisms for permanent immobilization and 'burial', but we do not know what they are, still less the rate at which this may take place, if it does.

For this reason, even in the absence of quantitative evidence of toxic effects on human health, it seems foolhardy to allow continued dissipation of arsenic into the environment, where it continues to accumulate.

4.8.   SILVER SOURCES, USES AND LOSSES

Silver is a relatively rare metal. It constitutes about 0.2 parts per million, by weight, of the earth's crust. Silver (and gold) are often found in association with other non-ferrous metals, such as lead, copper and zinc. Even high-grade silver ores contain very little silver — typically a few ounces per ton of ore. Thus, of the order of 10 tonnes of non-ferrous metal ores (Cu, Zn, Pb, Mo) must be moved and processed to yield 1 kg of silver. All commercially important silver minerals at present are sulfides.

About two-thirds of silver output is now obtained from copper and zinc ores (in the US), with the remaining third from ores classified by the Bureau of Mines as silver ores (USBuMines 1975). The latter are primarily underground. Gold is usually a minor byproduct in all cases. Silver is recovered commercially from copper during the final electrolytic refining stage. (In the case of zinc and lead, it is recovered at the smelting stage.) Silver ores *per se* are first treated by cyanidation. (Mercury was used for the same purpose in the 19th century.) The silver and gold are precipitated from the cyanide solution by adding zinc dust, leaving a silver-gold alloy called doré metal.

In 1993, world mine production was 14 900 tonnes. In the US 1700 tonnes of silver were recovered from ores. In 1989, 2007 tonnes were recovered from 405.7 MMT of non-ferrous ores, of which 230.56 MMT were copper ores. The biggest producer in the world is Mexico (2200 tonnes), followed by the US (1700 tonnes). Others producing more than 1000 tonnes, in order, were Peru, Australia and Canada. Europe produced declining and minor quantities. Figures for 1989 were Spain (350 tonnes), Sweden (195 tonnes), Italy (93 tonnes) and Germany (70 tonnes).

Silver is used, today, primarily for its chemical and electronic properties. In the past, this was not the case; most silver was mined for its own sake and was used in metallic form as bullion (backing for currency), coinage, or jewelry, 'silverware' and for *objets d'art*. Except for sterling silverware, plateware, jewelry and coinage, the uses are largely dissipative, although some spent silver batteries and wastes from film-processing facilities can be recycled. Consumptive uses of metallic silver have included solders, brazes, plated bearing surfaces, electrical contacts, and silver gauze catalysts, silver impregnated glass used for protective spectacles. Metallic silver is relatively unreactive except in the presence of sulfur, and most silver salts are quite insoluble.

Chemical uses include pharmaceuticals (especially silver nitrate), which are still used to treat warts, boils, bites, small growths, ophthalmia, gastric ulcers, gonorrhea and chronic dysentery. Silver chemicals are also used in specialized electric batteries (e.g. silver-zinc cells), and photographic films. By far the most important chemical use today is in photography, with silver-based batteries and catalysts distant runners up.[4]

Photographic film is a multilayer material consisting of a colloidal dispersion of silver halide (chloride, bromide, chloro-bromide or iodide) grains in a special gelatin that performs the functions of mechanical binder, and sensitizer. The gelatin is usually supported by a paper backing. The manufacturing process is extremely complex and many of the details are proprietary. However, the starting point is a solution of sodium or potassium halides and gelatine. Silver nitrate ($AgNO_3$) and ammonia are added at 40–50°C and the silver halides grains are precipitated under suitable conditions.

In the 'black and white' era much of the developing was done in small laboratories and significant quantities of silver-containing chemicals were discarded. Color film was, and is, more likely to be processed in a centralized facility where silver recovery is practicable. The movie and publishing industries are major users of film, and much of this is recycled in small 'film-stripping' facilities to recover silver. Thus silver loss in photography has not by any means been proportional to total film production. However, consumptive — and dissipative — usage has ranged around 30% of net industrial consumption of silver (in the US) since the 1950s.

Silver losses to the environment from mine tailings and slag are not significant, since most of the silver is recovered. Most losses are probably attributable to photographic film developing (especially in smaller facilities) and disposal of used film in refuse, to landfills and incinerators. Use and disposition of other silver-based products such as mirrors, batteries, solders, brazes and electronic equipment can be considered to be secondary sources. Silver is also dispersed into the environment via the combustion of coal and oil, but to a very minor degree.

Silver is not one of the most important environmental hazards, though neither is it negligible. But it is a useful illustration of an important point. Silver is 50–100 times more valuable than copper, for instance (roughly $4 per ounce, as compared to $0.40–$1.20 per pound), and yet dissipative losses remain significant. This is because the amount of silver required to perform a useful and economical valuable function can be extremely small. Thus, for many metals used in small quantities for specialized purposes, to achieve anything close to 100% recycling by means of market forces alone is, at best, a very distant prospect.

NOTES(4)

1. To be sure, the US is actually an importer of arsenic despite its large copper mining and smelting sector. This is because US copper ores are relatively low in arsenic and imports are cheaper than recovery. The only arsenic recovery facility in the US (Tacoma Washington) was shut down a few years ago, partly for economic reasons and partly for environmental reasons. However, unrecovered arsenic must therefore remain in tailings, slag, baghouse dust and other process wastes.
2. In 1981 it was estimated that magnets accounted for 16% of worldwide cobalt use (Voigt 1982). German industry consumed 210 MT of cobalt for magnets in 1981.
3. Since 1973 only one US smelter recovers arsenic commercially (ASARCO, at Tacoma, WA). This plant processes arsenical ores and flue dust from other US smelters.
4. Important chemical processes (mostly partial oxidation) utilizing silver-based catalysts include the following:

    - acetaldehyde from ethanol;
    - acetone from isopropanol;
    - acrylonitrile from propylene;
    - ethylene oxide from ethylene;
    - formaldehyde from methanol.

    Silver use for catalytic purposes apparently peaked in 1976 or 1977 at a level of 9 million ounces per year (net). It would appear that net consumption, in this case, is tantamount to loss.

5.   Chromium sources, uses and losses

5.1.   SUMMARY

Chromium (along with cobalt) is the archetypical 'strategic metal' because of
its importance in corrosion and heat resistant alloys, especially 'stainless'
steel and so-called 'superalloys'. Stainless steel is needed for chemicals
processing and storage, nuclear power plants, pollution control equipment —
such as catalytic convertors for automobiles — and a host of consumer
products. Superalloys are used for jet engines and other applications in aerospace technology requiring strength and corrosion resistance at high temperatures. 'It is by no means an exaggeration to assert that modern technology is
largely built on chromium in general, and stainless steel in particular' (Bennett
and Williams 1981, p. 28).

Because production and known reserves are concentrated in a few countries, there is at least some theoretical possibility of a supply interruption. In
the 1970s, when the two major sources of world supply were the Soviet
Union and South Africa, this was a serious concern for the industrial countries. The UN Security Council instituted mandatory sanctions against Rho-
desian exports in 1966. (Rhodesia is now Zimbabwe.) The US complied until
the end of 1971; the embargo against Rhodesia was reinstituted in 1977. In
the same year an embargo against South Africa was imposed and continued
in place until 1994, although chromite and ferro-chromium exports were
excluded from the embargo and continued. This concern led to a number of
studies of the economic impact of a possible supply disruption. These, in
turn, resulted in a significant increase in the US strategic stockpile of chromium. Today these geo-political concerns are much reduced, although they
could be rekindled by untoward political developments in the world.

However a newer concern has arisen, namely the public health and ecological impacts of dissipative losses (and uses) of chromium compounds to
the environment. Hexavalent chromium (Cr VI) is particularly toxic. This fact
provides a further incentive to minimize losses of chromic acid (chromium
trioxide) and its compounds. Yet, while some historical uses of chromium
chemicals (e.g. as pigments and for electroplating) have declined, others have
grown. In particular, chromium sulfate is still the major leather tanning
chemical, while copper–chromium–arsenic chemicals have become the most

important wood preservative (replacing pentachlorophenol in most countries). Virtually all chemical uses are inherently dissipative.

A more subtle danger has also appeared on the horizon. While the more common trivalent form of chromium (Cr III) is non-toxic and immobile in soils and sediments, it has been demonstrated that under some (i.e. oxidizing) conditions Cr III can convert to toxic Cr VI (Bartlett and James 1979). Different forms of manganese (Mn) may serve as oxidizing agents. In soils with high organic matter content, this is unlikely to occur because oxygen is rapidly consumed. However, in soils with little organic matter the turnover of Cr III to Cr VI is a distinct possibility. Hence, it may be necessary to worry about accumulations of Cr III in soils and sediments due to past industrial activities, as well as current ones (Bergbäck *et al.* 1989).

For all these reasons, there are strong arguments for increasing the rate of recycling of chromium alloys, while reducing dissipative uses of chromium chemicals.

Public policy goals: reduce dependence on imports of raw materials; reduce dissipative uses, especially of chromic acid and its derivatives (Cr VI); increase recycling of chromium-containing products, especially stainless steel.

5.2. SOURCES OF CHROMIUM

Chromium constitutes 185 ppm (0.0185%) of the earth's crust (Taylor and McLennan 1985, pp. 15–16). It is obtained, in practice, entirely from so-called chromite ore, which consists of variable chromium oxide (Cr_2O_3), ferrous and ferric iron oxides (FeO and Fe_2O_3), and alumina (Al_2O_3), plus traces of TiO_2, MnO and V_2O_5. This ore is found in commercially viable grades in relatively few locations. The two largest producers, by far, are Kazakhstan (2.9 MMT in 1993) and South Africa (2.84 MMT) (Papp annual 1993, Table 22). Other significant producers are India (1.07 MMT), Turkey (490 kMT), Zimbabwe (400 kMT), Finland (500 kMT) and Brazil (430 kMT). Total world production of ore was 9.3 MMT in 1993 (10.99 MMT in 1992), of which only 500 kMT (from Finland) came from Western Europe (see Appendix A, Table A.3).

The ore currently being mined averages about 44% Cr_2O_3 or 30% chromium (Cr) content. Chromium content of US imports was 29.5% (Papp 1994, Table 9). Apparent chromium content of the chromite ore produced globally in 1992 was therefore 3.309 MMT (Papp annual 1993).

5.3. PRODUCTION AND MAJOR USES OF CHROMIUM

Chromite ore is classified by the US Bureau of Mines as refractory, metallurgical or chemical, depending on its intended use. Chromite is used in its raw (oxide) form in the manufacture of refractory bricks for high temperature furnace liners, such as electric steelmaking furnaces, reverberatory copper-refining furnaces, and heat-exchanger sections of glass-making furnaces. It is also used as an abrasive. This 'route' involves physical processing (grinding, compaction and sintering) only. It accounts for 8% of total global chromite consumption (3% in the US), or 265 kMT of contained chromium (ibid.). We have no data on refractory chromite usage in Europe. However, it probably bears the same relation to electric steel production in Europe as in the US.

The metallurgical route involves smelting with coke and fluxes in an electric furnace to yield ferro-chromium, an alloy of iron and chromium used mainly as an alloying component in the production of stainless steel, other chromium wrought or cast alloy steels. Ferro-chromium is classified by carbon and silicon content. In general, chromite is smelted with coke and a silica (quartz), limestone, dolomite or alumino-silicate flux. The iron in the ore (and some silicon) remains with the ferro-chromium product, while the slag consists mostly of alumina and the other impurities. Ferro-chromium slag could potentially be used as a source of aluminum, though residual iron and silica constitute a disadvantage as compared to bauxite.

Ferro-chromium accounts for 87% of total US chromite consumption (Papp annual 1993). The percentage of world chromite production used for ferro-chromium has been variously estimated at 77% to 80% (Papp 1994). However, if refractories account for 8% and chemicals for 8% or 9% (discussed later), it would seem to follow that ferro-chromium accounts for as much as 83% or 84% of world chromite output. Total world output of ferro-chromium in 1992 was 3.579 MMT, of which 619 kMT was produced in Western Europe (Roskill Cr 1993, p. 37). The other large producers are South Africa, the former USSR and Japan, with annual capacities of 791 kMT, 223 kMT and 218 kMT (Cr-content) respectively. The US was a major consumer of chromium alloys (367.2 kMT in 1991 but only a relatively small (and declining) producer: 68.3 kMT (43 kMT Cr-content) in 1991, down from 146.8 kMT (90 kMT Cr-content) in 1989 (USBuMines 1991).

Assuming ferro-chromium accounted for 79% of the chromite ore, with a recovery of 78% (Papp 1994), it would have contained 2.036 MMT Cr in 3.425 MMT ferro-chromium. That is to say, ferro-chromium would, on the average, consist of 60% Cr, the remainder being iron, carbon, silicon and/or trace quantities of other metals. Losses in the production of ferro-chromium are obviously significant, amounting to 583 kMT (Cr) in 1992. If ferro-chromium accounts for 84% of chromite, the imputed loss of chromium would be closer to 610 kMT (Cr).

Both refractory production and ferro-chromium production generate fairly large quantities of chromium emissions. In fact, on a gross tonnage basis, these are by far the dominant sources of environmentally mobile chromium. In 1970, in the US more than 50% of all uncontrolled chromium emissions (and 68% of post-control emissions) were due to ferro-chromium production in electric furnaces (GCA 1973). Another 20% arose from the production of chromite-based refractory bricks and chromium alloy steels. It is important to point out, however, that emissions from these metallurgical operations are of the non-hazardous trivalent (Cr III) form.[1]

Major producers of ferro-chromium and other chromium ferro-alloys in 1991 were the former USSR (CIS) and South Africa, which accounted for 52% of the total output (down to 44% in 1992, because of a temporary cutback in South African output to reduce stocks). The other major producers of ferro-chromium in 1992/1993 were China (400/190 kMT), Japan (266/215 kMT), India (220/244 kMT), Finland (187/218 kMT), Zimbabwe (186/140 kMT), Sweden (135/128 kMT) and Norway (114/80 kMT) (Roskill Cr 1993, p. 38). It is noteworthy that ferro-chromium production is increasingly co-located with mining. Significant capacity cutbacks have occurred in countries lacking chromite ore resources. Nevertheless, capacity in Western Europe still stood at 521 kMT (Cr-content) as of year-end 1992 (ibid., p. 48).

Ferro-chromium is used predominantly (70%) in the manufacture of stainless steel. On the average, chromium constituted 17% of the mass of stainless and heat-resisting steels produced in the US between 1962 and 1983. Recently the unit requirement for chromium in steel has declined slightly because of increased use of Type 409, a ferritic low chromium steel used for automotive exhaust systems with catalytic convertors (Papp 1991). Nevertheless, demand for stainless steel drives the market for chromite.

Chromium metal is produced in relatively small quantities. Total world capacity is estimated at 25 kMT/yr of which 9.5 kMT/yr (from three producers) is in Western Europe (Roskill Cr 1993). Recent production has been well below capacity. It is made by two routes, electrolytic (one-third of world production capacity) and alumino-thermic (two-thirds of production capacity). The first of these routes starts from ferro-chromium. The second starts from chromic oxide, using metallic aluminum as a reducing agent. All European producers of chromium metal use the alumino-thermic process. Output is used in so-called superalloys (with nickel and cobalt), mainly for jet engines and gas turbines.

Metallic uses of chromium and chromium alloys *per se* do not cause significant environmental risks. Metallic chromium that cannot be recycled is ultimately embodied as a tramp contaminant in iron or steel foundry products, or is discharged to slag heaps and landfills in insoluble form; very little gets into air or water (GCA, 1973). The main concern is that, under some conditions, dispersed chromium as Cr III may be oxidized to the toxic Cr VI form. Thus, both criticality and potential toxicity argue for increased emphasis on recycling metallurgical chromium to the maximum feasible extent.

5.4. MAJOR USES OF CHROMIUM CHEMICALS

According to the US Bureau of Mines, *Minerals Yearbook* (USBuMines 1991, p. 370) chemical uses account for 13% of worldwide chromite consumption. However, this figure has been corrected in a more recent study. Apparently, chemical uses currently account for 8% (or 9%) of total global chromite consumption, or about 280 kMT of contained chromium (Papp 1994).

Chromium chemicals ('the chemical route') begin with the manufacture of sodium dichromate (or bichromate), $Na_2Cr_2O_7$. This is done by a hydrometallurgical process involving roasting of chromite ore with sodium carbonate and lime to yield sodium chromate, followed by leaching with sulfuric acid, then evaporation and crystallization of the sodium dichromate (with sodium sulfate as a byproduct). Identified world production capacity for sodium dichromate was estimated at 329 kMT (Cr equivalent) in 1992 (USBuMines 1991; Roskill Cr 1993, p. 55). Gross world sodium dichromate capacity (329 kMT) corresponds to just under 10% of gross output of contained chromium in 1992 and a little less for 1991. The largest producer is Russia (62 kMT) followed by the US (55 kMT), the UK (51 kMT) and Kazakhstan (42 kMT). Total capacity located in Western Europe was 82 kMT. Production has seemingly been very close to capacity in recent years, because of very strong demand (ibid.). The ratio of sodium dichromate (dihydrate) weight to its chromium content is 2.87:1. Thus US production capacity of 55 kMT (Cr) translates into 158 kMT sodium dichromate ($Na_2Cr_2O_4 \cdot 2H_2O$). Capacity in the rest of the world may have been underestimated, since new capacity has been added in the UK, India, China, Brazil and other developing countries, in recent years.

Actual production of sodium dichromate (equivalent) in the US was 130.8 kMT in 1990 (Roskill Cr 1993, p. 57). This production rate is 83% of nominal capacity. Domestic US consumption in 1991 appears to have been about 115 kMT (see below). The US was a net exporter of 13 kMT of sodium dichromate in 1989, 15 kMT in 1990 and 12 kMT in 1991 (Papp annual 1991). There is no direct data on chromium chemical production or consumption in Europe *per se*. However, assuming the same capacity utilization rate as the US, this implies a European production level of 173 kMT (sodium dichromate) for 1991. Gross world production, at the same level of capacity utilization (83%), would have been 273 kMT (Cr-content).

Recovery of chromium by the chemical industry in the US apparently averages about 81% (Papp 1994), implying losses at this stage of 19%, or 8.8 kMT (Cr-content) in the US for 1992. On this basis, downstream chromium chemicals produced and consumed in 1992 (US) can be assumed to have contained roughly 36.8 kMT (Cr), of which some was exported. Assuming the same recovery rate, losses from dichromate production in Europe were presumably about 13.6 kMT. The global loss in production would have been $0.19 \times 73 = 52$ kMT (Cr), on the same basis. Downstream chemicals presumably contained the remainder of the chromium, or 221 kMT (Cr). Production and use of these chemicals accounts for a high proportion of environmentally harmful and toxic chromium emissions.

Subsequent chemical conversions (US) were as follows (Papp annual 1991): chromic acid 55%, chromic oxide 10%, leather-tanning chemicals 8%, pigments 7%, wood preservatives (other than chromic acid) 2%, drilling mud additives 2%, other uses 3% and export 13%. Chromic acid (more precisely, chromium trioxide, CrO_3), in turn, is used to manufacture wood preservatives 70%, for metal finishing 27%, and to make chromium dioxide 3% (used in magnetic recording tapes). (See Figure 5.1.)

There is considerable confusion among various data sources with regard to chromium chemical production and use. This arises from the fact that there are only a few manufacturers, and that they typically sell both sodium dichromate and its derivatives. For instance, the biggest producer in the Western world, Harcros Chemicals (UK) — which has subsidiaries in many countries — reports sales of sodium dichromate as 28% of output, along with derivatives such as chromic acid (31%), chromium oxide (24%) and chromium sulfate (14%). In terms of end-uses, 40% of its worldwide sales go to leather tanning, 20% to pigments, 17% to metal treatment, 14% to wood preservation and 6% to chromium metal (Roskill Cr 1993). This allocation is quite different from that reported above by the US Bureau of Mines for the US, for instance. The Harcros allocation is also quite different from the Japanese allocation, discussed below.

One of the largest single uses of chromium chemicals, globally, is for waterborne wood preservatives, primarily copper-chromium-arsenate (CCA). The most common formulation in countries with stringent environmental regulations consists of 47.5% hexavalent chromium (measured as chromic oxide CrO_3 equivalent), plus 18.5% copper (as CuO) and 34% arsenic (as As_2O_3) (Roskill Cr 1993, p. 474). The actual chemical composition, however, is a mixture of 44.7% sodium dichromate ($Na_2Cr_2O_7 \cdot 2H_2O$), 33.2% copper sulfate ($CuSO_4 \cdot 5H_2O$) and 22.1% arsenic pentoxide ($As_2O_5 \cdot 2H_2O$). Contained chromium in wood preservatives is about 17% (ibid., p. 475). Chromic acid is

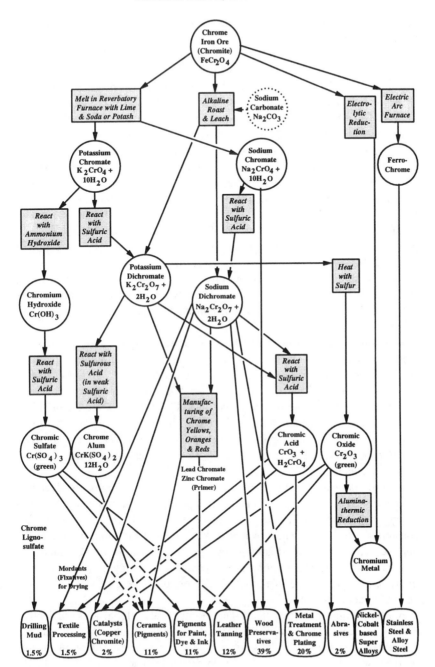

Figure 5.1: Chromium process-product flows (Europe 1992)

also used in wood preservatives, which depend largely on the toxicity of hexavalent chromium.

This use accounted for 43% of US chromium chemical consumption in 1991, and the market has been growing at 10% per annum. In that year US consumption of sodium dichromate for wood preservation was 47.230 kMT (ibid., p. 482). Global consumption of CCA in 1991 was estimated to be 118 kMT (or 20 kMT Cr-content) assuming the US accounted for 40% of the global CCA market and Europe 33% (ibid.). The European market of 39 kMT (sodium dichromate equivalent) was further broken down as follows: UK 28%, Scandinavia 26% and (West) Germany 23% (ibid., p. 483). Apparently there is also a large market for chromium-based wood preservatives in Australasia, where tropical conditions cause rapid deterioration of unprotected wood.

Japan, the world's largest importer of wood, used 96.5 kMT of CCA wood preservatives in 1980, although the dichromate content was not reported (ibid., p. 481). Apparently, however, usage of chromium chemicals for this purpose in Japan has declined sharply. By 1989 it was less than 2 kMT, evidently because of substitution by other types of wood treatment. This illustrates the difficulty of extrapolating consumption patterns from one country to another.

The single biggest use of chromium chemicals in Japan (40%) was for metal treatment, especially chromium plating for the automobile industry (which starts with chromic acid). Plating accounted for 15.98 kMT dichromate equivalent in Japan in 1990 (ibid., p. 505), or 40% of total Japanese consumption of chromium chemicals (40 kMT, sodium dichromate equivalent). The same use accounted for 17.27 kMT in the US in 1991,[2] which was only 15% of total consumption (ibid.) but 27% of non-CCA consumption. For Europe, these would translate to 21–31% of total consumption (sodium dichromate equivalent).

A third major use of chromium chemicals has been in pigments, dyes and colorants (e.g. for ceramics and glass). Japanese consumption for this category of uses was 8.378 kMT (about 21% of total) in 1990, while US consumption in this category was 9.16 kMT (8% of the total or 14% of the non-CCA total) in 1991. Lacking any specific data, it seems reasonable to estimate European consumption in this category to be intermediate between the two, as a percentage of non-CCA use, or somewhere between 11% and 16% of total consumption.

A fourth significant use of chromium chemicals, globally, is for leather tanning. As noted above, this use accounts for 40% of the output of Harcros Chemicals Co., the largest Western producer. Japanese consumption for this purpose was about 7 kMT (18% of domestic demand) in 1990, while US consumption was about 10.3 kMT (9% of domestic demand, and 15.7% of non-CCA demand) in 1991 — down from 13.4 kMT in 1988 and 30 kMT in the early 1980s. On a proportional basis, it seems reasonable to assume that tanning would account for 16–17% of non-CCA chromium chemical consumption in Europe, or 12–13% of total consumption (sodium dichromate equivalent) in 1991. However, leather tanning has been declining in the industrialized world, and moving to the so-called developing countries where environmental regulation is much less stringent. Global consumption for tanning was 180 kMT (sodium dichromate equivalent) in 1988, of which US consumption was only 7%. India, alone, consumed 25 kMT in 1991, up from only 5 kMT just five years earlier.

Chrome tanning requires 22.2 kg of chromium sulfate per tonne of 'bovine raw stock' (i.e. cattle hides). This yields 645 kg of 'wet blue leather' and 149 kg of solid wastes (scrapings and trimmings) (Roskill Cr 1993, p. 509). Only 40% of the chromium is embodied in the product (leather); 25% remains with the solid waste, while 35% is left in 5000–10 000 liters of liquid tannery waste (ibid.). The latter also contains 206 kg of organic materials. On a global basis, this waste stream amounted to 108 kMT (sodium dichromate equivalent) in 1988. Tanning activity is increasing at the world level, though declining in the industrial countries. Cattle hides are now imported, and finished leather goods are re-exported in large quantities by Thailand, China, India, Brazil, South Korea and Turkey (ibid., p. 512).

Glass and ceramics constitute another significant use of chromium chemicals. Chromium compounds are used mainly as colorants. In Japan, this use accounted for 4.2 kMT in 1990, or 11% of domestic demand. In the US the glass and ceramic category is lumped together with abrasives and chromium metal production from chemicals. The total of all these amounted to 13.08 kMT in 1991. (Of the latter, 3.3 kMT is estimated, below, to have been for abrasives, leaving 9.8 kMT or 15% of non-CCA demand for use in glass, ceramics and chromium metal.) The glass and ceramics industry in Europe could have taken 9–11.5% of all chromium chemicals.

Oil-well drilling muds are another (highly variable) use of chromium chemicals, namely chromium ligno-sulfonates. They act as thinning and anti-corrosion agents. Consumption depends on the number of wells drilled, and on a variety of other factors. US consumption in 1984 (when 72 138 wells were drilled) was 5 kMT; in 1992 only 23 813 wells were drilled in the US, and chromium chemicals for drilling muds probably dropped to 2.3 kMT (sodium dichromate equivalent). Most petroleum exploration around the world is carried out by US or Western European firms, so it would not be unreasonable to assume that specialized chemicals like chromium ligno-sulfonates would also be produced in the US or Western Europe. However, we have no further information on this point. Other miscellaneous small uses of chromium chemicals include catalysts (2.2% Japan; 1.9% US);

abrasives (2.3% Japan, 3% US); mordants for textile dyeing (1.3% Japan and US).

As noted, there are no direct data for chromium chemical consumption or trade in Western Europe, but capacity was previously estimated to be 82 kMT (Cr-content) or 235 kMT (sodium dichromate equivalent), with actual production of 173 kMT in 1991. On this basis, we estimate that wood preservatives (CCA) accounted for 22.6% (39 kMT), metal plating and finishing 21–31%, leather tanning 12–13%, pigments 11–16%, glass and ceramics 9–11.5%, with miscellaneous uses taking up the difference. Since the 'misc' category should probably not exceed 10%, it would seem that the actual numbers are likely to be near the upper ends of their ranges. It must be emphasized that the ranges given are little better than guesses, with a considerable margin of error.

It is interesting to note that Western Europe, the US and Japan among them appear to have consumed about 338 kMT of chromium chemicals (sodium dichromate equivalent) or 118 kMT (Cr-content). The rest of the OECD countries and Asian 'Tigers' might conceivably account for a further 20–25 kMT (Cr). If Papp's lower estimate of 8% of chromite consumption is accurate, this leaves 130 kMT (Cr) that is presumably consumed — and mostly produced — elsewhere. Unquestionably, significant quantities of chromium are used for leather tanning outside the OECD (roughly, 80% of the total used for this purpose, or 52 kMT, chromium content).

This would still leave 78 kMT (Cr-content) for other uses in the rest of the world, which seems somewhat excessive. True, the CIS (former USSR) has the largest nominal production capacity for these chemicals (104 kMT, Cr-content), which admittedly does suggest a comparably large domestic demand. But the allocation of domestic uses and exports is very unclear. We would speculate that metal plating and finishing, pigments, wood preservatives and tanning may be the largest uses in the CIS. The large market for wood preservatives in Australasia has been mentioned. Oil-well drilling may also be a significant use. China is also probably a significant user of chromium chemicals, today. Nevertheless, we suspect that chemicals account for slightly less than 8% of total chromite production.

5.5.   RECOVERY AND RECYCLING OF CHROMIUM

From a strategic point of view (perhaps not important at present) the problem has been seen as how to increase the recovery and recycling of stainless steel and other chromium-bearing alloys. Recycling of industrial scrap is already very efficient. However, annual losses of chromium from scrappage of manufactured products is quite large. For instance, the use of stainless steel (Type

409) in automotive exhaust systems has been mentioned. However, few, if any, scrap dealers are prepared to remove and recycle the stainless steel components of automobiles. This situation may improve, however, as 'take-back' legislation — actual or threatened — induces automobile companies to pay more attention to the potential for remanufacturing and resource recovery in future years. This is an obvious candidate for design innovation ('Design for Environment', or DFE).

An interesting but minor area of potential for chromium recycling is refractory furnace liners. In principle, refractory materials can be recycled for the same use. At least one supplier of refractories to the steel industry (Cookson Group Ltd.) offers a rental service for furnace liners, retaining actual ownership of the refractory materials.

Chromium plating and other uses of chromium chemicals are essentially dissipative. Metal-plating operations are notorious polluters, and have been among the earliest targets of environmental controls. There has been a substantial reduction in pollution from this source in the more advanced industrial countries (but not all). Decorative chrome plating for automobiles and other products has also been sharply reduced in recent years, as other materials — including stainless steel — have increasingly been used. Here is another potential application of DFE. However, 'hard' chromium plating is still used for many engineering purposes and the chromium that is used in this way is essentially unrecoverable by present methods.

Use of chromium pigments has fallen sharply in the US, but much less so in Europe because of lack of effective environmental regulation in this field. Use of chromium for tanning has also fallen, though not nearly as rapidly as it might. Chrome-tanned leather is eventually worn to powder and washed into rivers and streams, or it becomes a household waste and is disposed of in landfills or incinerators where it would largely end up in the ash. On the other hand, chromium-based wood preservatives now dominate the market in both Europe and the US (though not in Japan). This use has no immediate harmful consequences, but the chromium compounds bound to cellulose (in wood) are not permanently immobilized. Eventually the wood will still decay, at least if it is exposed to water and weather. The accumulation of chromium and other toxic metals in wood structures will eventually result in metals being incorporated into demolition waste, if not burned. Either way, there is a potential for remobilization. Alternatives to the use of toxic heavy metals for wood preservation would seem to be a particularly appropriate objective for research. In this context, we call attention to the possibilities of developing synthetic wood from recycled plastics (see Chapter 12, Packaging).

NOTES(5)

1. Chromium takes both trivalent and hexavalent forms. Chromic oxide Cr_2O_3 and trivalent chromic salts are not classified as toxic. According to the American Conference of Government Hygienists chromates and dichromates (e.g. CrO_4, Cr_2O_7), on the other hand, are toxic and a confirmed human carcinogen. (See also Windom and Duce 1977, Chapter 12.)
2. Consumption for this purpose in the US had dropped by 50% between 1976 and 1988, because of reduced use of decorative chromium plating and environmental concerns with regard to the electroplating industry. Consumption is still declining at about 1% per annum.

6. Zinc and cadmium

6.1. SUMMARY

Zinc is an important industrial metal. Zinc is mined primarily from sulfide ores (sphalerite, ZnS), often associated with ores of copper and/or lead. Zinc ores normally contain significant quantities of copper and lead plus traces of arsenic and cadmium (see Chapter 4, Copper). Zinc ores are sulfides, so smelting releases significant quantities of sulfur, unless it is recovered for use.

Zinc is extensively used both in metallic and chemical forms, predominantly the former. It has useful electrochemical properties, forms useful alloys (e.g. with copper and tin) and makes a good protective coating for iron or steel. It is also easy to smelt and easy to cast. However, zinc is not a 'strategic' metal in the sense that chromium or cobalt are. It is produced in many countries. There are satisfactory substitutes for most, if not all of its uses. Only the fact that its uses are so widespread, and many of them are dissipative, gives cause for concern about zinc *per se* from an environmental point of view.

Cadmium has been used in the past mainly because of its low cost (as a byproduct of zinc smelting and refining) and because some of its compounds are highly colored. Cadmium has many dissipative uses, as well as being a contaminant of some zinc chemicals, notably zinc oxide. In recent decades cadmium has found an important 'niche' market for rechargeable batteries. These batteries are getting smaller and smaller, and they are being used in more and more small appliances. Eventually they find their way into household — thence municipal — wastes, which may be incinerated. This is a legitimate cause for concern.

Zinc is an element required by growing plants, in trace amounts, and is found at the active sites of many enzymes. Zinc is moderately toxic in some forms, like copper, but it is not one of the more dangerous heavy metals. The major environmental problem of zinc is that cadmium (along with arsenic, copper and lead) is usually a co-product of zinc. It is, however, much more toxic than zinc. Because cadmium is chemically similar to zinc, it can be taken up and accumulated by plants and animals via the same biochemical mechanisms needed for zinc. The sulfide CdS and the oxide CdO are nearly insoluble, and not bio-available. However, 'immobile' cadmium sulfide in soils and sediments may be remobilized by oxidation. The latter is promoted by increases with acidity (pH) and conversion to the bio-available Cd^{+2} cation. Thus, as in the case of chromium III, cadmium can be 'toxified' by changing conditions (Stigliani undated; Enquete 1994).

Because cadmium is a byproduct of zinc, its supply tends to be proportional to the supply of primary zinc. It follows that there are two strategies for reducing environmental releases of cadmium. The first is to find and promote non-dissipative uses of cadmium that can 'soak up' the available supply. In principle, nickel-cadmium (nicad) batteries might be such a use, provided they can be remanufactured or recycled effectively. The technology is not too difficult. Unfortunately, the problem of logistics (i.e. collection and return) remains unsolved. Most nicad batteries, currently, are discarded with household solid wastes and find their way to landfills or incinerators. The only practical solution is to create a market for used batteries, probably by means of a returnable cash deposit.

The other viable strategy for reducing cadmium pollution is to cut back on primary zinc production/consumption of zinc itself. Here two complementary approaches suggest themselves. One is to discourage unnecessary uses of zinc by raising its price, via a severance tax on the mine output (or a corresponding tariff at the border). The other would be to discourage certain purely dissipative uses of zinc by regulatory means. For instance, zinc-based white pigments, zinc 'dry cells', and most zinc chemicals could be replaced quite easily by other materials. It is also likely that the use of zinc oxide as an accelerator in tire production could be replaced by some other chemicals.

Goals of public policy: reduce import dependence for raw materials; reduce zinc, arsenic, sulfur and cadmium emissions from mining, smelting and refining zinc; reduce dissipative uses of zinc; encourage recycling of zinc; reduce dissipative uses of cadmium; encourage recycling of cadmium.

6.2.   ZINC SOURCES AND USES

Zinc is slightly more abundant than copper (70 ppm in the earth's crust, vs. 60 ppm for copper). Cadmium is much scarcer than zinc (0.12 ppm in the earth's crust). Production of zinc ores, smelter output, zinc chemicals and cadmium are summarized in Appendix A, Table A.4. The world's biggest producers of ore and concentrate are Canada and Australia, followed by the former USSR, China and Peru. Europe produces relatively little ore, but smelter output is considerably larger than mine output, because of imports and secondary production.

Zinc metallurgy is comparatively straightforward (compared to copper). Zinc emissions from mining and milling operations have been estimated at 0.1 kg per tonne of zinc mined (MRI 1980). Zinc emissions from primary metallurgical operations have been estimated at 60 kg/tonne of zinc for electrolytic plants, 80 kg/tonne of zinc for vertical retort plants and 170 kg/tonne of zinc for horizontal retort plants. Emissions of sulfur, arsenic, cadmium, copper and lead are also significant. In North American and European refineries, most of the sulfur is recovered, as in the case of copper.

Slab zinc (from refineries) is the starting point of all metallurgical uses. The metallurgical uses are: galvanizing (coating) of sheet iron and steel to provide enhanced corrosion resistance, accounting for 50% of slab zinc; zinc-based thin-walled (hollow) die castings for a variety of purposes, especially in the auto industry (21%); brass and bronze products (14%), and other uses (15%), including rolled zinc for 'dry cells', weather stripping and lithographic plates. The zinc content of an average US-made car (1991) was 18 kg, of which die-castings accounted for about 8.6 kg, galvanizing 8.1 kg and other uses (including rubber), 1.3 kg. This consumption pattern is probably similar in Europe.

A significant amount of zinc is consumed in non-metallic form. Processing stages are shown in Figure 6.1. A small amount of slab zinc is used in the manufacture of zinc chemicals, but zinc oxide is made directly from ore concentrate or from scrap (by the so-called French process). Zinc chloride ($ZnCl_2$), is made from metal (either slab or secondary). Zinc sulfate ($ZnSO_4$), or 'white vitriol', is made either from ore or from secondary zinc.

The single most important zinc chemical is zinc oxide (ZnO). Zinc oxide (ZnO), 'zinc white' is a white, insoluble powder that was once widely used as a pigment for paints. Today it is mainly used as an accelerator/activator for hardening rubber products (e.g. tires). Roughly half of the output of lead-free zinc oxide has been used (since the early years of the 20th century) as an activator for vulcanizing rubber; it constitutes about 2% of the weight of a finished tire (see Chapter 13, Tires). Zinc oxide is dispersed to the environment by tire wear at the rate of 25 kg per million vehicle miles (Huntzicker *et al.* 1975). Because it is made directly from ore, the cadmium contamination of the ore is not removed and accompanies the zinc. As a consequence, tire wear is a significant source of cadmium dispersion into the environment. Consumption of zinc oxide in 1991 was as follows: rubber (58.6%), chemicals (21.2%), paints (4%), ceramics (3.1%), agriculture (19%) and other (12.5%).

Other major tonnage zinc chemicals include zinc chloride and zinc sulfate. Zinc chloride is used for vulcanizing rubber, in dry batteries as a mordant, for mercerizing cotton, and as a disinfectant. Zinc sulfate is used to manufacture the insecticide 'Zineb' and in galvanizing by the electrolytic method. It is

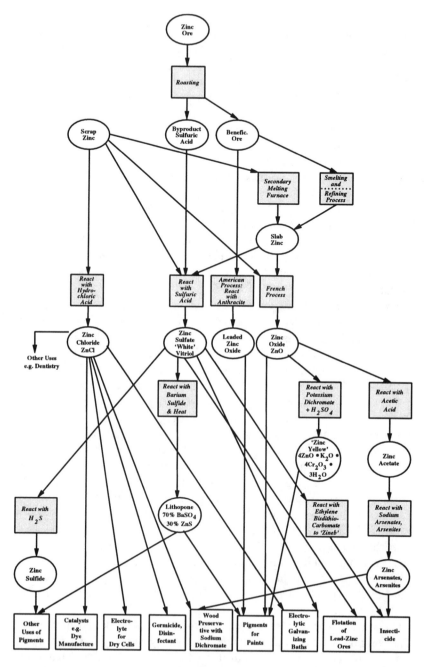

Figure 6.1:   Zinc process-product flows

also a component of fertilizers and fungicides. Agricultural uses account for
65% of consumption in 1991. Zinc sulfide, $ZnS \cdot H_2O$ is used as a pigment (in
lithophone, a mixture of 70% barium sulfate and 30% zinc sulfide. Lithophone, in turn, has been largely displaced by titanium dioxide). It is also used
for whitening rubber, for paper coating, and as the major component of
phosphors. Zinc dithiophosphates are common additives to automotive motor
oils. A typical zinc content for motor oil is 0.1% by weight (ibid. 1975). This
implies that motor oil contains as much as $3800 = 0.001 \times 0.45 \times 8.44 \times 10^6$
tonnes of zinc. In this case, too, a significant amount of associated cadmium
contaminant is dispersed into the environment annually by the loss (by burning or dumping) of motor oil.

6.3.   CADMIUM SOURCES AND USES

Cadmium is a very scarce element (0.1–0.2 ppm in the earth's crust), only
slightly less scarce than silver (0.075 ppm). It is obtained primarily as a
contaminant of zinc ore and thus as a byproduct of zinc smelting. The Cd/Zn
ratio varies; for purposes of estimating cadmium reserves, the US Bureau of
Mines uses the recovery ratio 0.36% cadmium to zinc reserve (USBuMines
1991, p. 312). World refinery production of cadmium was 20 673 tonnes in
1991. Japan was the biggest producer of refined metal, followed by the
former USSR, Belgium and the US (see Appendix A, Table A.4).

A number of techniques are used for cadmium recovery, depending on
the method being used in the copper or zinc refinery. Efficiency of recovery
is not especially high; the Bureau of Mines estimates 75% (USBuMines
1975). About 4.4 kg of cadmium are typically recovered per tonne of
refined zinc. Unrecovered cadmium remains in tailings, slags or sludges, in
the metallic zinc itself, or is emitted to the atmosphere during zinc smelting
or refining. Emission controls at refineries have only been implemented
since 1970 or so.

The ratio of cadmium recovery to zinc smelter production in all market
economy countries from 1950 to 1989 has ranged from a high of 1:260 in
1960 to a low of 1:343 in 1950 and a more recent low of 1:341 in 1983
(Roskill Cd 1990, Table 9). In short, the relationship has been fairly stable,
despite fairly significant changes in markets and technology.

Despite sharply declining use of cadmium for metal plating and in pigments, in recent years (because of environmental restrictions) demand has
been relatively stable, though spot prices have fluctuated significantly. Usage
varies somewhat from country to country, but the major uses at present are
for rechargeable batteries, pigments, electroplating, stabilizers for plastic
(PVC) and special alloys (see Table 6.1).

Table 6.1:   Cadmium consumption patterns (MT/year)

Use	West Germany 1989	United States 1991	United States 1993	Market Economy 1988
Nickel-cadmium batteries	427 (48%)	1450 (45%)	(65%)	10 175 (55%)
Pigments	282 (32%)	520 (16%)	(15%)	3 700 (20%)
Stabilizers	94 (11%)	390 (12%)	(12%)	1 850 (10%)
Electroplating	35 (4%)	650 (20%)	(7%)[a]	1 850 (10%)
Glass manufacturing	26 (3%)			
Alloys	21 (2%)		(5%)[b]	555 (5%)
Other	1 (0%)	230 (7%)		

Notes:
a.   Plating and coating.
b.   Alloys and other.

Sources: Germany (Enquete 1994); US (USBuMines 1991), Cadmium Association; Market Economy (Roskill Cd 1990).

The use of cadmium in batteries, mainly rechargeable nickel-cadmium cells, has grown steadily since the 1960s. In 1970 it accounted for only 8% of consumption. It reached 37% on a worldwide basis by 1985, 50% in 1988 and 55% in 1989 (12 000 tonnes) (Roskill Cd 1990, p. 214). In Japan, this use is even more dominant, since Japan is the major producer of these batteries. Battery use accounted for 12% of Japanese consumption in 1970, 78% by 1986, and 91% in 1988, though the trend may have peaked temporarily (ibid., p. 214). Data for Europe is extremely scattered. For Germany, batteries accounted for 35% of demand in 1988 (ibid., p. 207). The only other country for which there is explicit data is the UK, where batteries were included with 'misc.' uses at 17% in 1988 (ibid., p. 211).

The biggest use of cadmium, historically, is for anti-corrosion protective electroplating of iron and steel.[1] Cadmium is consumed in the electrolytic plating process as metallic ball anodes; cadmium oxide is added to plating baths, while cadmium chloride is the usual electrolyte (NMAB 1979). An OECD study concluded that very little cadmium is lost to the environment from the electroplating process *per se* (OECD/ED 1974). However this comforting conclusion is sharply disputed by others. In 1973, Ottinger (Ottinger *et al.* 1973) estimated that up to 18% of the cadmium used in electroplating or nearly 500 tonnes/ yr was lost as a liquid, solid or sludge during the plating operation, mostly to sewers. In 1976, Yost re-estimated the loss to water at 49.4 tonnes/yr (BCL 1977). Application of pollution-abatement practices, presumably implemented since 1976, would have cut even this loss rate by over 90% in the last decade, with two-thirds of the formerly lost cadmium recovered for re-use and most of the remainder concentrated to sludge and shipped to landfills. Plating accounted for 29% of 1991 US consumption (USBuMines 1991), 7% of Japanese consumption in 1988 (Roskill Cd 1990, p. 208), 13% of UK consumption in 1988 (ibid., p. 211) and 6% of German consumption in 1988 (ibid., p. 207).

The second most important cadmium use category until the mid-1960s was in pigments, based on cadmium sulfide and cadmium sulfo-selenide. Cadmium yellows (ZnS–CdS), and reds (CdSe–CdS and HgS–CdS) are exceptionally brilliant, stable in the presence of heat, light, moisture and oxygen, insoluble in water and most paint solvents, and modest in cost. These pigments are widely used in plastics, rubber, paints, enamels and printing inks. Cadmium acetate is used to produce iridescent effects on porcelain and pottery ware, while cadmium nitrate imparts a reddish-yellow luster to glass and porcelain. Pigment uses have fluctuated considerably from year to year, but appear to be declining on the average since the 1960s. Still, pigments accounted for 16% of US consumption in 1991 (USBuMines 1993). According to Roskill (Roskill Cd 1990) pigments accounted for 5% of Japanese consumption and 26% of German consumption in 1988. Pigments and stabilizers were combined in UK statistics (58% in 1988). For the market economies as a whole, pigments continued to hold a 20–29% market share in the 1980s, despite increasingly tight environmental restrictions.

Organic cadmium salts (notably cadmium stearate and cadmium benzoate) have been used in significant quantities as stabilizers for clear polyvinyl chloride (PVC) plastic packaging material. Cadmium salts are generally used in combination with barium salts. Other metal salts (of zinc, aluminum and lead) are also used for this purpose. Apparently other stabilizers, including purely organic systems and tin-based organic compounds have partly, but not totally, displaced cadmium-based stabilizers since the early 1970s (NMAB 1979). Use for this purpose peaked in the US in 1971, and declined because of concern about cadmium in the environment. However, it has increased again since the mid-1980s to about 10% of total consumption in 1988 (Roskill Cd 1990, p. 252).

The other important use of cadmium is metallurgical. Cadmium-nickel and cadmium-silver alloys (98.5% Cd) were introduced for high-speed, high-pressure bearings in the 1930s. This use was continued into the 1950s, but has declined since (USBuMines annual). Cadmium is a component of various low-melting alloys, including silver-brazing alloys (18–20% Cd) that are widely used in the electrical and electronics industries. Cadmium is also alloyed with silver in most electrical contacts. The most popular composition is 10% cadmium oxide, dispersed in silver. An alloy of cadmium (0.2%) with copper was introduced by the automobile industry in some 1969 models to improve the performance of copper radiators.

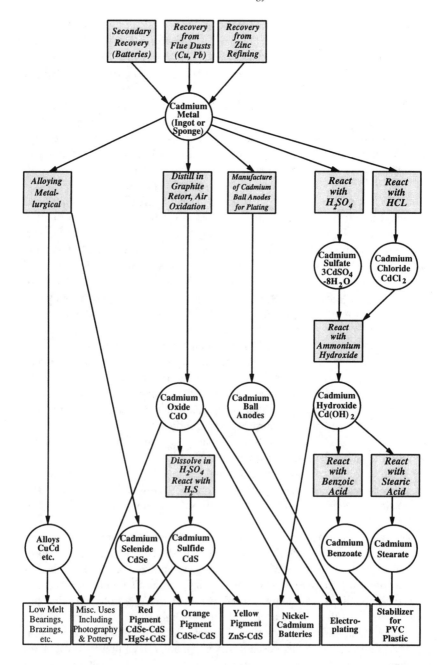

Figure 6.2:   Cadmium process-product flows

It is not known how much of this alloy is used at present. Cadmium is alloyed with copper to increase strength and wear resistance (0.5% to 1.2%) Overall, metallurgical uses of cadmium have fluctuated around 3–6% of total demand in market economies for the past two decades.

A graphical summary of cadmium process-product flows is shown in Figure 6.2. Virtually all uses of cadmium are inherently dissipative. Only about 5% is recycled (from batteries) in the US. We have no figures on recycling for Europe. In Germany, dealers will take back worn-out batteries, but the recycling figure is also less than 10%, though battery recycling is quite feasible (batteries contain up to 19% cadmium by weight) (Enquete 1994). In Europe some cadmium pigments are being recycled from yellow and red beer bottle cases (ibid.). There is a proposal by the Association of Window and Facade Manufacturers to take back and recycle cadmium stabilizers in PVC window frames, on a voluntary basis (ibid.).

Much cadmium in the past was embodied in anti-corrosion plating or alloys, and some of this ends up in solid waste in landfills. The fate of cadmium-plated or -alloyed items once they are discarded is still in doubt. However, cadmium, even in metallic form, is currently regarded by USEPA as a hazardous waste; even the presence of a few cadmium plated bolts or cadmium-alloyed bearings can render an automobile carcass unsuitable as a feedstock for secondary steel production. When cadmium-plated iron or steel items are remelted as scrap, some of the cadmium escapes into the atmosphere, as vapor or dust, while some is ultimately trapped in slags. Cadmium in silver-brazing or electrical contacts may escape into the environment by a similar route when scrap copper and brass containing equipment is remelted. Cadmium-containing pigments are likely to be disposed of in land fills or incinerated.

6.4. OPPORTUNITIES FOR RECYCLING ZINC AND CADMIUM

It is important to emphasize that until recently most uses of zinc, even metallurgical ones, were essentially dissipative (the major exception being brass/bronze). Nevertheless, there has always been a significant secondary zinc sector, recycling both new and old scrap. Some scrap, such as fragmented castings, are remelted (along with virgin material) for new castings. For instance, brass castings are about 50% based on scrap. Some scrap is converted into chemicals. The remainder is redistilled to slab zinc. New scrap comes mainly from galvanizers' dross, 'skimmings and ashes' and steelmaking dust. Old scrap is partly steelmaking dust and flue dust, partly castings and partly 'miscellaneous'.

Most zinc-containing products end in scrap iron/steel, batteries, tires and pigments being the major exceptions. Because of its volatility, the zinc (and cadmium) is easily recoverable as zinc calcine in baghouse dust from electric arc furnaces (EAFs) processing iron/steel scrap. As recently as 1985, only 15% of this dust was reprocessed to recover zinc (and cadmium); the remainder went to landfills for disposal. At present, much more — perhaps over 50% — of the zinc in EAF baghouse dust is recovered. The first US EAF baghouse dust reprocessing facility opened in 1981, with a capacity of 245 kMT (dust) and a zinc recovery potential of 75 kMT; a second plant followed in 1988. Eight more facilities came on stream between 1989 and 1992. Total capacity reached 533 kMT with potential zinc recovery of 93.7 kMT. The increasing interest in this process in the US can be attributed to a change in USEPA regulations (1991) making it harder to dispose of zinc-containing baghouse dust in landfills. There are at least six reprocessing plants in Japan, 10 in the US (as of 1992), one in Mexico, three in Germany, two in France, one each in Spain and Sweden.

A new source of secondary zinc is fly ash from the incineration of used tires for energy recovery (see also Chapter 14, Coal ash). Oxford Energy Co. in the US was operating two plants in the US as of 1993, one in California burning 5 million used tires/yr and producing 14 MW and one in Connecticut that burns 10 million tires/yr producing 30 MW. These plants generate ash that is rich in zinc oxide, which is shipped to secondary zinc-processing plants. At full capacity these two plants would yield about 750 MT/yr of secondary zinc. Oxford Energy had plans for two more tire-burning energy recovery plants to be operational by 1995. All told, 26 million scrap tires (10.7%) were burned in the US in 1990, and the trend appears to be sharply up. Evidently most of the zinc oxide used in tire production can eventually be recovered profitably if the tires are burned for energy recovery. (It is interesting, but probably coincidental, that two plants producing zinc oxide from primary sources were closed in North America in 1991.)

Apart from baghouse dust, very little cadmium is recycled, even from nickel-cadmium batteries. In the latter case there is no technical difficulty, only an economic and logistical problem of collection. This situation may be improved in the US as a result of newly introduced (1994) legislation to encourage battery recycling. For the future, continued growth in the market for nickel-cadmium batteries, especially in larger sizes (e.g. for electric cars) would offer a relatively painless way to reduce cadmium emissions and increase recycling. The two French automobile companies, Renault and Peugeot, have both announced that they will introduce a small electric 'city car' in the spring of 1995, to be powered by a nickel-cadmium battery weighing 250 kg. These batteries would, most likely, be leased rather than sold, and would be 100% recycled. This is a promising development. One can hope that this trend will spread.

6.5. ZINC AND CADMIUM IN THE ENVIRONMENT

Zinc not recovered from baghouse dust in secondary iron/steel works is presumably still disposed of in landfills. In the latter case, an unknown but not insignificant amount of zinc may be leached by acidic surface water. A smaller fraction is vaporized and discharged to the atmosphere (where it condenses on dust particles). Major point sources of atmospheric zinc are smelters, hot dip galvanizing operations and waste incinerators. Other sources include tire dust, weathered paint, and auto exhaust (from burning of lube oil detergents) and incinerators. Also, zinc is emitted by coal and residual oil combustion. Fly ash is of the order of 7.5 ppm zinc (see Chapter 13, Tires).

It has been estimated that natural geological processes move about 330 kMT of zinc into the oceans each year, as compared to losses from mining alone of 4 MMT (Waldichuk 1977). This represents an anthropogenic increase in zinc mobilization by a factor of 12. For airborne emissions, anthropogenic contributions have been estimated at 132 kMT (mostly from mining and smelting) vs. natural processes (volcanoes, dust, fires, etc.) of 45 kMT, for a mobilization enhancement factor of 4 (Nriagu 1990).

In the case of cadmium, which is of greater concern, a global cadmium cycle (c. 1975) was compiled from various sources (see Figure 6.3). Waterborne cadmium flux (to the oceans) from anthropogenic sources was about 20 kMT/ yr as compared to about 11 kMT from natural erosion and runoff processes, for a ratio of 2:1 and a mobilization enhancement factor of 3. In the case of airborne emissions, the corresponding figures are 7.6 kMT (again, mostly from smelting and mining) vs. 1.4 kMT (ibid.). The mobilization enhancement factor for cadmium is over sixfold. For 1975 Nriagu provided a detailed estimated breakdown of the sources of airborne cadmium emissions, as follows (ibid.):   zinc smelting and refining (2.8); copper smelting and refining (1.6); lead smelting and refining (0.2); cadmium processing (0.11); phosphate production (0.21); secondary n.f. metals (0.6); waste incineration (1.4); wood combustion (0.2); coal combustion (0.06); other (0.1).

The picture is complicated, however, by the fact that cadmium is readily cycled by atmospheric processes and by living organisms. Cadmium emitted to the atmosphere is redeposited via precipitation on land (6.4 kMT) and oceans (2.7 kMT). Annual cycling of cadmium in the marine biosphere is estimated to be 240 kMT, while terrestrial plants take up 36 kMT and recycle 31 kMT to the soil in plant litter and humus, and 5 kMT to rivers and streams (Ayres *et al.* 1988).

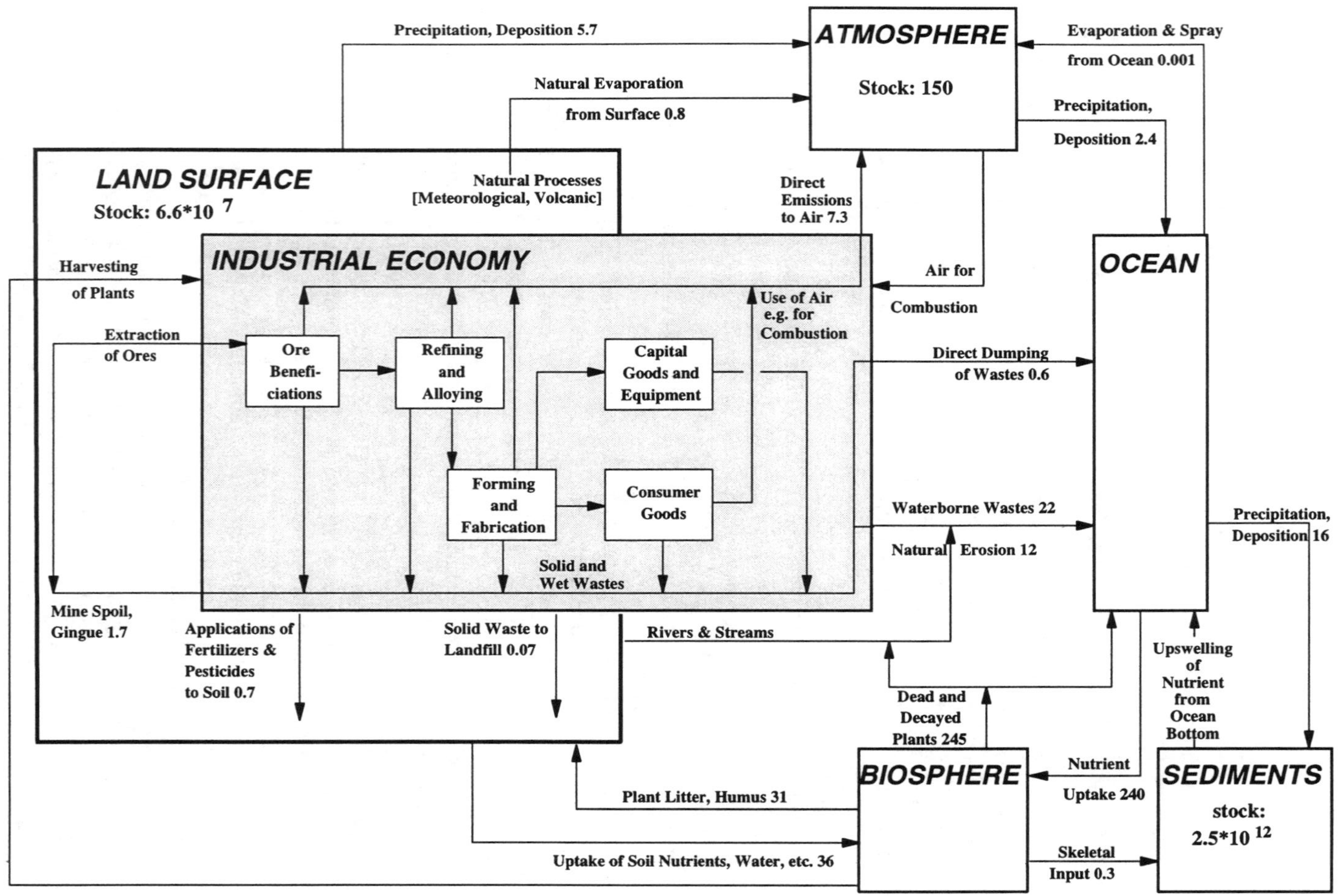

Figure 6.3: Global cadmium cycle, circa 1980 (kMT).

With this perspective, it is clear that while a large amount of biologically available cadmium has been moving around in the marine environment, a relatively small amount is being cycled by terrestrial plants where it can get into the human food chain. (Yet cadmium is taken up by plants, rather easily, precisely because of its chemical similarity to zinc, which is a necessary trace nutrient.) To this small stock of circulating cadmium, phosphate fertilizers alone add 0.7 kMT, while atmospheric deposition via rainfall adds another 6.4 kMT. The buildup of biologically available cadmium is, moreover, not uniformly distributed over the land surface, but heavily concentrated in industrial areas, especially northwest Europe. Thus the growing concern in Germany, the Netherlands and Sweden is more than justified.

It is important to distinguish the different cadmium-containing waste streams in terms of mobility. This issue has been investigated, particularly, by Harrison *et al.* (1981); Lum *et al.* (1982); Fraser and Lum (1983); and Stigliani (undated). Generally speaking, airborne cadmium particulates are 100% mobile; street dust and sewage sludge are 95% mobile; in rural soils 60% would be typical; incinerated sludge reduces the mobility to 10% (see Figure 6.4).

The Netherlands is a densely populated and heavily industrialized country. It is also the unwilling recipient of many pollutants from other countries by way of the Rhine river (which can hardly be excluded from the ground

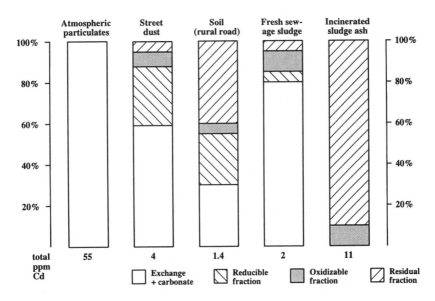

Source: Stigliani undated.

Figure 6.4: Mobility of cadmium in various environmental forms

water). Cadmium is one of the most worrisome. For soil, a cadmium content of 1 ppm defines it as contaminated. Calculations of cadmium buildup in Dutch soils are disquieting. Over the period 1960–80, the average for Dutch agricultural soils was 3 ppm (Stigliani undated). Based on emissions and mobility estimates undertaken by Dutch researchers and IIASA, cadmium content is expected to increase by 2010 to between 28 ppm (10% mobility assumption) and 44 ppm (60% assumed mobility) (ibid.).

The likely effects of this buildup will be seen in kidney damage to people over 50 years of age, and bone damage to those most acutely affected. Data suggest that the margin of safety for cadmium intake through food is already approaching a factor of two for much of Europe and North America. A sharp increase in mobilizable cadmium in soils would have serious public health consequences. In conclusion, it is clear that dissipative uses of cadmium, which contribute to this growing threat, must be discouraged to the utmost, and recycling must be promoted.

6.6. IMPLICATIONS

It can be concluded that cadmium is already on the way to becoming a public health hazard in the Netherlands. Some other regions, at least, must also be approaching their limits in terms of cadmium 'absorption' capacity. There are no feasible — even plausible — strategies to 'clean up' cadmium-contaminated soils or sediments. The only thing that can be done is to reduce the rate of input to a level below the annual level of cadmium dispersal to the deep oceans or other environmental sinks, then wait patiently for the cadmium 'overload' in the environment to fall. This means that we must focus on measures to reduce primary cadmium use, or — failing that — to reduce primary zinc use.

As regards the more direct approaches for reducing (dissipative) cadmium use, there are really two possibilities. The first is to use public policy to raise the price of cadmium *vis-à-vis* other competing metals (including zinc itself). A tax on cadmium at the zinc refinery would, however, tend to discourage cadmium recovery, leaving more unrecovered cadmium in tailings, slags, dusts and so on. A slightly cleverer approach would be to tax the *unrecovered* cadmium, being the difference between the cadmium content of the zinc ore and the cadmium recovered for sale. However, this would also be counterproductive unless accompanied by an effective restriction on dissipative uses of the recovered cadmium. An outright ban on the use of cadmium-based pigments, cadmium-based stabilizers for plastics, and other such chemical uses should be considered. A ban on the use of zinc chemicals contaminated with cadmium (such as zinc oxide used in tire manufacturing) would also be a possibility.

Still, the major single use of cadmium, namely in rechargeable nickel-cadmium (nicad) batteries, should not be banned or even heavily taxed. What is needed is a much more effective encouragement to remanufacture or recycle these batteries. A returnable deposit of several cents on each battery is probably the answer. The money would be collected from battery purchasers at the point of sale and returned (plus a bonus) by the manufacturer to the retailer–collector. Many retailers would probably object to having to undertake this additional responsibility, but experience with returnable bottles and other such items suggests that the scheme would be effective if put into effect. As a very strong inducement, retailers could be *required* by their suppliers to collect and return a certain quota of batteries previously delivered as a condition of obtaining additional supplies.

Of course, the returned batteries would simply accumulate unless an effective remanufacturing or recycling system were also developed. This is a fairly straightforward task from the chemical and metallurgical perspective, since the cadmium content of the batteries is significantly higher than the cadmium content of the original zinc ore, or even the zinc concentrate as it arrives at the refinery. The possibility of recovering zinc at the same time would be economically attractive, also. The major problem with implementing such a scheme is simply the lack of any existing incentive for manufacturers or retailers to do so. This would necessarily be the role of government.

The other general approach to reducing cadmium losses to the environment is to reduce the supply. This could be done by discouraging unnecessary uses of (primary) zinc. The obvious method for accomplishing this objective would be to tax primary zinc itself, either at the mine or at the refinery. The zinc content of imported materials and products would also have to be taxed as a tariff. The idea behind such a tax is to raise the price of primary zinc, both in absolute terms and *vis-à-vis* less harmful direct competitors. (The most obvious of the latter is secondary zinc.) The most immediate impact would be to encourage more efficient recovery and recycling of secondary zinc, especially from galvanized sheet and zinc-based primary cells. (The latter could be collected and recycled by the same basic mechanism suggested above in connection with nicad batteries, namely a returnable deposit.) To the extent that more zinc is recovered and recycled, less primary zinc would be needed and less cadmium would be produced as a byproduct. Apart from reducing the cadmium load on the environment, increased recycling of zinc would also reduce overall energy consumption, at least modestly.

NOTE(6)

1. Cadmium and zinc are direct competitors for this purpose. In fact zinc provides slightly better corrosion protection. Cadmium has always been more expensive than zinc, but the plating process for cadmium was more reliable and controllable until improvements in the zinc electroplating (galvanizing) process began to strongly favor zinc (see NMAB 1979).

7. Sulfur and sulfuric acid

7.1. SUMMARY

Sulfur is biologically and environmentally important because it can exist in valence states from –2 (e.g. hydrogen sulfide, H_2S) to +6 (sulfuric acid, H_2SO_4). Like nitrogen and phosphorus, it is essential to living organisms. It is a component of three of the 20 amino acids that are the 'building blocks' of all proteins, namely, cystine, cysteine and methionine. It seems to play a special part in cross-linking amino acid chains to give them their characteristic three-dimensional shapes (especially important for enzymes). On the other hand, a number of sulfur compounds are toxic, including hydrogen sulfide, sulfur dioxide and the mercaptans.

Sulfur is an important industrial substance. Sulfur is not intrinsically scarce; enormous quantities are theoretically available as a byproduct of fossil fuels, as well as in deposits of sulfide ores, pyrites and elemental sulfur. Virtually all sulfur used by industry today comes from elemental sulfur deposits or from refining oil, gas and non-ferrous metals. In some sense, the availability of large reserves of reduced sulfur is the core of the problem, since it is much easier, hence cheaper, to obtain sulfur in forms useful to industry from reduced sources such as H_2S or S than it is to recover it from coal, or from oxides.

Most industrial sulfur is converted initially to its most oxidized form, sulfuric acid. Sulfuric acid, because of low cost and its variety of uses as a powerful oxidizer and pH control in the chemical industry and other industries, is one of the most reliable indicators of general industrial activity. However, currently, the biggest and fastest growing single use of sulfuric acid, worldwide, is a specialized one: converting phosphate rock to phosphoric acid for fertilizer. In this case, the sulfur is combined with calcium as insoluble calcium sulfate (gypsum). (See Section 8.5, Gypsum sources and uses for a further discussion of gypsum.) The majority of chemical processes end up with sulfur (from the acid) combined with calcium (from lime) or sodium (from caustic soda). In the latter case, the material is soluble and biologically available.

The major source of anthropogenic volatile sulfur oxide emissions, today, is the combustion of fossil fuels — especially coal — and the smelting and refining of non-ferrous metals (Cu, Zn, Pb). In these cases, the sulfur is oxidized to SO_2 or SO_3. In the air, SO_2 and associated droplets of acid are irritating and harmful to the nasal passages and lungs. Sulfur dioxide was actually the first air pollutant to be subject to regulation, although its sharp and unpleasant odor may account for this early attention. The unreacted sulfur oxides remaining in the atmosphere are the major cause of a haze which reduces visibility and increases the reflectivity (albedo) of the earth to sunlight. Thus sulfur oxide emissions, other factors remaining equal, tend to cool the earth slightly.

The sulfur oxides are eventually deposited as dry sulfite/sulfate particulates, or dissolved in water droplets (producing sulfurous or sulfuric acid), or they react with ammonia, producing ammonium sulfite or sulfate. In any case, the sulfur is eventually deposited on land (or water) as sulfurous or sulfuric acid, or as sulfates. On the ground, ammonium sulfate is a fertilizer. Sulfurous and sulfuric acids are also biologically active. In effect, the natural 'sulfur cycle' has been significantly accelerated by industrial activity. One consequence is widespread acidification of forest soils, especially granitic soils in central and northern Europe. On the other hand, since many soils are sulfur deficient, there is also a general fertilization ('eutrophication') effect, especially in calcareous soils.

There are a few industrial processes where sulfur escapes in reduced forms. Reduced volatile forms of sulfur (H_2S and mercaptans) are particularly hazardous, although the quantities released in the industrialized countries (mainly from oil refineries and pulp mills) are comparatively minor. (The major source of reduced sulfur into the atmosphere is from volcanic eruptions, fumaroles, anaerobic decay in swamps, and vented natural gas.)

Goals of public policy: to reduce unnecessary surface mining (of coal and gypsum, for instance); to reduce atmospheric emissions of sulfur oxides, especially in areas where increased acidification is a problem; to minimize emissions of toxic reduced forms of sulfur, such as H_2S; to reduce the need for land disposal of wet flue-gas desulfurization (FGD) sludges; to recover elemental sulfur or sulfuric acid for industrial use from fossil fuels and non-ferrous metals smelters.

7.2.   INDUSTRIAL SULFUR SOURCES

Worldwide, there are currently three major primary sources for elemental sulfur and sulfuric acid: (1) native sulfur found in the limestone caprock of salt domes, volcanic deposits, or bedded anhydrite, (2) hydrogen sulfide present in 'sour' natural gas, refinery gas and other flue-gases, and (3) ferrous and non-ferrous metallic sulfides.

Total world production of elemental sulfur in 1991 was 55.592 MMT. Production in Western Europe was 7.081 MMT. Much sulfur is still mined in pure form (native sulfur) or from underground deposits (by the Frasch process), though not in Western Europe. Poland produced 4.4 MMT by the Frasch process and another 0.5 MMT from native sulfur deposits. Sulfur is also mined as iron pyrites, and as gypsum (only in Poland, however). In Western Europe pyrites accounted for 2.215 MMT in 1989, about half from Spain.

Crude oil refined in the US in 1980 averaged 1.5% S by weight. In the case of imported oil from Venezuela and Mexico, refined offshore, the average sulfur content was 5.5%. In the case of natural gas, the sulfur content was 0.003%. These percentages are rising, if anything, from decade to decade. The sulfur cannot be allowed to remain in the fuel, so it must be removed at the refinery, either as a waste or for beneficial use. Sulfur recovery from petroleum was negligible prior to the 1940s and is essentially a function of the complexity of the refinery. Much of the unrecovered sulfur — of which there is now relatively little in the industrialized world — was ultimately emitted as SO_x. This is still the case in some smaller refineries in less industrialized countries. Some so-called 'sweetening' processes to eliminate odors from hydrogen sulfide and mercaptans leave odorless sulfur compounds dissolved in the fuel. These are ultimately burned, yielding SO_2.[1]

In recent years, increasing amounts of refinery sulfur have been recovered for re-use. About 26% of the potential sulfur from crude oil refined in the US was actually recovered in 1974, mostly by the catalytic hydrogen de-sulfurization process (USBuMines 1975). About one-third (33.9%) of US petroleum distillation capacity included hydro-treating facilities for sulfur recovery as of January 1, 1980 (Gaines and Wolsky 1981). The sulfur recovery process itself is said to be 99% efficient. Petroleum refineries accounted for 28% of the domestic US sulfur supply in 1983 (USBuMines 1985). Natural gas accounted for 26% of the domestic US sulfur supply in 1983. These fractions are rising. Fuel processing accounted for 56% of the US sulfur supply in 1990 and 61% in 1991 (USBuMines 1991). Some sulfur is also recovered (as sulfuric acid) from copper, zinc, lead and nickel smelters. Western Europe now gets most of its sulfur from byproducts (see Appendix A, Table A.5).

Non-ferrous metals are almost exclusively obtained from sulfide ores. For instance, copper ore consists mostly of chalcopyrite ($CuFeS_2$) — which is the most common — followed by bornite (Cu_5FeS_4) and chalcocite (Cu_2S), although minor amounts of copper are also obtained from oxides and carbonates. Zinc and lead are obtained respectively from the minerals sphalerite (ZnS) and galena (PbS). Mercury ore is cinnabar (HgS). Nickel is also mined partly from sulfide ores (e.g. in Canada). Table 7.1 gives the ratios of sulfur to metal in major non-ferrous ores.

Table 7.1:   Ratio of copper, lead and zinc in ore, by weight

Copper	1.0[a]
	1.47[b]
Lead	0.15[c]
Zinc	0.49[d]

Notes:
a.   Preferred estimates. Based on chalcopyrite (CuFeS$_2$) as the ore. In the early 19th century a significant fraction of the copper mined was native (not combined with sulfur).
b.   Implied by *Mineral Facts and Problems* (1975) estimate of potential byproduct sulfur availability from copper ore.
c.   Based on the mineral galena (PbS) as the ore. This is quite consistent with *Mineral Facts and Problems* (1975).
d.   Based on the mineral sphalerite (ZnS) as the ore. The coefficient implied by *Mineral Facts and Problems* (1975) is 0.43.

Sulfur recovery from copper and lead smelters was still relatively incomplete until quite recently. It is motivated mainly by environmental concerns. As recently as 1974 the US Bureau of Mines estimated a 30% sulfur recovery rate for copper smelting and 43% for lead smelting (USBuMines 1975). However, the above estimate for copper assumes a sulfur content of copper ores equivalent to 1.47 tons of sulfur per ton of copper, which is inconsistent with the known composition of copper minerals and smelter feeds (Table 7.1). For this reason we suspect that the USBuMines recovery estimate for copper in that year was slightly too low. Using the lower figure for sulfur content in Table 7.1 the sulfur recovery rate for US copper smelters in 1974 would also have been 43%. This is consistent with the fact that about 60% recovery was easily achievable at the convertor stage, but the remainder (40% or so) requires scrubbers or the equivalent. It is estimated that sulfur recovery from copper smelters in the US has reached 95% (USBuMines 1994).

By contrast, complete sulfur recovery from zinc smelters in the US was much easier to achieve (81% by 1974). This was apparently because the zinc retorting process itself makes sulfur recovery straightforward and economical. If all byproduct sulfur recovery from copper and zinc smelters in 1911 (the first year for which we have data) is attributed to zinc smelting alone, the implied recovery rate would be 79% — close to the 1974 level. In 1983 copper smelting accounted for 6% of the US sulfur supply, while zinc, lead and molybdenum accounted for another 2% between them. In 1991 the non-ferrous metal smelters contributed 12% of domestic US supply, entirely in the form of sulfuric acid.

The efficiency of sulfur recovery (as opposed to emissions control) from non-ferrous metal smelters is not easy to determine. One study (Chapman 1989, Table 3) estimated the sulfur control indices for a number of exporting countries for 1985 as follows: Chile (14%), Peru (0%), South Africa (39%), Zaire (76%), Zambia (70%), Philippines (0%), Australia (0%) and Canada (26%). It estimated the average control level for copper exporters as 32%, compared to an average of 89% for the major copper-importing countries. A more recent study of 8 US and 29 non-US copper smelters around the world, commissioned by the US Bureau of Mines, concluded that sulfur control (i.e. recovery) at US smelters for the year 1988 was 90.4%, but that only 55% of the available sulfur was recovered by the non-US group (Towle 1993). However, of the non-US smelters surveyed, three were located in Western Europe (Ronnskar in Sweden, Hamburg in Germany and Huelva in Spain). The first two, at least, are at the 90% recovery level.

In principle, all of the world's needs for elemental sulfur and sulfuric acid could easily be met by recovering the sulfur from metals, gas, oil and coal. Yet only a small proportion of the sulfur in coal is actually recovered, and most of that is disposed of as a semi-liquid, hydrated sludge of mixed calcium sulfite ($CaSO_3$) and calcium sulfate ($CaSO_4$). Virtually none of the sulfur in coal is used industrially. (As of 1989, only 2000 tonnes was recovered from coal in Europe, in a Spanish gasification plant.) Most coal-bound sulfur is still emitted to the atmosphere as SO_X.

7.3. POTENTIAL SULFUR RECOVERY FROM COAL

Coal contains, on average, 0.5–5% sulfur, depending on the mine. Coal traded internationally must have a maximum sulfur content of 1%, though some coals being burned locally are significantly higher in sulfur (WEC 1992). The sulfur oxidizes to SO_2 which (if not removed) is the major source of environmental acidification. In turn 'acid rain' from coal combustion (mainly in electric power plants) is largely blamed for forest die-back (*Waldsterben*) in many parts of Europe. US coal averages 1.85% S (ibid.). Coal from the Saar and Ruhr areas ranges from 0.9% to 1% (ibid.). British coal is 1.66% sulfur (ibid.). Some coals have much higher sulfur content. French sub-bituminous coal averages 5% sulfur (ibid.). Spanish coal has a high sulfur content. Hungarian coals are also high in sulfur (2.5–3.8%). Virtually none of the sulfur emitted from coal combustion in Europe is being recovered today, though there is some emissions control.

The total quantity of sulfur that could be potentially recovered worldwide from coal (assuming a conservative 1% sulfur content) approaches 40 MMT. In fact, this is a lower limit. This is more than enough to replace all the 'mined' sulfur currently produced in the world (25 MMT). Since mining is itself an environmentally damaging activity, and uncontrolled emissions of SO_2 cause serious health hazards as well as acidification, it would be very beneficial to solve two problems at once by recovering the sulfur from coal in an industrially *useful* form, either as elemental sulfur, carbon disulfide or sulfuric acid.

The need to capture the sulfur from coal combustion is becoming clear, at least in Western Europe. Indeed, Western Europe will be forced to subsidize Poland and the Czech Republic, and perhaps others, as the most economical way to reduce the sulfur emissions that would otherwise cross the border from east to west. But current means of flue gas desulfurization (FGD) are almost exclusively limited to variations of one theme: the use of lime (or limestone) 'scrubbers' that capture the sulfur as wet calcium sulfite ($CaSO_3$). This is a material that has no market as such, and which is only convertible, with some difficulty, into hydrated calcium sulfate, essentially wet plaster-of-Paris. Synthetic gypsum for use in plaster-boards and building materials can be produced from wet FGD wastes from coal-burning plants. One viable approach seems to be the so-called lime-sinter process (Motley and Cosgrove 1978), although there are several variants. At least one such plant is already operational, on an experimental basis, in the Czech Republic, using German technology.

In general, the synthetic gypsum product is moderately costly to make and there is a limited market for it. In the more general case, wet FGD waste is difficult and costly to dispose of. Moreover, the limestone or lime used for the scrubber must itself be mined and shipped, at some cost to the environment. Finally, a typical wet scrubber installation consumes about 4% of the electric power produced by the plant.

Since disposal of wet FGD sludges from electric power plants will become increasingly costly, there will be strong incentives to extract a more useful and valuable byproduct from the process. But, at present, the capital and energy cost of doing so, in the short term, is fairly high, but not entirely certain. In short, either capital subsidies or energy subsidies, or both, are needed. It is not entirely clear how big these subsidies need to be, or who will provide them.

A number of dry FGD processes have been tested and some have been installed. Dry FGD systems require less equipment because there is no need for thickeners, centrifuges, slurry pumping and so on. They produce a dry solid waste that can be handled and disposed of in the same way that ash is normally handled and disposed of. They use less energy, for the same reason. The major disadvantage is that the sorbents are mostly sodium carbonates and bicarbonates, which are more expensive than limestone. Also, the sodium-based wastes have a greater potential for leaching than calcium-based wastes.

One dry process that has the advantages mentioned above, without the disadvantages, is the so-called 'Trimex' process. A dry powder, consisting mainly of the clay known as calcium montmorillonite (bentonite), is injected into the firebox. The clay material has a very strong affinity for water and captures water vapor on its surface, where a catalytic reaction with SO_2 in the combustion product stream takes place. The sulfurous and sulfuric acids adhering to the clay particle surface, in turn, react immediately with the alkaline metals in the fly ash particulates. In other words, the fly ash becomes the sorbent for FGD in this case. The final product (collected by an electrostatic precipitator) would consist of dry metallic sulfites and sulfates. Certain additives, namely trisodium phosphate and borax, support or activate the catalytic function of the clay.

Recovery of elemental sulfur directly from flue gas is a further possibility. As applied to coal gasification, this could utilize a variant of hydro-gasification technology, where the sulfur combines initially with hydrogen to form H_2S. The latter is easily reduced to elemental sulfur by the Claus process. This is much less straightforward in an oxidizing environment, where solid coal is burned. The most useful product that can be extracted is probably a low-grade sulfuric acid.

An interesting process for co-producing sulfur, alumina and Portland cement was proposed by TRW Inc (Motley and Cosgrove 1978). A plant utilizing this process would have to be co-located with a large coal-burning power plant fitted with a limestone scrubber. Inputs might be 1.365 MMT of scrubber waste (50% solid), 317 kMT of kaolin, 250 kMT of coal, 12 kMT of soda ash and 5 kMT of lime. Direct outputs would be 70 kMT of alumina, 156 kMT of sulfur and 652 kMT of dicalcium silicate (input to a cement plant yielding 858 kMT of Portland cement). Unfortunately, the process chemistry involved in the process was non-standard and partially hypothetical at the time of the Motley–Cosgrove study. In particular, there are unresolved questions about the reaction rates of soda, alumina, calcium and silica to form dicalcium silicate and sodium aluminate under reducing conditions, and the likely percentage of completion. Further laboratory work and bench testing was needed (and may still be needed).[2] A variant of the above scheme was also suggested, in which the kaolin input is replaced by silica and the product is tricalcium silicate (cement) rather than dicalcium silicate.

In summary, there is a need for more research on FGD, not just as an 'add-on' process for existing coal-fired power plants, but in the context of an integrated system, such as 'coalplex'. For more detailed discussion see Chapters 14 and 15. The need is for sulfur recovery, not just for emissions control by itself. This need can best be met by treating the combustion unit as a source of raw materials, of which sulfur (in some form) is one, and integrating several down-stream processes in such a way as to take advantage of synergistic mutual interactions.

7.4.   SULFURIC ACID AND SULFUR-BASED CHEMICALS

Sulfuric acid is by far the most important sulfur-based chemical. It accounts for 92% of total US sulfur use, and 77% of non-fertilizer sulfur use. In the US (the largest consumer) phosphates alone account for 66% of the total demand for sulfuric acid. However, the US is a major exporter of phosphates, whereas Europe is a major importer. For Western Europe non-fertilizer consumption of sulfuric acid dominates in percentage terms (58.5%). This is because there are virtually no sources of phosphate rock in Western Europe; a great deal of the phosphoric acid consumed in Europe is imported, from a variety of places, including the US, Israel, South Africa and North Africa. Quite a lot of the processing is done outside Europe.[3] For the world as a whole, fertilizer accounts for 61.7% of total sulfuric acid consumption, mostly for phosphates.

The primary product is wet-process phosphoric acid, which is the source of phosphate fertilizers. The sulfur in this case ends up as hydrated calcium sulfate ('phospho-gypsum') and is discarded as waste. (See Chapter 8, Phosphorus for a further discussion.) The waste from phosphate rock processing is, essentially, a somewhat contaminated form of the mineral gypsum. Similarly, the waste from flue-gas desulfurization (FGD) is also gypsum. Yet, most byproduct gypsum is a waste that poses a disposal problem. At the same time, approximately 100 MMT of natural gypsum is mined, each year. Uncalcined gypsum is used in the manufacture of Portland cement and in agriculture as a soil condition for alkaline and saline soils. Calcined gypsum is used for conversion into plaster-of-paris and plasterboard products.

Production and consumption statistics for sulfuric acid are summarized in Appendix A, Table A.6. Elemental sulfur (23% of non-fertilizer use) is used to manufacture carbon disulfide, an intermediate in the production of fluorocarbons. It is also used in petroleum refineries (see below), to vulcanize rubber[4] and in a number of unspecified uses, mostly agricultural (USBuMines 1989, Table 12). The latter include traditional soil conditioners such as 'lime-sulfur' mixture.

Sulfuric acid is not only used for phosphatic fertilizers. It is also used in the manufacture of ammonium sulfate (see Appendix A, Table A.7, sulfuric acid end-uses). There are no detailed statistics on non-fertilizer sulfuric acid use in Europe. However, non-fertilizer use in Europe is very similar in absolute magnitude to non-fertilizer consumption in the US. It is reasonable to assume that the sectoral breakdown of non-fertilizer use of sulfuric acid in Europe would also be similar. A detailed sulfur balance accounting for most sulfur uses is summarized in Figure 7.1.

Sulfuric acid (H_2SO_4) is produced from elemental sulfur or byproduct SO_2 from gas processing, petroleum refining or non-ferrous metal smelting. It is

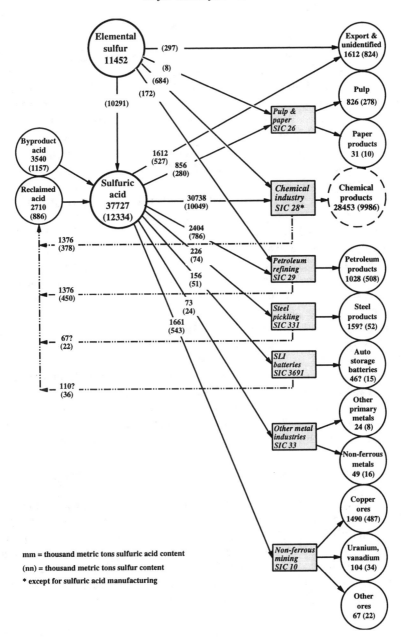

Data source: US BuMines 1989.

Figure 7.1:   US sulfur product flows, 1988

the starting point for most sulfur-based chemicals. What is recovered in petroleum refineries is mostly also consumed there. Sulfur is used in refineries for several purposes, both as elemental sulfur and as acid (Gaines and Wolsky 1981, p. 76). Refinery uses as S include solvent extraction with liquid SO_2, and as an additive to high sulfur metal-cutting oils. Acid is used especially as a catalyst for alkylation of iso- and normal butane to produce high-octane blending stock, and for polymerization of cracking-still gases to produce so-called 'poly-gasoline'. These uses accounted for about 14.7% of elemental sulfur and 16.7% of non-fuel consumption of sulfuric acid, in the US in 1988. Over half of the 'spent' acid from US refineries is reclaimed, however and sold in the market (USBuMines 1991).

Similarly, acid recovered from US copper smelters is mostly used for the so-called hydro-metallurgical process of copper and other non-ferrous ore leaching (e.g. uranium, vanadium). This use accounted for 16.3% of non-fuel consumption of sulfuric acid in the US in 1988, but is much less important in Europe. Crude copper sulfate is recovered from the leach piles, and this is recycled, but some of the leaching acid remains in the ore heaps where it presumably reacts with other minerals and remains as insoluble sulfates. In Europe, acid from smelters not co-located with mines (i.e. those not in Finland) is presumably sold on the market.

Inorganic chemicals manufacturing accounted for 10.75% of US sulfuric acid consumption in 1988. Major quantity uses included production of titanium dioxide from ilmenite, chromic acid, hydrofluoric acid from fluorspar, copper sulfate, lead sulfate, zinc sulfate and other pigments.

The next largest use of sulfuric acid in the US (9.85%) is in the manufacture of synthetic rubber, plastics and synthetics. Since very few organic chemicals actually contain any sulfur, it is likely that the most important contribution of sulfur (i.e. sulfuric acid) is to maintain reaction pH. In general, it is not embodied in products. Wastes are discharged, mostly as dilute or insoluble sulfates.

A further 1.3% of sulfuric acid consumption was used to make cellulosic fibers (e.g. rayon) yielding sodium sulfate as a byproduct. Detergents — sulfonated fatty acid esters — accounted for another 2.5% of non-ferrous sulfuric acid. This is virtually the only category of products (apart from vulcanized rubber) in which sulfur is actually embodied. Minor amounts of sulfuric acid are used in other chemicals manufacturing processes, adding up to 9.3%. Agricultural and water treatment chemicals are the biggest categories.

Another important non-fertilizer use of sulfuric acid — about 12.2% of US consumption — is in the sulfate (Kraft) pulp-bleaching process. Sulfuric acid is used to convert sodium chlorate to chlorine dioxide, with sodium sulfate as a byproduct. The byproduct sodium sulfate is used in the dominant Kraft pulping process. Sulfuric acid may also be used to produce sodium sulfate by direct reaction with sodium hydroxide. In the case of Kraft pulp mills there are increasing efforts to recover sodium sulfate and other chemicals from the waste stream ('black liquor') by using electrostatic precipitators at recovery furnaces. But the annual makeup requirements represent that which is discharged, either into the air as H_2S and other non-condensible gases (mercaptans, DMS, DMDS), or into streams and rivers as complex ligninsulfonates (from the sulfite process).

The 'pickling' process for cleaning rolled steel prior to galvanizing or tinplating uses a small amount of sulfuric acid (1.5%). In this case the waste is mostly ferrous sulfate, which is easily recoverable but has few markets. Sulfuric acid is used in small amounts by other metallurgical processes (such as plating). Automotive storage (lead-acid) batteries accounted for 1.3% of non-ferrous uses. All the above items add up to 92.7% of the total. Unidentified uses, including exports, account for the rest (7.3%). The unidentified uses are probably distributed more or less in proportion to the identified uses.

Summarizing, 77% of non-fertilizer uses of sulfur are based on sulfuric acid. The remainder is diverse. Other starting points are SO_2 (used in the sulfite pulp process), and carbon disulfide (CS_2) which is used in the manufacture of chlorinated methanes. Elemental sulfur is used as such in agriculture (as noted previously) and in rubber processing (as a vulcanizing agent). Sulfur is also used in the manufacture of some pesticides. In most cases, the sulfur is eventually oxidized and released or neutralized. However, when organic sulfur compounds enter anaerobic environments, trouble (i.e. reduced sulfur gases) can ensue. In particular, this is a problem that has been associated with paper pulping, for instance.

Virtually all uses of sulfur are dissipative. Most of the dissipative losses occur in agriculture (as elemental sulfur or ammonium sulfate), within the chemical industry itself, or in the petroleum refining or pulp and paper sectors. The final form of production waste is normally either insoluble calcium sulfite/sulfate, soluble (dilute) sodium sulfate, organic sulfonates, or SO_2 or reduced sulfur gases (H_2S, mercaptans, etc.) emitted into the air. Consumption wastes include sulfur-cutting oils and sulfonated detergents. Only a small amount of sulfuric acid is recycled (about 0.864 MMT S, or 7.3%), also mostly from petroleum refineries and synthetic materials. It is likely that the non-fertilizer sulfur consumption pattern for Europe is very similar to that for the US.

7.5. ATMOSPHERIC EMISSIONS OF SULFUR OXIDES (SO_x)

Aggregate emissions of sulfur dioxide can be best estimated by using a materials balance calculation. Sulfur emitted (as SO_2) can be estimated fairly accurately as the *difference* between sulfur associated with ores and the sulfur recovered at refineries or smelters, with appropriate adjustments for imports or exports of sulfur containing fuels or minerals.

The sulfur mobilized by the industrial economy in Western Europe for non-combustion uses is compared to the atmospheric sulfur emissions from combustion and the total anthropogenic sulfur budget in Table 7.2. The percentage of sulfur metabolized by the European and US industrial economy (non-combustion uses) is much higher than the global average. For Western Europe as a whole, industrial uses account for just over half of the total sulfur budget. Numbers for the US are comparable.

7.6. EMISSIONS TO OTHER MEDIA

Much has been written about the sources of atmospheric sulfur emissions and their detrimental environmental effects. Less information is available on industrial sulfur waste disposal in water and on land. It is important to emphasize here that the majority of the sulfur used in industrial processes is used for processing and is not embodied in the end product. That which is not recycled becomes a waste.

Having concluded that the industrial use of sulfur is a significant portion of the Western European anthropogenic sulfur budget, two new questions arise: in what form is the emission? And, is it an environmental hazard? Currently, sulfur does not appear to be a problem pollutant in large international rivers. However, humans have had an impact on the sulfur concentration in rivers. It is estimated that, globally, man-induced sulfur runoff is roughly equal to the natural flow (Schlesinger 1991). In industrialized regions, such as the eastern US or Western Europe, the ratio of anthropogenic to natural sulfate in runoff is much higher (up to 8) (Husar and Husar 1985).

The common opinion about non-atmospheric sulfur wastes from industry is described in a passage from Meyer (1977).

> Industrial sulfur is almost totally converted to sulfate, is used as an acid, and promptly returns to the sediment as sulfate. So far, only comparatively little sulfur enters industrial products. It is possible that in the future a much larger fraction of sulfur will be incorporated into industrial products. If this becomes the case, it will be mainly in elemental form or in the form of sulfite, both of which readily biodegrade to sulfate, which reenters the sedimentary cycle. We need not dwell

Table 7.2: Atmospheric emissions of anthropogenic sulfur, 1980–1990 (kMT of sulfur)

		IIASA Data			WRI Data	
	industrial as % of total	*from combustion*	*from industry*	*total emissions 1980*	*total emissions 1980*	*total emissions 1990*
Austria	17	30	147	177	199	45
Belgium/Lux	16	73	375	448	426	215
Denmark	0	1	226	227	225	91
Finland	42	122	170	292	292	130
France	19	343	1 434	1 777	1 676	601
Germany(W)	14	223	1 377	1 600	1 599	470
Greece	4	15	333	348	200	250
Iceland					5	4
Ireland	3	3	105	108	110	94
Italy	16	293	1 512	1 805	1 607	1 204
Netherlands	38	86	139	225	251	104
Norway	48	33	36	69	71	27
Portugal	13	19	130	149	133	106
Spain	37	609	1 020	1 629	1 690	1 096
Sweden	35	86	157	243	245	64
Switzerland	2	1	63	64	63	32
United Kingdom	11	250	2 089	2 339	2 451	1 892
Western Europe	**19**	**2 183**	**9 310**	**11 493**	**11 243**	**6 424**
Bulgaria					518	516
Czechoslovakia					1 552	1 283
Germany(E)					2 164	2 381
Hungary					817	506
Poland					2 052	1 610
Romania					901	901
Turkey					138	199
Yugoslavia					589	741
Eastern Europe					**8 730**	**8 136**
Canada					2 324	1 665
Japan					632	438
US					11 902	10 541
USSR					6 407	4 465

Sources: IIASA data is from IIASA Transboundary Air Pollution Project. Combustion includes combustion from power plants, district heat generation, domestic and service sectors, transportation and industry. Industrial sulfur includes non-combustion industrial process emissions and all emissions (combustion and non-combustion) from the conversion of fossil fuels (refinery coke production). It was not possible to divide the data from this project into combustion and non-combustion emissions for this sector.
WRI data is from WRI 1994, Table 23.5. It is not broken down by source.

here on the use of gypsum, which is mixed and used as such, because in it sulfur does not change oxidation state. (Meyer 1977, pp. 161–2)

This reassuring view leaves several questions unanswered. Much of the sulfuric acid used in industry which is not recycled (and not discharged into the atmosphere) is eventually converted to calcium sulfite or calcium sulfate. Clues about the potential problems caused by the disposal of calcium sulfate and calcium sulfite wastes can be found in the extensive literature on flue-gas desulfurization and other methods used for the control of sulfur dioxide emissions from fuel combustion (Ellison and Luckevich 1984; Morrison 1986). These sulfate wastes pose three potential problems.

One problem is disposal *per se*. The calcium sulfite and sulfate wastes are often in a sludge form which is difficult to dewater. In addition, the disposal of these materials on land makes the site unusable for other purposes for an indefinite period. The sheer magnitude of such wastes over the long term can create serious disposal problems, at least locally.

The second concern is the possibility of environmental mobilization and secondary damages. The pathway for environmental mobilization is through leaching. The leachate from these dumps can contain concentrations of sulphate, chloride, calcium and magnesium several orders of magnitude greater than natural background concentrations. In addition, in the case of wastes from fuel emissions (and possibly some industrial processes) the leachate may also contain traces of heavy metals.

The third, and perhaps the most serious, concern has to do with the fate of concentrations of sulfates in anaerobic environments rich in organic materials. In the absence of oxygen, nitrates or manganese or iron oxides, but given the availability of organic materials, decay bacteria can extract oxygen from the sulfate (SO_4) radical for their own metabolic purposes, releasing toxic hydrogen sulfide. The basic (equivalent) reaction is

$$SO_4^- + CH_2O + H^+ \rightarrow CO_2 + H_2O + H_2S$$

Concern over the long-term accumulation of solid or liquid sulfate wastes is of particular importance, because of the trend (prompted by environmental regulation) towards reduced atmospheric emissions of sulfur. This trend means that increasingly the anthropogenic sulfur wastes are being disposed of on land or waterways. We can expect this trend to continue and possibly accelerate.

7.7. THE GLOBAL SULFUR CYCLE

Biologically available sulfur is apparently 'scarce' on land, because its commonest forms (calcium and magnesium sulfates) are extremely insoluble. Unfortunately, soluble (i.e. bio-available) forms of sulfur like ammonium sulfate are continuously depleted by erosion and runoff to the oceans, where sulfur accumulates. To close the cycle, sulfur is recycled back to the land by atmospheric flows of volatile sulfur compounds such as hydrogen sulfide, mercaptans, dimethylsulfide (DMS) or dimethyldisulfide (DMDS), produced by marine organisms.

$$SO_3 + H_2O \rightarrow H_2SO_4$$

Dissolved in water, sulfurous and sulfuric acids then react with ammonia, derived from the decay of nitrogenous organic materials (e.g. animal manure) forming ammonium sulfate. Thus, the natural sulfur cycle interacts strongly with the natural nitrogen cycle here.

The global sulfur cycle (Figure 7.2) consists of a set of oxidation reactions balanced by reduction reactions. Reduced forms of sulfur (S, H_2S) are gradually oxidized by atmospheric oxygen, ending in sulfur oxides (SO_2, SO_3) and finally sulfate SO_4^{++}. Sulfate is deposited on the earth's surface in wet or dry form (e.g. as ammonium sulfate). The reverse part of the cycle, which converts sulfur back to reduced forms — states of higher thermodynamic potential — is accomplished either by biological activity or possibly by high temperature magmatic reactions in the earth's mantle.

From another perspective, of course, it can be seen as a cycle in which insoluble and biologically unavailable forms of sulfur — notably sulfides (pyrites) and calcium and magnesium sulfates — are converted to biologically available forms, utilized, and finally returned once again to unavailable forms. From this perspective, the cycle can also be seen as a complex set of transfers between air, land and sea (Figure 7.2). Assuming the pre-industrial version of the cycle was really balanced, the controlling rate, or 'bottleneck' in the system must have been the rate at which insoluble sulfides or sulfates were deposited in oceanic sediments. In the very long run (on the average) this deposition rate must have been equal to the rate at which sulfur was remobilized by pre-industrial geo-chemical processes, with or without biological assistance. It must also equal the pre-industrial net rate of deposition of sulfur compounds on the ocean surface, plus the pre-industrial runoff from rivers, abrasion of shores, and so on.

Various estimates of sulfur fluxes are shown in Table 7.3. Estimates of the impact of human activity are most explicit in the work of Ivanov and Freney (Ivanov and Freney 1983). These authors estimated that globally 113 teragrams

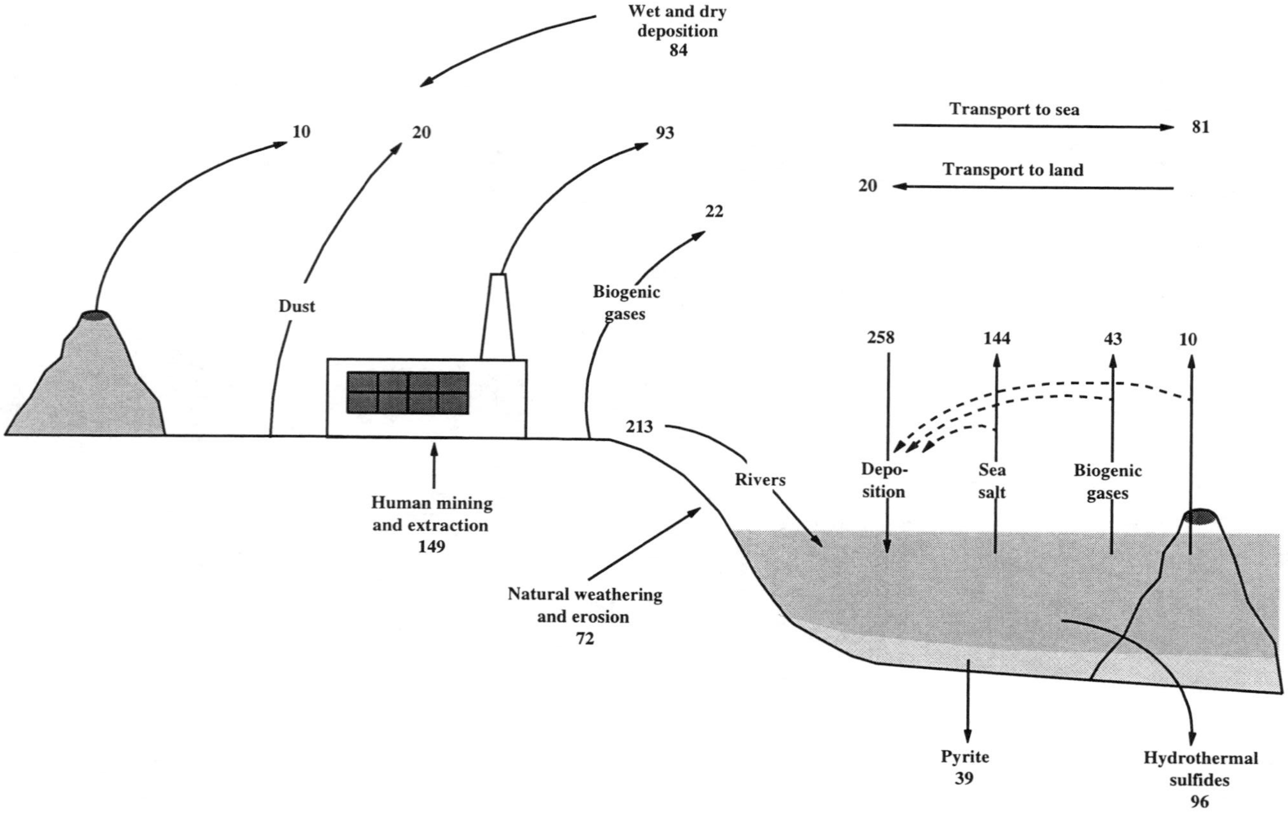

Source: Schlesinger 1991.

Figure 7.2: Global sulfur cycle (teragrams/year)

Table 7.3: Global sulfur fluxes

(Tg/yr)	Eriksson 1960	Junge 1963	Robinson and Robbins 1970	Kellogg et al. 1972	Friend 1973	Granat et al. 1976	Ivanov and Freney 1983	Brimblecombe et al. 1989
Combustion, smelting, etc.	39	40	70	50	65	65	113	93
Fertilizer	–	–	–	–	–	–	28	
Volcanic gases	–	–	–	1.5	2.0	3.0	28	land 10 ocean 10
Aeolean emission (dust)	–	–	–	–	–	0.2	20	20
Biogenic, land	77	70	68	90	58	5	16	22
Biogenic; coastal and ocean	190	160	30	43	48	27	20	43
Sea spray	44	–	44	43	44	44	140	144
Long-lived reduced S-compounds	–	–	–	–	–	–	5	
Uptake of SO_2 by land and terr.veg.	77	70	26	15	15	28	17	–
Washout of SO_4 over land	57	55	70	86	86	43	51	84
Dry sulfate deposit over land	–	15	20	10	20	–	16	
Uptake of SO_2 by oceans	70	70	25		25	10	11	
Washout of SO_4 over ocean	146	60	71	72	71	63	230	258
Dry SO_4 deposition over ocean						–	17	
River runoff: natural							104	213
River runoff: anthropogenic							104	
Abrasion from shores							7	
Underground river seepage							11	
Erosion and runoff								72
Ocean sediments, SO_4							28	–
Ocean sediments, reduced (pyrite)							111	135
Atmospheric transfer, land to sea							total 102	81
Atmospheric transfer, sea to land							anthropogenic 65	20

of sulfur was emitted into the atmosphere (as SO_2) through the combustion of fossil fuels and the smelting of ores. By comparison, 28 teragrams was used for phosphate fertilizer production, and 28 teragrams was used in other chemical industries. Thus, about one-third of the sulfur extracted from the lithosphere is used in industrial processes, half of this being used in the manufacture of phosphate fertilizer. In this connection, it is important to emphasize that relatively little sulfur is embodied in final products. In the case of fertilizer, just mentioned, the sulfuric acid is used to convert insoluble calcium phosphate into soluble phosphoric acid, leaving calcium sulfate as a by-(waste)-product.

Ivanov and Freney's estimate of current industrial atmospheric inputs and outputs is 342 Tg/yr. Removing the anthropogenic emissions (113 Tg/yr) from the input side (from land) should be compensated by a corresponding reduction in wet/dry deposition on the output side during the pre-industrial period. Assuming the anthropogenic contribution falls disproportionately on land (58 Tg/yr vs. 65 Tg/yr), the overall current ratio of oceanic to terrestrial deposition (258:84) implies that sulfate deposition from natural sources is allocated between oceans and land in the ratio 193:26. In other words, the pre-industrial inputs to the land surface must have been about 26 Tg/yr, as compared to 84 Tg/yr from atmospheric deposition (c. 1980) and a further 28 Tg/yr as fertilizer. In short, the sulfur flux to land has more than quadrupled since the beginning of industrialization.

The pre-industrial situation with regard to both sulfur and nitrogen has changed radically in the last two centuries. The net impact is not clear. The original cycle was presumably stable. It is not clear how the system will react to anthropogenic disturbances, mainly in terms of increased availability of sulfur to the terrestrial biosphere. (See also Chapter 9, Nitrogen.)

7.8. REDUCING GLOBAL SULFUR FLUX

Sulfur dioxide pollution is sufficiently hazardous to health to warrant the imposition of pollution controls at the local level. In addition, acid rain appears to be sufficiently harmful to some forests and lakes to warrant controls at the regional level. However, the problem of anthropogenic disturbance of the global sulfur cycle, still largely unrecognized, may be even more serious in the long run. Unfortunately one cannot pinpoint any specific ecological consequences. It is only possible to point out that humans appropriate most of the surplus productivity of the entire biosphere, a system that has reached a stable evolutionary balance over eons. To disturb such a balanced system is inherently risky, especially to humans, who are the most vulnerable to any change in the balance. The chances are great that any changes will be adverse rather than beneficial in human terms.

By far the most effective way of reducing the excess flux of biologically available sulfur in the biosphere is to stop burning coal. This does not seem to be a realistic option for decades to come, however. The best alternative is to permanently immobilize sulfur oxides at the point of combustion (by flue-gas desulfurization) or — still better — to recover the sulfur oxides and convert them to reduced sulfur or to industrially useful sulfuric acid. It is evidently environmentally beneficial to recover and use sulfur from petroleum, natural gas and from the smelting of non-ferrous metals, as long as the latter are to be exploited in any case. The sulfur recovery activities should be encouraged still further. On the other hand, it is extremely undesirable from an environmental standpoint to extract large amounts of reduced sulfur from the earth's crust (by mining pyrites and elemental sulfur) while simultaneously allowing large amounts of fuel-bound sulfur to escape into the atmosphere in oxidized form without recovery.

The technologies for doing these things are relatively straightforward, but the economics are unfavorable — as long as reduced forms of sulfur are commercially available and inexpensive.

There is no need to comment further on the technology of recovery. To alter the economics will require government intervention. An obvious possibility would be to tax sulfur dioxide emissions on a progressive scale. At the same time it would be sensible to tax sulfur mined from underground deposits (Frasch process) and sulfur recovered from pyrites, but *not* sulfur recovered from oil and gas refineries or non-ferrous smelters. Taxes of this kind would fit into a program of shifting the major source of government revenues from taxes on labor to taxes on resources and pollution.

NOTES(7)

1. However, some other refinery processes leave the sulfur in liquid wastes or in asphalt and road oils.
2. Actually, much of the proposed testing could probably be bypassed by computer simulation, using software (e.g. ASPEN+®) that has become relatively standard since 1978.
3. It is noteworthy that in 1988 Morocco produced 8.085 MMT of sulfuric acid, which was consumed entirely for phosphate rock processing. (In 1989, Moroccan production and consumption both dropped to 3.965 MMT, of which only 15 kMT were used for non-fertilizer applications.)
4. Sulfur constitutes about 1.5% of the weight of tires (see Chapter 13). Data on this specific use is not published. However, in the US 1988 tire production amounted to about 3 MMT, of which about 50 000 tonnes was presumably sulfur, equivalent to 5% of the total use of elemental sulfur (i.e. sulfur not converted to acid).

8. Phosphorus, fluorine and gypsum

8.1. SUMMARY

Phosphorus (like nitrogen and sulfur) is an essential element for all living systems. It is depleted from the soil by modern agriculture, because harvested crops are removed from the place where they are grown. For this reason, phosphorus must be replaced by synthetic fertilizer. There is, effectively, only one source of phosphorus for fertilizer, and that is from deposits of 'phosphate rock' — one of several variants of the mineral apatite, consisting of calcium phosphate with traces of iron, silica and fluorine — located in several parts of the world.

Both phosphate rock and fluorspar are depletable resources. There is only a finite quantity that can be mined, and eventually it will run out. Phosphate rock is of biological origin, and phosphorus is recycled by geological processes, but only over millions of years. However, current consumption rates will exhaust the known reserves in two or three generations, at most. Of course there are undoubtedly some additional undiscovered reserves. But even on a shorter time scale, other problems arise. One such problem is over-fertilization ('eutrophication') of rivers, lakes and estuarine zones, by the addition of phosphorus from runoff and sewage plants.

Another problem is that phosphate rock processing yields enormous quantities of wastes that are potentially recoverable, but which are virtually unrecovered at present. This results in unnecessary destruction of land, both for the disposal of phosphate process wastes and for the mining of other materials (gypsum and fluorites) that could easily be extracted from these wastes. A further problem of concern is that phosphates contain trace quantities of cadmium, a very toxic metal, that is not removed by the fertilizer manufacturing process and consequently ends up in agricultural soils where it can enter the human food chain (see Chapter 6, Zinc and cadmium). Some phosphates also contain traces of radioactive uranium and thorium.

Similarly, fluorspar mining and processing generate significant wastes that could be avoided if fluorine were recovered from phosphate wastes. Fluorine is an extremely reactive element, which makes it uniquely valuable as an intermediate for many chemical processes. Its very reactivity also makes its organic compounds (e.g. CFCs) extremely inert. Many of its inorganic compounds are toxic. It plays very little role in biological processes, except that it seems to have an affinity for phosphates, especially teeth.[1] The beneficial effects of small amounts of fluorides in drinking water as a tooth decay inhibitor are well known, if not entirely understood. In any case it would be prudent to utilize available sources of byproduct fluorine in preference to mining virgin ores.

Technologies for recovering both fluorine and gypsum products from phosphate rock are known, but not widely employed. To some extent this might be changed by public investment directly in technology development. However, the most potent instrument for encouraging the needed development would be to increase the prices of virgin fluorspar and gypsum *vis-à-vis* the secondary product recovered from phosphate rock processing. A tax on phosphate rock waste disposal would probably be helpful in this regard, but a properly constituted resource-based tax on gypsum and fluorspar as well as phosphates (shifting taxation away from labor and more towards raw materials) should accomplish the same result more equitably.

Goals of public policy: reduce emissions from phosphate mining and phosphoric acid production; maximize recovery of useful byproducts (fluorine compounds, gypsum); reduce emissions of cadmium.

8.2. SOURCES AND BYPRODUCTS OF PHOSPHATES

Phosphate rock is the only significant source of phosphorus chemicals, including fertilizers.[2] The composition of phosphate rock varies only slightly from source to source, as indicated in Table 8.1, except for trace elements like cadmium. Note that fluorine is a relatively constant proportion of most samples, averaging 3–4% by mass. Phosphoric acid (H_3PO_4) is the end product of phosphate rock processing (see Appendix A, Table A.8). The world's largest producer is the US. US production of crude phosphate rock in 1992 was 154.9 MMT (1988, 162.3 MMT). This was beneficiated by washing and flotation to yield 47 MMT (1988, 45.4 MMT) of marketable rock. This material contained 14.1 MMT (1988, 13.8 MMT) of phosphorus pentoxide (P_2O_5).[3]

The phosphate rock was reduced by the so-called 'wet process' — essentially digestion by sulfuric acid. In 1992 39.2 MMT (1988 37.4 MMT) of phosphate rock were reduced to 33.8 MMT (1988, 30.6 MMT) of fertilizer grade phosphoric acid with 11.2 MMT (1988, 10 MMT) of phosphoric acid content. A schematic diagram of the 'wet process' is shown in Figure 8.1. Phosphate rock processing in 1992 consumed about 25.4 MMT (1988, 25.5 MMT) of 100% sulfuric acid or 8.4 MMT of sulfur. This was more than 67% (1988, 68%) of total US sulfur consumption in 1992 (see Chapter 7, Sulfur).

Table 8.1: Composition of phosphate rock from US producing fields for use in superphosphate manufacture

Constituent	In Florida land pebble[a]		In Tennessee rock[b]		In western rock[c]	
	66–68 BPL percent	70–83 BPL percent	66–68 BPL percent	70–83 BPL percent	60–68 BPL percent	70–83 BPL percent
P_2O_5	30.5–32.6(21)	32.8–36.5(40)	27.9–32.4(15)	32.8–37.5(25)	27.5–32.5(30)	33.0–37.9(34)
CaO	45.0–47.4(7)	46.1–50.2(18)	41.9–45.2(4)	45.3–50.8(13)	43.7–45.2(7)	44.2–52.2(8)
MgO	0.1–0.5(6)	0.8–1.0(5)	0.1–0.3(3)	0.0–0.2(5)	0.0–1.2(7)	0.0–0.5(2)
Al_2O_3	0.7–1.1(6)	0.8–1.8(18)	1.4–3.1(4)	1.2–2.7(13)	1.0–1.9(7)	0.3–1.7(8)
Fe_2O_3	1.5–2.6(6)	0.6–1.9(18)	01.8–3.4(4)	0.9–3.4(13)	0.8–2.7(7)	0.3–1.3(8)
K_2O	0.1–0.5(6)	0.1–0.3(5)	0.4–0.6(3)	0.2–0.4(5)	0.2–0.6(7)	0.1–0.3(2)
NA_2O	0.4–0.6(6)	0.1–0.6(5)	0.1–0.3(3)	0.1–0.3(5)	0.2–0.8(7)	0.4(2)
CO_2	3.6–4.4(6)	1.5–3.3(18)	1.0–2.4(4)	1.1–3.7(4)	0.8–4.1(7)	1.2(1)
SO_3	1.1–1.3(6)	0.2–0.9(5)	0.0–1.2(3)	0.4–0.8(5)	0.1–1.4(7)	0.3–1.8(2)
SiO_2	7.3–9.8(6)	7.4–8.4(5)	8.6–16.8(3)	1.9–8.1(15)	5.6–17.3(7)	2.5–5.6(8)
F	3.3–3.9(21)	3.4–4.0(40)	2.9–3.7(15)	3.4–4.0(25)	[d]2.9–3.8(30)	3.8–4.4(30)
Volatile matter[e]	4.8–7.0(6)	3.0–6.1(5)	2.8–4.0(3)	2.7–5.9(5)	2.2–8.4(7)	1.9–7.2(8)

Notes:

a. Data from USDA 1964. Figures are on moisture-free basis (105°C); the samples contained 0.2–1.3% moisture.

b. Figures in parentheses show number of analyses included in the range.

c. Total Fe.

d. One analysis showed 6.9%; the specimen contained considerable fluorite.

e. Water, organic carbon, carbonate carbon, and nitrogen.

Source: Meister 1994.

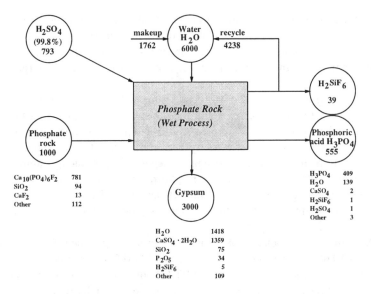

Figure 8.1: Materials balance for wet-process treatment of phosphate rock concentrate

It is worth noting that approximately 1.8 kg of water is used in the process for each kg of phosphate rock processed. The sulfur content of the acid is disposed of as calcium sulfate ('phospho-gypsum') waste. According to Figure 8.1 about 3 kg of gypsum is produced per kg of phosphate rock, while 1.8 kg of process water used, of which 1.4 kg is discharged. The remainder is water of hydration combined with calcium sulfate. The sulfur content of the sulfuric acid is disposed of as calcium sulfate (phospho-gypsum) waste. On this basis, phospho-gypsum production for 1992 would have been 72 MMT (1988, 75 MMT).

Actually, the US Bureau of Mines reports that phospho-gypsum generated by the wet process and disposed of on-site in the US only amounts to 30 MMT per year (USBuMines 1991). This seems too low, and may be an underestimate. In addition, other mineral (mainly silica) wastes from phosphate rock processing in 1988 (1992) amounted to approximately 117 MMT (108 MMT), dry. Evidently this one process also accounts for virtually all of the waste from the entire fertilizer sector in the US and most of the waste (in mass terms) from the whole US.[4]

The phospho-gypsum component of the waste is recoverable in principle and could be used for Portland cement and/or for building materials (e.g. plasterboard). That is to say, the byproduct phospho-gypsum could used for exactly the same purposes as natural gypsum. It is not recovered for use in the US because of the presence of contaminants. In fact, it is classified as a hazardous waste because of contamination by phosphoric acid and traces of radio-active elements. It is thus a major disposal problem for the phosphate fertilizer industry. In practice, natural gypsum is still mined on a large scale (see below).

At present, in the US (also Morocco, Tunisia, Jordan and Israel) sulfuric acid is generally produced on-site at the phosphate rock processing facility. The waste heat from the exothermic sulfuric acid production process can then be utilized to co-generate electricity and concentrate the phosphoric acid product from 30% to higher strengths needed for producing ammonium phosphates (MAP, DAP) or merchant phosphoric acid (54%). However, in Europe, the practice has been to import beneficiated phosphate rock to a convenient continental site such as Hamburg, Rotterdam or Antwerp, where the sulfuric acid is also produced.

A significant byproduct of phosphate rock processing in the US is fluosilicic acid. In 1988 recovery was 46 565 MT (0.047 MMT) of fluosilicic acid, with a fluorine content equivalent to 90 000 MT of fluorspar. This was largely (75%) used for municipal water fluoridation; the remainder was mostly consumed by the aluminum industry to produce aluminum fluoride, which is used in the Hall process (see Chapter 3, Aluminum). A very small amount of fluosilicic acid is consumed in Europe, apparently from Swedish sources. However there is obviously no technical reason for failing to recover fluorine from Moroccan and other phosphates imported into Europe.

8.3.   USES OF PHOSPHORUS

Fertilizers (SIC 2873) accounted for 94% of all phosphorus used; of this 31% was consumed domestically and 63% was exported. Chemicals accounted for the other 6%, of which 5% was consumed domestically. Most of the phosphate rock that was processed domestically (94%) was converted into 'wet-process' phosphoric acid (H_3PO_4). Elemental phosphorus production accounted for the remainder. Phosphorus production in the US in 1991 was 0.25 MMT (0.615 MMT P_2O_5 equivalent), of which 85% is reconverted to 'furnace-grade' phosphoric acid for chemical manufacturing. Some of this phosphoric acid goes back into fertilizer (to make triple superphosphate), but about 40% of it was used to manufacture sodium tripolyphosphate, or STPP ($Na_5P_3O_{10}$), a detergent builder.

US production of all sodium phosphates in 1991 was 0.4 MMT, with a phosphorus content of about 0.1 MMT. Detailed data for Europe are not available. Production of these chemicals has been declining since at least 1980. This appears to be due to the introduction of a competing type of

Table 8.2: Composition of detergents

Components	Standard detergents			Compact detergents			
	With phosphates (%)	Without phosphates (%)	Difference	With phosphates (%)	Compared to standard detergent	Without phosphates (%)	Compared to standard detergent
Sodium tripolyphosphate (STPP)	20–25	0	–	50	++	0	0
Zeolite	0	25	++	0	0	20 to 30	+
Polycarboxylates (PCA)	0	4	++	0	0	5	+
Organic phosphonates	0 to 0.2	0.4	+	0	–	0.2	–
Sodium silicate	6	4	–	5	–	4	0
Sodium carbonate	5	15	++	4	–	15 to 20	++
Surface active agent	12	15	+	14	+	15	0
Sodium perborate	14*	18	+	10**	*	13	*
Activator	0 to 2	2.5	++	3	++	5	++
Sodium sulfate	21 to 24	9	–	4	–	5	–
Enzymes	0.3	0.5	+	0.8	++	0.8	+
'Antiredeposition' agents	0.2	0.2	0	0.3	+	0.3	+
Perfume	0.2	0.2	0	0.2	0	0.2	0
Water	10	5	–	8	–	5	0
Total	100	100		100		100	0

Notes:

* Tetrahydrate Perborate is used in standard detergents.

** Monohydrate Perborate is used in compact powders. Its power is much higher than Tetrahydrate Perborate.

Source: Information Chimie n°341, Sept. 1992.

121

detergent builder, namely zeolites together with polycarboxylic acid. These have virtually taken over the market in Germany, Italy, Switzerland and the Netherlands, because of concerns about the eutrophication of lakes, rivers and streams. Phosphate detergents have also lost some market share in the UK from 67% in 1991 to 54% in 1993. Declining use of phosphates also occurred in France, Belgium, Sweden and Denmark.

However the so-called 'compact detergents', introduced in 1988, may have actually reversed the trend. Whereas traditional detergents contained 20–25% STPP, the compact detergents increase this to 50% (*Info Chimie*, September 1992) (see Table 8.2). The effect is that some consumers use less detergent, but with a higher phosphorus content. On the other hand, some European countries (e.g. Switzerland) do not permit phosphates to be used in detergents because of concerns about eutrophication of lakes.

Some phosphoric acid is used as a flavoring agent in the food and soft drink industry. A minor but growing use of phosphorus is in the manufacture of lubricating oil additives such as zinc dithiophosphate, which starts from phosphorus pentasulfide (made by direct reaction of phosphorus metal and elemental sulfur). This use accounted for 0.015 MMT of phosphorus metal in 1974; it is probably greater today.

The starting point for organic phosphate synthesis is phosphorus trichloride (PCl_3). Production figures are not published, but on the basis of absorbing 1% of chlorine output (see Chapter 10, Chlorine), we can conclude that about 0.03 MMT of phosphorus metal would have been required. The trichloride is later converted to phosphorus oxychloride ($POCl_3$) by direct reaction with chlorine and phosphorus pentoxide P_2O_5. The oxychloride, in turn, is the basis of organic phosphate esters that now have many uses. The most important of them is the plasticizer tricresyl phosphate (TCPP). Phosphate esters are also used as flame retardants and fire-resistant hydraulic fluids. Such phosphate esters totalled 0.043 MMT (P_2O_5) in 1990 (USITC 1991); detailed data for each chemical are not published, but the phosphorus content is rather small (8.5% in the case of TCPP). TCPP is also used as a gasoline additive.

All of the uses mentioned above are inherently dissipative. No more than 0.2 MMT of elemental phosphorus is embodied in chemicals used to manufacture other chemical products (mainly detergents). Uses of phosphorus are summarized in the pie-chart, Figure 8.2. In most cases the dissipation does not occur within the chemical industry itself (SIC 28), however.

The only practical way to cut down on phosphate demand would be to discover ways of remobilizing biologically unavailable phosphates in the soil. This is a worthwhile object of agricultural research, but at present it appears to be rather a distant prospect at best. Thus, the most promising approach to minimizing environmental harm associated with the use of

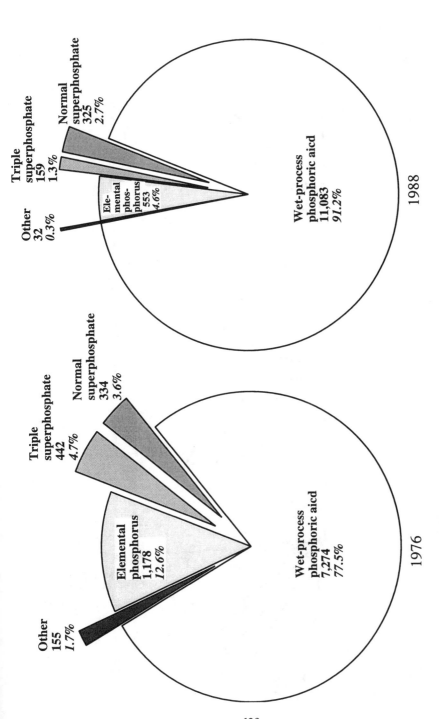

Source: USBuMines 1977, 1989.

Figure 8.2: *US phosphorus production by end-use, 1976 and 1988 (kMT)*

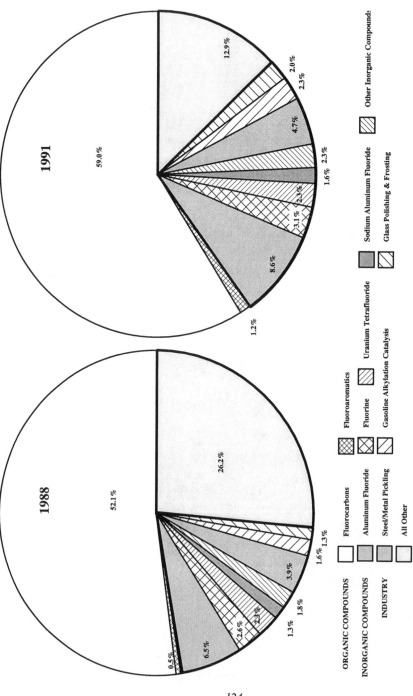

Source: EcoPlan 1992.

Figure 8.3: Western European consumption of hydrofluoric acid by end-use

phosphates in industry is to focus on opportunities to utilize wastes and byproducts from mining and production.

Fluoride emission factors for phosphate rock processing have been estimated by the US Environmental Protection Agency (USEPA) (Martin 1974). Their relevance to other countries (e.g. Morocco) can be inferred from the fact that the same factors were adapted by the World Health Organization for its guidebook for *Rapid Assessment of Sources of Air, Water and Land Pollution* (WHO 1982). The averages for wet-process phosphoric acid plants with holding ponds for waste gypsum, with supernatant water recycling, are assumed to be 11.2 kg/tonne of anhydrous P_2O_5. For wet-process plants with no ponds, dissolved fluoride emissions in waste water are assumed to be 22.2 kg/tonne. Based on the composition of phosphate rock (Table 8.1), however, available fluorine should be closer to 100 kg/tonne of P_2O_5.

Based on Western European production (1991) of 2.34 MMT of phosphoric acid, mostly from imported phosphate rock, it can be inferred that 234 kMT (F) was lost in processing, of which at least 52 kMT of dissolved metallic fluorides were generated, probably containing less than 20 kMT of F. Of this, about half may be stored in holding ponds and the rest was probably dumped into rivers. Thus, 234 kMT (F) may have been potentially recoverable, of which only about 10 kMT (F) was actually recovered (as fluosilicic acid) and perhaps 20 kMT (F) was emitted as dissolved fluorides. An additional 200+ kMT was apparently discarded in solid form, mostly as a contaminant of phospho-gypsum.

We do not know the fluorspar equivalent of this potential resource, but it seems possible that fluosilicic acid recovery could be considerably increased, replacing a significant fraction — perhaps all — of the imported fluorspar. See Appendix A, Table A.9. on fluorspar mining and hydrofluoric acid production. Hydrofluoric acid uses in Europe are shown in Figure 8.3.

8.4. SOURCES AND USES OF FLUORINE

Fluorine is commercially extracted from a single mineral fluorspar, consisting of calcium fluoride, and various contaminants, notably silica. It is mined in a number of countries, especially China (by far the largest producer), Mongolia, Mexico, the former USSR and South Africa. Identified world resources of the mineral (as of 1991) were 365 MMT of contained fluorspar — of which 239 MMT were classified as 'reserves' and the remainder currently sub-economic — as compared to 325 MMT in phosphate rock deposits. (Only 32 MMT of the latter are in domestic US phosphates.)

Most mined fluorspar must be beneficiated, usually by gravity separation or froth flotation. The beneficiation process generates significant wastes. There are three commercial grades, metallurgical grade (> 60% 'effective' CaF_2), ceramic grade (85–96% CaF_2) and acid grade (> 97% CaF_2). Metallurgical grade fluorspar is used as a flux in iron- and steelmaking, and in foundries. It reduces the melting point of slag, making it more liquid and also more reactive, thus making it more soluble for lime and other fluxes which can react with undesirable impurities (such as sulfur) in the metal. For this purpose silica is an undesirable contaminant, whence effective CaF_2 is calculated as actual CaF_2 minus 2..5 times actual silica content. Ceramic grade fluorspar is also used as a flux, mainly in the glass industry (it is also an 'opacifier' for certain types of glass); small amounts are used in other industries.

Acid grade fluorspar is used to manufacture hydrofluoric acid (HF), from which most fluorine chemicals are derived. The process involves direct reaction with sulfuric acid, yielding calcium sulfate (gypsum) as a waste product. Approximately 3.6 tonnes of $CaSO_4$ is generated per tonne of anhydrous HF product.

By far the largest use of HF is in the manufacture of chloro-fluorocarbons (CFCs). The three major CFCs (CFC 11, CFC 12 and CFC 113) are in the process of being phased out, because of their ozone-depletion potential. Some of the possible substitutes are so-called HFCs, which are more completely fluorinated molecules that contain no chlorine. Thus, the phaseout of CFCs does not necessarily imply a sharp reduction in demand for HF. In fact, the reverse is actually a (slight) possibility.

The technology for producing HF from impure fluosilicic acid (H_2SiF_6) — the most likely fluorine-containing byproduct of phosphate rock processing — is apparently not yet fully developed. One process that has been described in detail is a two-stage reaction. The first stage is to react the acid with ammonia, yielding ammonium fluoride and silica (SiO_2), which precipitates out of solution. In the second stage ammonium fluoride reacts with calcium hydroxide (from lime and water), regenerating the ammonia and yielding solid CaF_2. The process is, of course, somewhat more complex than this simple description, because of the various filtration and drying stages that are needed in practice.

Another process that has recently been developed by the Phosphate Engineering and Construction Co., of Lakeland Fla., is to react fluosilicic acid with phosphate rock itself. This yields marketable phosphoric acid and calcium silicon hexafluoride ($CaSiF_6$) (USBuMines 1989). The latter is hydrolized to produce silica and calcium fluoride, which is identical to the natural mineral fluorspar. These byproducts are separated by gravity (settling) and/or centrifuging. The calcium fluoride (i.e. fluorspar) is then converted to hydrofluoric acid (HF) in the usual way.

The virtue of the above schemes is that they produce the equivalent of commercial acid-grade fluorspar, which has a ready market. A short cut that avoids the production of solid CaF_2 would, however, make sense. There are two possibilities. One is to develop fluorination processes that utilize ammonium fluoride as a starting point. This seems rather a distant prospect, at best. The other is to produce HF directly from ammonium fluoride. This could be done, in principle, by reacting it with sulfuric acid, yielding ammonium sulfate — a valuable fertilizer — and HF.

The aluminum industry has developed a process to make aluminum fluoride (for the Hall–Heroult electrolytic smelting process) directly from fluosilicic acid, by reacting it with aluminum hydroxide. We do not have any further details of this process, however.

Another potentially interesting possibility, explored by SRI International, is to neutralize fluosilicic acid with caustic soda, yielding insoluble sodium fluorosilicate ($NaHSiF_6$). This, in turn, can be reacted directly with metallic sodium, namely,

$$2NaHSiF_6 \rightarrow 2SiF_4 + H_2$$
$$SiF_4 + 4Na \rightarrow Si + 4NaF$$

It is claimed that this process can produce ultra-pure silicon metal (suitable for electronic uses) at a lower cost than the current Siemens process (see Chapter 11, Silicon).

Although Figure 8.1, describing phosphate processing in the US, indicates fluosilicic acid recovery, this is apparently not much practiced outside the US. Enhanced fluorine recovery would have two immediate and direct advantages. First, it would reduce both the need for mining and processing fluorspar, and the waste emissions from those processes. Second, recovery of fluosilicic acid (or silicon tetrafluoride) from phosphate rock processing would automatically reduce harmful fluorine emissions from phosphate rock processing facilities. We have no data on health problems arising from this activity in Europe. However anecdotal evidence suggests that the problem may be quite severe in some less-developed countries.

A third possible benefit suggests itself: more sophisticated processing to increase the recovery of fluorine chemicals from phosphate rock might also increase the technical and economic feasibility of removing the undesirable cadmium contamination from phosphate fertilizers. This could also make the byproduct phospho-gypsum more usable.

8.5. GYPSUM SOURCES AND USES

As noted previously, about 100 MMT of the mineral gypsum ($CaSO_4 \cdot 2H_2O$) was mined globally in 1989. Production has been increasing at a steady pace. It is mined in over 80 countries. Reserves are large. Production in most countries is consumed domestically, although the US is also a large importer (from Canada and Mexico). Some countries have no known gypsum resources (e.g. Scandinavia). (See Appendix A, Table A.5 on gypsum mining.)

The US is the largest producer of natural gypsum (16 MMT/yr). Other large producers include Canada, China and Iran. Production in Western Europe as a whole in 1989 was 19.426 MMT while Eastern Europe accounted for another 4.5 MMT. In the US about 8% of mined gypsum was used without calcination in agriculture (as a soil conditioner for excessively alkaline soils). The remainder is calcined, by the low-temperature process (at 159 degrees Celsius):

$$CaSO_4 \cdot 2H_2O \rightarrow CaSO_4 \cdot 1/2(H_2O) + 3/2(H_2O)$$

Of this, one-seventh (13% of the total) was used as a cement additive and the rest (79% of the total) was used to make prefabricated wallboard products. Use of calcined gypsum as 'plaster-of-Paris', for manual application, is declining rapidly.

Europe can be assumed to have a roughly similar use pattern, except that plaster for manual application continues to have a significant market, especially in housing renovation. Yet, it should be recalled that plaster-of-Paris once enjoyed a much wider range of uses. Before the discovery of Portland cement (c. 1815) it was used as mortar for stone buildings, as the basis for a form of concrete, and as a fireproofing agent.[5]

The French phosphate producer APC has a plant at Ottmarsheim, in Alsace on the Rhine river. At few years ago at this plant a new process was tried out, to purify the phospho-gypsum byproduct by double crystallization. The product was calcined and used to make plasterboard by PREGYPAN (Pichat 1982). Subsequently APC also claimed to have developed a satisfactory single-crystallization purification process (ibid.). However, apparently these processes were never exploited commercially, for reasons we do not know.

APC also has a phosphoric acid plant on the Seine river, near Rouen, in France. In the 1970s wastes were towed by barge to the mouth of the Seine and dumped, causing pollution and distress to the local fishermen and tourists at Deauville. To avoid this necessity, APC developed a new product called 'foamed' or 'cellular' gypsum. It is very light (specific gravity 0.5), yet has good compression strength (10–15 bars) and good thermal insulation (0.12 watts per square meter per degree Celsius). It is also fire resistant, a good acoustic absorber, and an effective humidity regulator (since it takes up water from the air at high levels of external humidity, and releases it at low external humidity levels (ibid.). It can be poured into molds on a building site, or cast into blocks.[6] The material hardens in 15 minutes. Houses have been built from this material in Douvrin and Rennes, France, and in Senegal (ibid.). However, for various reasons the process has not been commercially exploited.

Other uses of phospho-gypsum have been reported (e.g. at the International Symposium on Phospho-gypsum, Orlando Florida, November 1980). Examples that do not require calcination include the following (ibid.):

- Cement production. Gypsum regulates the setting of Portland cement. About 5% of the mass of clinker typically consists of gypsum.
- Phospho-gypsum (PG) can be mixed with slag or fly ash (see Chapter 14, Coal ash) to make a quick-setting binder, as a partial substitute for lime. The combination 90% fly ash, 5% lime and 5% PG has been successfully used for roadbuilding in several locations.
- Paper filler (e.g. as a substitute for kaolin). APC has a proprietary process for this use.
- Soil conditioner for tight clay soils. The Ca++ neutralizes the charges on the clay particles and encourages flocculation into a more granular form.
- Reclamation of salt buildup in alkaline-clay soils. PG can displace the sodium ions that bind to clay particles, thus allowing them to be removed by percolation with ground water.
- Drainage clearing. Pipes draining marshy lands can be clogged by ferric clay complexes. These can be flocculated by PG, reopening clogged drains.

To substitute wet phospho-gypsum for natural gypsum would primarily require dehydration. (The presence of trace quantities of uranium or thorium would also be a problem in some locations.) The major requirement, however, is heat. Much of the needed heat could be waste heat (or low-grade fuels) from other processes, such as steel mills or petroleum refineries. The key to success is almost certainly to integrate the phosphate rock processing with other heat-generating activities.

Thus, it would make particular sense to integrate phosphate rock processing in Europe with petroleum or gas refining and/or non-ferrous metal refining. This would seem to be quite feasible, given that all of these processes tend to be located near major seaports or riverports. This would make it possible to convert the sulfur recovered from fuel processing directly to sulfuric acid at the same location where it will be used subsequently. In so far as possible, in view of the above uses for phospho-gypsum, it would make sense for a phosphate producer to locate near an agricultural area characterized by clay soils. Finally, it would also make sense to co-locate with a building materials producer, a paper manufacturer, and possibly a fluorine chemicals user.

At least one plant in Europe manufactures plaster wallboard from another kind of byproduct gypsum, namely flue-gas desulfurization (FGD) wastes from a coal-burning power plant. This plant is GYPROC in Kalundborg, Denmark (see Section 15.4, the Kalundborg example). Flue-gas desulfurization is also a very large potential source of synthetic gypsum, although there are probably better ways to utilize the available sulfur in coal.

NOTES(8)

1. There seems to be evidence that some deposits of the mineral apatite were formed by metamorphic geological processes on accumulations of sharks' teeth! This seems bizarre, but it might explain why apatite usually contains fluorine.
2. Some phosphorus is recoverable from high phosphate iron ores. These ores were not usable for steelmaking until the so-called Thomas process was invented in the later 19th century.
3. Phosphorus pentoxide dissolved in water is phosphoric acid, the active ingredient in most phosphate fertilizers (e.g. 'superphosphates'). It is not used, generally, in pure form.
4. It is important to emphasize this fact; to associate an undifferentiated 'waste coefficient' with the 'fertilizer sector' as a whole, in a country without a phosphate rock processing industry, would be grossly misleading. By the same token, it must be recognized that most countries (such as Morocco and Algeria) with significant phosphate rock processing sectors do not bother to control fluoride emissions, still less recover the fluorine for beneficial use. In most of the world this industry is extremely hazardous to workers and nearby residents.
5. Many 17th-century buildings in Paris, especially the Marais district, were constructed — foundations included — from plaster-based concrete and mortar. These buildings have survived to the present day, with continuous occupancy and little or no need for renovation. In fact, these old buildings appear to be as durable, or more durable, than current construction.
6. The on-site pouring technology has been developed by the French construction firm, BOUYGES; the casting technique was developed by the construction firm GTM.

9. Nitrogen-based chemicals

9.1. SUMMARY

Inorganic nitrogen (N_2) is a colorless, odorless, tasteless gas that constitutes almost 80% of the atmosphere. In this form it is chemically rather inert and inaccessible to living organisms, as well as to other key chemicals in living cells. However, nitrogen is essential to organic life. Amino acids are nitrogenous compounds that are the basic building blocks of all proteins. Similarly, the basic building blocks of DNA (thymine, cytosine, adenine and guanine) all consist of single or double rings of carbon and nitrogen atoms, with various side chains. Nitric oxide (NO) is a neuro-transmitter.

Nitrogen occurs in all valence states from -3 to $+5$. The most reduced (-3) form of nitrogen, ammonia (NH_3), is a strong alkali. It is also quite toxic to animals at high concentrations. However, all known bio-fixation pathways convert di-nitrogen first to ammonia. Similarly, all pathways to the synthesis of amino acids begin from ammonia and evolve glutamic acid and aspartic acid as the primary building blocks for amino acids and proteins.

On the other hand, the most oxidized stable form of nitrogen is the compound N_2O_5, which reacts with the water molecule to form nitric acid HNO_3. Nitric acid deposition is one of the two chief causes of soil acidification and problems like forest die-back (*Waldsterben*). Nitric acid reacts with alkaline salts to form nitrates. Either ammonium salts or nitrates (most are soluble) can be taken up by plants. Thus, nitric acid deposition is also a kind of fertilization (eutrophication) of the environment.

Unfortunately, both types of bio-available nitrogen compounds (i.e. ammonium salts or nitrates) are rather easily lost from soils, either by runoff and erosion, or by bacterial conversion to unavailable forms such as molecular nitrogen. The latter process, called denitrification, probably created the nitrogen atmosphere in the first place. Thus the balance between denitrification and nitrogen fixation is one way of characterizing the 'nitrogen cycle'.

Thus, the limiting factor for life, in most environments — both terrestrial and marine — is bio-available nitrogen. Most biomes are N-limited, despite the evolutionary 'invention' of nitrogen-fixing bacteria and their symbiotic relationships with certain plants known as legumes. However, few legumes produce food directly consumable by humans (soya beans being the main exception). This is why nitrogen fertilizers are effective. It is also why N-fertilizers are essential to support agricultural production at the levels needed to support the current human population, and why still further increases will be needed to support expected population increases.

The natural tendency towards thermodynamic equilibrium, in an oxidizing environment, is for reduced nitrogen in the -3 valence state (NH_3) to be oxidized gradually to the $+5$ valence state (nitrate ion, NO_{3-}). In short, without living organisms to cycle the nitrogen between the reduced state (ammonia) and the neutral unoxidized molecular (di-nitrogen) state, all the oxygen in the atmosphere would eventually combine with the nitrogen to form nitric acid. The eventual result would be an acid ocean, leaving an atmosphere with no free oxygen left in it. No life on such an earth would be possible.

Life on the earth actually depends on the continuing stability of the nitrogen cycle. This cycle evolved over billions of years to a (nearly) balanced and quasi-stable state. However, as will be seen, the N-cycle is now being rapidly unbalanced — and possibly destabilized — as a result of large-scale industrial fixation of nitrogen, both as NH_3 and as NO_X. The use of nitrogenous fertilizers to enhance the fertility of agricultural soils is probably unavoidable, in view of growing populations and rising standards of living. This being so, it is of utmost importance to minimize unnecessary losses of nitrogen in biologically available form, including wasteful uses of fertilizer itself, losses in chemical processing, dissipative uses of N-based chemicals (such as pesticides, explosives, etc.) and inadvertent NO_X production. A few of these emissions, such as cyanides and nitrosamines, are extremely hazardous as such. But it is the cumulative total of N-emissions that may constitute a major threat to the environment.

To minimize unnecessary nitrogen emissions will be a difficult task, since they are so various. A detailed analysis of policy approaches to bring this about is beyond our scope. However, a few comments are relevant. Certainly, a very high priority should go to the development of genetically engineered crop plants capable of N-fixation. Second priority should go to improved means of delivery of fertilizer nutrients directly to crop plants. Strictly enforced worldwide controls over NO_X emissions from electric power plants and internal combustion engines is another necessary starting point. Since virtually all nitrogen-based chemicals are derived from ammonia, a resource tax (or emissions fee) on ammonia production would tend to reduce wasteful consumption. A targeted tax on other nitrogen-based chemicals, such as explosives, materials of all kinds (virtually all of which are dependent on nitrogen) would have a number of beneficial effects.

Goals of public policy: highest priority to develop plant species capable of N-fixation; strict minimization of NH_3, N_2O and NO_X emissions from all sources.

9.2. SOURCES OF FIXED NITROGEN

The first commercial process for direct nitrogen fixation was the so-called Birkeland–Eyde process, developed in Norway and first commercialized in 1904. This process emulated the natural process by which nitrogen is oxidized in the atmosphere in the presence of an electric arc (i.e. lightning). A competing process, developed around 1905, was the cyanamid process, yielding calcium cyanamide ($CaCN_2$) from limestone, coke and atmospheric nitrogen. The calcium cyanamide is dissolved in water to form urea and ammonia.

It is interesting to note that in 1920 there were five different anthropogenic sources of biologically available ('fixed') nitrogen, producing a world total of just over 1.55 MMT of N-content.[1] Of this, Chilean saltpeter was the largest, accounting for 30%. The second largest (26.6% in 1920), was ammonium sulfate from byproduct coking of coal. This was a process developed in Germany in the 1880s by Koppers, which is still in use, although nowadays the main byproduct is coke oven gas. In fact, about 0.86 kg of NH_3 can be extracted from a ton of bituminous coking coal (Russell and Vaughan 1976, Table 3.2), along with 178 kg of high-BTU gas (8800 cubic feet). Thus, production of 1 mcf of gas also yielded up to 98 kg of NH_3. Later ammonia was produced in larger quantities from the coking of coal for the steel industry, but still as a byproduct. Its output could not be expanded above the limited amounts available from coal usage.

By 1920 the third-largest source of synthetic fixed nitrogen (20.9%) was calcium cyanamid. This process was still commercially significant in the 1950s, but it was then obsolescent. The last cyanamid plant in the Western world closed in June, 1971. The fourth largest was the Haber–Bosch process (below). Fifth and last, by 1920 the original Birkeland–Eyde process was already obsolete, because of its dependence on very cheap electricity, and then accounted for only 1.5% of synthetic nitrogen.[2]

The so-called Haber–Bosch process, was first developed by the German firm BASF and commercialized in 1913. The process involves direct combination of nitrogen and hydrogen at high pressure, in the presence of a catalyst of iron oxide plus small quantities of cerium and chromium at high pressure and temperature. There have been many improvements to the basic process utilizing various catalysts and increasingly high temperatures and pressures.

Before 1950 the major source of hydrogen for the synthesis of ammonia was the reaction of coal or coke and steam via the water-gas process. A small number of plants used water electrolysis or coke oven byproduct hydrogen. Since 1950 the major source of hydrogen has been natural gas obtained by steam reforming of natural gas (or, less commonly, oil, coal or lignite). The partial oxidation process is also used to produce hydrogen from natural gas and other liquid hydrocarbons. As of 1975, 75 to 80% of the world supplies of hydrogen for the manufacture of ammonia came from steam-reforming of hydrocarbons, of which 65% was from natural gas. The importance of natural gas has continued to grow.

The original source of synthetic nitrogen chemicals has always been air, which is already 70% pure. It is fairly easy to purify the nitrogen further by letting the oxygen react with some other substance, leaving an oxide (H_2O is the simplest) that is easy to remove by condensation or solvent extraction. Originally, the nitrogen was obtained either from a liquid-air separation plant or by burning a small amount of hydrogen in the synthesis gas. Modern ammonia plants eliminated the above process steps by the use of secondary reforming, a process in which methane is burned in air in the amount required to produce a 3:1 mole ratio of hydrogen to nitrogen synthesis gas.

The Haber–Bosch process as used in most of the world today is based on the passage of a mixture of air and natural gas over a catalyst at very high pressure. Under the required conditions the methane in the gas is cracked and the carbon reacts with oxygen to form CO_2 while the hydrogen and nitrogen combine in the presence of a catalyst to form ammonia (NH_3) (see Figure 9.1). The subsequent processes to obtain key derivatives are shown in Figure 9.2. There are several variations of the basic process depending on (1) the separation of air to produce nitrogen or (2) the removal of the oxygen by combustion to leave a nitrogen CO_2 material that can then be separated. While the wartime plants were mainly in the 200–300 tonne/day range, in the 1960s the introduction of efficient single-stage centrifugal compressors made possible a new industry standard of 1 kMT per day. The new technology increased capacity and cut costs sharply and further expanded the market.

There are several known processes for nitrogen fixation which are not currently exploited commercially. These include ionization and chemo-nuclear reactions to obtain oxides of nitrogen, fixation of nitrogen as metal nitrides or di-nitrogen complexes of transition metals, and reducing nitrogen bound up in certain transition metal complexes to ammonia. In addition, biological fixation by nitrogen-fixing microbes through genetic engineering is being developed for agricultural applications.

Nearly all forms of fixed nitrogen are currently derived from synthetic ammonia. Fixed nitrogen (in the form of ammonia and its derivatives) is an interesting case, since the nitrogen is obtained from the atmosphere, combined with hydrogen from natural gas. Most fixed nitrogen is consumed in fertilizer. Ammonia production and consumption in Europe is shown in Appendix A, Table A.10. In 1991, world production of synthetic ammonia was 94 MMT (N-content). A more detailed breakdown of Western European fertilizer production and consumption is given in Appendix A, Table A.11.

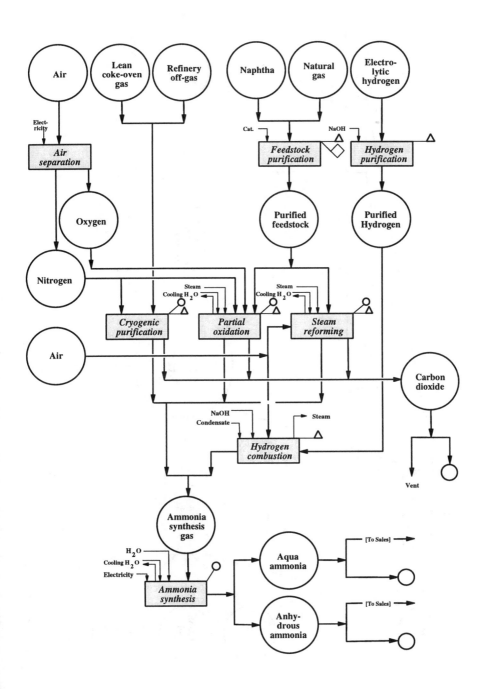

Source: Muelberg *et al.* 1977, p. 30.

Figure 9.1: *Materials–process relationships for ammonia synthesis*

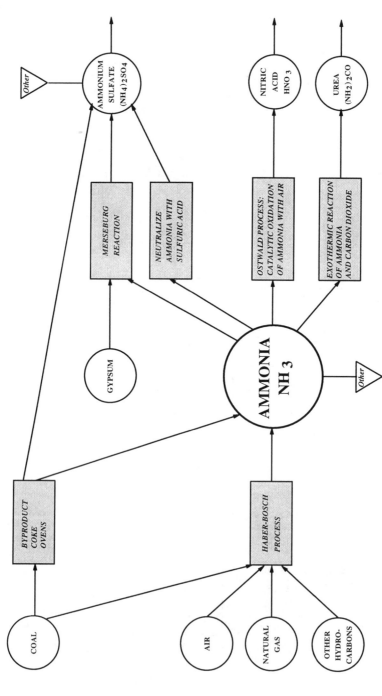

Figure 9.2: Production of ammonia and some key derivatives

9.3. USES OF FIXED NITROGEN

Apart from fertilizers, nitro-chemicals are the main basis of most explosives, both industrial and military. Nitrogen-based chemicals are also building blocks for an important class of synthetic fibers, such as nylon. Because a very large number of chemical pathways is involved, and because of secrecy — both industrial and governmental — it is impossible to account fully for nitrogen chemical usage.

9.4. MATERIALS BALANCE FOR N-BASED CHEMICALS (US)

Apparent US consumption of ammonia in 1988 was 14.746 MMT (N-content), taking into account imports, exports and stock changes (USBuMines 1989, p. 741). Of this amount, known domestic fertilizer use accounted for 9.536 MMT (N). However, a more detailed accounting by chemical suggests that 10.241 MMT (N) was used for domestic fertilizer purposes, or about 70% of apparent consumption. To confuse matters, 1.150 MMT (N) in the form of mono- and di-ammonium phosphates was produced and exported by the US for fertilizer use outside the US. This presumably counts as part of 'domestic consumption' for statistical purposes, and raises the fertilizer fraction to 77%. Fertilizers are spread on the land and are not normally counted as pollution, although nitrogenous fertilizers are known to contribute to nitrate pollution in ground waters.

Ammonia, as such, enjoys a significant share of the US fertilizer market; 3.422 MMT (N) was used in anhydrous form and 86 kMT (N) in aqueous solutions in 1988. In addition, ammonia is used as a household cleaning agent, as an industrial refrigerant, in metallurgy, in pulp production, and in NO_x reduction equipment. These uses constitute a significant part of the 'unaccounted for' fraction.

The major intermediate between ammonia and 'downstream' chemicals is nitric acid. Production of nitric acid in Europe is shown in Appendix A, Table A.12. End-uses are indicated in the pie chart, Figure 9.3.

Nitric acid production in 1988 in the US was 1.611 MMT (N) (CEN 1992). About 5% of the ammonia input is lost in production, so 1.690 MMT (N) of ammonia was used as an input. The nitric acid, in turn is used mostly to produce ammonium nitrate; 1.191 MMT (N) was used for this purpose in 1988, along with an equal amount of ammonia. Most of the ammonium nitrate was used as fertilizer (1.795 MMT (N)), while the remainder — 587 kMT (N) — was almost exclusively used as an industrial explosive in the mining sector (USBuMines 1989, p. 745).

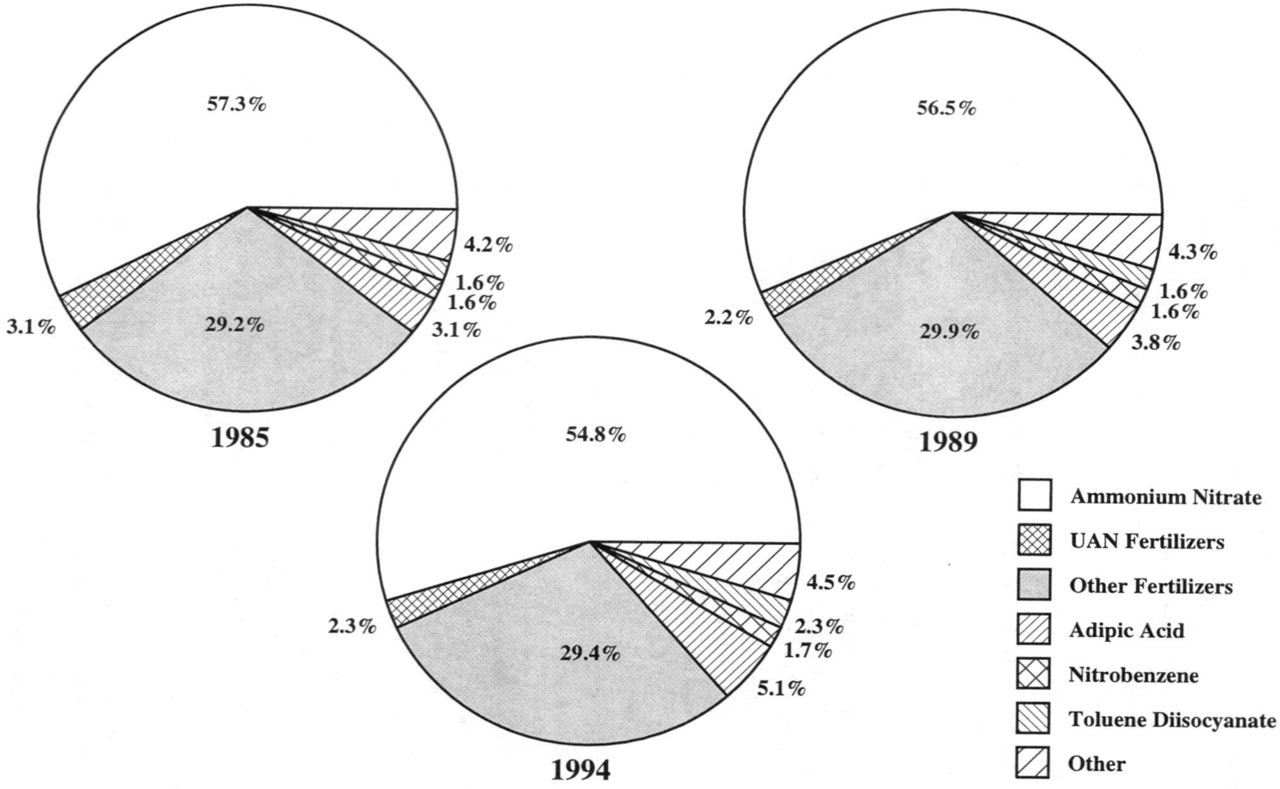

Legend:
- Ammonium Nitrate
- UAN Fertilizers
- Other Fertilizers
- Adipic Acid
- Nitrobenzene
- Toluene Diisocyanate
- Other

1985
- 57.3%
- 29.2%
- 3.1%
- 4.2%
- 1.6%
- 1.6%
- 3.1%
- 2.3%

1989
- 56.5%
- 29.9%
- 2.2%
- 4.3%
- 1.6%
- 1.6%
- 3.8%

1994
- 54.8%
- 29.4%
- 2.3%
- 4.5%
- 2.3%
- 1.7%
- 5.1%

Source: EcoPlan.

Figure 9.3: Western European consumption of nitric acid

Other industrial uses of nitric acid in the US amounted to 420 kMT (N) according to the Bureau of Mines (ibid.). Such uses include the manufacture of military explosives (other than ammonium nitrate), nitrobenzene, nitrocellulose, other 'nitro' compounds (such as dinitrotoluene used in the manufacture of isocyanates) and steel pickling. Nitrobenzene, used entirely in the manufacture of aniline, for the dye industry, alone accounts for 5.2% of US benzene consumption; based on 1988 benzene use data this implies 68 kMT (N) (IEI 1991), but a probable nitric acid requirement of 75 kMT (N). We also estimate that 0.080 MMT (N) was consumed in the production of dinitrotoluene for the manufacture of toluene di-isocyanate (below), of which 60 kMT (N) remained in the product. Nitric acid is used as an oxidant in the production of adipic acid, probably accounting for 60 kMT (N) (below). We somewhat arbitrarily assign 100 kMT (N) of nitric acid to military use, leaving 105 kMT (N) for all other uses, including steel pickling and metal treatment.

Nitric acid is used as an oxidant in some chemical reactions, notably adipic acid (a nylon 6,6 precursor). To manufacture 1 kg of adipic acid from either cyclohexane or phenol (the main routes in the US) requires 0.37 kg of nitric acid (HNO_3). Adipic acid production for 1989 was reported as 744 kMT (CEN 1990, cited by Thiemens and Trogler 1991). This implies total HNO_3 consumption (as N) of 60 kMT. More than half of the nitrogen seems to be converted into nitrous oxide (N_2O) as a waste (Thiemens and Trogler 1991). Hence adipic acid production may contribute significantly to the atmospheric buildup of nitrous oxide, a greenhouse gas with a long atmospheric residence-time.

Total US nylon resin production in 1988 was 1.466 MMT (CEN 1992); the total for nylon 6 and nylon 6,6 together was 1.090 MMT, the remainder (nylon tape) consisting mostly of other polyamides (see Figure 9.4). Subtracting 566 kMT for nylon 6 leaves 534 kMT as the output of nylon 6,6 and 476 kMT for other polyamide resins. Nylon 6,6 is a co-polymer of adipic acid and hexamethylene diamine (HMDA), with a kg of product requiring 0.65 kg of adipic acid plus 0.521 kg of HMDA (Gaines and Shen 1980). Thus, 534 kMT of nylon 6,6 would require only 331 kMT of adipic acid (direct) and 281 kMT of HMDA. This leaves 413 kMT (or 55%) to be accounted for.

We have no information on how much (if any) adipic acid may be used for other purposes. In 1974 'other uses', as plasticizers and polyols for polyurethanes, accounted for only 10% of output (Lowenheim and Moran 1975, p. 52). One possible process, to manufacture HMDA via ammonylation, uses about 1.4 kg of adipic acid plus 0.33 kg of NH_3. If the 281 kMT of HMDA needed for nylon 6,6 were entirely derived from adipic acid by this route, most of the latter would be accounted for. This is unlikely, since other processes to make HMDA are certainly in use. However, there are also some

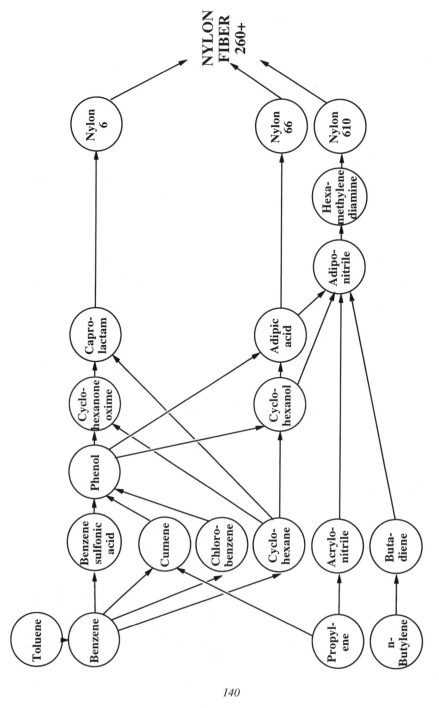

Figure 9.4: Steps in the production of nylon

other uses of HMDA (e.g. to produce hexamethylene di-isocyanate) as well as some other uses of adipic acid.

Hydrogen cyanide (HCN) is another major nitrogen chemical intermediate. US production in 1988 was 282 kMT (N), of which 90% was used captively by producers (IEI 1991). Of this, 110 kMT (N) was apparently used in the manufacture of adiponitrile, an intermediate in the production of hexamethylene diamine used, in turn, to manufacture nylon 6,6. Unfortunately, HMDA cannot account for all of the adiponitrile (see above). We cannot reconcile this discrepancy.

According to one source, 87 kMT (N) of HCN was consumed in 1988 in the production of methyl methacrylate, via the acetone cyanohydrin process (ibid.). Another source reported 1990 cyanohydrin production in the US as 610 kMT or 100 kMT (N). The two figures are reasonably consistent, bearing in mind that they do not refer to the same year. Methyl methacrylate is the most important acrylic monomer, used to manufacture 'plexiglass', 'Lucite' and acrylic latex paints. As it happens, none of the nitrogen is embodied in the monomer or the polymer; it is almost entirely converted to ammonium sulfate, used as a fertilizer. All other uses of HCN (28% of production, or 85 kMT (N)), are converted into sodium cyanide, 18% or 51 kMT (N), or miscellaneous chemicals. Of the sodium cyanide, 62% or 0.031 MMT (N), was used in the mining industry, mostly for the extraction of gold from ores. The rest of the sodium cyanide was used for electroplating or metal treatment.

It is noteworthy that HCN is a co-product of vinyl cyanide, better known as acrylonitrile (ACN), one of the major nitrogen chemicals, accounting for 308 kMT (N), in 1988 (USBuMines 1989, p. 745). There is only one process for ACN, the ammoxidation of propylene, which consumes 0.46 kg of ammonia and generates about 0.11 kg of HCN per kg of ACN. This process therefore consumed roughly 443 kMT of ammonia and produced 65 kMT (N) HCN as a byproduct. The process also generated other byproducts and wastes containing 0.070 MMT (N), partly consisting of acetonitrile, which is potentially recoverable but not very valuable. Working back, it appears that the N-content of ammonia consumed directly for HCN production would have been $282 - 65 = 217$ kMT (N).

ACN is an alternate source of adiponitrile; it is also used directly to make ABS (ACN–butadiene–styrene) rubber, SAN (styrene–ACN), nitrile rubber and acrylic fibers. If no ACN was converted into adiponitrile in 1988, a maximum of 308 kMT (N) was embodied in polymers, disregarding process losses.

Urea production in 1988 was about 7.0 MMT (46% N-content), mostly for fertilizer — 3.311 (N) — and animal feed supplements (SIC 28732). About 46 kMT (212 kMT N-content) was used for industrial purposes (USBuMines 1989, p. 745). These were for amino-resins, urea-formaldehyde (UF) and melamine. Total production of melamine resins in 1988 was 93 kMT (CEN 1992), or 62 kMT (N). Melamine is made by a complicated process (Stamicarbon) involving approximately 1.4 kg N-input (as urea) per kg melamine (Lowenheim and Moran 1975). Incidentally, melamine production also consumes about 0.2 kg anhydrous ammonia per kg of melamine, or about 16 kMT (N). Thus, urea input to melamine must have been 130 kMT (N), with part of the difference of 68 kMT (N) being recycled as aqueous ammonia of which 84 kMT (N) was consumed as fertilizer (USBuMines 1989, p. 746).

US production of urea-formaldehyde (UF) resin in 1988 was 0.646 MMT. UF resin is a straightforward condensation polymer in which the urea is entirely embodied in the product, which has 26% N-content. On this basis UF resin production accounted for 168 kMT (N). The two resins together embodied 230 kMT (N), disregarding losses and byproducts; this is slightly larger than the figure reported by the Bureau of Mines for 'industrial use' of urea (212 kMT (N)) (USBuMines 1989, p. 745).

Another important N-chemical is caprolactam, an intermediate in nylon 6 production. (In fact, the nylon is a straightforward polymer of caprolactam, so it contains all of the nitrogen in the monomer. Although nylon 6 output is not separately published, we can conclude that it must have been very close to the weight of caprolactam, or about 566 kMT for the US in 1988.) The nitrogen content of US caprolactam output in 1988 was 68 kMT (N) (ibid.). There are several production processes in use, but the most common in the US begin with cyclohexane or phenol. Based on the major process in use a few years ago, about 0.62 kg of ammonia is consumed, and 1.7 kg or ammonium sulfate is produced per kg of caprolactam. The ratio of nitrogen embodied in ammonium sulfate to nitrogen embodied in caprolactam is slightly less than 3:1, while the ratio of input nitrogen in ammonia to nitrogen in caprolactam is almost exactly 4:1. On this basis, 68 kMT (N) in caprolactam — ultimately in nylon 6 — requires 272 kMT of nitrogen in ammonia and yields about 200 kMT (N) as ammonium sulfate, plus some dilute nitric acid and wastes.

Based on the above calculation, we can account for 87 kMT (N) of ammonium sulfate as byproducts of caprolactam and methyl methacrylate production, plus 50 kMT (N) as byproducts of coke ovens, out of a total US ammonium sulfate output in 1988 of 498 kMT (N) (ibid.), leaving 161 kMT (N) as imputed primary production from ammonia and sulfuric acid. It happens that 243 kMT of sulfuric acid (100%) was consumed in the manufacture of nitrogenous fertilizers in 1988 (USBuMines 1989, p. 1034). Assuming all of this was used to make ammonium sulfate, it would account only for 69 kMT (N) as ammonia, leaving a shortage of 92 kMT (N) that must have been obtained from byproducts from other industrial processes. Actually, one possible candidate is caprolactam, since there is at least one newer process that yields a 40% higher ratio of ammonium sulfate to caprolactam. Consequently, we assume this process has supplanted the older one, adding an additional 8 kMT (N) to the byproduct supply. This would account for most of the missing byproduct source. The remaining discrepancies are probably statistical.

Methylenediphenyl di-isocyanate (MDI) and toluene di-isocyanate (TDI) are the other major N-containing intermediates in the manufacture of plastics and synthetic fibers. In 1988 TDI alone accounted for 10.4% of all toluene output (IEI 1991), or 215 kMT of toluene. The toluene di-isocyanate molecule substitutes two NCO radicals for two of the H atoms on the benzene ring. The conversion sequence is

toluene $\rightarrow$ dinitrotoluene $\rightarrow$ toluene diamine $\rightarrow$ toluene di-isocyanate

The overall yield is probably not above 80%. There is no published information on the production of dinitrotoluene, but it is certainly a direct reaction with nitric acid, as noted above. The nitrogen embodied in toluene di-isocyanate can be estimated on the basis of molecular weights (28 units of N per 92 units of toluene input), or 56 kMT (N) embodied in the product. This would have required at least 60 kMT (N) as nitric acid, assuming minor losses in the process. Obviously MDI accounted for some additional nitric acid (or equivalent nitrogen).

The N-content of monomers embodied in plastics and resins in 1988 (US) added up to at least 0.669 MMT. Nitrate and nitro-explosives (excluding amines) accounted for about 0.777 MMT (N). Dyes (aniline, etc.) account for at least 0.007 MMT (N). Other uses of nitric acid in the US — including small amounts used in phosphate rock processing and steel pickling — accounted for 0.135 MMT (N). Part of the missing 11% of ammonia goes into other 'final' chemicals, including military explosives, pesticides, plasticizers, rubber chemicals and so on. Over 4 MMT of miscellaneous nitrogenous compounds were produced in the US in 1988, including a little less than 1 MMT in the form of alkyl and other amines. We cannot estimate the nitrogen content very accurately, except to say that it is likely to be in the range 10–20% (higher for explosives). Thus somewhere between 0.4 MMT and 0.8 MMT might consist of nitrogen. We tentatively estimate 0.5 MMT, or approximately one-third of the missing 1.6 MMT of nitrogen.

A partial materials balance of the N-chemicals, accounting for 13.144 MMT (N), or about 89% of total ammonia supply, is shown in Figure 9.5. In fact, apparent 1988 US consumption of ammonia (in terms of contained nitrogen) was 14.746 MMT. In addition, there were net imports of about 520 kMT (N) of N-chemicals (excluding the ammonium phosphates). We can account for over 90% of the total, but with some uncertainties. Our total of 13.144 MT does not include chemicals for which we have no recent data, such as amides, alkylamines,

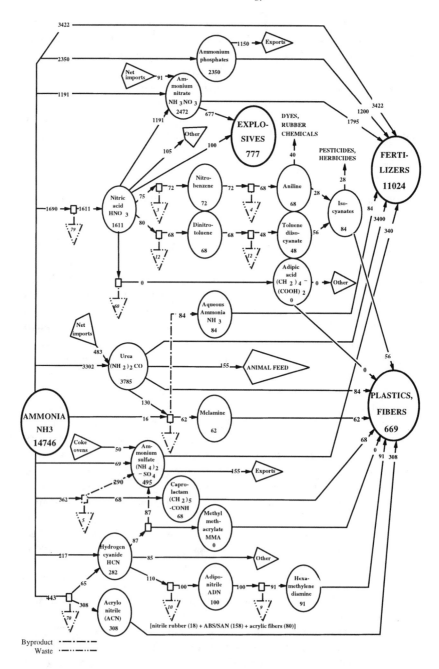

*Figure 9.5:   Materials balance of ammonia-based chemical production in
            the US, 1988 (1000 MT N-content)*

ethanolamines, nitro-paraffins, acrylates, ammonium chloride, hydrazine, ethylene diamine and hexamethylene tetramine, nor does it include household uses of ammonia, or uses of ammonia in other sectors (such as pulp and paper).

For 1990 it was reported that approximately 4.73 MMT of 'nitrogenous compounds' was produced in the US; the major sub-categories were 'amides' 139 kMT, 'amines' 897 kMT, 'ethanolamines' 330 kMT, 'nitriles' (including acrylonitrile and acetone cyanohydrin), unreported, and 'all other' 1.515 MMT. We can estimate the total for nitriles as roughly 1.835 MMT (by subtraction). Caprolactam is technically an amine (oxyhexamethyleneamine), and should be included in this total, although it is not listed separately for unknown reasons. The same is true of hexamethylene diamine (HMDA).

Because so much data is withheld, we cannot account for specific uses of nitrogenous chemicals beyond the foregoing. However, it would appear that at least 3 MMT of nitrogenous organic chemicals are not included in our listing. Assuming 10% N-content, on average, would not be unreasonable. This would account for another 300 kMT of N-content with a probable uncertainty of 100 kMT (N).

9.5.   LOSSES OF FIXED (ODD) NITROGEN

It is difficult to estimate chemical process wastes with any precision, because of the uncertainty about ammonium sulfate. The following, in kMT (N) is our best estimate, based on taking differences between published input N requirements and N embodied in products:

HNO_3 production (5% loss)	79
Adipic acid production	30
Acrylonitrile production	70
Caprolactam	5
Toluene di-isocyanate	12
Others	38
Subtotal of the above	234

This subtotal identifies probable losses in production amounting to 234 kMT (N). This is certainly an underestimate, however, since we have neglected the large number of products made in small quantities via batch reactions that are considerably less efficient than the large-scale continuous processes. Our best guess is that process losses (unreacted feedstocks or contaminants) amount to at least 3% of the total, or 450 kMT. If this is so, to a reasonably good approximation, we have accounted for 95% of the synthetic fixed nitrogen produced and consumed in the US in 1988.

The 5% remainder unaccounted for would probably be ammonia used for non-chemical purposes, such as household cleaning agents, as noted above. However, there is some possibility of under-counting of the use of nitrogen in mixed fertilizers, where published data seems to be incomplete. Lacking further information, we assume the remaining nitrogen is allocated mostly to household cleaning agents and other consumer products.

It is of some interest that the major waste streams from nitric acid and adipic acid manufacturing are in the form of NO, while a significant fraction of the latter, at least, takes the form of nitrous oxide N_2O, one of the more potent 'greenhouse' gases. It has been suggested that the N_2O emissions from adipic acid manufacturing is nearly equal to the quantity of product (Thiemens and Trogler 1991). However, process data suggests that the maximum output of N_2O from adipic acid manufacturing (even assuming 100% conversion of 60 kMT (N) to N_2O) would be about 94 kMT. However a 50% conversion rate is more plausible.

We have not been able to determine the reaction products of nitrate explosives such as ammonium nitrate. It is not clear how complete the oxidation of nitrogen would be under non-equilibrium conditions. However, it is interesting to note that an old commercial process for producing nitrous oxide (laughing gas) has the simple formula:

$$NH_4NO_3 \rightarrow N_2O + 2H_2O$$

It would not be surprising if use of ammonium nitrate as an explosive generated significant quantities of N_2O. A straightforward estimate of the reaction products of ammonium nitrate decomposition using ASPEN-PLUS software, suggests that as much as 9% of the N-content could be converted to N_2O (Axtell 1993). Assuming 777 kMT (N-content) of nitrate explosives produced in the US, mainly ammonium nitrate, this suggests that 110 kMT of N_2O might be generated by explosives.

In terms of pollution of the environment, the 3% loss rate suggested above would be insignificant in comparison with dissipative uses of nitrogenous chemicals. Apart from fertilizers and animal feeds, these include industrial explosives, pesticides and herbicides, dyes, surfactants, flotation agents, rubber accelerators, plasticizers, gas conditioning agents, and so on. In fact, except for the plastics and resins (and plasticizers), it is safe to assume that virtually all nitrogenous chemicals are dissipated in normal use, but mainly by other sectors, or final consumers. Over a slightly longer time span — 5 to 10 years — the same is also true of plastics, synthetic rubber, fibers and military explosives.

The ultimate forms of nitrogenous wastes, and even the environmental media into which they are dispersed, are not particularly well known. One soluble waste generated by many processes is ammonium bisulfate $(NH_4)HSO_4$. This can be converted to ammonium sulfate, in principle, but the conversion is not economic in most cases. Many processes probably dissipate some N as ammonia, some as cyanides (e.g. gold mining) and some as NO_X. The latter contributes to environmental acidification. Adipic acid production, and possibly nitrogenous explosives, seem to produce emissions of N_2O.

9.6. EMISSIONS OF TOXIC NITROGENOUS CHEMICALS

It is important to consider the ultimate fate of nitrogen-containing chemicals. It is reasonable to assume that most of them — especially the explosives — will ultimately be oxidized. When this occurs, the carbon and hydrogen are converted to carbon dioxide and water vapor, respectively, while the nitrogen goes to NO and NO_2 or, in some cases, N_2O. However, there will undoubtedly be traces of ammonia, HCN, and other volatiles such as carcinogenic Peroxy-Acyl Nitrates (PAN), one of the intermediates produced by photolytic reactions between NO_2 and hydrocarbons in the atmosphere.

Cyanides are found in many industrial wastes, especially quench waters from coking operations and metal heat treating operations. Sodium and potassium cyanides are also used in both gold and silver mining, in the 'heap leach' process to beneficiate low-grade ores to the point where smelting is feasible. Cyanides are extremely toxic. The cyanide ion CN^- is toxic to most fish at a level of 0.1 mg per liter (kg) of water, for instance. Fortunately, cyanides easily form metallic complexes, such as ferrous cyanide $Fe(CN)_2$, ferric cyanide $Fe(CN)_3$, ferro-cyanides, and so on. These complexes are much less toxic. However, there is a possibility that complex cyanides could revert to the simpler forms under certain circumstances, such as increased acidity (lower pH), increased temperature, or UV radiation. This means that accumulations of metallic cyanide complexes in the surroundings of old gold and silver mining operations are still potential 'chemical time bombs'.[3]

One of the most toxic and carcinogenic of all groups of compounds are the nitrosamines, characterized by the $N-N = O$ linkage. It is known that amines, such as dimethylamine, can be nitrosated in the atmosphere, by reaction with nitrous acid vapor, in equilibrium with NO and NO_2, to yield nitroso-dimethylamine. All the amines can apparently be nitrosated under appropriate conditions. It is believed that nitrosamines become active carcinogens after being decomposed by enzymes. Of the first 100 nitroso compounds studied, over 80 were carcinogenic in test animals, sometimes after a single dose.

These compounds were first detected in the environment in the mid-1970s. The first confirmed atmospheric detections were in Baltimore, in the vicinity of a plant that manufactures methyl amines and hydrazine. Other amine plants have subsequently been associated with atmospheric nitrosamine findings. Later research discovered nitrosamines in the expired air of rats that had been fed on amines and nitrates. There is some reason to suspect that rocket engine exhaust (from hydrazine) may also be a source of nitrosamines. There is also reason to think that nitrosamines can be formed in food, e.g. bacon, that has been preserved by nitrites. Nitrosamines are also found in tobacco smoke, and may be one of the cancer-causing agents.

A few nitrosamines were manufactured, as such, in the 1970s, mainly for use as a retardant in the rubber industry. However, amines have been produced in fairly large quantities for many years. Total US amine production in 1972 was about 910 kMT. This included hexamethylene diamine, aniline, ethanolamine and melamine. For 1991, the totals for these compounds was 806 kMT, plus aniline and melamine. The presence of these in the environment, in conjunction with NO_X seems to be conducive to the formation of nitrosamines.

9.7. AGRICULTURAL EMISSIONS OF NITROGEN

As mentioned in the opening paragraph, nitrogen is an essential element for protein production. It can only be ingested (by plants) as soluble ammonium (NH_4^-) ions, nitrate (NO_3^+) ions, or soluble organic molecules such as amino acids. There are many routes by which soluble nitrogen finds its way into the soil.

Nitrogen oxides are created in the air either by electric storms or fuel combustion. These oxides then react with water vapor and create nitrous or nitric acid (HNO_3) which falls as a component of acid rain. Nitric acid subsequently reacts with metallic salts to form nitrates. Ammonia is also emitted by volcanoes.

Rhizobia bacteria in the root nodules of legumes (such as soybeans) are able to fix nitrogen from the air. Some other varieties of bacteria can also fix nitrogen. A third source — from a practical point of view — is the recycling of plant and animal matter. Some of this nitrogen from decaying organic matter is released in the form of ammonia (NH_3), and, along with ammonia from anthropogenic sources, is returned to the soil in rain.

For centuries nitrogen fixation by atmospheric electrical discharges, from legumes and from decayed matter (manure) were the only means of restoring lost fertility to soil. Gradually, the recycling process was accelerated through composting and distribution. Organic matter in the soil may contain as much as 5–6% nitrogen, but this is not available to plants until it has been released by bacteria or fungi in the form of ammonia or nitrates. Soils with plentiful organic matter can retain much of this for future use by plants.

With increasing pressure on farmers to increase crop yields, the available nitrogen in the soil was used more rapidly than it could be replaced by the available plant and animal materials. In 1930 the annual nitrogen deficit for the US was estimated at 3.4 MMT, despite some use of nitrogen fertilizers (Shreve 1956, p. 397). However, fertilizer use has increased very rapidly since then. In recent years a growing proportion of nitrogen has been applied by direct injection of anhydrous ammonia into the soil, particularly in the large farms of the Mississippi valley. However, the major portion is still applied either in solid or liquid form that can be handled more easily and applied in combination with other plant nutrient materials.

Crutzen has estimated the partitioning of 100 units of agricultural fertilizer into ultimate sinks as follows (Crutzen 1976, cited in NAS 1978): (1) accumulation in the soil, ground water or sediments: 38 units; (2) active recycling through the soil-biosphere system as manure or plant residues: 39 units; (3) denitrification to N_2 or N_2O which return to the atmosphere: 23 units. In this picture about 17 units escape as ammonia, 4 from the point of fertilizer application, 12 from manure and 1 from sewage. Another 6 units escape as N_2 (5.6 units) or N_2O (0.4 units). Crops initially take up 50% (50 units) of the N-content of the fertilizer; of this 47 units are consumed by livestock, and 42 units end up in manure and animal urine, of which 15 units go back to the soil, along with 30 units of nitrogen from plant residues and 4 units from local deposition of gaseous emissions. But, during each cycle, 10 units of organic N are lost to waterways and ground water, so the amount of organic N 'permanently' added (i.e. for the next cycle) is 15 units, while 24 units of inorganic N are also added for the next cycle. This represents accumulation within the terrestrial biosphere and cultivated lands. Crutzen's allocation neglects NO emissions from soil, which are not well documented, but known to be significant (see below).

Of the 50% of nitrogen in fertilizer not taken up by the harvestable parts of plants and removed in crops, a small amount (possibly 10%) is lost immediately to runoff or ground water. A considerable part (Crutzen estimates 30%, which we accept for purposes of discussion) returns to the soil in organic root, stem or leaf material that gradually decays. Some of the fertilizer and some of the organic material is, in turn, converted to N_2 (or N_2O) by denitrifying bacteria: Crutzen estimates 15%, which is consistent with other data (see below).

In well-ventilated soils having low organic matter (with a carbon/nitrogen ratio of less than 15) when the quantity of ammonium ions exceeds the absorption by plants and microbes, the excess ammonia is oxidized to nitrates by a nitrification process. The first step (to nitrite) is brought about by bacteria such as *nitrosomas*. The second step (to nitrate) is carried out by other bacteria such as *nitrobacter*. These nitrates remain in the soil for plant use, up to certain limits depending on temperature, and so on. Most nitrate compounds are soluble and can be leached from the soil — particularly in permeable soils having low organic matter and high rainfall. However, in soils with high levels of decaying organic matter, air circulation, and a high microbial population, the microbes consume the nitrogen in the form of ammonia and effectively store it in their body-mass for future use by plants — resulting in very little loss by leaching.

Bacterial action also continuously removes organic nitrogen from soils altogether by converting organic nitrogen to volatile NH_3, some of which escapes into the atmosphere. However, denitrification is the dominant process. In clogged soils having insufficient air circulation, fertilizer nitrates may be denitrified (reduced to gaseous nitrogen) by anaerobic microbes which break up the molecules to satisfy their demand for oxygen. Crutzen's estimate was 6% direct loss by denitrification at the point of application and another 9% from subsequent decay of organic materials.

Bacteria in the soil convert nitrates to di-nitrogen (N_2) and nitrous oxide (N_2O) in a ratio of about 16:1. The ratio is highly variable, and depends strongly on local conditions. Fertilizer use is, however, reckoned to be one of the major sources of atmospheric N_2O emissions, accounting for roughly 1.5 MMT globally in 1988 according to several estimates.

The rest of the applied fertilizer not otherwise taken into account returns to the atmosphere directly as ammonia. Ammonia emissions depend on fertilizer type. In the case of urea, the ammonia emission factor is apparently about 0.2 (20%); for ammonium sulfate it is 0.1 (10%); for other fertilizers — including anhydrous NH_3 injected directly into the soil — it is about 0.03 (Schlesinger and Hartley 1992, Table 6).

Direct emissions of ammonia would seem to account for about 9% of total N-content of applied fertilizer or 18% of the nitrogen not embodied in harvested crops. On the other hand, Crutzen estimates that about 20% of ammonia emissions (including emissions from animal excreta) are redeposited on agricultural soils.

Following this line of reasoning, but without going into all the details, one is forced to conclude that — in a balanced system that is not deficient in nitrogen — crop removals can be larger than 50%. (In other words, Crutzen was considering a system in which nitrogen was accumulating in the soil, presumably to compensate for prior deficits.) Indeed, we have seen estimates from the US Department of Agriculture that nitrogen uptake by crops in the US during the early 1970s was in the range of 64–80% (depending on the year) with an average of 72%. The unbalanced case is applicable to many parts of the world where nitrogen has been 'mined' from the soil, but the balanced case is more applicable to the US and Europe today.

Animal wastes are a major ammonia pollution problem, especially in the vicinity of animal feed lots and large-scale poultry producers. Per capita annual NH_3 emissions from animal metabolism have been estimated as follows: 15.5 kg for cattle and horses; 2.4 kg for sheep, 2.35 kg for pigs and 0.21 kg for (average) chickens and turkeys (Schlesinger and Hartley 1992, Table 4). Populations of these animals in the US for 1988 were 99.6 million cattle, 55.5 million pigs, 10.9 million sheep and lambs and 5.7 billion (5.7×10^9) chickens (including broilers) and turkeys. This implies total NH_3 emissions from animals of 2.91 MMT, or 2.4 MMT (N), of which at least three-quarters, or 1.8 MMT (N) would have been emitted at feeding stations or feedlots in the US. Such mass-feeding stations are uncommon in Europe, except in the Netherlands. The bulk of this NH_3 was volatilized directly into the atmosphere, although some gets into ground water.

Because of the rapid increase in nitrogen fertilizer use, runoff from agricultural areas is now the dominant source of aggregate nitrogen emissions to the water (and has been since the 1960s). In addition, large-scale animal feed lots have become major point sources of nitrogen emissions (both to water and air) by way of manure and urine.[4] In the extreme case of a heavily urbanized region, however, most N-emissions can evidently be attributed to food-processing and consumption wastes (sewage).

As noted above, more than half of the nitrogen in fertilizer added to agricultural soils (in countries where there is a reasonable balance between annual inputs and losses) is taken up by crops and removed by harvesting. Nevertheless, 30% or 40% of that nitrogen is lost unnecessarily to runoff or volatilization. That loss is not only wasteful of a costly (and energy-intensive) resource, but it contributes significantly to the growing disequilibrium of the nitrogen cycle. Opportunities to deliver fertilizer more efficiently do exist. One recent study in the Netherlands has estimated that fertilizer application could be reduced by 44% (minimum 28%, maximum 51%) by the adoption of more rational techniques (Worrell *et al.* 1994). This is an area of research that could pay important dividends, both in terms of immediate energy savings and in terms of long-term sustainability.

9.8. EMISSIONS OF OXIDES OF NITROGEN (N_2O, NO_X)

Oxides of nitrogen are formed naturally by electrical discharges in the atmosphere. They are also formed when either atmospheric or fuel-bound nitrogen are 'burned' in air. This is the major anthropogenic contribution. The major nitrogen oxides are N_2O, NO and NO_2. In the absence of fuel-bound nitrogen, typically 95–98% of the NO_X in combustion exhaust gas consists of NO. Incompletely oxidized nitrogen is oxidized further to NO_2 in the atmosphere. NO_2 is eventually dissolved in water and precipitated as nitrous acid, or oxidized further to nitric acid. In either case it is a major contributor to acid rain and acidification of soils. In addition, NO_2 reacts with hydrocarbons and oxygen (especially in the presence of UV radiation) to form peroxy-acyl-nitrates (PAN), one of the most irritating and carcinogenic ingredients of urban smog.

The reaction chemistry for NO_X formation by fossil fuel combustion is not completely known, but the most probable sequence for thermal NO_X seems to be the following (Lim *et al.* 1981).

$$N_2 + O \rightarrow NO + N$$
$$N_2 + O_2 \rightarrow NO + O$$
$$N + OH \rightarrow NO + H$$

where oxygen and hydrogen concentrations are in equilibrium.

$$O_2 + N_2 \rightarrow O + O + N$$
$$H_2O + O_2 \rightarrow H^+ + OH^- + N_2$$

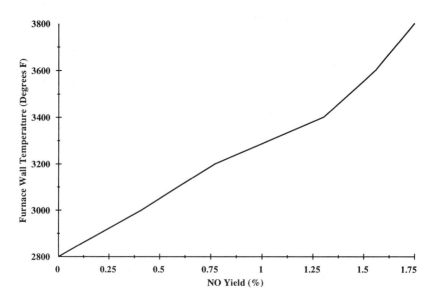

Source: Ermenc 1956, cited in Engdahl 1968.

Figure 9.6:   *NO_X formation vs. temperature, based on measurements at furnace wall*

The reaction rate for NO_X formation is determined by two factors. The activation energy of the initial endothermic reaction step is quite large (317 KJ mole) and probably determines the overall reaction rate. The reaction is, therefore, highly temperature dependent: equilibrium NO levels in heated mixtures of N_2 and O_2 at atmospheric pressure is an increasing function of temperature (Figure 9.6).

Because of the high activation energy for the nitrogen oxidation reaction, it will only occur after all available carbonaceous fuels are exhausted. Thus, the rate of NO_X production also depends on the amount of excess oxygen that is present beyond the stoichiometric air/fuel ratio (14.6 for the case of gasoline). The equilibrium NO level is also proportional to the product of N_2 concentration times the square root of O_2 concentration, times residence time in the flame. Because of these relationships, air/fuel ratio is a dominant factor in determining NO_X emissions in the absence of fuel-bound nitrogen. Figure 9.7 shows typical NO_X (NO, NO_2) emissions as a function of air/fuel ratio for automobile gasoline engines (Jackson 1968).

For smoldering fires, or 'rich' fuel air mixtures, NO_X production is negligible. However, for 'lean' fuel air mixtures it becomes increasingly significant. Thus, NO_X is, for practical purposes, not significantly produced in low-

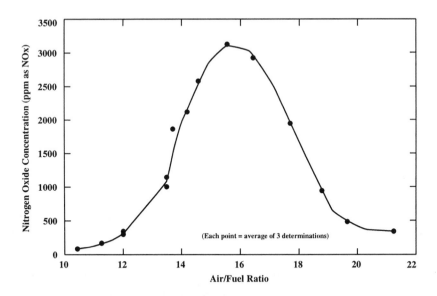

Source: Adapted from Jackson 1968, Figure 5a.

Figure 9.7: *Influence of air–fuel ratio on concentration of NO_X in exhaust gas*

temperature combustion processes, except to the extent that fuel-bound (or-ganic) nitrogen is present.

However, organic nitrogen is present in coal and residual oil and in biomass.[5] Thus, fuel-bound nitrogen in all organic materials, as well as in fossil fuels (in coal and residual oil) also contributes to both N_2O and NO_X emissions. Apparently N_2O — one of the most potent greenhouse gases — is associated *only* with fuel-bound nitrogen.

Median nitrogen content of US coals corresponds to approximately 1350 mg/KJ of NO_2, assuming 100% conversion; the 25–75 percentile range is fairly narrow, namely, 1250–1400 Ng/J (Lim *et al.* 1981). Figure 9.8 shows measured relationships between coal nitrogen content in percent by weight and *measured* NO_X emissions. The median NO_X (as NO_2) emission level is about 270 Ng/J. The 25–75 percentile range for bituminous coal combustion corresponds to NO_X (as NO_2) emissions in the range of 240–300 Ng/J (ibid.). Based on this data, it appears that if there were thermal contribution to NO_X, the average conversion fraction for fuel-bound nitrogen to NO_X would be $270/1350 = 0.2$.

The relative contribution of fuel-bound nitrogen to NO_X emissions from combustion is not yet completely understood. However, studies have shown that the contribution of fuel-bound N to total NO_X may be as high as 50% for

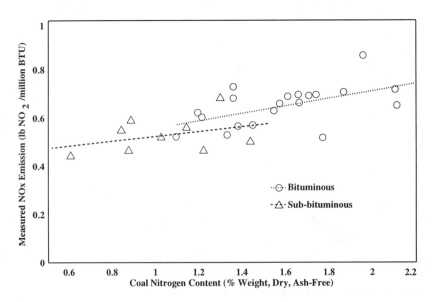

Figure 9.8:   Nitric oxide emission as measured vs. coal nitrogen content

residual oil, and 80% for coal. Looking at it another way, 20–90% fuel-bound nitrogen in oil and 10–60% in coal may be converted to NO_x, depending on conditions of combustion. No data for wood combustion is available.

Emissions vary widely according to the type of combustion equipment, so test data is limited and generalizations are difficult to make. Taking into account the contribution from atmospheric nitrogen, USEPA has developed estimates of NO_x emissions for most fuel uses (USEPA 1978 and undated). The USEPA emissions coefficients for coal burned in electric utilities and other industrial boilers, respectively, are about 10.4 kg/tonne and 8.6 kg/tonne. Natural gas and residual oil combustion emissions by electric utilities are slightly lower than emissions from coal (9.95 and 6.6 kg/tonne, respectively). Industrial boilers emit a little less NO_x than utility boilers, on the average, because they are smaller and operate at lower temperatures. Railroad uses of coal can be assumed to be very similar to industrial boilers. Fuel wood is used primarily in residences, or by the paper/pulp industry. High water content tends to keep temperatures low and minimizes NO_x.

9.9. ENVIRONMENTAL IMPACTS OF FIXED (ODD) NITROGEN

There are three long-term impacts of importance. First, N_2O is a greenhouse gas, contributing up to 10% of the total impact. Second, NO_x contributes about one-third of the environmental acidification impact (the other two-thirds being due to SO_x). Third, large-scale emission of NO_x as well as large-scale use of synthetic nitrogen fertilizers may be significantly enhancing the amount of biologically available nitrogen on land. (In fact, the multiplier cannot be stated precisely, but it could easily by 200%.) Runoff, in turn, causes — or may cause — eutrophication effects in offshore waters.

Long-term consequences of these effects cannot be foreseen accurately, absent a reliable and quantifiable model of the N-cycle and its interaction with the sulfur-cycle and the carbon-cycle. Such a model may not be possible, given the complexity and non-linearity of the system.

9.10. TECHNOLOGIES AND POLICIES

The overall task of public policy must be to minimize unnecessary human interference with the natural N-cycle. This means, in effect, to minimize total emissions of synthetic nitrogen-based chemicals into the environment, from any source whatever.

The first, and most obvious, source of N-emissions is the use of synthetic fertilizers. Whereas natural N-fixation processes synthesize only what is necessary and make it directly available to the plant, the industrial analog is rather inefficient and allows much of the nitrogen to go to waste. What this means, in practice, is that the excess fertilizer moves into other environmental media, whether the air, the surface waters or the ground water. The end result of surface runoff is likely to be eutrophication of lakes or streams — especially estuarine zones offshore. Denitrification bacteria can eliminate the excess, but some is emitted to the air as nitrous oxide, N_2O. This can lead to anoxia and fish kills, among other problems. Nitrates and nitrites in ground water are potentially harmful to animals that may eventually drink the water. Nitrogen (as ammonia) volatilized to the air generally ends up by reacting with sulfur oxides, ending as ammonium sulfate, a fertilizer. This is deposited with the rain, over both land and sea, as does the NO_X from fossil fuel combustion (which is deposited as acid, and helps to acidify the soil). Acidification of agricultural land can be countered — albeit not inexpensively — by spreading limestone, but acidification of forests cannot be reversed, except by very slow natural processes.

The long-term solution must be to stop using synthetic nitrogen fertilizer at all. The technical solution is biological nitrogen fixation by 'engineered' bacteria or other organisms. In principle, this should be within the domain of genetic engineering. Unfortunately, up to now very little R&D investment has been directed to this end. One way to change this would be for government to subsidize this type of research directly. Another approach would be to raise the price of synthetic fertilizers enough to induce farmers to return to the use of animal manure and leguminous crops. This would also create a much more attractive market for genetically engineered N-fixing crops.

Other nitrogen-based chemicals should also be banned or discouraged over time. For one thing, explosives are largely based on nitrogenous compounds. To ban some explosives and heavily tax others would have several beneficial effects. It would be a form of indirect arms control, for one thing. It would also increase the costs of mining virgin ores and fuels in comparison to recycling metals and energy conservation. An outright ban on some uses of nitrogen chemicals (such as cyanidation in gold and silver mining) would probably be helpful, for instance.[6]

Obviously radical changes of this magnitude cannot be accomplished quickly. Quite apart from the impact on chemical producers, the disruptive effects on agriculture will be enormous. But if the relative prices of N-chemicals were to rise gradually (*vis-à-vis* human labor) over a long period of time, the end result would eventually occur automatically through the agency of the 'invisible hand' of the market. This change in relative prices (or costs, depending on one's point of view) is the domain of government. It can be accomplished through a combination of regulation and tax policy, especially by reducing direct and indirect taxes on labor and increasing taxes on fuels and natural resources.

NOTES(9)

1. For a detailed discussion and breakdown see A.J. Lotka (Lotka 1956, Chap. XVIII).
2. However, in a hypothetical future world in which hydrocarbons are scarce but electricity (from fusion reactors or the sun) is inexpensive, the Birkeland–Eyde process could conceivably be revived.
3. The terminology is due to William Stigliani (Stigliani 1988).
4. Animal urine accounts for at least 50% of excreted nitrogen, in the form of urea. Under typical feedlot conditions urea is rapidly hydrolyzed to carbon dioxide and ammonia.
5. In coal the range is between 0.6% and 2% by weight (Figure 9.8). In terrestrial biomass, it has been found that the nitrogen/carbon molar ratio is fairly constant (1:80), which means that the C/N weight ratio is 68.5. This is about the same as the average ratio for coal.
6. The objection will be made that to ban cyanidation would invite the use of mercury for extracting gold and silver from low grade ores, as was done in the 19th century. This should not necessarily be banned, however, but rather taxed at a rate high enough to ensure virtually 100% recycling of metallic mercury.

10. The chlor-alkali sector

10.1. SUMMARY

Chlorine is a chemically active element that is invariably combined with other elements, usually sodium, but occasionally with calcium, iron, magnesium or potassium. Its major compound is sodium chloride (NaCl) or ordinary salt, which constitutes roughly 3.7%, by weight, of seawater. There are large underground deposits of evaporite salt left over from earlier seas that have since dried up. However, apart from this one mineral, chlorine is comparatively rare in the earth's crust, although it is apparently released in significant quantities by volcanoes as hydrochloric acid, HCl.[1]

Chlorine's role in biochemistry is equally limited. While salt (sodium chloride) is a necessary component of every diet, its role appears to be mainly that of maintaining the internal electrolyte composition and osmotic pressure of cells at an equilibrium level. It is also, of course, the source of hydrochloric acid released in the animal stomach to assist with digestion. Until recently it was thought that chlorine is rarely, if ever, found in organic molecules of natural origin.[2]

Perhaps it is for this reason that decay bacteria tend to metabolize chlorinated organics very slowly, and higher organisms metabolize them scarcely at all. Yet, a number of organo-chlorines are biologically active in the sense that they are capable of interfering with certain normal biochemical functions, especially in the endocrine systems of animals and humans. In other words, organo-chlorines may be toxic, carcinogenic, teratogenic or even mutagenic. In some cases these characteristics were deliberately exploited, as in the development of a whole family of chlorinated pesticides and herbicides during the 1950s and 1960s. In other cases, the toxic or carcinogenic effects turned up by accident, as in the case of the widely used solvents such as trichloroethylene (TCE) and methylene dichloride, or the chemicals ethylene dichloride (highly toxic to aquatic systems), and the monomer vinyl chloride (a potent carcinogen).

The exact mechanisms whereby these biological effects occur are not yet understood, for the most part. (If they were, it would be much easier to design both chemical agents for particular purposes, and also to design effective antidotes or therapies.) All that can be said at present, with some confidence, is that the biological activity of organo-chlorine molecules is probably related to their physical structures (i.e. the shapes of the molecules). This follows with a high degree of probability from the fact that organo-chlorines differing only by the exact placement of a chlorine atom on (say) a benzene ring can have totally different biological effects. Evidence has been accumulating of malign biological consequences of long-term low-level exposures to chemicals that mimic the effects of the hormone estrogen on cells. Among the possible effects are birth defects (such as those associated with use of the drug diethylstilbestrol or DES, now banned), breast, prostate and testicular cancers, and a range of male reproductive problems, including a widely observed decrease in male sperm counts (*Scientific American*, September 1993, p. 16). Some of these estrogen-like chemicals may be organo-chlorines, though there is no evidence that the chlorine *per se* plays any part.

Moreover, since persistent organo-chlorines are not actively metabolized, but simply stored (mainly in fatty tissue) and passed on, many of them are bio-accumulated through the food chain. Thus, what would be an insignificant concentration in a simple organism (such as a mosquito larva), may become a lethal concentration in a top predator three steps up the chain. This is why eagles, ospreys, falcons and game fish were the main victims of dichloro-diphenyl-trichloroethane (DDT) and other chlorinated pesticides, even though they were never its targets. Much the same sort of problem has been identified for other classes of organo-chlorines, notably the polychlorinated biphenyls (PCBs).

It is not only the organo-chlorines that are manufactured for specific biocidal (or other) purposes that have been implicated in undesirable side-effects. On the contrary, it may be the unexpected byproducts of reactions that occur in incineration furnaces (and accidental fires) that cause the greatest public concern — justified or not. Here we refer to the poly-chlorinated dioxins (PCDDs) and poly-chlorinated dibenzyl furans (PCDFs) that may be the most carcinogenic compounds yet discovered, at least based on animal tests (Gough 1988). The US Environmental Protection Agency (USEPA) has been working on a new report on dioxin that is expected to say that dioxin is a serious potential threat to human health (*Time*, September 19, 1994).

Apart from its biological activity, chlorine has been implicated in the destruction of stratospheric ozone. The details of the chemical mechanism involved need not detail us here. It is only of interest that chlorine is mainly transported into the stratosphere in the first place by virtue of the great stability (i.e. persistence) of chloro-fluorocarbons (CFCs) in the presence of atmospheric oxygen and OH radicals. Whereas most organic chemicals are rapidly oxidized in the lower atmosphere (or washed out by rain), this is not true of the CFCs.[3] These are compounds used widely as refrigerants, foam blowing agents and solvents (and formerly as aerosol propellants) precisely because of this stability.

Because of all of these problems, the industrial use of chlorine itself is being increasingly questioned by some environmental organizations, notably Greenpeace. The chlorine industry, feeling threatened, is mounting an active defense. This chapter is not intended as an intervention in that debate, either for the unrestricted use of chlorine, or for a total ban. Because of the debate, there has already been a rather intensive examination of potential technological alternatives to the use of chlorine. It is indisputable that alternatives can be found to most of them, at some cost. What is much less clear is how costly the substitutes would be and whether the costs would be justified by the presumed benefits.

We acknowledge the validity of some of the environmental/health arguments against the use of chlorine for bleaching paper pulp, and against the dissipative use of chlorinated pesticides, chloro-carbon solvents and chloro-fluorocarbons. We also believe that a total ban on chlorine use would be extremely disruptive and probably excessively costly in relation to the benefits achieved. In effect, we argue for a much more complete and sophisticated life-cycle analysis of the chlorine industry than anything yet attempted along these lines. We wish to focus attention here on the need for the industry to release accurate quantitative information on the production, consumption, trade and stockpiling of individual chemicals. Without such data the requisite analysis cannot be carried out and intelligent public policy cannot be made

Goals of public policy: reduce mercury emissions and electricity consumption; reduce dissipative uses of chlorine, chlorinated hydrocarbons, especially solvents, pesticides and other organics; increase recycling of chlorine, both internally to the chemical industry and recycling of products like PVC, to minimize the escape of chlorinated organics into the environment (see also Chapter 12, Packaging); increase public understanding of the costs and benefits associated with pending proposals such as the proposed ban on all chlorine use.

10.2. SOURCES AND USES OF CHLORINE

Chlorine and caustic soda (sodium hydroxide) are co-products of the electrolysis of sodium chloride (salt), mainly in the form of brine made by solution mining of underground salt (halite) deposits. World production and consumption of virgin chlorine in 1990 was 37.433 MMT, of which the US accounted for 29% and Western Europe 25%. The output of caustic soda is essentially proportional to that of chlorine, in the ratio of their respective molecular weights (40:35.5 = 1.12). Thus 1.12 tonnes of (100%) caustic soda are produced by electrolysis per tonne of chlorine, or 42.1 MMT for the world. However, the situation is slightly confused by the existence of several alternative minor routes to chlorine (mainly, electrolysis of HCl and MgCl). In Europe, these routes altogether account for only 3.4% of 1988 chlorine capacity.

There are three important variants of the basic electrolytic process for chlor-alkali production, namely, the de Nora mercury cell (63.1% of 1988 European capacity; 17% of 1989 US capacity), the diaphragm cell (28% of European capacity) and the membrane cell (5.3%). The mercury cell is a significant source of environmental pollution, since some mercury is lost in the process. Historical data on the use of mercury for this process is shown in Appendix A, Table A.13.

The diaphragm cell is also a source of pollution, namely asbestos fiber. The membrane cell is the most efficient and least polluting, but the chlor-alkali industry has been surprisingly slow to adopt it, because there has been little growth in demand since the early 1970s and because existing facilities are fully depreciated but still functional. The three processes are summarized in Table 10.1(a,b,c).

Production and consumption of chlorine and caustic soda need not be (and are not) proportional in any given country. See Appendix A, Table A.14 for 1988, which is the last year for which we have a breakdown by country. A recent survey of the chlorine chemistry sector as a whole, in Europe, reveals some interesting facts. One is that about 47% of the chlorine that enters the system (from electrolysis of salt) is embodied in chlorinated end-products — solvents, polymers, pesticides, etc. — averaging 56.8% chlorine by weight (Ecotec 1995). Another 3% or less is sold as such for use in water treatment. The other half of the chlorine is discharged into process waste streams. Salt is the final form for just about 33% of the input chlorine and 66% of the wastes (ibid.). Most of the remainder is discharged as calcium chloride $CaCl_2$. These figures are probably also approximately correct for the US.

Major uses of chlorine and hydrochloric acid in Western Europe are summarized for 1989 and 1992 and for the US in 1989 in Figures 10.1 through 10.4. Unfortunately, these pie charts use different categories, in some cases, so they are difficult to interpret. For instance, VCM in Figure 10.1 refers to the vinyl chloride monomer, whereas vinyl chloride in Figure 10.2 refers to the polymer. This is confusing because, in the US most chlorinated ethanes (1,1,1 trichloroethane, trichloroethylene and perchloroethylene) are actually derived from VCM. This may not be the case in Europe. Another difficulty is that allyl chloride (Figure 10.1) is an intermediate consumed entirely in the production of epichlorohydrin, which is the category shown in Figure 10.2. But, in terms of chlorine consumption they are not equivalent, as noted below.

Table 10.1: Processes for the production of chlorine

A. Chlorine: by electrolysis of NaCl in diaphragm cells

Utility inputs and outputs			Other uncounted	
Water (cooling) (input)	69	tonnes	Hydrogen (as fuel) (T-Cal)	906
Steam (input)	2.4	tonnes		
Electricity (input)	2811	kWh		
INPUTS (metric tonnes)			OUTPUTS (metric tonnes)	
Sodium chloride	1.712		Caustic soda	1.128
Sulfuric acid	0.009		Sulfuric acid (65%)	0.009
Calcium chloride	0.013		CHLORINE	1.000
Hydrochloric acid (20BE)	0.056		(caustic soda byproduct)	
Carbon tetrachloride	<0.000			
Water (process)	0.010			
INPUTS ACCOUNTED FOR	1.800		OUTPUTS ACCOUNTED FOR	2.134
Source: SRI #110.	−0.337		=Difference = −18.70% of input	

B. Chlorine: By electrolysis of NaCl in membrane cells

Utility inputs and outputs			Other uncounted	
Water (cooling) (input)	152	tonnes	Membrane (sq. cm)	166.9
Steam (input)	0.89	tonnes	Hydrogen (as fuel) (T-Cal)	916
Electricity (input)	2798	kWh		
INPUTS (metric tonnes)			OUTPUTS (metric tonnes)	
Sodium chloride	2.430		Caustic soda	1.143
Sodium carbonate	0.035		Sulfuric acid (65%)	0.009

Sulfuric acid	0.009	
Hydrochloric acid (20BE)	0.011	
Water (process)	3.700	
CHLORINE (caustic soda byproduct)	1.000	
INPUTS ACCOUNTED FOR	6.185	4.033
OUTPUTS ACCOUNTED FOR	2.152	
= Difference = 65.20% of inputs		

Source: SRI #111.

C. Chlorine: By Electrolysis of NaCl in mercury cells

Utility inputs and outputs		
Water (cooling) (input)	208	tonnes
Steam (input)	2	tonnes
Electricity (input)	3575	kWh
Other uncounted		
Hydrogen (as fuel) (T-Cal)	898	
INPUTS (metric tonnes)		
Sodium chloride	1.711	
Sulfuric acid	0.009	
Calcium chloride	0.014	
Sodium carbonate	0.039	
Hydrochloric acid	0.040	
Sodium sulfide (flake)	<0.000	
Mercury	<0.000	
Water (process)	0.030	
OUTPUTS (metric tonnes)		
Caustic soda	1.118	
Sulfuric acid (dilute)	0.009	
CHLORINE	1.000	
INPUTS ACCOUNTED FOR	1.843	-0.284
OUTPUTS ACCOUNTED FOR	2.127	
= Difference = -15.42% of inputs		

Source: SRI #112.

Note: The inputs and outputs do not balance exactly because only about 98% of the sodium chloride in the brine is consumed, and because some of the chlorine is lost in the process. Based on Toxic Release Inventory data for the US (1990), air emissions of chlorine amounted to 45 KMT (fugitive) and 290 KMT (stack), or 0.42% and 2.7% of output respectively (Kostick 1994).

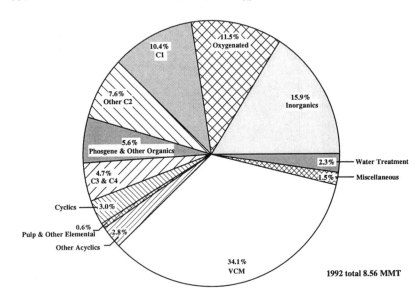

Figure 10.1:   *Western European consumption of chlorine, 1992*

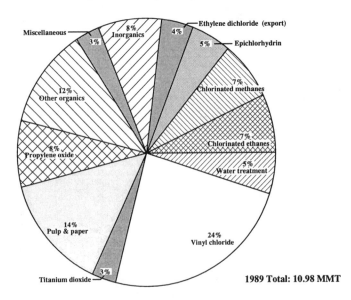

Source: MIT 1993.

Figure 10.2:   *US consumption of chlorine, 1989*

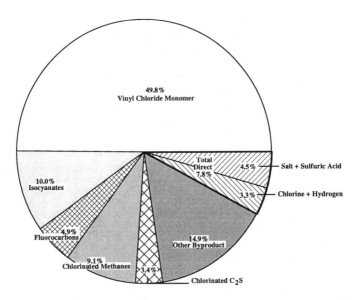

Source: EcoPlan.

Figure 10.3: *Western European production of hydrochloric acid, 1989*

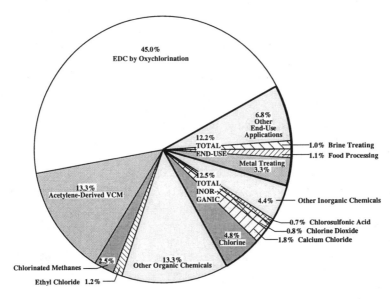

Source: EcoPlan.

Figure 10.4: *Western European consumption of hydrochloric acid by end-use, 1989*

Another point of possible confusion arises in connection with phosgene ($COCl_2$). Phosgene itself is classified as an inorganic chemical, but it is used to produce a number of important organic compounds, including cyanuric acid, isocyanates — especially toluene di-isocyanate — (the basis of most polyurethanes), polycarbonates, pesticides (e.g. 'Sevin'), and dyes. Use for these purposes in Europe has been growing, from 6.4% in 1988 to 8.7% in 1992. Isocyanates and polycarbonates contain no chlorine. The chlorine is either recycled as HCl (in isocyanate production) or discarded as sodium chloride (in the case of polycarbonates).

Other uses of elemental chlorine include water treatment, titanium dioxide production (see below), HCl by direct synthesis from natural gas and phosgene ($COCl_2$). Other unspecified inorganic chemicals accounted for 10.7% of total Cl consumption in Europe (1988), but dropped down to 5.8% by 1992. (It should be noted that several large tonnage chlorides are either natural products (e.g. KCl), byproducts (e.g. $CaCl_2$, Fe_2Cl_3), or are made directly from sodium chloride (e.g. sodium chlorate).

Ethylene dichloride (EDC) is the most important single organic chlorine compound in tonnage terms, as shown in Table 10.2 and Appendix A, Table A.15. Most EDC in Europe is consumed in the production of vinyl chloride monomer (VCM), with byproduct HCl. Altogether, EDC accounted for 36.5% of European Cl consumption in 1988 and 40% in 1992. Roughly 10% of the EDC is converted into solvents (trichloroethylene and perchloroethylene) or exported.

Another large user is propylene oxide by the chlorohydrin process (see below). This accounted for 7.8% of Cl consumption in 1988, up to 8.25% in 1992. Chlorinated methane (solvents) accounted for just under 10% of 1988 chlorine consumption, but only 7.6% in 1992. Chlorinated ethanes and ethylene accounted for 5.1% in 1988, dropping to 3.2% in 1992. Chlorinated benzenes declined slightly, from about 1.25%, to 1.06% while the big winner

Table 10.2: World demand for chlorine by end-use, 1994

Use Category	Europe	US	Japan	Rest of World
Organic chemicals	37%	32%	26%	38%
EDC/VCM	35%	34%	29%	20%
Pulp and paper	1%	9%	5%	8%
Inorganic chemicals	13%	12%	10%	14%
Water treatment	4%	5%	5%	11%
Miscellaneous	10%	8%	25%	9%

Source: Consulting Resources Corporation (for the US Bureau of Mines).

was allyl chloride (leading to epichlorohydrin and epoxys), up from 1.37% in 1988 to 1.74% in 1992. Other uses held roughly steady, in percentage terms.

There are several interesting and important examples of the use of chlorine (and HCl) as an intermediate in the production of chemicals that do not themselves contain chlorine. The case of *epichlorohydrin*, a co-polymer in epoxy resins and polyamides, is exemplary. The entire sequence has three stages. The first stage is propylene chlorination, yielding allyl chloride and some byproduct dichloropropylene. Approximately 1.3 tonnes of chlorine are needed per tonne of allyl chloride produced. The second stage is another chlorination, leading to epichlorohydrin. In this stage, for each tonne of allyl chloride used, about 0.925 tonnes of additional chlorine is needed, along with about 0.78 tonnes of lime. The outputs consist of 1.03 tonnes of epichlorohydrin and 1.55 tonnes of calcium chloride, plus roughly 0.14 tonnes of other chlorinated hydrocarbons (waste). In the final stage, polymerization, all of the chlorine contained in the epichlorohydrin — 38.4% by weight — is lost in the form of sodium chloride. The final products (polymers) contain no chlorine at all. Yet, apparently this process sequence alone accounted for 5% of US chlorine consumption in 1989 (Figure 10.2).

Other examples include the following:

- *Toluene di-isocyanate*, the basic feedstock for polyurethanes is made by reacting toluene diamine with a chlorine-containing intermediate (phosgene, CCl_2O), with HCL as a byproduct. (Some of this HCl is recycled back to hydrogen and chlorine by electrolysis.)
- *Propylene oxide (epoxipropane)*, itself an intermediate feedstock for polyesters and polyurethane, is made by two processes. The older 'chlorohydrin' process proceeds via dichloropropane (DCP). HCl is a byproduct of the second stage. It can be used as such or neutralized and recycled as brine through the chlorine cells in an integrated facility (Dow). The newer process (Oxirane) does not require chlorine, but it is used primarily to produce tert-butyl alcohol (TBA), from i-butane and/ or ethylbenzene en route to the gasoline octane additive methyl-tert-butyl ether (MTBE). Propylene oxide is only a minor byproduct, whence the Oxirane process accounts for only about 4% of worldwide capacity as of 1989–90 (Fonds Chem 1992)
- *Silicones* are polymers based on a chain of molecules with the composition $(CH_3)_2SiO$, containing no chlorine. However, the starting point is a reaction between silicon metal Si and methyl chloride (CH_3Cl) which produces methylchlorosilane ($(CH_3)_2SiCl_2$). The latter reacts with water yielding the silicone monomer plus byproduct HCl (Fonds Chem 1992).

- *Tetrafluoroethylene (TFE)* is C_2F_4, the monomer for the polymer best known as 'Teflon®'. It contains no chlorine, but is made by high-temperature pyrolysis of the solvent monochlorodifluoromethane ($CClF_2H$), releasing chlorine as HCl for recycling.
- *Ultra-pure electronic grade silicon (EGS)*, the starting point for virtually all semiconductor products ('chips'), is produced by a process in which impure metallurgical grade silicon (MGS) is chlorinated to trichlorosilane ($SiHCl_3$), which is subsequently reduced again (by reaction with hydrogen) to silicon and hydrochloric acid. The latter reacts with trichlorosilane to yield silicon tetrachloride ($SiCl_4$) and hydrogen gas. In principle the hydrogen can also be recycled. The byproduct $SiCl_4$ is an intermediate for virtually all silicon chemicals. This complex system is described in more detail in Chapter 11, Silicon.
- *Titanium dioxide* is by far the most important white pigment for paint, paper and other products. It contains no chlorine. Titanium is obtained from two ores, ilmenite and rutile. The process for extracting titanium dioxide from rutile involves chlorination as an intermediate step. In this case HCl is not recycled, but is neutralized; the waste product is sodium chloride (salt).

A less detailed usage breakdown for 1994 is shown in Table 10.2. The biggest single use of chlorine in all countries is in the manufacture of vinyl chloride, the monomer for the plastic polyvinyl chloride or PVC. A few major regional differences are worthy of comment. For one thing, 25% of Japanese chlorine consumption is used for inorganic chemicals, as compared to only 8–10% for Europe, the US and the rest of the world. Another difference between Western Europe (Figure 10.1) and the US (Figure 10.2) appears to be the much smaller proportion of European chlorine production being used for pulp bleaching. In fact, elemental chlorine use for pulp and paper bleaching accounted for 5.8% of European chlorine consumption in 1987, 2.9% in 1992 and 1% in 1994 vs. 14% in 1989 in the US (9% in 1994) and 5% in Japan (1994). On the other hand, water treatment accounted for 4% in Europe, 5% in the US and Japan, but 11% in the rest of the world.

The complexity of the chlorine 'system' is not fully captured by tables and pie charts, of course. We have attempted to reconstruct more detailed chlorine flow charts for Europe and the US in Figures 10.5 through 10.8.

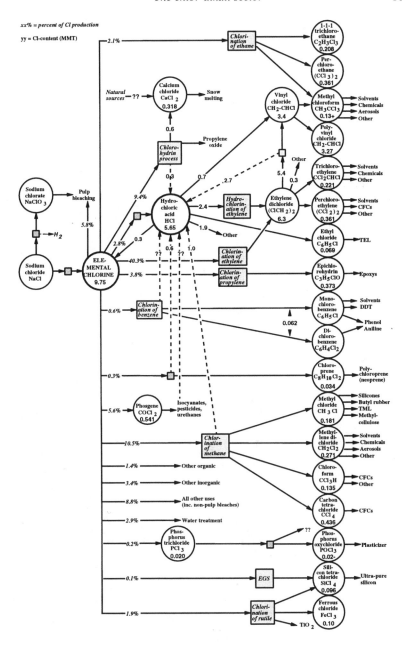

Data Source: EcoPlan.

Figure 10.5: *Chlorine process-product flows: Western Europe, 1987*

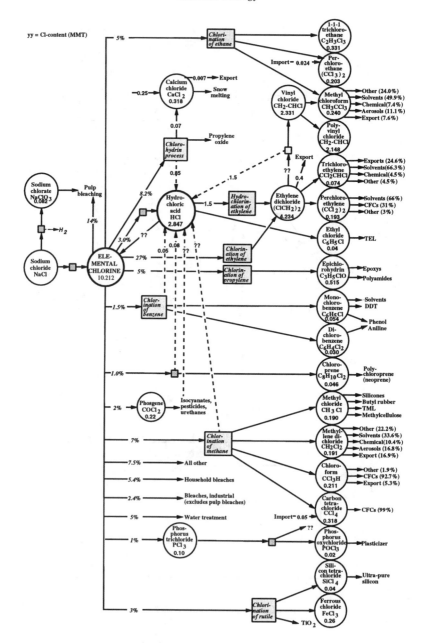

Data Sources: USITC 1992; IEI 1991.

Figure 10.6: Chlorine process-product flows: US, 1988

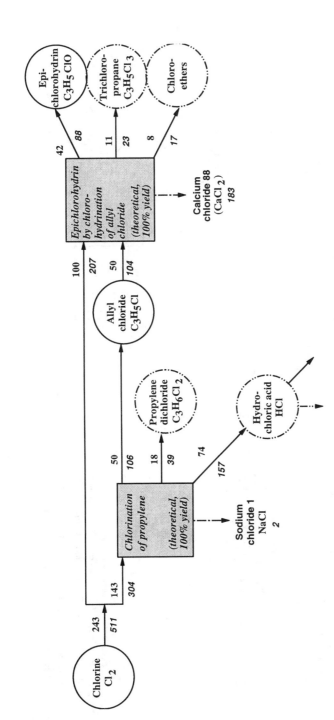

Figure 10.7: Chlorine to epichlorohydrin process-product flow: US and Europe, 1988 (kMT of Cl)

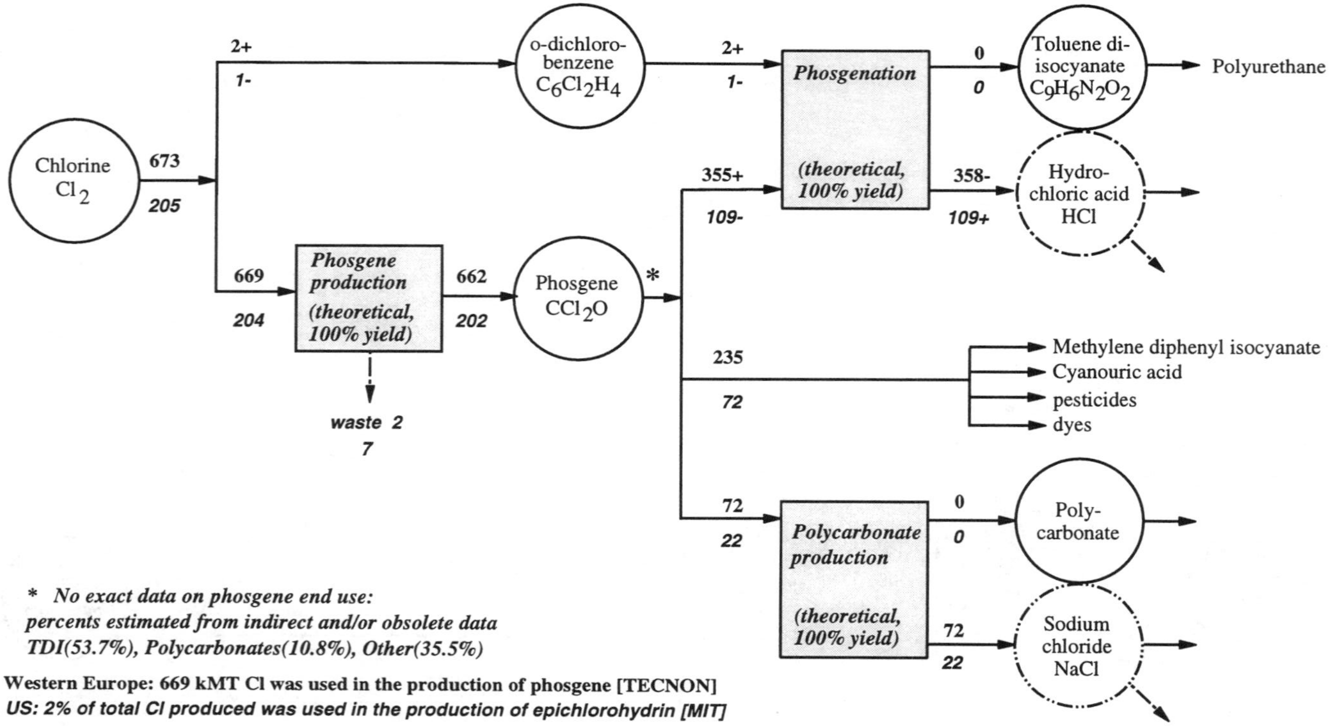

* *No exact data on phosgene end use:*
percents estimated from indirect and/or obsolete data
TDI(53.7%), Polycarbonates(10.8%), Other(35.5%)

Western Europe: 669 kMT Cl was used in the production of phosgene [TECNON]
US: 2% of total Cl produced was used in the production of epichlorohydrin [MIT]

Figure 10.8: Chlorine through phosgene process-product flow: US and Europe, 1988 (kMT of Cl)

10.3. WASTES AND RECYCLING LOOPS IN THE CHLOR-ALKALI SECTOR

Wastes are obviously candidates for byproducts and/or recycling. One surprising recycling loop is a link between propylene oxide manufacture via the chlorohydrin process. While HCl is a potential byproduct of the process, there are a few plants where the HCl is neutralized by caustic soda and recycled as NaCl through the electrolytic cell. (In this case the caustic soda is also recycled.) Obviously there would be some potential benefit in recycling the salt waste from titanium dioxide production in the same manner, if chlorine were produced on site.

Chlorine itself is recycled in at least two processes, the toluene di-isocyanate process and the pyrolysis of monochlorodifluoromethane to yield TFE.

Most HCl (over 97% in Europe) is recovered as a byproduct of one of the many chlorination processes (Ecotec 1995). This is an important form of recycling. This happens because chlorination is often an intermediate step in a complex process, often followed by a subsequent step in which (some or all of) the chlorine is released as HCl. The best-known example is probably the production of vinyl chloride (VCM) via direct chlorination of ethylene to ethylene dichloride (EDC), which is then catalytically split to yield VCM and HCl. The HCl is normally used in a complementary process in which HCl reacts with ethylene and oxygen to yield more EDC (and water). These two processes are normally balanced to consume all the HCl that is produced. (In Europe, some VCM is also produced by reacting HCl with acetylene — an older process that has been phased out in the US because of the much lower cost of ethylene.) HCl is derived as a byproduct of other processes, especially the production of VCM from EDC and from phosgene production. Other examples include allyl chloride production (below), silicon purification by the Siemens process and silicone manufacturing.

Apart from process waste, a small amount of HCl is now recovered by burning chlorinated hydrocarbon (CHC) wastes. This seems to be relatively recent. According to the survey, about 81% of HCl is used as a feedstock for manufacturing chlorinated compounds, 14% is used for pH control or neutralization of alkaline wastes, and 5% is sold as such for use outside the sector (Ecotec 1995). For purposes of comparison, data from another consultant gives HCl sources and uses in Europe for 1989 were shown in Figures 10.3 and 10.4.

Another small but interesting recyclable chlorine carrier is Silicon tetrachloride, $SiCl_4$. This is a byproduct of the Siemens process for silicon purification, mentioned above. Most of the $SiCl_4$ is apparently used in manufacturing other silicon chemicals. (See Chapter 11, Silicon for more discussion of this possibility.)

There are a number of chlorination processes in which the yield of useful main product is not a very high fraction of the chlorinated material, resulting in either significant waste or a very complex set of internal recycling loops. The chlorination of propylene to allyl chloride and thence to epichlorohydrin (a co-polymer for epoxy resins) is a good example. In this process 0.71 tonnes of propylene and 2.2 tonnes of chlorine, plus 0.76 tonnes of lime (CaO) are required as inputs, to yield 1.0 tonnes of epichlorohydrin, 0.62 tonnes of HCl and 0.26 tonnes of dichloropropylene, plus roughly 1.8 tonnes of wastes. (Of this, about 1.50 tonnes is $CaCl_2$, but the remainder, 0.3 tonnes, consists of other organo-chlorines.) It is worth noting that, for every tonne of chlorine embodied in the final product, between 4 and 5 tonnes are lost in waste streams.

In the first step the main products are allyl chloride and HCl, along with excess propylene. The organic fraction consists of a number of fractions, which can be separated by distillation. The lowest-boiling fraction is rich in saturated chlorides such as 1,2 dichloropropane. The heavy boiling fraction is rich in 1,3 dichloropropene, as well as breakdown products such as benzene, tars and carbon. It is sometimes used as a feedstock for fumigants or pesticides (e.g. *DD*, or *Telone II*). In the second stage of the process, the intermediate fraction is reacted with hypochlorous acid (chlorine dissolved in water) yielding another stream that must be gravity separated once again. The heavier fraction goes on to the final stage of the reaction (with lime) to yield epichlorohydrin and trichloropropane, which must be separated. The latter can be recycled internally as a solvent. The waste stream consists mostly of calcium chloride, which can be recovered in principle, but rarely in practice, because of lack of markets.[4]

A more dramatic (but small tonnage) example is the pesticide *lindane*, which is the purified gamma isomer of hexachlorocyclohexane (HCH), also called benzene hexachloride (BHC). The biologically active element accounts for only 14% of the BHC; the remainder must be converted to some other useful product, or else burned to recover HCl. According to Ecotec, a very tiny fraction is actually disposed of in other ways, such as landfill. Possible conversion products include hexachlorobenzene, perchlorbenzene and trichlorobenzene. The latter can be used as a starting point to produce other biocides, such as the herbicide *dicamba*. It is also used as a transformer fluid (replacing PCBs).

10.4.   USES OF CAUSTIC SODA

Major uses of caustic soda in Western Europe (1992) are summarized in Figure 10.9. World data is given on an aggregated end-use basis, for 1994 in

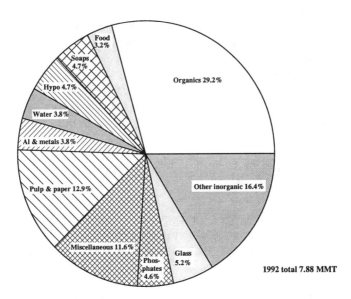

Source: Detournay 1993.

Figure 10.9: Western European consumption of caustic soda by end-use,
1992

Table 10.3: World demand for NaOH by end-use, 1994

Use Category	Europe	US	Japan	Rest of World
Organic chemicals	29%	36%	35%	34%
Pulp and paper	13%	21%	13%	15%
Inorganic chemicals	27%	16%	15%	13%
Miscellaneous	31%	27%	37%	38%

Source: Consulting Resources Corporation (for US Bureau of Mines).

Table 10.3. The 'miscellaneous' category includes neutralization of acid chemical wastes, manufacture of cellulosics (rayon and cellophane); soaps and
detergents; textiles; gasoline refining; water treatment; household products;
tertiary oil recovery (in the US) and exports.

Taking into account neutralization of acid wastes, soap/detergent manufacturing and some miscellaneous chemical products, 56–60% of caustic soda in
Europe is consumed within the chemical manufacturing sector. Except for
detergents, virtually all sodium chemicals based on caustic soda (or, for that

matter, on sodium carbonate) are dissipative, either within the chemical sector or in other manufacturing processes. Virtually none, except detergents, is actually embodied in products. The ultimate fate of most of the sodium hydroxide consumed in the chemical industry is to react with either sulfuric acid, yielding sodium sulfate, or with hydrochloric acid, yielding sodium chloride as a waste. Sodium sulfate has more uses (notably in the manufacture of pulp for paper), whence sulfuric acid is the preferable reagent where either acid could be used.

10.5. FACTORS AFFECTING CHLORINE SUPPLY/ DEMAND

In both the US and Western Europe the demand for chlorine has historically been stronger and less elastic than the demand for caustic soda. In effect, chlorine was the primary product and caustic the byproduct. However, the situation has been changing. In 1984 nearly 18% of caustic soda produced in Europe was exported. This has declined rather steadily to 10.5% in 1991 (Detournay 1993). Meanwhile, caustic soda spot prices have increased sharply, from a range of $40–$80 per tonne in the years 1984–86 to a peak of nearly $500/tonne in 1987. Subsequently the spot price declined moderately, but by 1992 it still remained about $300/tonne (ibid.).[5]

This peculiar price behavior is a consequence of both real and anticipated declines in the demand for chlorine in certain applications. The peak price for sodium hydroxide coincided with the signing of the Montreal Protocol (1987), which called for the gradual phasing out of chloro-fluorocarbons, because of concern about the 'ozone hole'. Meanwhile, the use of chlorinated pesticides and herbicides, polychlorinated biphenyls (PCBs) and several major chlorinated solvents had already been declining for a number of years. Demand for chlorinated solvents from 1986 through 1992 is shown in Appendix A, Table A.16.

Another factor depressing demand for chlorine has been the discovery of traces of highly carcinogenic dioxins in paper. This was traced to the chlorine pulp bleaching process. A major public outcry arose in Europe against chlorine-bleached paper (led by Greenpeace in Germany). The Scandinavian pulp and paper industry quickly responded to consumer demand for 'chlorine-free' paper by publicly committing itself to eliminate the use of chlorine bleaching. The primary alternative to chlorine is some form of oxygen bleaching, initially using chlorine dioxide (from sodium chlorate),[6] but perhaps eventually using ozone or hydrogen peroxide. This trend has spread. As noted above, already by 1987, only 5.5% of chlorine produced in Europe was used for pulp bleaching, as compared to 14% in the US. By 1994 these figures were down to 1% and 9% respectively.

10.6. ENVIRONMENT, HEALTH, TECHNOLOGY AND POLICIES

The environmental dangers associated with chlorinated pesticides (such as DDT), PCBs, CFCs and so on are rather well known by now and need not be reviewed here. They are relevant, however, in so far as they constitute the background for an increasingly determined effort by the environmental group Greenpeace (with support from others) for an across-the-board ban on all production and use of chlorine, on the grounds that it is implicated in so many toxic, carcinogenic, mutagenic or ozone-destroying substances that its use — at least in organic form — should be eliminated altogether. The main focus of this effort is on the ubiquitous plastic PVC.

In support of the anti-PVC argument, it is true that both major intermediates in PVC production, ethylene dichloride (EDC) and vinyl chloride monomer (VCM) are classed as hazardous. VCM, however, is polymerized to make the durable and harmless plastic PVC.[7] PVC accounts for nearly 31% of European elemental chlorine output. On the other hand, PVC does not lock up the chlorine permanently. All PVC products have finite lifetimes, ranging from a few weeks for bottles to more than 30 years (perhaps much more) for structural products such as pipes.

The only significant hazard associated with PVC, after it has been produced, is fire. This hazard applies largely to short-lived PVC products, primarily bottles and other containers that may be incinerated (see Chapter 12, Packaging). There is a lesser but not negligible hazard associated with PVC embodied in structures. Though it is not particularly combustible, PVC will burn. In a fire the chlorine in PVC is largely converted to hydrochloric acid (HCl), and plasticizers, stabilizers and other additives, if any, can be released.[8] This contributes slightly to environmental acidification. However the major environmental concern is the possibility of generating traces of toxic phosgene and carcinogenic dioxins.

To put this into perspective, a German study estimated the average annual intake of PCDD/PCDF (toxic equivalents) from various combustion sources as follows (Fonds Chem 1992):

Household refuse incineration	432
Non-ferrous metal refining	380
Household coal burning (for heat)	164
Gasoline (leaded)	20.9
Medical wastes	5.4
Cable insulation smoldering	4.6
All other	4.4
Total identified	1011.3

It is probably fair to say that PVC is the major (but not the only) source of dioxins from household waste (mainly packaging products) incineration, medical wastes (also packaging) and electrical cable insulation. On the other hand there are other significant sources, especially coal-burning and non-ferrous metal refining.

There are also other threats that might lead to further regulation of chlorine use. All of this has combined to create an apparent potential shortage of caustic soda. Prices in the spot market reflect such expectations.

In response to the Greenpeace attack, the chemical industry — through the Chlorine Institute — has rallied strongly in defense of chlorine as an indispensable component of modern technological society. The truth is that some uses are surely not indispensable. Indeed, several have been banned outright for a number of years. The chances of a total ban still seem remote, at this point. Restrictions on certain uses of chlorine (e.g. solvents and PVC packaging) would seem to make more sense. But such things are not always decided rationally, and there is always the possibility of further scientific discoveries implicating chlorine.[9] It would therefore be advisable for government and academia to begin consideration, in cold blood, of the possible implications of such a ban.

To permit such a study, however, the chemical industry will have to cooperate by making available much more data than it has traditionally been willing to release to the public. The industry consistently refuses to publish production, consumption, trade and stockpile data even for extremely toxic compounds that have long been banned (such as DDT and PVCs). The argument that such information must remain proprietary for 'competitive reasons' rings hollow. The more likely explanation is that the industry prefers to keep the numbers hidden for fear of embarrassment. It seems very unlikely that the public will be persuaded to support the industry position on the basis of technical and economic arguments that depend entirely on 'proprietary' data that cannot be released for scrutiny. In the present circumstances, Greenpeace may be able to make a persuasive case that the industry must have something nasty to hide. The only way for industry to take and hold the 'moral high ground' is to release the data.

NOTES(10)

1. One source calculates that annual volcanic emissions amount to approximately 11 MMT of HCl.
2. However, the presence of organo-chlorine molecules in the environment may have been overlooked.

   According to Dr. Gordon Gribble of Dartmouth, there are nearly 2000 different organo-chlorides and organo-halogen chemicals that naturally occur in our biosphere, 700 of which were discovered in the last 10 years. For example, about 100 different halogen compounds are in one species of edible Hawaiian seaweed. One species of Florida Gulf acorn worm produces 20 different organo-halogen compounds. ... He states that biomass generates about 5 million tons of natural methyl chloride annually. (Kostick 1994)

3. In this connection, chlorine from industrial activities is not necessarily the only source. As mentioned in a previous note, as much as 11 MMT of HCl is liberated annually by vulcanism. While HCl is normally washed out of the troposphere by rain, volcanic eruptions can (and do) sometimes pierce the troposphere and inject quantities of material into the stratosphere where it has the potential of interacting with ozone. This problem is most acute in the polar regions, where the stratosphere is closer to the earth's surface than in the tropics.

4. A more detailed discussion of possibilities for reducing waste and emissions in this process sequence can be found in Noyes (1993, pp. 438–40).

5. In the early 1990s several Wyoming producers of sodium carbonate (from evaporite Trona deposits) began producing sodium hydroxide by reacting sodium carbonate with lime, with byproduct calcium carbonate (that is recycled to lime by calcination). This continued until the market for electrolytic caustic soda returned to balance (Kostick 1994).

6. The surprisingly large production of inorganic chlorine chemicals in Japan may be partly attributable to large-scale production of sodium chlorate.

7. There may be some hazard associated with plasticizers and other additives, including cadmium.

8. The most important PVC plasticizers are Di (2 ethyl hexyl) phthalate (DEHP) and t-dioctyl phthalate (DOP). Production of DEHP in Germany in 1986 was 360 kMT, with net exports of 150 kMT. Production of DOP in 1986 was 234 kMT, with net exports of 141 kMT. Both domestic production and exports were used primarily in PVC (Balzer and Rauhut 1987).

9. In this connection, recent epidemiological evidence of a decline in male fertility, among both human and non-human species, has convinced some scientists that the likely culprit is not one chemical but a whole class of 'estrogen-like' chemicals including poly-aromatic hydrocarbons (PAHs) and especially their chlorinated derivatives. The latter — of which DDT and PCBs are examples — seem to cause problems primarily by virtue of being very stable and nearly immune to attack by micro-organisms. As a consequence of both properties they tend to bio-accumulate in the fatty tissues of higher animals where they can interfere with normal hormonal functions, including reproductive functions.

11. Electronic grade silicon (EGS) for semiconductors

Paolo Frankl, Howard Lee and Nichole Wolfgang

11.1. SUMMARY

The electronics industry is a very large and important one based very largely on the special semiconductive properties of a single element: silicon. For use as a semiconductor this material must be extremely pure. Silicon itself is the commonest metal and the second-commonest element in the earth's crust, so it will never be scarce. On the other hand, the purification process is extremely demanding and energy intensive. The cost of ultra-pure electronic grade silicon (EGS) is many times higher than the cost of the 'raw' material from which it is made, metallurgical grade silicon (MGS). At the same time, the wastes from this process — including a mix of chlorinated compounds — far exceed, in volume, the quantity of the finished material. This is a situation probably unique in all of industry except for the case of pharmaceuticals manufacturing.

The quantity of EGS consumed today, worldwide, is only of the order of 1000 tonnes. This is because the pace of miniaturization has been keeping up with the expansion of the industry in terms of unit sales. Thus, even though the silicon purification process and the subsequent chip manufacturing processes are extraordinarily 'dirty', the overall quantities of wastes generated are not enormous by industrial standards. Nevertheless, there are important opportunities for waste recycling that are apparently not being fully exploited at present.

Starting with 100 units of MGS, we can expect no more than 20 units of polycrystalline EGS. This, in turn, yields about 10 units of finished monocrystalline wafers and 3 units of finished semiconductor chips. Putting it another way, for each 3 units of finished chips (used in final products) to be disposed of at the end of a useful life of perhaps 3 years, there were 7 units of unusable chips and chip fragments, 10 units of contaminated wafer fragments and 80 units (silicon content) of chlorinated silicon chemicals that had to be

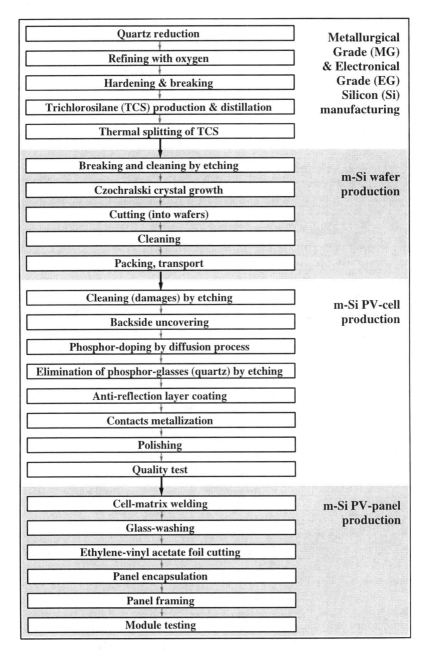

Figure 11.1: *Process chain for monocrystalline silicon PV-panel manufacture*

disposed of, or sold as byproducts. The chlorine content of these unaccounted-for chemicals amounts to 320 units, more or less. On a global basis, this amounted to about 100 kMT of chlorine in 1988 — not a trivial amount. In addition, on the order of 600 units of etchants and solvents were consumed (and disposed of) in the chip-making process. In tonnage terms, this adds up to 192 kMT in 1988.

These numbers raise major concerns, especially in view of the likely future penetration of PV in the energy market and the consequent rapid growth of silicon consumption and processing. In fact, today's PV cell manufacturing process (both for mono- and poly-crystalline silicon cells) is very inefficient and causes much more pollution (and higher costs) than necessary. The EGS standard of purity is not really needed for energy production purposes; indeed, PV cell producers are currently exploring ways to manufacture so-called 'solar grade silicon' (SGS) polycrystalline cells. These cells would be only slightly less efficient than monocrystalline silicon cells, but their manufacturing process would avoid the intermediate steps of EGS and monocrystalline wafer production, thus being simpler, less material and energy intensive, less polluting, and much cheaper.

The development of more efficient silicon purification processes for PV cell manufacturing, either chlorine free (see Figure 11.1) or at least sufficiently integrated to recycle the chlorine internally, constitutes a major technological challenge. It may also be a real business opportunity. But more than that, it is a worldwide necessity if significant damage to the environment is to be avoided. Here is a case where process change and pollution prevention would be far more cost-effective than 'end-of-pipe' treatment of toxic and hazardous wastes.

Goals of public policy: increase materials use efficiency in the silicon purification and manufacturing processes; reduce toxic and hazardous emissions associated with these processes, especially in view of potential future growth in the PV and semiconductor industries.

11.2.   INTRODUCTION

The electronics industry, of which the semiconductor industry is a part, has had a record of extremely fast growth over the past 40 years. It is surely the fastest-growing manufacturing industry. To give a sense of this growth, about 8 million copies of Intel's 286 microprocessor were sold in the peak year of 1988. Its successor, the 386, peaked at about 19 million in 1991. The 486 was expected to reach sales of 35 million units in 1994, with the Pentium taking over leading-edge markets in 1995 (*The Economist*, October 15–21, 1994, p. 79). However, growth in tonnage terms appears to have ceased, at least for the moment. In recent years miniaturization trends appear to have outstripped volume demand trends. As a result, in 1988 world output of electronic grade silicon (EGS) accounted for barely half of capacity, and the situation has barely changed since.

The production of silicon chips requires relatively trivial amounts of physical materials. Worldwide production of metallurgical grade silicon (MGS) in 1990 was about 800 000 tonnes. Of this, about 4% (32 000 tonnes or 32 kMT) was converted to ultra-pure electronic grade and used for semiconductor devices. Of that, only about 10% (or 0.4% of MGS) was devoted to photovoltaic (PV) cells (LES/ETH 1994). The silicon purification process is very inefficient: only about 750 tonnes of silicon are embodied in the total (1988) world chip production.

This means that more than 31 kMT (97%) of the silicon metal was lost *en route* to the final product. We are unable to determine how much (if any) of this lost material is chemically recycled or used for other products. However, the concern with ultra-purity makes recycling dubious. More worrisome: about 4 tonnes of chlorine is used for each tonne of MGS processed. We cannot account for the fate of this chlorine; some may be utilized beneficially or recycled, but there are indications that much of it is wasted.

Looking ahead, the use of silicon for PV cells has barely begun, although growth is rapid (Figure 11.2). Worldwide PV market penetration in 1990 was

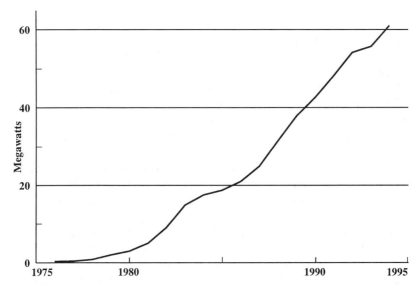

Data Source: ENEL (Italy).

Figure 11.2:   *World photovoltaic shipments, 1972–1994*

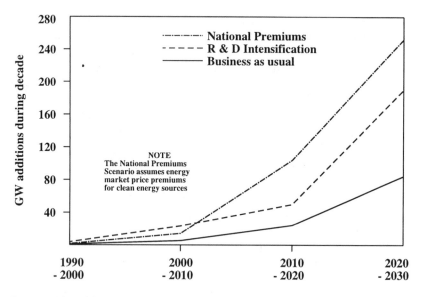

Source: Adapted from SERI 1990.

Figure 11.3:   Incremental market penetration of photovoltaics in the US

about 50 MW of additional capacity added per year, which corresponds to a 1990 share of 0.4% of world MGS production (3.2 kMT). A recent projection by the Solar Energy Research Institute (SERI) of the US Department of Energy is shown in Figure 11.3 (SERI 1990). According to an optimistic DOE scenario, PV capacity could grow annually by as much as 20 gigawatts (GW), in the US alone, during the decade 2020–30. This could correspond to a worldwide growth of 100 GW per year.

Assuming current PV technology and current silicon production processes and yields, this scenario would imply an increase in current EGS output levels by a factor of 2000 over a few decades! PV uses would then far outstrip computer, communications and other electronic uses. It would require an annual output of MGS of 6.5 MMT (8 times the present level). Requirements for other chemicals used to convert MGS to EGS (notably hydrochloric acid) would also increase in proportion. Admittedly, a much smaller rate of growth of the PV market, coupled with more efficient use of silicon (e.g. in thin films) is regarded as much more probable, according to most experts. But this could still easily increase current levels of demand for silicon feedstock by a factor of 100 or more from present levels.

Fortunately, PV cells do not require the extremely high purity degree needed for electronic circuit elements ('chips'). Indeed, such a large amount

Table 11.1: Typical semiconductor fabrication gases, scrubbers and chemicals

Process	Material	Typical Chemicals	Formula	Recommended Scrubbing Stages	Recommended Scrubbing Liquid
D e p o s i t i o n	Silicon nitride (Si_3N_4)	Ammonia Arsine Dichlorosilane Phosphine Silane	NH_3 AsH_3 SiH_2Cl_2 PH_3 SiH_4	Spray chamber, venturi, and packed bed	KOH and NaOCl
	Silicon dioxide (SiO_2)	Arsine Diborane Phosphine Silane	AsH_3 B_2H_2 PH_3 SiH_4	Spray chamber, venturi, and packed bed	KOH and NaOCl
	Poly-crystalline silicon (Si)	Dichlorosilane Silane	SiH_2Cl_2 SiH_4	Spray chamber, venturi, and packed bed; or multi-stage spray chamber and venturi	KOH
E t c h i n g	Polysilicon (Si)	Carbon tetrachloride Carbon tetrafluoride Fluorine/chlorine-based compounds	CCl_4 CF_4 CCl_2F_2 C_2F_6	Venturi and packed bed	KOH
	Silicon dioxide (SiO_2)	Trifluoromethane Carbon tetrafluoride Fluorine-based organic compounds	CHF_3 CF_4 CCl_2F_2 C_2F_6	Spray chamber, venturi, and packed bed	KOH
	Aluminum (Al)	Boron trichloride Carbon tetrachloride	BCl_3 CCl_4	Multi-stage spray chamber and venturi	KOH
	Aluminum oxide (Al_2O_3)	Boron trichloride Carbon tetrachloride	BCl_3 CCl_4	Multi-stage spray chamber and venturi	KOH
	Tin oxide (Sn_2O_3)	Carbon tetrachloride	CCl_4	Venturi and packed bed	H_2O
	Gallium arsenide (GaAs)	Carbon tetrachloride Dichlorofluoromethane Chlorine	CCl_4 CCl_2F_2 Cl_2	Venturi and packed bed	KOH
	Epitaxial Deposition	Arsine Dichlorosilane Phosphine Silane	AsH_3 SiH_2Cl_2 PH_3 SiH_4	Spray chamber, venturi, and packed bed	KOH and NaOCl

185

of silicon could not be supplied by scrap EGS. Thus, at some point, the cart will necessarily cease to drive the horse and silicon for PV will become a product in its own right: so-called solar grade polycrystalline silicon (SGS). Several MGS purification processes into SGS have been developed and are currently being successfully tested in PV industries (for more details see Figure 11.1).

Apart from EGS production *per se* the semiconductor fabrication industry consumes a number of extremely toxic and hazardous chemicals for processing, including cyanides, toluene, xylene, hydrofluoric acid, arsine, phosphine, diborane, boron tetrachloride, chlorinated solvents (carbon tetrachloride, dichloroethylene, trichloroethylene, trichloroethane), and chloro-fluorocarbons (CFCs). The latter have been identified as a primary cause of ozone depletion in the stratosphere. A list of the major chemicals used is shown in Table 11.1.

11.3.   SILICON-BASED ELECTRONICS: OVERVIEW

For clarity, the electronics equipment industry can be subdivided as shown in Figure 11.4. Waste emissions are concentrated in the five subsectors shown, which involve chemical processes and surface finishing operations. The remainder of the industry consists largely of assembly operations.

The first part of this chapter focuses on monocrystalline silicon wafer preparation and on process chemicals. This is unfortunately not a recognized subsector of the chemical industry. Hence detailed data on the industry are extremely scarce (most of the data we have relates to 1989 and earlier). Thus, we can only consider individual chemicals. Further sections deal with chip and solar cell fabrication stages, as summarized schematically in Figures 11.4 and 11.5.

Figure 11.5 summarizes the necessary steps for photovoltaic cell and module manufacturing. At present PV technology mainly relies on the same silicon purification processes used for the electronic devices industry. However, in principle several other silicon (and other semiconductor) preparation processes are possible, because of lower semiconductor purity requirements

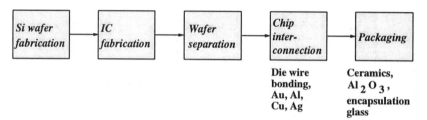

Figure 11.4:   Manufacturing process for semiconductor integrated circuits

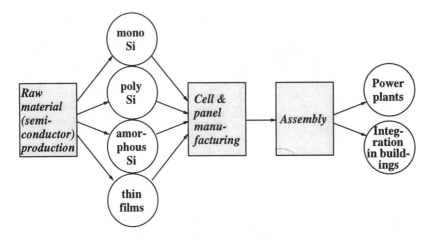

Figure 11.5:   Manufacturing process for photovoltaics

for power production. PV cell and module production steps also cause an environmental impact through the chemical and physical processes involved (doping, junction and electrical contact formation, anti-reflection surface treatment, cell encapsulation, and so on).

11.4.   MONOCRYSTALLINE SILICON WAFER PRODUCTION

As shown in Figure 11.6, there are three steps in the production of monocrystalline silicon wafers from crude metallurgical grade silicon (MGS). The latter is manufactured in large quantities for the steel industry by reducing silicon dioxide (sand) with coke in an electric furnace (top left). The next step consists of preparing ultra-pure polycrystalline electronic grade silicon (EGS) by a process of hydrochlorination and decomposition (top right), described later and shown in more detail in Figure 11.7.

As noted previously, world consumption of impure silicon metal (MGS) for polysilicon production in 1990 was roughly 32 kMT. This was 4% of total global output of metallurgical grade silicon (MGS). World consumption of electronic grade polysilicon (EGS) for wafer production in 1988 and 1989 was estimated at 6 to 7 kMT (Roskill Si 1991). Thus, assuming 1990 production levels to have been comparable, the apparent average yield of ultra-pure polysilicon from MGS was roughly 20%. In other words, 80% of the silicon metal input is lost in the purification process leading to polysilicon. (Estimates from other sources are discussed later.)

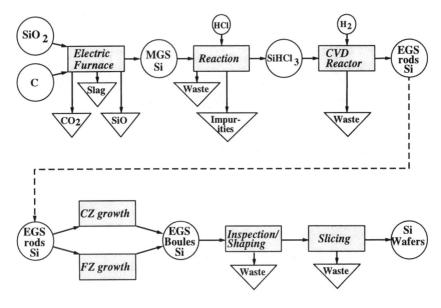

Figure 11.6:   Silicon wafer production process

The third stage in wafer production (Figure 11.6, bottom) is to break and
etch the polysilicon, melt and recrystallize rods of EGS into single crystal
silicon ingots or boules, and slice them into wafers. Again, there are two
processes for silicon crystal-growing: the (dominant) Czochralski (CZ) process or the so-called float-zone (FZ) process. Details of the last few steps are
provided later and summarized in Figure 11.8.

Worldwide consumption of finished silicon wafers in the same year (1988)
was reported to be 2.182 kMT, from a polysilicon input of 6–7 kMT (SRI
1989). This implies a very significant loss of nearly 4.4 kMT of polycrystalline
silicon along the process chain. Thus, the apparent average yield of the wafer
production process, starting from polycrystalline EGS and yielding
monocrystalline silicon wafers, was evidently about 33%. According to SRI's
market data, the *combined yield (MGS to usable wafers) was about 7%.*
Idealized process data discussed later give a slightly higher estimate (10%).
But this merely confirms the extremely low efficiency of this production
sequence.

One reason for the low efficiency of these processes is that they are still
batch processes being implemented on a small scale, at least in chemical
industry terms. Another reason is that the raw materials have low value. A
third reason is relative lack of competition. Only a few companies produce
the basic chemicals. Silicon wafer production in 1988 (worldwide) had a

market value of approximately \$2.13 billion (\$2.13 × 10⁹), or \$976 per kg. This was produced from inputs of MGS valued at \$48 million (about 1.5 \$/kg) (Roskill Si 1991; LES/ETH 1994). Thus the value *added* by the purification, crystallization and slicing processes — as reflected in part by the very low yield — was more than forty times the value of the raw material (MGS) consumed. This provides some indication of the technological difficulties involved in the purification process.

As noted above, 2.182 kMT of silicon wafers (1988) was the raw material used to fabricate all integrated circuits (ICs) and discrete semiconductor devices, including PV cells. In the case of Japan, single crystal silicon wafer consumption in 1988 was 1200 tonnes, including 90 tonnes of imports. It is possible to estimate the mass of the resulting products, as shown in Table 11.2 and the accompanying notes. The probable mass of ICs and discrete

Table 11.2:   Weight estimates for discrete semiconductor devices and integrated circuits, Japan, 1988

Type	Typical size (cm × cm)[1]	Quantity produced (million units)[2]	Estimated total mass (MT)[3]
Discrete devices			
Si diodes	0.25 × 0.25	20 519	136.6
Si rectifiers	0.50 × 0.50	5 309	141.3
Transistors (< 1 Watt)	0.10 × 0.10	16 533	17.6
(> 1 Watt)	0.25 × 0.25	2 532	16.9
Field effect	0.25 × 0.25	914	6.1
Thermistors	0.10 × 0.10	523	1.1
Varistors	π(0.15 × 0.15)	1 039	7.8
Thyristors	0.25 × 0.25	357	2.4
		47 726	329.9
Integrated Circuits	0.25 × 0.25	14 296	98.3
TOTAL		62 022	428.1

Notes:
1. Dr S. Wojtzcuk, Spire Corporation, provided data on typical dimensions.
2. Source: EIAJ 1990, Electronic Industries Association of Japan, *Annual Data Book*.
3. Typical thickness is assumed to be 18 mils (0.0457 cm). The density of silicon is 2.33 g/cm³. From this and the average cross-sectional area it is possible to estimate the mass.
4. SRI gives the consumption of silicon wafers in the production of these devices in Japan in 1988 as 1200 MT (including net imports of 90 MT). Thus the yield efficiency is 428.1/1200 = 35.7%.
5. Worldwide Si wafer consumption in 1988 is given by SRI as 2182 MT. On the assumption that the same efficiencies are achieved worldwide, we can calculate the worldwide production of silicon devices as 0.357 × 2182 = 779 MT.

devices made in Japan in 1988 can be estimated from data on the numbers of each type of device, the average area in square cm (estimated), and the average wafer thickness, or density. The result of this calculation was 428 tonnes of 'chips', plus or minus a few.

This calculation implies an apparent 'yield' for the Japanese semiconductor industry in 1988 of 35.7% (chips from wafers). It further implies a total conversion rate from MGS to chips ranging from 2.5 to 3.55% for the entire sequence, starting with MGS, depending on the yield assumed for the previous process steps. If the rest of the world achieved the same yield in the fabrication stage as the Japanese, the total mass of semiconductor products produced in 1988 must have been in the range of 750–800 tonnes. This is consistent with recent estimates of about 1200 tonnes for 1993–94.

The total market value of Japanese semiconductor products in 1988 was 2.968 billion yen (¥2.968 × 10^9), according to official Japanese government statistics (*Electronics Facts and Figures*, 1988). The Japanese, then, accounted for about 40% of world (merchant) output of chips (*The Economist*, February 18, 1989). Assuming an exchange rate for 1988 of 128.15 yen/dollar, we estimate the value of worldwide semiconductor production for that year at $57.9 billion ($57.9 × 10^9), or about $75 000 per kg of silicon embodied in finished chips (excluding packaging and support materials).

According to the method of estimation illustrated above it was noted that Japan apparently produced 425 tonnes of chips in 1988, out of a world total of perhaps 750 tonnes, or nearly 57% of the total mass of chips.[1] At first sight this appears inconsistent with Japan's 40% market share in dollar terms. However, the apparent inconsistency is partly explained by the fact that Japan held a much larger market share of the discrete devices and low-value semiconductor chips (used, primarily, in the consumer electronics industry) and of the mass-produced memory chips. By contrast, Japan held a significantly lower share of the market for very high-value custom chips and microprocessor chips (such as those produced by Intel and Motorola), which were predominantly made in the US. A summary is given in Table 11.3.

Quantitative data on inputs to the chip manufacturing process as a whole is extremely scarce, though some figures are available for Japan (Appendix A, Table A.17). On the order of 35 kMT of strong acids and alkalis, plus 27 kMT of organic solvents were used in Japan for semiconductor manufacturing processes in 1988/89. World totals would have been at least double (assuming the Japanese had 50% of the market in terms of mass). In any case, negligible quantities of these chemicals are actually embodied in the final product. Virtually all are finally discarded as wastes. We discuss the question of toxic and hazardous wastes later.

Table 11.3: Silicon price and market summary

	MGS	Poly-EGS	Mono-Si wafers	Chips
Tonnage worldwide for chip production (MT)	32000 (1990) (LES/ETH 1994)	6581 (1988) (SRI) 6000—7000 (1988—90) (Roskill)	2182 (1988) (SRI)	about 750 (our estimate from Japanese data assuming same yield)
Tonnage Japan 1988 (MT)	—	—	1200 (SRI)	428 (our calculation)
Market worldwide 1988	$48 million ($1.5/kg * 32000 MT)	$283 million (SRI)	$2.13 billion (SRI)	$57.9 billion (our estimate from Japanese data assuming 40% market share)
Market Japan 1988	—	—	—	¥2968 billion (Electronics Facts…) ¥3104 billion (The Inter. Electr. Ind.) (about $23.16 billion)
Specific price ($/kg)	1.3–1.5 (1988–90) (Roskill)	75 (1980) (Roskill) 40–60 (1992) (Brenneman et al.)	$976 = $2.13 billion/2182 MT (our calculation from SRI data)	77200 = $57.9 billion/750 MT (our calculation from (Japanese data)

11.5. SILICON PROCESSES AND PROCESS CHEMICALS

We now return to consider the wafer production process, *per se*, in more detail. As noted earlier, the wafer manufacturing process can be split into three sub-processes: (1) production of metallurgical grade silicon (MGS), (2) MGS purification into polycrystalline electronic grade silicon (EGS), and (3) recrystallization of polycrystalline EGS into monocrystalline EGS boules, which are then cut into monocrystalline Si wafers.

Metallurgical Grade Silicon (MGS) Production

The first step in the sequence is production of metallurgical grade silicon (MGS) from quartzite (sand) in an electric furnace.[2] Yields at this stage are said to be about 90%, based on inputs. The product is silicon metal with a purity of 98–99%. The process is very similar to that for manufacturing ferro-alloys. It need not be described further here.

MGS Purification into Polycrystalline EGS

Next, there are several extant processes for producing ultra-pure[3] polysilicon (EGS) from 98–99% pure metallurgical grade silicon metal (MGS). The major process accounting for 98% of 1988–89 output of polysilicon is the Siemens process. This process produces polycrystalline EGS by the reduction of trichlorosilane ($SiHCl_3$) with hydrogen gas (Figure 11.7, right).

Gaseous trichlorosilane ($SiHCl_3$) is made by reacting crude silicon with hydrogen chloride gas (HCl) in a fluidized bed (Figure 11.7, left). The 'once through' yield is about 90%, with hydrogen gas and silicon tetrachloride ($SiCl_4$) as dominant byproducts (O'Mara *et al.* 1990). The latter can be partially recycled to recover additional trichlorosilane, bringing the overall yield up to 92% or 93%. Other waste products include other chlorosilanes, silane (SiH_4) and chlorides of phosphorus, boron, arsenic and antimony, arising from impurities in MGS.

Subsequently the trichlorosilane can be catalytically decomposed in a chemical vapor deposition (CVD) reactor, yielding pure polycrystalline EGS and other waste products including $SiCl_4$ and HCl for recycling. This process is rather inefficient; a 'good' conversion rate is said to be about 23% (ibid.). Thus, 100 units of MGS yields, at most, about 21 units of polycrystalline EGS. A more detailed German estimate (Hagedorn and Hellriegel 1992; LES/ETH 1994) set the overall yield figure lower, at 18%. These figures compare reasonably well with the apparent 20% industry average calculated previously from the EGS/MGS ratio.

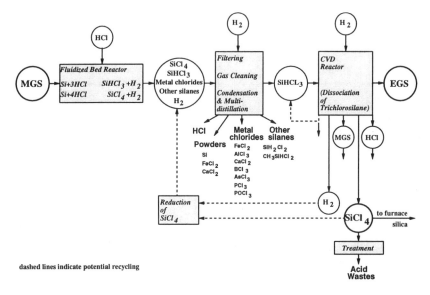

Figure 11.7: Preparation of ultra-pure polycrystalline EGS silicon from crude MGS

In an attempt to verify data provided on processes described by Hagedorn and Hellriegel (Hagedorn and Hellriegel 1992), we did several calculations. The calculated numbers were obtained by working through the process from output to inputs. For a single monocrystalline silicon wafer, 16.86 g of polysilicon are required. For this, a stoichiometric minimum of 243.9 g $SiHCl_3$ is needed. Taking into account a reported 43 g of unreacted $SiHCl_3$, a total input of 286.9 g is implied. This corresponds to an 85% conversion of $SiHCl_3$ to Si. This reaction produces, as a byproduct, approximately 204.0 g $SiCl_4$. Using Hagedorn's estimate of 12.6 g H_2 as an input, we have an excess hydrogen output of 1.2 g. This result deviated less than 1% from Hagedorn's H_2 output data. For HCl, our calculated value was 21.9 g; Hagedorn's, which includes the output from the fluidized bed reactor, was 27.0 g.

Our computed output of $SiCl_4$ from the fluidized bed reactor is 335.2 – 204.0 = 131.2g of $SiCl_4$, where the first number is the total output given in Hagedorn and Hellriegel (ibid.) and the second number is the calculated output of the CVD reactor (in addition to the calculated 286.9 g $SiHCl_3$). The MGS input was calculated to be at least 81.19 g, not taking into account additional amounts needed to generate the outputs of Si powder and other silanes. The HCl input was determined to be at least 351.4 g. We emphasize that the numbers obtained are rough estimates at best and do not take into account all possible outputs from the reaction, since the data necessary to describe the

Table 11.4:   Verification

	Hagedorn (grams)	Calculated (grams)
Reactants		
MGS	93.4	>81.2
Hydrochloric acid	368.7	>351.4
Hydrogen	12.6	see col. 1
Main product		
EGS	16.9	see col. 1
By-products		
Silicon tetrachloride	335.2	see col. 1
Trichlorosilane	43.0	see col. 1
Hydrogen	13.7	13.8
Atmospheric emissions		
Hydrogen	13.7	13.8
Waste water		
Metal chlorides	3.8	see col. 1
Hydrochloric acid	27.0	21.9

reactions was not all available. The calculated values differ from those given by Hagedorn and Hellriegel by a maximum of 13% for any mass stream, effectively verifying their results. The simulation results are shown in Table 11.4.

Silicon tetrachloride can be recycled by reduction to trichlorosilane. There are two major methods. One method is the reaction of $SiCl_4$ with H_2 in a fluidized bed of MGS. This reaction takes place in the presence of a copper catalyst at an approximate temperature of 800 K and an approximate pressure of 3 megaPascals (MPa), resulting in a conversion rate of up to 37%:

$$3SiHCl_4 + 2H_2 + Si \rightarrow 4SiHCl_3$$

Another method, described by Weigert, Meyer-Simon and Schwartz, involves heating a mixture of $SiCl_4$ and H_2 to about 1175°K. The chemicals approach thermal equilibrium at this temperature. This results in a conversion of up to 37% to $SiHCl_3$. (We worry, however, about the composition and disposition of the remainder.)

Simulations of both methods were performed. A conversion of 23% was achieved when 335.2 g $SiCl_4$ and 13.0 g H_2 reached equilibrium at 1175°K. The Weigert, Meyer-Simon and Schwartz method produced approximately 60 g of $SiHCl_3$. This shows that the recycle of $SiCl_4$ is technically feasible. However, at present one can expect to achieve relatively low yields, at best. Nevertheless, it is possible, at least in theory, to improve on the present system.

Monocrystalline Silicon Wafer Preparation

The product of Siemens silicon purification process is polycrystalline silicon. However, polycrystalline silicon is full of electronically-active defects (dislocations, dangling bonds, etc.) which affect the semiconductor conductivity and thus the device speed. In other words, electronic devices require single-crystal semiconductor material for optimal operation.

The conversion of polysilicon EGS to wafers (Figure 11.8) involves three further steps, breaking and etching (cleaning) by a mixture of hydrofluoric and nitric acids, Czochralski crystal growth (in order to produce exceptional purity monocrystalline silicon, sometimes Float-Zoning is also used), and cutting. The losses in these two steps (largely in cutting) amount to slightly over 50% of the input material (Hagedorn and Hellriegel 1992; LES/ETH

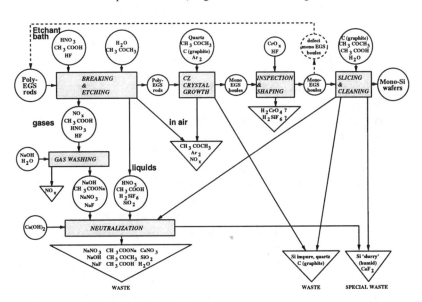

Figure 11.8:   Monocrystalline silicon wafer production from polycrystalline EGS

1994). Thus, the overall efficiency of conversion of MGS to usable wafers is about 10% at maximum.

11.6. SILICON CHIP FABRICATION

The last stage of the manufacturing process, chip fabrication, starts from monocrystalline wafers. Wafers undergo five major processing steps which transform them into semiconductor devices. These steps may be repeated a number of times in various sequences, depending on the specific design.

1. *Oxidation* is the process in which wafers are heated in the presence of air or oxygen (or distilled water) leaving a thin layer of SiO_2 on the surface of the wafer.
2. *Photo-lithography* is the process that transfers the circuit design from a master pattern to the wafer. The first step in this process is surface cleaning, using acids, caustics or solvents. The next step is to coat the clean wafer with hexamethyldisilane (HMDS) in a solvent — usually a CFC, at least until recently. This improves the adhesion of a film (coating) of an organic polymer, added next, known as the 'photoresist'. Either the circuit element, or its complement, is then 'masked'. The masked photoresist is then exposed to ultraviolet radiation (or X-rays) to 'develop' (or 'undevelop') the film (there being two cases). Finally, either the undeveloped photoresist, or the developed photoresist is removed by a chemical 'stripper' leaving the desired pattern as a 'negative' or as a 'positive'.

     The usual photoresist for positives is ortho-diazo-ketone, which becomes soluble after exposure to UV, in a developer solution of alkaline and phenolic strippers. Negative photoresist is soluble to start with, but becomes insoluble after UV exposure. Organic solvents are difficult to neutralize and can be carcinogenic or toxic. Thus there is a trend towards increasing use of positive photoresists.
3. *Etching* is the next step. It involves removal of the silica surface that is not covered by photoresist. Various strong acids are used, including sulfuric, hydrochloric, hydrofluoric, nitric, phosphoric and chromic acids.
4. *Doping* is the process that alters the resistivity of the semiconductor. There are two methods. The first is *diffusion*. The second is *ion implantation*. The diffusion process is analogous to baking the wafer in a quartz chamber in an atmosphere consisting of some appropriate impurity-carrying gas (such as arsine, phosphine, diborane, etc.). The implantation process is essentially a very precise ion 'gun' that shoots ions to the desired location.

5. *Metalization* is the last step, in which a metallic conductor (such as gold) is deposited on the pattern, to interconnect the circuit elements.

The various processes above are carried out in various sequences, but each process may be repeated several times in manufacturing a single chip. For example, for a typical sequence to manufacture an n-channel polysilicon-gate MOS IC device the oxidation step occurs 4 times, ion implantation 5 times, vapor deposition 4 times, etching 9 times, lithography 6 times, doping (diffusion) 2 times and annealing (heat treatment) once. For our present purposes, additional details of these processes are not needed.

11.7.   TOXIC EMISSIONS AND WASTES

Several of the fabrication processes, especially photo-lithography and etching, generate significant quantities of toxic and hazardous wastes, including acids, solvents and heavy metals. In particular, five chemicals have been found consistently in wells (both public and private) in areas adjacent to semiconductor fabrication plants, especially around 'Silicon Valley' in California. These five are listed below.

- *Trichloroethylene (TCE)* was used as a degreaser (cleaning agent) until the 1970s. Levels as high as 2000 ppm have been measured in ground water. Extended exposures at 75 ppm probably cause liver damage and have been implicated in damage to the central nervous system (CNS).
- *1,1,1-Trichloroethane (TCA)* was a replacement for TCE. It, too, is suspected of causing liver damage. Has been measured at levels of up to 140 parts per million (ppm) in drinking water. The USEPA proposed a limit of 1 ppm, to drop eventually to 200 parts per billion (ppb).
- *Dichloroethylene (DCE)* causes kidney cancer in mice. Suspected of causing liver and CNS damage in humans at levels above 70 ppb. USEPA wants to phase it out completely.
- *Toluene* is thought to cause breakdown in red blood cells at levels of 350 ppb in water.
- *Xylene* (actually a mixture of three isomers) is suspected of being dangerous, though long-term effects are unclear. USEPA wants to set the upper limit at 620 ppb.

Other chemicals used in the industry are also extremely hazardous. For example, silane is pyrophoric (it was blamed for a fire that destroyed a semiconductor plant in Japan). Arsine, phosphine and diborane are among the most toxic compounds known (far more toxic, for instance, than hydrogen cyanide).

Table 11.5:   *Hazardous waste generation by responding semiconductor*
manufacturers, 1985[1]

Waste type[2]	California manufacturers		Total, US	
	Quantity (tons)[3]	Percentage of total (%)	Quantity (tons)[3]	Percentage of total (%)
Hydrofluoric acid waste	3 800	62	10 100	41
Non-halogenated solvents	1 270	21	6 300	26
Halogenated solvents	460	7.5	2 200	9
Metal-bearing liquids	29	0.5	360	1.5
Stripper	120	2.0	1 830	7.3
Contaminated solids[4]	125	2.0	225	0.9
Photoresist (+) and (−)	80	1.3	285	1.2
Fluoride sludge	85	1.4	2 530	10
Vacuum pump oil	45	0.7	100	0.4
Lab packs	75	1.2	230	0.9
Gallium arsenide	20	0.3	20	0.1
Waste cyanide	3	0.05	600	2.5
Total, excluding dilute waste acid[3]	6 100	100	24 800	100

Notes:
1. Data from 43 facilities representing 16 manufacturers.
2. Excludes dilute waste acid, which is 95–99% water, and is normally neutralized on site.
3. Data for wafer fabrication processes only.
4. Primarily gloves and wipes.

Source: SIA 1987, Table 17.

A 1985 survey of the semiconductor industry in the US yielded the results shown in Table 11.5. Note that only 40% of the firms surveyed responded, and the table does not include dilute waste acids. The survey also covered disposal practices. Weak acids are generally neutralized on site (15%). Other disposal methods cover the spectrum from off-site neutralization (17%) to incineration (17%) to landfilling (10%) and deep well injection (10%). Recycling accounts for 12% of reported wastes and 'unspecified' for 16% (SIA 1987). It is noteworthy that in the case of non-halogenated solvents (such as toluene and xylene, both carcinogens) by far the major disposal method was by deep well injection (ibid.).

In some communities, notably Silicon Valley between San Francisco and San Jose, California, hazardous chemicals from semiconductor-processing operations have been stored in underground tanks. Increasingly, some of these chemicals have been found in ground water, especially wells (from which many homes and businesses obtain drinking water). For example, a

Table 11.6: Hazardous waste survey of National Semiconductor facility, South Portland, Maine

Waste category	1984	1987
Ammonium hydroxide solution	10 000 g	
Alpha flux (contains ethanol)	2 255 g	
Boiler soot	915 g	4 400lb
Mixed solvents and Speedi-Dri from spill cleanup	2 892 g	
Empty drums previously containing ethanol	800 lb	
Oil, solvent, water mixtures	440 g	
Liquid with butyl cellulosic glycolic acid and ammonium chloride	330 g	
Liquid with xylene, acetone and isopropanol	220 g	
Waste oil	385 g	
Waste mixed solvents	531 890 lb	117 496 lb
1,1,1–Trichloroethane	6 775 g	86 984 lb
Freon TF	165 g	1 560 lb
Arsenic trioxide filter media	2 540 lb	904 lb
Rags, gloves and glass contaminated with antimony trioxide	1 339 lb	2 274 lb
Copper hydroxide sludge and filter paper	8 143 lb	
Hydrofluoric acid solution	1 0085 g	
Hazardous waste solid (molding compound)		216 800 lb
Waste butyl acetate for reclamation		68 850 lb
Waste isopropanol for reclamation		6 600 lb
Cyanide contaminated debris		43 560 lb
Xylene mixture (waste photoresist)		1 320 lb
		7 040 lb

Sources: USEPA 1984, 1987, *Annual Hazardous Waste Generator Reports*.

major underground leak of trichloroethylene (TCA) caused public attention to focus on this problem. From 1981 to 1985 over \$100 million was spent by Silicon Valley firms to clean up toxic spills (ibid.). In 1985 the San Francisco Bay Regional Water Control Board attempted to rank the relative danger of toxic leaks and spills in the Bay area (Barney 1985). As a result, over 50 private and public wells in the Silicon Valley area were forced to close.

Concerns about toxic and hazardous materials use and disposal have spread to other states. Firms in the US are required to report their toxic and hazardous emissions on a regular basis. (For instance, Table 11.6. gives emissions data for the National Semiconductor manufacturing facility in S. Portland, Maine, for the years 1984 and 1987 (USEPA 1984, 1987).) It will be noted that in 1984 most waste quantities were reported in gallons, a volume unit. In 1987 all wastes were reported in mass units. The Toxic Release Inventory (TRI) assembled by USEPA is comparable in its level of detail. However, the data provided in Table 11.6 (and in TRI) is clearly inadequate for any serious analytic purpose, since several waste streams are defined only in terms of the presence of one of the components, but not its actual quantity.

11.8.   CHEMICAL WASTE REDUCTION AND RECYCLING OPPORTUNITIES

The principal recycling and byproduct allocation opportunities within the overall silicon wafer manufacturing process are concentrated in the silicon purification section (MGS to EGS by the Siemens Process). The main chemicals involved are trichlorosilane ($SiHCl_3$), silicon tetrachloride ($SiCl_4$) and hydrogen chloride.

Because of its high purity and because it is the major feedstock for polycrystalline EGS production, $SiHCl_3$ is recycled to the maximum extent whenever possible. For the same reason, it is desirable to re-use $SiCl_4$ and HCl for $SiHCl_3$ production. However, polysilicon and trichlorosilane manufacturing plants are usually not located at the same site, and transportation has to be taken into account. An alternative is to sell both silicon tetrachloride and hydrogen chloride as byproducts. Byproduct silicon tetrachloride is of particular interest, since it is the intermediate for most silicon-based chemicals.

In the Siemens Process, in addition to the final product (poly-EGS), the output gases are $SiHCl_3$, $SiCl_4$, HCl, and H_2. These remain unchanged in the two simultaneous reactions occurring in the process, namely:

$$(1375°K)$$
$$SiHCl_3(g) + H_2(g) \rightarrow Si(s) + 3HCl$$

and

$$SiHCl_3(g) + HCl(g) \rightarrow SiCl_4(g) + H_2(g)$$

leading to the overall chemical equation

$$3SiHCl_3(g) \rightarrow Si(s) + 2SiCl_4(g) + HCl(g) + H_2(g)$$

There are several possible levels of intervention, leading to different recycling and byproduct allocation opportunities. The first step, common to any of these processes, is to separate the effluent gases.

The one-step $SiHCl_3$ dissociation yield is quite low (only 8% to 25%, as compared to the unreacted $SiHCl_3$ dissociates). Thus, the process has to be repeated several times. Because of its high purity, it is possible to recycle $SiHCl_3$ completely as a feedstock for polycrystalline EGS production. In addition, (less pure) trichlorosilane can be used as a coupling agent for glass-to-metal bonding (O'Mara *et al.* 1990). In principle, if $SiHCl_3$ is completely recycled (purified and returned as feedstock to the reactors, according to the above equations) approximately two-thirds of it is converted to $SiCl_4$. In this process, hydrogen is usually repurified and recycled as carrier gas in the dissociation reactor.

Silicon tetrachloride $SiCl_4$ can be purified and blended with $SiHCl_3$ to be used as reactor feedstock. Moreover, it can be converted back to trichlorosilane ($SiHCl_3$), which remains the main feedstock for polysilicon production. $SiHCl_3$ is produced from $SiCl_4$ by reacting with hydrogen in a fluidized bed of MGS in the presence of a copper catalyst. The latter process has a conversion efficiency up to 37% (ibid.). Also hydrogen chloride can be re-used to react with MGS to produce $SiHCl_3$ (Figure 11.7).

It should be noted that neither $SiHCl_3$ nor $SiCl_4$ production plants are located at major polysilicon manufacturing sites. For example, Huels AG, a subsidiary of the German Veba group, the world's second-largest silicon chemical manufacturer, produces polysilicon at Novara, Italy, yet manufactures silicon tetrachloride, trichlorosilane and fumed silica at Rheinfelden in Germany (Roskill Si 1991).

Silicon tetrachloride ($SiCl_4$) is the intermediate for most silicon-based chemicals. Almost all silicon-based chemicals are produced by a small number of multinational companies. The world's largest producer is Wacker Chemie of Germany (ibid.). Byproduct $SiCl_4$ from the silicon purification process is used to make fumed silica, fiber optics, or for semiconductor epitaxy.[4]

Fumed silica is an extremely fine silica powder. It is obtained by hydrolyzing $SiCl_4$ at high temperature in a hydrogen–oxygen flame. It is used as a filler in toothpaste, a thickener in sealants, or to reinforce silicone rubber for high-temperature, structural applications.

The case of German Degussa (a major silica producer) and General Electric is an example of byproduct opportunities and synergistic interests. In Waterford, New York, Degussa has built a fumed silica manufacturing plant to supply General Electric's silicone rubber facility, and even a wider market in silicone rubber sealants, coatings and printing inks. In turn, General Electric will supply the Degussa plant with chlorosilane. Another example is Dow Corning which produces fumed silica but not enough to satisfy its internal needs, which are met by Wacker, Degussa, and Cabot Corp (ibid.).

In principle, $SiCl_4$ can be also used for the production of silanes by reaction with lithium aluminum hydride. However, we have found no report of any polysilicon manufacturing plant using or selling $SiCl_4$ for this purpose. The byproduct HCl can be diluted and sold as muriatic acid to swimming-pool or plating industries, or it can be sold to the semiconductor industry as an etchant gas.

There are three levels of chemical recovery systems. The potential profitability of each is strongly dependent on the plant capacity:

1. Small plants find it convenient to buy $SiHCl_3$ and to sell both $SiCl_4$ and HCl. The capital costs of the plant are lower and additional revenues are gained by the sale of the byproducts.

2. As the size of the plant increases, the number of potential buyers of $SiCl_4$ decreases. Also, the costs and the risk of safe transportation of large quantities of $SiHCl_3$ and $SiCl_4$ become much higher. To a rough order of magnitude, it can be estimated that on-site conversion of $SiCl_4$ into $SiHCl_3$ for re-use as a feedstock becomes economically feasible above 500 tonnes per year of poly-EGS production. At this level, byproduct HCl is still sold to the market.

3. Finally, the third level of vertical integration (Figure 11.9) involves buying MGS, using byproduct HCl to produce $SiHCl_3$, converting on-site $SiCl_4$ to $SiHCl_3$, and selling only poly-EGS as final product. This last solution, efficiently recovering chemical byproducts, reduces potential environmental problems associated with the Siemens Process to near zero (O'Mara *et al.* 1990). However, it should be remembered that in the $SiHCl_3$ production step from MGS, chlorosilanes are released to the environment. This type of plant, although requiring higher initial investment, allows a reduction of total polycrystalline silicon production costs per unit mass.

Generally speaking, it appears that the silicon industry is moving towards this third level of integrated chemical recovery system. However, there is no

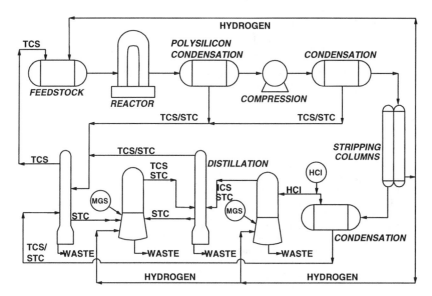

Source: O'Mara *et al*. 1990.

Figure 11.9:   *Chemical recovery system – polysilicon plant using purchased metallurgical grade silicon and hydrogen chloride with no byproduct sales*

published information on what the silicon industry has already done or will do in the near future.

11.9. PHYSICAL WASTE REDUCTION AND RECYCLING OPPORTUNITIES

Monocrystalline silicon wafer preparation from polysilicon is rather wasteful (65% loss), as noted earlier. However it seems to be unavoidable for the silicon-based semiconductor industry in the near/mid-future. The waste material at this stage consists of powder and scraps, contaminated by cutting oils and abrasives. Some scraps can apparently be 'recycled' for manufacturing photovoltaic cells, but not for computer chips.

At present the PV industry actually uses scrap from the micro-electronic ('chip') industry. However, if the PV sector grows significantly, alternative processes for low-cost PV cell production will be needed. Such processes should not be based on monocrystalline silicon preparation. They should also be less energy intensive and material intensive (especially in terms of hazardous chemicals like chlorine) than chip manufacturing. Alternative manufacturing processes should be studied and developed as a high priority. To some extent this is already happening. Because of extremely limited information about the industry, we cannot comment further on possible waste reduction or recycling opportunities in chip fabrication.

NOTES(11)

1. All such estimates are questionable because semiconductors manufactured for in-house use by IBM, AT&T, GM (Delco) and other vertically integrated firms are not included.
2. Currently only 4% of MGS production is used to manufacture chips.
3. The definition of 'ultra-pure' is that the concentration of electrically active impurities is less than 0.3 ppb for n-type impurities (phosphorus, arsenic), 0.15 ppb for p-type impurities (boron, aluminum, gallium, indium), 0.4 ppm for carbon impurities (O'Mara *et al.* 1991).
4. The epitaxial growth of semiconductors is a chemical deposition process: the semiconductor is grown, layer by layer, on a substrate, keeping its crystalline orientation. This kind of process allows the construction of so-called junction devices; namely structures made by layers of different doping or types of semiconductor.

12. Post-consumer packaging wastes

12.1 SUMMARY

Every package consumes raw materials. Packaging materials (for the most part) have notoriously short useful lives. Thus, while the quantity of raw materials (and energy) required to produce a single bottle, can or carton are not very great, the numbers of such items produced are cumulatively very large.[1] The wastes and emissions generated by the production processes are correspondingly great. Moreover, the bulk and weight of packaging adds significantly to goods transportation requirements, thus amplifying the environmental impact.

This argument is especially pertinent with regard to aluminum cans and foil. Aluminum is extremely energy intensive to produce from virgin materials (see Chapter 3, Aluminum). For this reason it is especially important not to use aluminum for frivolous purposes, and to recycle that which is used. The US and Swedish experience verifies the feasibility of achieving very high levels of recycling. No new technology is really needed for this. The problem is clearly administrative and organizational.

Disposal of waste packaging materials is a growing problem. Old landfills are filling up and it is becoming very difficult to find new sites that are both physically and economically suitable and acceptable to nearby residents. In effect, landfill space is becoming scarce in urbanized areas. Packaging materials constitute 30% of municipal waste by weight but 50% by volume. Meanwhile incineration for energy recovery also generates significant emissions to the air, including heavy metals (e.g. mercury, cadmium) and dioxins. Incineration is currently unacceptable in some countries (e.g. Germany), although it is regarded as a useful source of energy in others (France, Switzerland, UK).

The current situation with regard to recycling of packaging wastes in Europe is far from equilibrium, and probably unsustainable. The 'green dot' program in Germany has created a major new avenue for waste disposal (by users), and a sharp increase in the available supply of recyclables. However, it is by no means clear that this program alone will lead to significantly more recycling. Recycling requires both supply and demand. The German program has been criticized justly for greatly increasing the supply of recyclables without doing anything to increase the demand for them. As a consequence, the added supply (supplemented by exports of recyclable paper from the US) has disrupted existing markets for secondary materials and harmed existing enterprises in the recycling business. Partly in response to these concerns, the French Eco-Emballages program, beginning in 1993, finances demonstration projects and is voluntary and organized on a regional basis, involving local communities as well as firms.

Recycling of packaging wastes in general is not making much headway. In fact, re-use of glass bottles is declining, and recycling is still not economically feasible for most types of packaging materials (with the exception of glass and aluminum cans). For several reasons, more cost-effective and more efficient means of sorting and separating mixed municipal wastes are needed. There seems to be no fundamental technical barrier. However, most of the re-use and recycling options for waste materials cannot be justified economically in small-scale applications, and large-scale sorting and separating facilities require significant markets for the output.

A new and more systematic approach is also needed to facilitate energy recovery from municipal wastes (including chlorinated plastics). Assuming that chlorinated plastics will not be banned from use in packaging any time soon, the next best alternative would be to develop an effective low-temperature gasification technology suitable for mixed municipal wastes.

What has not yet been given sufficient consideration up to now is an integrated system operating on quite a large scale, that could accept mixed wastes from a large region, and utilize the most advanced possible technologies for separation and beneficiation to produce a number of secondary materials, plus energy. The problem is high cost. This can only be reduced by gaining experience and operating on a larger scale. Subsidies to users may be needed at the beginning.

There is a need for much more innovation on the demand side to rectify the current imbalance between supply and demand. Having created the problem, in large part, governments will have to intervene to solve it. This can be done, in part, by mandating the use of recycled materials in certain applications. However that is a very blunt instrument, since bureaucrats are not the best judges of technical or economic feasibility. A much more appropriate form of intervention would be to subsidize R&D on new applications of recyclables. A less attractive, but possible approach would be for governments to offer tax relief for materials producers that convert virgin materials processing facilities to recycling facilities. This might be appropriate in the paper industry, for instance, where a new paper recycling plant costs $500 million and even a retrofit costs $50 million. At the same time, governments must begin the (admittedly difficult) process of cutting back on direct and indirect subsidies that favor the use of virgin materials, especially aluminum.

Goals of public policy: reduce consumption of non-renewable raw materials; reduce energy consumption; reduce pollution associated with disposal of packaging wastes; increase recycling of energy-intensive materials, especially aluminum; develop new uses for mixed packaging wastes; develop improved means of energy recovery from mixed wastes.

12.2. INTRODUCTION

Packaging materials are extremely diverse. Major categories of packaging include rigid containers (glass, metal cans, plastic bottles), flexible containers (paper bags and cartons, plastic bags, toothpaste tubes) and flexible wrapping materials (paper, plastic film, aluminum foil) as well as bottle caps and seals, string, tape and wire. Each type includes several different materials and combinations, depending on the nature of the substance being contained. Liquids and dry materials constitute one major dichotomy, since packaging materials for the former must be airtight and impermeable. Food products and beverages must also be packaged in airtight (and, in some cases, lightproof) containers to inhibit contamination and spoilage. Toxic or hazardous materials, on the other hand, must be packaged in such a way as to prevent escape and/or corrosion. Some packaging materials should be transparent to allow the contents to be seen, as in the case of fresh fruits, vegetables and meat. Some packaging materials need to be very strong and tough, to facilitate handling, but need not be rigid. Some are needed only for a very short period (e.g. a grocery bag) while others should preserve the contents for a long time.

A material that is ideal for one application will not serve the purpose in others. Packaging materials compete against each other only in particular markets, e.g. alcoholic beverages, non-alcoholic beverages, prepared foods, detergents, paints and solvents, shipping containers (i.e. containers for other containers), and so forth. The potential for re-use and recycling depends very much on the specific application. However, by far the greatest share of used packaging materials end up in municipal solid wastes. This type of waste constitutes a particularly difficult challenge for re-use or recycling.

To compound the difficulties, published data on the supply side is scarce and inconsistent. On the other hand, market data from unofficial sources (mainly consulting companies) is voluminous but expensive and unverifiable. A significant degree of uncertainty is unavoidable. Nevertheless, there are several good reasons for considering possibilities for increased re-use and recycling.

According to one source, the rate of paper recycling in the EU was 38.3% in 1991 (CEPI, cited in Renaux 1992). However, this is a little misleading, since paperboard packaging materials such as cartons are probably the chief consumer of recycled paper, whereas they themselves are not very suitable for recycling. On the other hand, used paper packaging materials themselves are not as easily recycled as printing grades of paper. Only in the cases of glass and aluminum is recycled material of comparable quality with the original, although the recycling rate for aluminum cans in Europe is still very low except in Sweden.

12.3.   THE PACKAGING SECTOR, IN PHYSICAL TERMS

Because of the diversity of package types, also, it is very difficult to characterize the packaging market as a whole in physical units. In monetary terms, paper products and plastics each account for about 30% of the total packaging market, while metals (tinplate, steel and aluminum sheet) account for 16%, glass for 7%, and the remaining 8% is divided between wood pallets and steel drums (Eurostat 1990) (see Figure 12.1, top). We neglect the latter two categories hereafter, bearing in mind that they are virtually exclusively industrial. In tonnage terms, of course, the distribution among materials is somewhat different (see Figure 12.1, bottom).

Total paper and paperboard consumption in the US for 1993 was about 80 MMT, or 310 kg/capita. Consumption in the EU (11 countries) for 1993 was 54.5 MMT, for a per capita consumption, about two-thirds the US level. This undoubtedly reflects the relatively high availability and low cost of wood and paper products in the US as compared to Europe. (In contrast, Europeans use more plastics.) A summary of available data on paper production, consumption, recovery and recycling is given in Appendix A, Table A.18. Paper products and cartons used for packaging purposes in the EU (11 countries) amounted to 22.882 MMT in 1991 and 23.574 MMT, or 43% of total consumption (ibid.). To include Austria, Greece, Ireland, Scandinavia and Switzerland would increase the total consumption roughly in proportion to the additional population,[2] or 12.5%. Thus, we estimate total paper and paperboard consumption for packaging purposes of 25.7 MMT in Western Europe in 1991 and 26.5 MMT in 1993.

As regards plastics, total consumption in Western Europe (1991) was 24 MMT (Matthews undated) as compared to 27.74 MMT in the US (*Modern Plastics*, January 1993); the total used for packaging purposes was 9.4 MMT, or 39% of total European plastics production (ibid.) (see Figure 12.2). Unfortunately, detailed data on production and consumption are available in Europe, from the Association of Plastics Manufacturers in Europe (APME) only for 6 major tonnage resins (LLDPE, LDPE, HDPE, PVC, PP, and PS) (APME 1993).

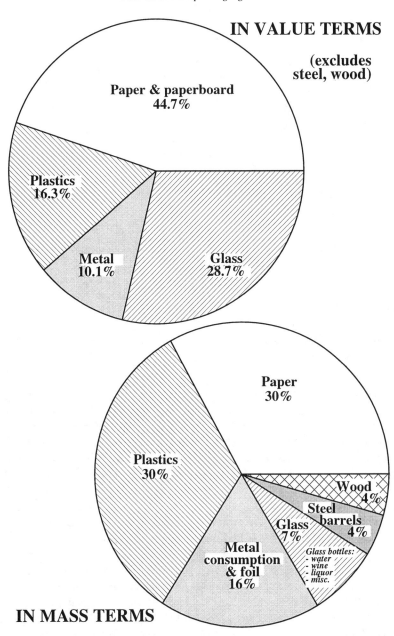

Source: Renaux 1992.

Figure 12.1: *The packaging market in Europe, 1991*

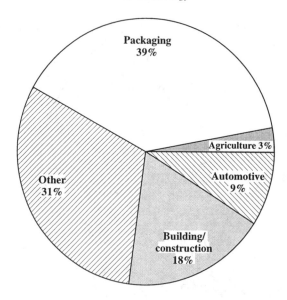

Source: APME 1993.

Figure 12.2:   *Western European plastics consumption by industry sector,*
                1991

The Association Professionelle des Producteurs Européens d'Acier pour
Emballages (APPEAL, cited by Renaux 1992) estimated the use of steel
(mostly tinplate) for packaging at 4.87 MMT in 1990 and 5 MMT in 1991.
The recycling rate for steel cans was estimated at 25% (ranging from 6% in
Italy to 50% in Germany and the Netherlands). (It was 34% in the US, as
compared to an overall recycling rate of 66% for the US steel industry.) We
have no information on the rate of recycling of tin (detinning) from used tin
cans in Europe. However, this technology seems to have advanced considerably in the last few years. As a matter of interest, tinplated steel produced in
the US amounted to 2.47 MMT, with a tin content of 11 482 tonnes, or 4.7 kg
per tonne (USBuMines 1991, Table 4). (This accounted for 23% of total tin
consumption in the US in 1991.) Based on 5 MMT production in Europe, and
assuming the same average tin content, tin consumption for this purpose in
Europe would have been about 23 000 tonnes, virtually all imported.

Aluminum for beverage cans amounted to 780 kMT for Western Europe in
1991. Aluminum captured 50% of the European beverage can market in
1991, with individual countries ranging from 100% for Sweden and Switzerland and 96% for Italy to 60% in the UK and only 12% for Germany (Renaux
1992). The recycling rate for aluminum cans averaged 21% for Western

Europe as a whole; it ranged from 93% in Sweden to only 7% for the average of the original six EU countries, none of which had recycling programs in place as of the end of 1991 (ibid.). Tinplate still dominates the non-beverage market. (This is also true in the US, where aluminum cans have captured 73% of the total market of 130 billion — 130 × 109 — cans shipped (USBuMines 1991).) Packaging materials — mostly cans — account for 31% of aluminum produced in the US; we do not have a comparable figure for Europe.

Glass bottles were much heavier, adding up to 12.63 MMT, which is 65% of the total production of the EU(9) glass-manufacturing sector (ibid.), and 80% in France (Briant 1990). Again, one should extend the estimates to include the massing countries, in proportion to their population. In this case, the missing countries (including Spain and Portugal) add 31% to the base number. Assuming consumption and production are roughly equal for these countries, total packaging glass for Western Europe should be about 16.54 MMT. Adding up all the above we arrive at a total of 57.5 MMT for European consumption of packaging materials in 1991, not including any allowance for steel drums or wooden pallets used by industry.

Within each of the major materials categories there are significant differences in usage. For instance, glass bottles are overwhelmingly used for beverages, especially wine and beer, with a minor fraction going to food products

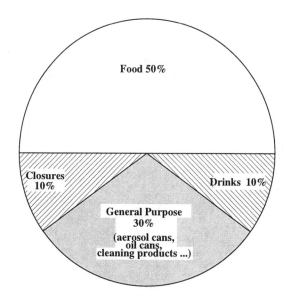

Source: Renaux 1992.

Figure 12.3: Western European packaging uses of metal cans, 1991

(like baby-foods and jams and jellies). In the case of metal cans, 50% are used for foods, 10% for beverages and 30% for non-food products such as aerosols, paints, and motor oil (ibid.). The remaining 10% is aluminum foil, bottle-tops and closures (see Figure 12.3). Paper products are being increasingly used for drinks, especially fruit juice and milk, but most paper packaging products are cartons and wrapping materials for dry products other than food.

12.4.   PLASTICS IN PACKAGING

Because of their diversity of composition, and the significant quantities of metals and other chemicals used for plasticizers, stabilizers and colorants, plastics cannot be aggregated for purposes of recycling. They therefore constitute a special case requiring more detailed analysis.

Plastic packaging materials are conventionally subdivided into four categories: (1) containers, (2) film and sheet, (3) coatings (mostly used in composite multilayer materials and inside cans) and (4) bottlecaps or closures. Unfortunately, we do not have a detailed breakdown of European plastics consumption in a way that correlates directly with the above catego-

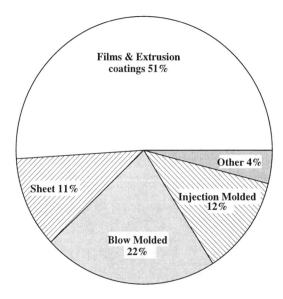

Source: *Modern Plastics International.*

Figure 12.4:   Western European packaging use of plastics, 1991

ries. The usual classification allocates plastics partly by process (e.g. blow molding, extrusion coating) and partly by material form (e.g. rigid sheet) (see Figure 12.4). While containers are *ipso facto* 'packages', neither film and sheet, nor coatings, are necessarily used for packaging purposes. In fact, in Europe a great deal of plastic sheet is used in agriculture and in construction. Similarly, while bottles are usually blow moldings or injection moldings, not all moldings are bottles.

A breakdown of plastic use within the packaging sector, as such, does exist for the US, for 1989, as shown below (*Modern Plastics*, June, 1990):

	kMT	
Containers	3393.5	52.1%
Film and sheet	2354.5	36.2%
Coatings	393.8	6.0%
Closures	368.9	5.7%

The total use of plastics for packaging purposes in the US in that year was 6.514 MMT, significantly less than the EU total.[3] The largest subsector, containers, can be further subdivided by plastic, namely,

	kMT	
High density polyethylene (HDPE)	1604.0	47%
Polystyrene (PS)	602.0	18%
Polyethylene terephthalate (PET)	451.5	13%

with the remaining 22% divided up among polypropylene (PP), polyvinyl chloride (PVC), low density polyethylene (LDPE and LLDPE) and 'other'. For film and sheet, LDPE and LLDPE are the main materials, followed far behind by PP, HDPE and PVC, and other. For coatings LLDPE is dominant and for closures PS and PP are the dominant plastics (see Figures 12.5 and 12.6).

The European pattern is certainly fairly similar, given the internationalization of the brand-name packagers. There is one major difference, however. In areas where plastic and paper compete, the US uses more paper for packaging whereas Europe uses more plastics. This suggests that the use of plastic film, in particular, may be considerably higher in Europe. Europe also probably uses more plastic bottles than the US, especially for mineral water. PVC is widely used for this purpose in Europe.

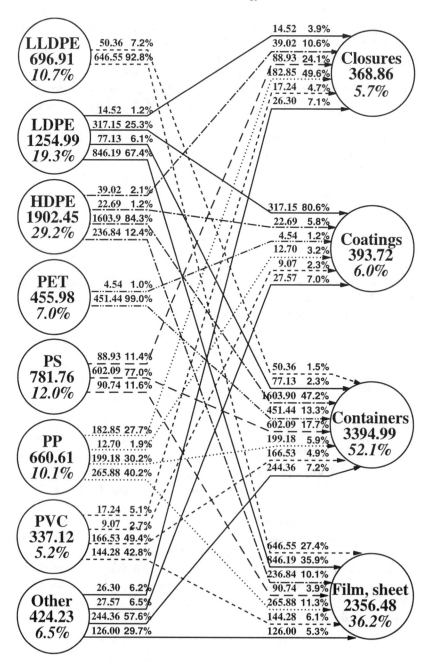

Figure 12.5:   US plastics use in packaging, 1989 (kMT)

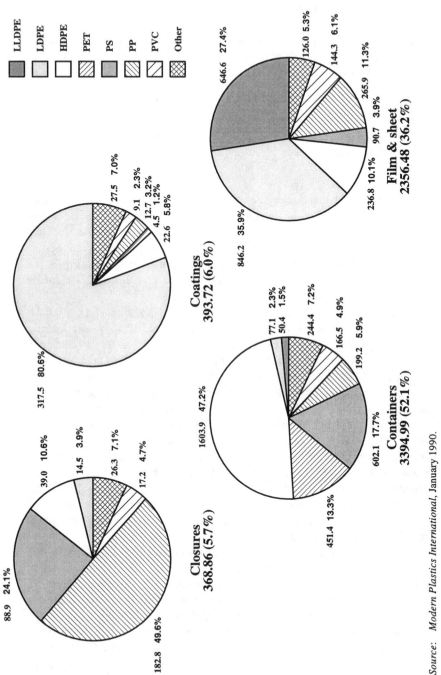

Source: *Modern Plastics International*, January 1990.

Figure 12.6: *US plastics use in packaging by end-use, 1989 (kMT)*

12.5. PACKAGING WASTE

Packaging waste produced in Western Europe as a whole has been estimated as 154 kg/capita or 50.5 MMT for 1990 (OECD 1991). This total is subdivided as follows:

	MMT	recycled
Domestic waste	25.0	10%
Commerce and services	15.0	17%
Industrial waste	10.5	43%
Total	50.5	19%

Based on the fact that packaging materials lifetimes tend to be very short, with little or no change in inventory, the sum total of materials apparently consumed for packaging purposes (57.5 MMT), should be very nearly equal to the annual waste flow. To be sure, some packaging materials are burned on farms or used for domestic heating purposes, thus never appearing in the 'official' waste stream. Nevertheless, we suggest that the OECD estimate (admittedly incomplete) may be about 10% too low.

A slightly more detailed breakdown of plastic waste, in particular, by country and major sector of origin is shown in Table 12.1. Detailed breakdowns of packaging waste by material are not available for all European countries, as we have noted. Data for the major northern European countries is given in Table 12.2. Details on the disposal of plastics wastes *per se* are not available for Europe as a whole. However, the Netherlands is probably reasonably typical of Northern Europe. In 1986 total plastic waste for that country was estimated at 763 kMT (1% of the total volume of solid wastes); of this 90% was incinerated or disposed of in landfills, and only 10% was recycled (Starreveld and van Ierland 1994). By 1994 the quantity of plastics waste was expected to increase to 850 kMT absent additional waste-prevention measures. Dutch authorities had hoped to reduce this by 6% (to 800 kMT) by means of effective waste prevention, with recycling up to 26% in 1994 and 42% by 2000 (ibid.). Yet, as of 1992, the recycling percentage remained at about 10% (ibid.).

Municipal solid wastes are the main avenue for disposal of packaging materials, other than those generated directly by industry. In terms of weight distribution, we have at least three inconsistent sources to choose from, as summarized in Table 12.3. It seems to be agreed that municipal wastes in Europe (1990) averaged between 33.5% and 35.5% packaging wastes. Miscellaneous organic products (food and yard wastes) accounted for 25–34%; paper and cardboard accounted for 28–39%; ashes and dust for 9.6–16%; plastics 7.3–10%; glass 8–12%; metals 5–8%, and textiles 2–4%. Of the

Table 12.1: Western European post-user plastic waste, 1990 (kMT)

Country	Total post-users plastics waste	Agricultural sector wastes	Automotive wastes	Construction/ Demolition civil works wastes	Large distribution and industry wastes	Municipal solid wastes
Austria	246	13	19	11	61	142
Belgium-Lux	372	8	30	31	89	214
Denmark	208	6	10	11	46	135
Finland	164	2	11	11	40	100
France	2311	123	176	58	454	1500
Germany	2363	38	160	51	446	1668
Greece	272	8	9	6	54	195
Ireland	106	4	6	3	22	71
Italy	1996	139	118	54	465	1220
Netherlands	781	6	37	25	133	580
Norway	216	14	11	6	35	150
Portugal	283	7	8	7	66	195
Spain	1426	138	49	59	250	930
Sweden	326	11	22	15	68	210
Switzerland	325	16	19	10	55	225
UK	2199	52	161	73	513	1400
TOTAL	**13594**	**585**	**846**	**431**	**2797**	**8935**

Source: PWMI.

217

Table 12.2:   Package material recovery and recycling rates, 1991 (%)

Country	Paper recovery	Paper recycle	Glass	Steel	Aluminum
Austria					24
Belgium	31.4	13.1	55	30	*
Denmark	39.1	27.8	35		
France	34.3	38.0	41	31	*
Germany	47.2	40.1	63	50	*
Greece			22		25
Ireland			23		8
Italy	27.8	37.3	53	6	10
Netherlands	53.2	57.9	70	50	*
Portugal	40.4	43.5	30		*
Spain	37.8	48.5	27		*
Sweden					93
Switzerland					40
UK	33.0	31.4	21	10	5
AVERAGE	**38.2**	**37.5**	**40.0**	**29.5**	**17.6**

Note: *   No data by country: average for all those with * = 7%.

Source: Renaux 1992.

paper waste, a fairly large fraction is newspapers, magazines and advertising materials sent through the mail. The rest is packaging.

The plastics and glass are almost all packaging wastes. In the case of metals, there are some non-packaging wastes. The major difference between the ANRED estimate (column #2 of the table) and the other two estimates (columns #3, #4) appears to be in the assumed split between packaging paper and non-packaging paper. (See, however, further discussion below.)

Annual packaging waste generation should be in proportion to annual production of new packaging materials, adjusted for recycling and re-use. Glass appears to be under-represented in the municipal waste stream, compared to both metals and plastics. Extrapolating from EU data, the weight of glass bottles manufactured and consumed in Western Europe as a whole in 1991 was about 16.5 MMT. This compares to 5.75 MMT of metal cans and 9.4 MMT of plastic packaging materials. Discards into municipal wastes should be roughly in the same proportions, other factors being equal. That is, the ratio of glass bottles to metal cans in the municipal waste stream should

Table 12.3: Municipal waste estimates for Western Europe, 1990

	ANRED (Renaux)	APME (I) (Matthews)		APME (II) (Anon)	
		source[a]	author's	source[a]	author's
Paper and board	5.5%	30.0%	17.5%	28.0%	15.5%
Plastics	10.0%	7.4%	7.4%	7.3%	7.3%
Glass	12.0%	8.0%	8.0%	8.0%	8.0%
Metals	6.0%	8.0%	2.5%	5.0%	2.5%
Packaging subtotal	33.5%	53.4%	35.4%	48.3%	33.3%
Other paper	24.5%	NA	12.5%	NA	12.5%
Other metals	NR	NA	5.5%	NA	2.5%
Textiles	2.0%	4.0%	4.0%	4.0%	3.0%
Ashes, minerals and misc.	16.0%	9.6%	9.6%	9.6%	15.0%
Organics	25.0%	33.0%	33.0%	33.0%	33.7%
Total	100.0%	100.0%	100.0%	100.0%	100.0%

Notes:
NR = Not Recognized.
a. Original source did not separate packaging paper and metal from other paper and metal. These allocations have been made by the author (see also text).

be about 3.6 to 1. In fact, glass and metals appear to be present in ratios of 2:1, 1:1 and 8:5 in the three cases cited above. Similarly, the ratio of glass to plastics should be roughly 16:9, based on relative consumption levels of glass and plastics. In fact, only slightly more glass than plastic is found in munici-pal waste. (In this case, all three estimates show similar ratios.)

Two strong implications can be drawn from these disparate numbers. First, compare glass with plastics, since both are essentially pure packaging wastes. The fact that less glass is present than one would expect based on consump-tion levels, it follows that some glass bottles are being collected for re-use and recycling *outside* the municipal system, whereas plastics are not recycled at all. In fact, the numbers suggest that about 20% of glass bottles are re-used or recycled through external channels. This is consistent with general obser-vation, though we have no precise confirming data. The second implication of the above numbers is that a considerable fraction of the metals going into municipal wastes are not packaging wastes (cans) but miscellaneous items such as wire, light bulbs, fasteners, pipe, small bits of hardware from domes-tic repairs, and so on. The non-packaging *fraction* would have to be about one-third (ANRED), two-thirds (APME I) or one-half (APME II) to make everything consistent. Interestingly enough, the end result in all three cases is that non-packaging metal accounts for 2–2.5% of total municipal waste.

The same logic should also lead us to an estimate for the packaging paper fraction. The proportionality principle implies that we should compute the ratio of paper consumption in packaging to plastics consumption in packaging, namely, 25.8/9.4 = 2.7. This is to be multiplied by the actual plastics percentage (10% or 7.4%, respectively). We thus estimate that either $10 \times 2.7 = 27\%$ or $7.4 \times 2.7 = 20\%$ of the waste stream consists of packaging paper and paperboard. Subtracting 20% or 27% from 30% or 28%, as appropriate, this implies that either 3%, 12.5% or 10.5% of the municipal waste stream must consist of 'other paper', e.g. newspapers, magazines and advertising materials. There is a major inconsistency with the figures shown in the ANRED estimate (column #2), which allocate only 5.5% to packaging and 24.5% to 'other paper'. We cannot explain or resolve it except in terms of survey error.

12.6.   RE-USE AND RECYCLING OF PLASTIC PACKAGING WASTES

The potential for re-use of packaging materials *per se* is largely limited to re-use of steel drums and wooden pallets by the industrial sector, and refillable glass and plastic bottles. The former problem is one of organization and incentives; we need not consider it further. The situation with regard to refillable bottles is similar. There are minor technical difficulties, but it must be remembered that, in the case of milk, local delivery, collection and refilling was the norm at one time. It would not be unreasonably difficult to reconstitute a local delivery and pickup service for a wider variety of liquids in refillable glass or plastic bottles, including mineral water, beer, wine and soft drinks. Again, the logistical details need not be considered here. The public health authorities do not permit refillable plastic bottles in the US, but refillable PVC bottles have been used for mineral water in France for some time. Refillable PET bottles were introduced for the same purpose in 1994 by a Belgian mineral water bottler (Spadel). Refillable polycarbonate milk bottles made from GE's 'Lexan' are currently being introduced in Germany (WRF 1994).

As regards recycling, the logic is clear if we compare the energy required to produce a packaging material with the energy recoverable by combustion (Table 12.4). It is clear that glass and metal (being non-combustible under normal conditions) contribute nothing to energy recovery.[4] Paper and most plastics are highly combustible, by contrast.[5] However, it is worth noting that

Table 12.4: Potential energy recovery from packaging materials

Packaging material	Energyrecovery potential (heat of combustion per kg) kJ/kg	Production energy kJ/kg	Recoverable portion %
Paper	17 400	30 102	57.8%
Glass	—	—	—
Steel	—	—	—
Aluminum	—	—	—
LLDPE	41 000	63 960	64.1%
LDPE	41 000	76 260	53.8%
HDPE	41 000	72 570	56.5%
PS	37 800	68 040	55.6%
PET	27 600	82 800	33.3%
PVC	14 300	47 619	30.0%

Source: Gaines 1981.

PVC, because of its high chlorine content, yields less than half the energy per kg than most of the other plastics. But even for polyethylene, 36–46% of the energy required to produce the plastic is irretrievably lost. In the case of PET, a very complex plastic, and PVC, not more than a third of the energy required to produce the material in the first place can be recovered as heat.

There are three recycling cases to be distinguished. The first is recycling of primary materials to be used again for the same purpose. The second case is recycling into another use that requires less purity or performance. The third is recycling for energy recovery. In the first case, recycled materials must be comparable in quality to the 'virgin' material and usable for the original purpose. In practice, this is possible for aluminum cans and some glass bottles. Tinplate can easily be recycled in so far as both the tin and the steel can be recovered. This is already done to a significant degree. The tin coating, however, is only recoverable by a special detinning process. To the extent that used tin cans are aggregated with other scrap iron and steel and used as feedstock for foundries, for instance, the tin becomes a minor contaminant of the steel and is lost.

In the case of paper, there is an unavoidable and significant degradation of quality every time a paper product is recycled. This arises from the need to repulp, remove various inks, coatings, and fillers (amounting to 10% or more of the product weight) and rebleach. Cellulose fibers are shortened in this process, losing strength each time. Thus, while '100% recycled' paper is appealing to some environmentalists, 100% recycling of all paper products is not technically feasible. An optimum mix of virgin and recycled pulp would probably require at least 30% new pulp on average, and the optimum 'cascade' of products from high-quality to lower-quality uses is not yet clear.

The problem of recycling used plastics, for use as materials rather than for energy recovery, is even more difficult. Most plastic wastes are currently consigned to landfills (Figure 12.7). This is because most plastics appear in household and commercial (not industrial) packaging wastes, where sorting is difficult to do (and to enforce). Standardized markings, now being used by most packagers to distinguish various types of plastic, make it somewhat easier for householders to sort plastics. But voluntary sorting will not help much unless it is virtually universal, and it is very hard to imagine any effective enforcement system.

Recycling mixed plastic packaging materials is the final, and most challenging, aspect of recycling mixed municipal waste. It is comparatively easy to separate steel from other wastes by taking advantage of its magnetic properties. Other solids can be separated on the basis of their density or (in the case of glass) color. A generic sorting and separation system is shown schematically in Figure 12.8. Such systems are still relatively rare, but are becoming more common as the technology matures. For instance, the Triselec–

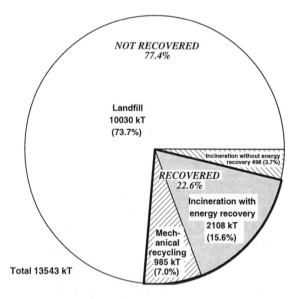

Sources: PWMI undated; APME 1993.

Figure 12.7: Destination of total post-user waste: Western Europe, 1990

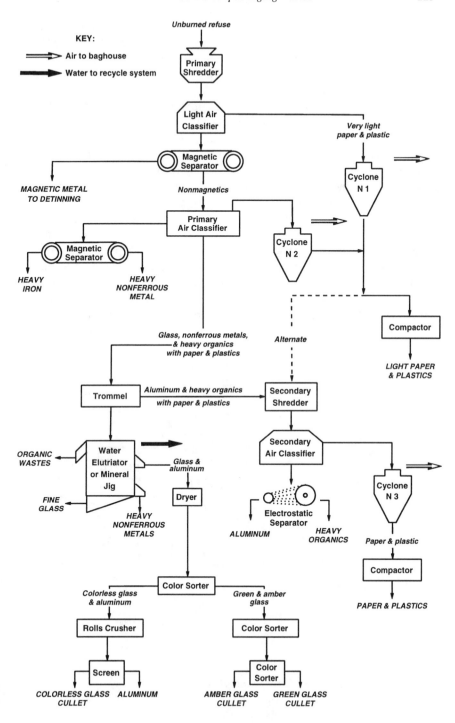

Figure 12.8: Raw refuse separation flow sheet

Lille facility processes 60 kMT/yr of mixed waste, which is sorted into 16
fractions for sale to industry (WRF 1994). The Austrian firm, Binder & Co.
has built a glass-sorting and recycling plant for the City of Berlin, that is
capable of processing 250 kMT of glass per year. It is sorted by color and
type and impurities are removed.

It is technically possible to separate different plastics, too, based on density and other characteristics. In particular, PVC is much denser than other
plastics and is therefore rather easy to remove by gravity concentration, once
the materials are broken up into small enough fragments. Electromagnetic
scanners can also specifically identify PVC by recognizing the presence of
chlorine (Manzone 1993). This also permits automatic separation, for instance, of bottles within a given size range. A separation scheme for plastics
(which would logically be an add-on to the system illustrated in Figure 12.8)
is shown in Figure 12.9. Systems like this have been implemented in a few
cases. PVC, in particular, is being recycled for a number of purposes, though
usually not the original ones. Other plastics sorting and recycling programs
exist, for instance the Tecoplast recycling plant in Italy, and Reprise in the
UK (ibid.). A facility built by Binder & Co. near Gleisdorf, in Austria,
processes 1200 kg/hr, distinguishes and separates all types of plastic used for
packaging and distinguishes 250 different colors and shades (WRF 1994).

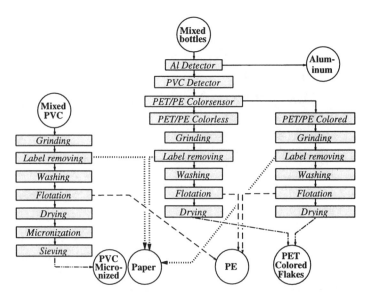

Source: Manzone 1993.

Figure 12.9:   TECOPLAST recycling plant

PET is also recyclable as such. In the US 30% of PET bottles are recycled (Rathje and Murphy 1992, p. 205). Half of the total is attributable to Wellman Inc. of Shrewsbury NJ. Wellman currently recycles PET bottles at two locations, Johnsonville SC and Mullagh, Ireland. The process involves removing aluminum caps and paper labels, then cutting off the black HDPE base cups. The latter are crushed and sold as flakes to be recycled into plastic handles for irons and other items. The PET itself is recycled as stuffing for sleeping bags and ski jackets (e.g. Patagonia Inc.) or as fibers for polyester carpets (ibid.). In 1990, the ultra-conservative Food and Drug Administration (FDA) in the US granted PET the first exception to its rule prohibiting the use of recycled plastic in food or beverage containers. Both Coca Cola and Pepsi Cola apparently plan to do this (ibid.).

Polystyrene foam, one of the most controversial packaging materials, can be recycled. The process starts with collection and sorting, followed by (1) quality check, (2) washing to remove food residue, (3) compaction and grinding, (4) drying, (5) melting, (6) filtration, (7) molding into pellets and (8) cooling. The most expensive equipment involved — after sorting — is an extruder which incorporates steps (5–7). The recycled polystyrene pellets have approximately the same market value as pellets of virgin material (Kuo 1990). Many polystyrene products are already made from mixtures of virgin and recycled material. One interesting product from Mandish Research, Florida, called 'lightweight concrete' is actually 90% recycled polystyrene (ibid.)

Polystyrene recycling was stimulated in the US by the widely publicized 'hamburger' controversy (between polystyrene foam and papier maché as containers for hamburgers and other 'fast food'). When McDonald's, under pressure from environmentalists, decided in favor of paper, the polystyrene industry saw a major threat. In response, National Polystyrene Recycling Co. (US) was created as a joint venture between several oil companies (Amoco, ARCO, Chevron, Mobil) along with several polystyrene producers (Dow, Fina, Huntsman, Polysar) in the late 1980s. The first operational recycling plants as of December 1990 were located in Brooklyn NY, Leominster MA, and Portland ORE, with plants in Chicago, San Francisco and Philadelphia scheduled to follow by mid-1991 (ibid.). (We do not have more recent information.) It is important to emphasize that polystyrene recycling is only practical in conjunction with an institutionalized collection and sorting system.

Another approach to plastic material recycling is being explored by several European manufacturers of monomers. Depolymerization can be accomplished by 'solvolysis' via certain alcohols (e.g. methanol) or glycols. Either methanolysis or glycolysis can be used to reduce polyesters, polyurethanes or polyamides to their constituent monomers. In particular, this approach is being investigated for PET by several major firms, including Hoechst-Celanese,

Dupont, and Eastman Kodak. Microwave depolymerization is another promising approach, now being applied by one firm both in Canada and the UK. Another proprietary system uses microwaves to break the polymer linkages, and is claimed to recapture enough heat from the dissolution process to provide the necessary electric power to keep going, once it starts. The initial application is for depolymerizing automobile tires (WRF 1994).

There are fundamental limits to plastics materials recycling, however, arising from the fact that even plastics using the same resin (e.g. PVC) can also use a wide range of different additives (see Table 12.5). Recovery systems are inherently complex and capital intensive. They will not compete economically with either landfill or incineration under present conditions (unless these alternatives are strongly discouraged).

There are some possible uses for mixed plastics that do not involve separation. One such use is to produce a kind of synthetic 'wood'. In principle, a plastic-based product similar to wood would be very attractive for many purposes, ranging from park benches and garden furniture to roof shingles, doors, floors and wall-panels. The plastic material would never rot, would never need to be painted (although it could be) and would not warp or twist. Minor technical problems need to be solved to make the material easier to cut, shape and fasten — like natural wood — but these do not appear to be serious. Such materials have already been produced and put to use. A German firm, EVD, makes a compressed board from packaging waste (combined with industrial waste) that can be used for brief-cases, clip-boards, office and kitchen furniture and wallboards. A vacation resort in St. Johns, US Virgin Islands, not only utilizes such materials exclusively in the construction of its villas, but advertises the fact to attract 'ecotourists'. Wal-Mart Inc., the biggest retailer in the US has built an 'eco-mart' near Lawrence Kansas that uses recycled materials for floors, roof, carpet and even paving in the parking lot. The major drawback to wider use seems to be market acceptance by consumers (and, of course, marketing by producers).

Nevertheless, practical difficulties must not be understated. The following story illustrates the sort of marketing problem that can arise:

> Syacon was originally conceived using recycled poly-butylene terephthalate (PBT) aggregate from GE which was available in white, gray, or black. The marketing group wanted, and got, colors of aggregate which were virgin plastic, rather than recycled. The reasoning was that we could then better compete against terrazzo, which was available in a wide range of colors, but nothing like the potential colors available for plastics. Unfortunately, that nearly doubled the cost of already very expensive (by construction floor industry standards) aggregate in the product. Despite the cost, we were able to compete for, and get, jobs because of our ability to provide special colors. What caused the removal of the product from the market was that we experienced a few 'popouts' of plastic aggregate in floors where spiked heels or other types of point loads were commonly found. The marketing

Table 12.5: Pollutants in plastics, 1989 (mg/kg)

Pollutant	Cd	Cr	Cu	Ni	Pb	Zn	Sn	Cl	F
PE-film									
● transparent	1	8	24	2	72	97	7	3 412	11
● white	<1	13	35	5	60	427	2	2 790	25
● yellow/red	20	347	55	4	1738	100	4	3 182	28
● blue/green	1	81	93	3	591	403	5	1 930	33
PE-hollow bodies									
● transp. /white	<1	0	12	0	15	247	6	1 070	5
● yellow/red	103	9	83	0	73	44	8	3 397	7
● blue/green	10	4	26	0	50	154	4	2 998	9
PP-cups	2	28	20	18	7	55	0	630	10
PP-cups									
● transp. /white	2	0	44	0	11	694	0	1 986	4
● colored	28	0	51	0	24	139	3	500	4
Polystyrene	2	0	32	0	21	151	3	7 100	8
Laminated foil	6	19	94	8	93	143	91	98 527	8
PE-nets	3	637	41	19	2 425	672	17	1 000	43
PVC									
● cups	1	0	20	1	13	46	371	454 250	9
● hollow bodies	15	0	14	0	12	58	452	434 000	10
● form pieces	2	4	47	10	22	88	362	418 866	36
PE-caps									
● transp. /white	4	69	66	59	14	381	4	750	12
● yellow/red	653	0	26	0	32	47	2	500	9
● blue/green	159	69	577	39	14	192	5	500	14
Other caps	40	0	245	0	17	370	2	750	11
Daily articles									
● PVC	420	156	26	13	1 679	393	78	283 250	35
● PE/PP	347	12	19	0	115	183	6	1 812	16
● Others	88	4	555	104	48	2 235	7	2000	

Source: After UBA report, January 1989.

group though aware of the potential for the problem before its introduction soon
stopped promoting the product because of the combined price and popout situation. (Mauerhofer 1993)

An exciting variant of this idea is to use recycled plastic in the form of tiny
solid balls to make synthetic 'snow' and 'ice' for ski-slopes and skating rinks
that could be used in summer. This is a high-tech (and rather expensive)
product that would not use much plastic material, but would help overcome
the reluctance of consumers to accept recycled plastics.

A last-resort method for reducing mixed plastic materials to their component hydrocarbons is also technically feasible. Pilot plants to do this have
been demonstrated by several petrochemical companies, including Shell and
British Petroleum (BP). BP Chemicals has built a pilot scale pyrolysis plant
for the conversion of mixed plastic wastes to hydrocarbon feedstocks. The
German utility VEBA has converted mixed plastic and household wastes to
synthetic fuel oil by hydrogenation. This oil is then recycled back to raw
materials for plastics in a neighboring refinery (ibid.). However, the economics are very unattractive compared to the use of virgin materials and will
probably remain so for decades to come.

An interesting study has been carried out recently by Dutch researchers at
the Wageningen Agricultural University in the Netherlands (Starreveld and
van Ierland 1994). They constructed an optimization model for plastics recycling, based on relatively standard and non-controversial assumptions about
technological alternatives and prices. The 'base case' assumed oil prices at
$20 per barrel, landfill dumping costs of $25 and incineration costs of $90
per tonne of waste plastics. Four major plastics were considered (PVC, PE,
PP and PS) which account for 85% of demand. Four categories of demand
were considered, namely packaging, construction, transport and miscellaneous. Within each category, demand was further subdivided by quality levels,
distinguishing 'virgin' applications (such as food and beverages), 'high-
quality' applications permitting a mix of virgin and recycled materials, and
'low-quality' applications for degraded or contaminated materials. Demand
schedules and elasticities of substitution characteristics were estimated roughly,
using 1986 as the base year. A standard linear programming software package was used. The model was used to explore the opportunities for recycling
under various assumptions about disposal charges.

The most controversial assumptions in the model concern the options (and
costs) for recycling plastic materials. Needless to say, the model considerably
simplifies the reality. For example, it assumes the cost of 'thermal conversion' of waste plastics for high-quality applications (exemplified in the real
world by the case of polystyrene, discussed above) to be $2400 per tonne on
a small scale, rising to $6500 per tonne as the scale of operation rises. Not

surprisingly, the model does not select this option under any circumstances, regardless of the charge for disposal. Nevertheless, the results of many optimization runs are interesting. Most interesting of all is the fact that product recycling is clearly preferable to materials recycling, under all conditions. Beyond this, the level of recycling vs. disposal is a strong function of the assumed disposal charge. For example, to achieve 25% recycling, the model calculates that a disposal charge of $300 per tonne would be needed — extremely high in comparison with the assumed costs of dumping or incineration (ibid.).

In some ways the model is clearly too conservative. For one thing, it probably underestimates the potential market for low-quality applications of plastics by an order of magnitude, having no way to take into account the potential for product improvement and the potential impact of serious mass marketing of such products as synthetic wood. For another, it (admittedly) does not reflect the likelihood of major technological progress in materials recycling.

12.7. ENERGY RECOVERY FROM PACKAGING WASTE

Incineration is the other form of 'recycling', to recover heat energy, as noted above. This is clearly the preferred option in some countries (e.g. Switzerland), despite the relatively low efficiency of the process (Table 12.4) and even though 80% of the cost of a modern 'high-tech' incinerator may be invested in pollution controls.

There are two particularly vexing problems associated with the incineration option. One is the fact that many plastics contain significant quantities of metals which either volatilize (like mercury) and are dispersed with the combustion products, or are retained in fly ash or bottom ash. Incinerator ash is notoriously toxic because of the high level of content of heavy metals such as cadmium and arsenic. Admittedly many of these metals are attributable to wastes (e.g. batteries) not associated with packaging materials. But significant quantities of cadmium, for instance, are used in inks and as plastic stabilizers. Table 12.5 indicates the extent of contamination of plastics by metals, many of which are toxic.

The other vexing problem associated with incineration is specific to plastics, especially PVC and others that contain chlorine. PVC, in particular, constitutes about 22% of total Western European plastics consumption. Of this, about 10% is coatings, 7% is flexible film and 9% for bottles, especially mineral water. Packaging uses account for 18% of PVC use in Europe, but only 7% in the US. Films, in particular, contain over 50% filler and 16% plasticizer (mostly di-2–ethyl-hexyl adipate, or DEHP). DEHP has been declared a 'probable carcinogen' in the US, but 'not a carcinogen' by the EU. This may account for the much larger use of PVC in packaging, especially of food and water, in Europe (MIT 1993). The combustion of chlorine-containing plastics, like PVC, generates hydrogen chloride, HCI, which is easily recovered from the gas stream and neutralized. The chlorine industry minimizes the dangers associated with HCI, pointing out that HCI accounts for only 2% of acidification in Europe, and PVC accounts for only about 10% of this (e.g. Manzone 1993). A second concern about combustion, of course, is the potential generation of carcinogenic dioxins and chlorinated poly aromatic hydrocarbons (PAHs).

This last issue is extremely controversial. Environmental groups, especially Greenpeace, have strongly criticized the use of PVC (and chlorine itself) on these grounds (e.g. Johnston and Troendel 1993). An independent life-cycle analysis of alternative packaging materials, by the Tellus Institute, was carried out for the State of New Jersey, the Council of State Governments and USEPA (Tellus 1992). This study assessed direct and indirect emissions for all major packaging materials, weighted by toxicity and carcinogenicity relative to lead. The dollar values were computed as multiples of the average dollar cost of controlling various types of lead emissions ($1600/lb). Using this approach, dioxins received an extremely high weight, as did vinyl chloride monomer (VCM) and mercury emissions from chlorine manufacturing. These emissions adversely affected the valuation of PVC *vis-à-vis* other materials. In the Tellus study, PVC was evaluated as 12–16 times as costly (in the above sense) as other alternatives (ibid.). In fairness, however, it must be acknowledged that both the data base and the valuation methodology are open to question and need further refining.

The Greenpeace assertions and the Tellus study were strongly challenged by the Vinyl Institute, the Chlorine Institute, Euro-Chlor and other industry groups. These groups have commissioned other studies, such as the MIT study (MIT 1993), and the recent TNO study (Wormgoor 1994). Most of the recent work tends to confirm that dioxins are less toxic to humans than to rats, and that they are generated (in small quantities, to be sure) by a large number of combustion processes, including forest fires. Apparently incineration of chlorinated plastics is, at best, a very minor and not very dangerous source of dioxins.

Nevertheless, concerns linger and waste incinerators are not popular. The fundamental problem with conventional incineration is that to achieve effective destruction of complex toxic organic molecules, not to mention thermodynamic efficiency, high temperatures are needed. But, at high temperatures metals like arsenic, cadmium, lead and mercury are volatilized. They can be recaptured only by cooling the exhaust gases and inducing the metallic vapors to recondense on particulates that are subsequently captured by electrostatic precipitators (ESPs). The precipitator technology is quite efficient and reliable, but not inexpensive. Moreover, it takes a significant amount of the energy that is supposedly being recovered. This problem is fundamental. The difficulties are compounded by the presence of chlorine compounds, especially corrosive hydrochloric acid, in the exhaust stream.

The long-term solution has to be to abandon conventional incineration altogether. It is a technological dinosaur. There are at least two generic alternatives, although neither has yet been taken seriously by either the electric utilities or the waste-disposal community. The first is to apply low-temperature thermo-chemical gasification technologies — similar, in principle to coal gasification technologies that have been under development for a number of years — to a mixed plastic waste input stream.[6] This would have to be followed by cooling (to condense metallic vapors), fly ash removal, desulfurization and hydrogen chloride removal of the gas prior to use as fuel for a two-stage combined cycle. The first stage would either be a small aero-derivative gas turbine, such as the GE LM2500, or a heavy duty industrial gas turbine designed for stationary applications. Some turbines of the latter type already have operating experience with low-calorific fuels such as blast furnace gas. The second stage would be a conventional steam turbine bottoming cycle, using the gas turbine exhaust as one of its heat sources.[7]

Gasifiers are of two types. The first type uses heat supplied directly by partial oxidation of the feedstock to yield carbon monoxide; this is normally accompanied by a 'shift reaction' in which steam reacts with carbon to yield more carbon monoxide plus hydrogen gas, along with nitrogen from the air. If pure oxygen is used (as coal gasification plants would do), the result is 'synthesis gas', a mixture of carbon monoxide, carbon dioxide, water vapor and hydrogen; if air is used for oxidation purposes the product is diluted with nitrogen and is, essentially, 'town gas' similar to the gas which was generated from coal to supply gas light and stove gas for cities before natural gas became widely available.

The second type of gasifier uses indirect heating through a heat exchanger. In this case the process is simple pyrolysis, at temperatures of 700–800°C with no oxygen present. The result, again, would be a mixture of carbon monoxide, carbon dioxide, water vapor, hydrogen, methane and tars. The amount of water vapor depends on the moisture content of the feed. Since municipal waste is quite dry in general, the resulting pyrolysis gas would consist mostly of carbon monoxide, carbon dioxide, hydrogen and hydrocarbons. Two indirectly heated gasifier designs have been tested to date: one uses circulation of hot sand as a heat exchange medium; the other uses a fluidized bed (Larson and Consonni 1994).

A third design is known as the Continuous Ablative Thermolysis Reactor (CAR), which is being developed in Canada by Castle Capital Ltd. A

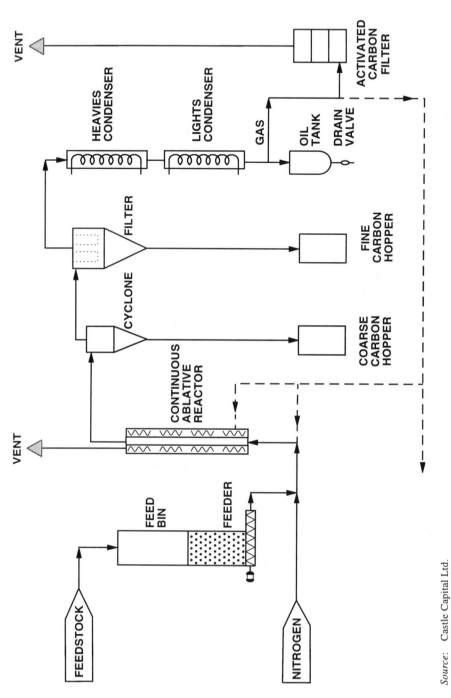

Source: Castle Capital Ltd.

Figure 12.10: Schematic for a Continuous Ablative Reactor (CAR)

232

schematic version is shown as Figure 12.10. It has been tested on a small scale on a variety of feedstocks ranging from shredded tires (see Chapter 12, Tires), sawdust, cow manure, sewage sludge, automobile shredder fluff, oil shale and municipal refuse. Here, too, the product would be a gaseous fuel to be used in a gas turbine along the lines described above. The CAR reactor is a proprietary version of the second type of indirect (heat exchanger) gasifier described previously. It achieves very high heat transfer rates in the reactor at pressures up to 100 atmospheres.

As applied to municipal wastes, the next step is gas cleaning and cooling. Aero-derivative gas turbines are very susceptible to erosion by particulates (Kurkela *et al.* 1993, cited in Williams *et al.* 1994). Ash remains solid at these gas temperatures, and easily volatilized metals (like arsenic, mercury, sodium and potassium) can be condensed and removed with particulates at temperatures below 400°C. The particulates, in turn, may be removed by ceramic filters or liquid scrubbers.

Tars must be removed or cracked. The former can be done by further cooling. However this is a loss of chemical energy and another disposal problem, so the better solution would be to crack the tar in a catalytic cracking unit using dolomite as a catalyst. Hydrodesulfurization is a standard off-the-shelf technology. Hydrogen chloride can be removed in the liquid scrubber. Further discussion of the technical details of low-temperature thermochemical gasifiers and gas-cleaning technology would take us too far afield for present purposes, however.

SPECIAL SOURCES(12)

A number of general sources have been used in this chapter in addition to those cited in the text; these are listed below as well as in the general reference section.

(Corradini 1990) Corradini, Roland, *Packaging in Europe: Belgium, the Netherlands and Luxembourg*, Special Report (EIU 2048), The Economist Intelligence Unit, London, November 1990.

(Duchin 1994) Duchin, Faye, *Household Use and Disposal of Plastics; an Input–Output Case Study for New York City*, Report to the AT&T Industrial Ecology Faculty Fellowship Program, Institute for Economic Analysis, New York University, New York, June 1994.

(Habersatter and Widmer 1991) Habersatter, K. and F. Widmer, *Ecobalance of Packaging Materials State of 1990*, Environmental Series (132), Swiss Federal Office of Environment, Forest and Landscape, Zurich, February 1991.

(Lushington 1990) Lushington, Roger, *Packaging in Europe: West Germany*, Special Report (EIU 2047), The Economist Intelligence Unit, London, August 1990.

(Lushington 1991) Lushington, Roger, *Packaging in Europe: The United Kingdom*, Special Report (EIU 2157), The Economist Intelligence Unit, London, November 1991.

(Lushington and Mills 1987) Lushington, Roger and Rowena Mills, *The European Market for Rigid Packaging*, Special Report (EIU 1100), The Economist Intelligence Unit, London, May 1987.

(PWMI undated) PWMI, *Weighing Up the Environmental Balance*, PWMI (European Centre for Plastics in the Environment), Brussels, undated.

(Reeves 1990) Reeves, Teresa, *Packaging in Europe: Italy*, Special Report (EIU 2049), The Economist Intelligence Unit, London, August 1990.

NOTES(12)

1. In the US per capita consumption of packaging materials in 1980 was over 275 kg/yr (Gaines 1981). The production of packaging materials of all kinds directly consumed 3% of the national energy budget in that year, while the transportation of packaged goods (and packaging wastes) probably consumed a higher proportion of transportation energy (being disproportionately concentrated in the retail and wholesale trade sectors). Figures for Europe are not available, but they would be comparable.

2. The population of EU(9) in mid-1993 was 349 million, while the other countries had aggregate population of 43.5 million, or 12.5%.

3. It is difficult to explain the difference, unless it reflects the fact that the US uses considerably more paper and paper products than Europe, presumably because of a price differential. As an example, grocery stores in the US routinely package goods in paper bags, whereas in Europe the same goods are likely to be packaged in plastic bags.

4. In the case of recycled (remelted) glass there is a slight — 15% — energy saving as compared to glass made from virgin materials.

5. Thermodynamic analysis shows that the 'quality' (i.e. usability) of the (heat) energy recovered in incinerators is comparatively low. Incinerators are only efficient if built on a very large scale; but direct use of the heat (e.g. for district heating) is then virtually impossible because of distributional difficulties. To reconvert this energy to electricity, a further 60% to 65% is lost.

6. Shell Chemicals and Leuna Werke are jointly exploring the gasification of plastic wastes to synthesis gas.

7. A recent discussion of the application of low-temperature gasification in the context of energy recovery from biomass by Williams and Larson describes the dimensions of the problem and gives numerous references (Williams and Larson 1993). See also Larson and Consonni 1994; Williams *et al.* 1994.

13. Scrap tires

Paul M. Weaver

13.1. SUMMARY

Scrap tires are becoming a major environmental hazard in all countries where there are large numbers of automobiles and trucks. In numbers, about 240 million used tires, weighing 3 MMT are discarded each year in the US alone (Noyes 1993, pp. 32–5). Figures for Western Europe (EU) are of the order of 195 million tires and 2.5 MMT, respectively. Retreading is on the decline, for passenger cars, though increasing for trucks. In the US, 18.6 car tires and 14.9 million truck tires were retreaded in 1990 — about 14% (ibid.). Another 25.9 million (10.7%) was burned for energy recovery in 1990. Of this, 6 million were burned by cement kilns and 12 million were burned for fuel by the pulp and paper industry; most of the rest were burned for electric power generation (ibid.). Another 7% of scrap tires in the US was used for a variety of other purposes, ranging from artificial reefs to paving (ibid.). Thus, only 32% of this material was recovered and recycled for any useful purpose. The situation in Europe is similar.

Accumulations of unusable old tires in the US amount to something like two billion (2×10^9) tires (24 MMT) (ibid.). Apart from being unsightly, these accumulations are public health hazards, being natural breeding grounds for mosquitoes and other insects that can carry disease. They are also extremely inflammable and regularly subject to 'accidental' fires that are virtually impossible to extinguish and that generate black clouds of acrid smoke containing a number of toxic or carcinogenic pollutants. Obstacles to recycling are numerous. Yet the only two major alternatives, at present — apart from accidental fires — are landfilling and burning (mostly by farmers) in open fields.

The hazards of open burning are obvious. Landfilling is, unfortunately, not a viable disposal method because buried tires tend to work their way to the surface and break through the surface liner. In effect, they refuse to stay buried. This means that landfills containing large accumulations of old tires are also potential fire and health hazards. (Moreover, a fire that starts on the surface of such a landfill can eventually work its way underground, where it may smolder for months or years.) Thus landfilling is not a practical long-term solution to the problem.

Apart from the environmental problems associated with scrap tires, they constitute a significant wasted resource. Tires are extremely energy intensive. In addition to the energy used in chemical processing and fabrication, the energy content of the rubber (including carbon black and other additives) is about 50% higher than that of coal.[1] In other words, the heating value of 2.5 MMT of tires is equal to that of perhaps 3.75 MMT of coal. Moreover, scrap tires can be used as fuel in cement plants, paper and pulp plants and electric power generating plants. Another technological possibility of interest is depolymerization to recover raw materials.

There are strong reasons for governments to reduce tire scrappage. This can be done by encouraging longer tire life, more remanufacturing (retreading), more recycling of the materials embodied within scrap tires and (as a last resort) energy recovery from scrap tires. As far as can be determined by an outsider to the industry, technology is not the barrier. The reasons for today's wasteful and environmentally damaging practices have more to do with industry structure and tradition. Indeed, truck and bus tires are mostly leased and routinely returned for retreading on a regular basis, with the result that the average truck or bus tire lasts five or six times as long as the average automobile tire in Europe.

Policies that would be effective in changing current practices are discussed later, but the key point would seem to be to make the manufacturer (or a designated agent) responsible for taking back the tire at the end of its useful life. This would induce manufacturers to design tires to last longer, on the one hand, and for easier retreading, on the other. Consumers would need an incentive to cooperate. There are two possibilities worth considering. One is the 'returnable deposit' which would be a sum of money retained by the seller and payable to the consumer on returning a *retreadable* tire. The other possibility is to create a tire-leasing system similar to that which now exists for trucks and buses. The two schemes might actually be combined, since the only way to induce people to lease their tires rather than buying them outright would be through price differentials. The returnable deposit would, of course, add to the apparent price of the tire to an individual buyer, whereas it could be waived for a leasing organization.

Goals of public policy: to minimize open burning of tires; to eliminate landfilling of tires; to recover valuable resources; to increase tire life; to increase tire recycling.

13.2.   TIRE PRODUCTION

Apart from Japan, the US and the EU are the major world tire-producing and -consuming regions. In gross output tonnage terms, France (727 000 tonnes) is the world's third most important tire producer (after the US and Japan). Germany's industry (641 000 tonnes) is almost as large. Spain, Italy and the UK each produce about 350 000 tonnes. With production in the Benelux countries (170 000 tonnes) and elsewhere in the EU (183 000 tonnes), total EU tire production is about 2.75 MMT.

Rubber constitutes more than half by weight of the materials used in tire production. The French and German tire industries each consume more than 300 000 tonnes of rubber annually. The Spanish, Italian and British tire industries annually consume about 180 000 tonnes each. Half of consumption is of natural rubber, which has to be imported. Since the main raw material for producing synthetic rubber is oil, much of which is also imported from outside the US and EU area, tire production relies heavily on imported raw materials.

The idea of recycling the materials represented by waste tires is not new. Initially, it was part of the tire life cycle. The rubber industry 'reclaimed' scrap tires; i.e. recovered the natural rubber from which the tire was made for use in a wide range of tire and non-tire applications. In essence, reclaiming attempts to reverse the vulcanization process at the heart of tire manufacturing. Natural rubber latex is a monomer that is plastic and tacky. Vulcanization is a chemical process that uses the chemical energy of sulfur to forge cross-linkages between the hydrocarbon chains of natural rubber latex. The result, vulcanized rubber, is a polymer. Vulcanization gives rubber the mechanical properties (especially, elasticity) needed for practical applications. Tires constitute the single most important such application.

Like vulcanization, reclamation is a chemical process. Its object is to reverse the vulcanization by splitting the sulfur cross-links to regenerate a viscous monomer comparable in character to latex. Initially, reclaiming rubber from tires was possible — and widespread — because tires were made from natural rubber, which is technically straightforward to reclaim. Several reclaiming processes were developed and widely used. However, with growth in demand for rubber products, concerns over natural rubber supplies (especially as a result of the Japanese invasion of Southeast Asia in World War II), and the need to improve the technical performance and useful lifetime of tires, there have been consistent pressures over the past 50 years for the development of synthetic rubbers and for their incorporation into tire products. R&D in this area has been extremely successful. A wide range of synthetic elastomers has been developed using petroleum-based feedstocks. Each has specific physical and chemical properties that offer different combinations of advantages and disadvantages.

With a wide choice of synthetics available, the tire industry has been able to select and blend materials for use in different kinds of tire and in different parts of tires to deliver products of ever higher performance. The disadvantage is that with the development and use of synthetic elastomers, reclamation has become more difficult and the reclaimed product correspondingly less functional as compared to the original. Synthetic rubbers do not devulcanize as well as natural rubber. Because tires are assembled from different components made from different polymers, reclaimed material is not pure. Its properties are not the same as those of virgin materials. Moreover, because different manufacturers use different blending formulae and the rubber content (by type of rubber) varies between types of tire, scrap tires are an 'unreliable' materials source. This means that reclaimed rubber lacks the necessary properties to meet the technical specifications of today's high-performance tires.

The use of steel-belted radial tires (which, because of their better road performance characteristics and longevity now dominate the passenger car tire market) has brought additional complications. While making the reclamation process for rubber more difficult, the development of safer, more durable tires has increased the possibilities for retreading. Commercial vehicle fleets and airlines exploit this by routinely retreading their tires. Retreading could potentially be expanded significantly within the passenger car sector. Unfortunately, a combination of economic, technical and 'image' factors has led to a steady reduction in the scale of retreading in the passenger car sector.

Retreading depends upon having a high-quality (reusable) tire carcass. Most scrap passenger car tires examined with a view to retreading are unsuitable because of damaged side walls or excessive wear. Also, the market for passenger car tire retreads is limited by their unfavorable image. They are widely regarded as inferior, if not unsafe (an image created, in part, by the advertising of new tire manufacturers). They have little price advantage, if any, over cheap, low-quality new tires imported from the Far East or from Eastern Europe.

13.3.   THE CURRENT TIRE LIFE CYCLE

In order to trace the fate of the materials involved, we can conceptualize a tire 'life cycle' from monomer production, through polymerization and tire fabrication to tire consumption, to scrap tire disposal. We do not consider the chemical processes hereafter. Production is made up of new and retreaded tires. During manufacturing, some materials are lost. There is also a fraction of mis-manufactured tires. Estimates place total manufacturing losses to be

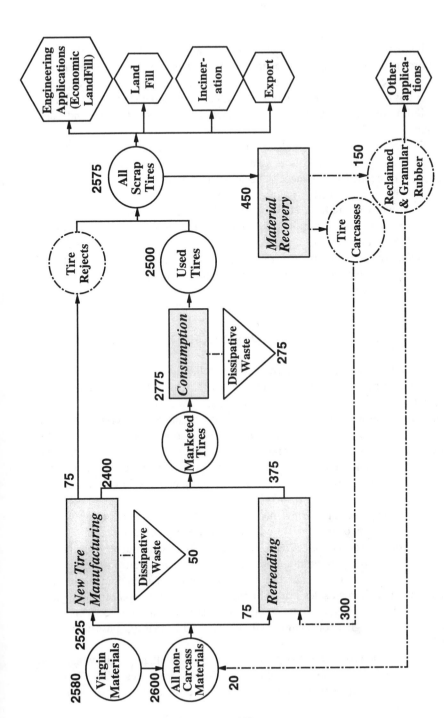

Figure 13.1: Provisional reconstruction of the EU tire life cycle (1000 tonnes)

239

about 5% (Guelorget *et al.* 1993). Further material losses occur as material embodied within a tire is worn away during use and is lost dissipatively to the environment. Losses here are estimated at between 5% and 15% depending on tire type. Average mass losses of about 10% are likely (ibid.). (Dissipative losses of tire material on the roads constitute a significant source of cadmium pollution of the environment, for instance. See Chapter 6, Zinc and cadmium.)

The remaining material ends up in the scrap tires. Scrap tires may be sent for retreading, for materials recovery, or (together with mis-manufactured tires) for secondary use in engineering applications. Some scrap tires are exported for use. Directly or indirectly, however, most scrap tires are incinerated (with or without heat recovery), buried in landfills, or stockpiled.

A provisional reconstruction of the tire cycle for Europe is given in Figure 13.1. Information has been pieced together from several sources to derive estimates of the quantity of scrap tires occurring annually, the levels and types of materials recovery/re-use within and outside the tire sector, and the pattern of final waste disposal.

13.4.   THE QUANTITIES OF SCRAP TIRES

Data on the quantities of scrap tires, noted earlier, have been collected for the US by the Environmental Protection Agency (Noyes 1993). Such data are not collected as such for the EU region. Estimates must be based on production data, tire sales in the replacement equipment market, vehicle scrapping levels and similar sources. From gross tonnage production data, it is possible to determine the split between production of passenger car tires, commercial vehicle tires, and other tire products. For France the tonnage split for the production year 1991 was 52%, 21% and 27% respectively. For Germany, the tonnage split was 58%, 25% and 17% respectively.

It is perhaps not surprising that passenger car tire production outweighs (by a factor of two) truck tire production. However, the surprising feature is the significance of the 'other' category. This includes motor cycle tires, heavy tires for industrial/agricultural/construction equipment, trailer tires, aircraft tires, inner tubes, and so on. The split between original equipment and replacement equipment sales is also instructive. In general, replacement equipment sales account for about 55–60% of total sales, in tonnage terms. The percentage is higher for commercial vehicles (60%) than for passenger cars (55%).

In 1990, the size of the EU passenger car parc (including light vans) was approximately 131 million (Table 13.1). For the countries of the EU for which we have replacement equipment (RE) sales data, the car parc was 113

Table 13.1: The EU vehicle parc and the replacement market for tires, 1990 (millions)

Country	Passenger cars in use	Replacement PC tire sales	Commercial vehicles (CVs) in use	Replacement CV tire sales
Benelux	9.53	6.0	0.92	1.2
Denmark	1.70			
France	23.55	24.4	4.74	3.0
Germany	35.52	23.1	2.25	2.2
Greece	1.60			
Italy	24.80	16.2	2.43	1.5
Ireland	0.80			
Portugal	1.90			
Spain	11.50			
UK	19.74	20.0	2.86	3.2
EU	130.65	*104.5*	*16.5*	*13.9*

Note: Figures in italics are estimates.

Sources: EIU, *Rubber Trends*, September 1991

million. Sales of tires to the replacement market in these countries amounted to 90 million units. This gives an average of slightly less than one (0.79) replacement tire per car per year. Since each car has a lifetime of 11–12 years (on the average) these statistics mean that, during the life of the car, about 9 replacement tires will be purchased, in addition to 5 tires as original equipment.

Applying this ratio to the EU car parc, we estimate replacement passenger car tire sales at 104.5 million units. For the countries for which we have commercial vehicle replacement equipment data, the commercial vehicle fleet was just over 13 million vehicles. Replacement equipment tire sales were just over 11 million units. The RE:CV ratio is 0.84. Applying this to the EU commercial vehicle fleet of about 16.5 million vehicles, we estimate replacement equipment commercial vehicle tire sales at 13.9 million units.

The number of tires discarded annually can be estimated as annual replacement sales plus 5× the number of vehicles scrapped. The latter number is slightly less than the number of new vehicles sold, or roughly 15 million per year for the EU. On this basis, total EU scrappage would be of the order of 195 million tires, about 20% less than the US total.

There is reasonable consensus that the average new passenger car tire weighs between 6 and 8 kg (e.g., Michelin 1993). Estimates of average commercial vehicle tire weight vary from 28 kg (e.g., EcoPlan 1993) to 65 kg (e.g., Guelorget *et al.* 1993). From data giving gross output by tire type in both unit and tonnage terms (e.g., EIU 1989), we have estimated the average weights of light commercial vehicle tires (21 kg) and heavy goods vehicle tires (50 kg). Specialist tires for aircraft, agricultural, industrial and construction machinery are significantly heavier. As a result of different approaches to data presentation, involving aggregations of vehicles into different categories, it is common to find discrepancies between studies in the weights assumed for different kinds of tire. If light commercial vehicle tires are grouped with passenger car tires, the class average tire weight would be about 8 to 10 kg. When light and heavy commercial vehicles are grouped together, the class average tire weight will likely be 30 to 35 kg. If heavy commercial vehicles are grouped with specialist tires, the class average tire weight will be 60 to 65 kg.

Since our data on replacement equipment sales are based on only two vehicle groupings, we have assumed average class weights of 8 kg (passenger cars) and 30 kg (commercial vehicles). Replacement equipment sales in the EU are therefore estimated at 836 kMT for passenger cars and 417 kMT for commercial vehicles. Scrap tires arising from vehicle scrapping are assumed to be an additional 684 kMT for passenger cars and 278 kMT for commercial vehicles. This gives a total scrapping weight of 2.2 MMT (almost 1.5 MMT for passenger cars and about 0.7 MMT for commercial vehicles). Assuming that this represents 80% of the total tire market (since about 20% of production is neither of passenger car nor commercial vehicle tires), total annual scrappage would be equal to annual production, or 2.75 MMT. However, assuming 10% weight loss through wear, this reduces to a little under 2.5 MMT tonnes. This is our estimate of the total annual quantity of scrap tires arising in the EU. On this basis, the corresponding figure for the US would be 3 MMT.

The quantity of scrap tires generated each year has been increasing. However, tire wear is essentially proportional to vehicle miles travelled, so it should stabilize as growth in total vehicle kilometrage slows. In the longer term, the quantity of scrap tires may decrease slightly as the market share of longer-lived, low-rolling-resistance (LRL) tires increases. However, these trends do not yet affect the broad picture.

13.5.   CURRENT FATE OF SCRAP TIRES

Data on the current fate of these scrap tires is not systematically collected. Several studies at national scale have tried to divide scrap tire generation among the range of recycling and final disposal alternatives e.g. Elm Energy and Recycling (UK) in 1993 and ANRED (France) in 1991. These national studies are not always consistent. For some countries, data from industrial sources on the quantities of materials recycled (i.e., the production of retreaded tires, 'reclaim' and ground rubber) are available and are likely to be reliable.

For the UK, Elm Energy and Recycling (EER) estimated total tire scrappage in 1991 at 450 kMT (EER 1994). It estimates disposal allocation as follows: landfill, 67% (301.5 kMT); incinerated with or without heat recovery, 9% (40.5 kMT); and materials recovery, 24% (108 kMT). Retreading/remolding accounted for 18% of scrap materials (81 kMT). Granulate/stamped rubber accounted for 6% (27 kMT).

The UK Retread Manufacturers' Association (RMA) in a 1993 publication suggests that retreads have about an 18% share of the replacement market for passenger car tires and a 34% share of the replacement truck tire market. Together with data on replacement tire sales (Table 13.1), these data imply that 28.8 kMT of scrap passenger car tires (8 kg average weight) and 54.4 kMT of scrap heavy commercial vehicle tires (50 kg average weight) are retreaded. The total, 83.2 kMT, is close to that suggested in the EER report (ibid.). Another study suggests total UK production of ground rubber (powder and crumb) to be 60 kMT, of which about half (30 kMT) is from scrap tires (Burlace 1991). This is also close to the EER estimate (EER 1994).

For France, an estimate of tire scrappage of 502 kMT is available for 1983 (ANRED 1985, 1986). Evidence on the fate of mis-manufactured and used tires in France is given in Table 13.2. With respect to mis-manufactured tires (which amounted to only 15 kMT of materials), a little over half of the material involved (53%) was recovered as 'reclaim'. A further 20% was used for other engineering applications. The remainder went to landfill or incineration. Of the 502 kMT of used tires in 1983, 72 kMT (14.3%) was sent for retreading. A further 8 kMT (1.6%) was used for direct raw materials recovery and 9 kMT (1.8%) was used for other engineering applications. Approximately 20 kMT of used tires (4.0%) was exported. All the remainder, 393 kMT (nearly 80%) was disposed of directly or indirectly through landfill or by incineration. The bulk of incineration was apparently by uncontrolled burning on open fields.

It is likely that the current figure for French tire scrappage is closer to 600 kMT. A breakdown of French production for 1991 by type of tire and weight

Industrial ecology

Table 13.2:   The fate of mis-manufactured and used tires: France, 1983

	Used tires		Reject tires	
	kMT	*%*	*kMT*	*%*
Material recovery				
a) carcass recovery	72	14.3		
b) powdered rubber	3	0.6	8	53.3
c) 'reclaim'	5	1.0		
Engineering applications	9	1.8	3	20.0
Landfill	236	47.0	2	13.3
Direct incineration	7	1.4	2	13.3
Indirect incineration	150	29.9		
Export	20	4.0		
TOTAL	502	100.0	15	100.0

Source: ANRED 1983, cited in Guelorget *et al.* 1993.

of output is given in Appendix A, Table A.19 (SESSI 1991). This shows that about 10% by weight of tires produced in 1991 were retreaded (i.e., less than in 1983). The ultimate fate of scrap tires is estimated as 40% (by weight) to landfill, 40% to incineration, 4% to export, and 16% to materials recovery (ANRED, unpublished, 1991). Recently, a tire-burning cement plant at La Malle (with an installed annual tire burning capacity of 20 000 tonnes) is estimated to incinerate 10 000 tonnes of scrap tires/yr.

Evidence from other EU countries points to a generally high and stable level of retreading in the commercial vehicle tire market and a low but still declining level of retreading of passenger car tires, as in the US. In Germany, approximately 70 kMT of old tires are retreaded annually (equivalent to about 12% of the scrap tires). For the Benelux countries we estimate that 12% of scrap tires go for retreading. In Italy, approximately 80 kMT of retreads are sold annually (equivalent to about 20% of scrap tires). In Italy, the decline of retreading in the passenger car tire sector was particularly marked during the 1980s. In 1980, 7.5 million car and light van tires were retreaded. By 1989, the level of retreading had halved to 3.5 million units. Over the same period, production of retreaded tires in the commercial vehicle sector fell only slightly, from 1.34 million units to 1.16 million units (EIU 1991).

Although incomplete and somewhat anecdotal, these data suggest that:

1.   Landfilling has been the dominant mode of waste tire disposal to date.

2. Incineration is the second likeliest fate. Incineration with heat recovery is on the increase, especially as political pressure to reduce or ban landfilling of tires mounts.
3. Current levels of materials recycling are very low and mostly attributable to the retreading of commercial vehicle tires. This activity is stable and may even be slightly increasing in some countries. Passenger car tire retreading is, however, on the decline.
4. Overall, the fraction of materials recycling via retreading is 14% in the US and not more than 20% in the EU. Evidence from France suggests that other forms of materials recovery and re-use may be associated more with mis-manufactured tires than with post-consumption (scrap) tire wastes.

13.6. MATERIALS AND ENERGY RECOVERY POTENTIAL

Tires embody valuable material resources. They are also very energy intensive. Table 13.3 (Guelorget *et al.* 1993) gives a breakdown of the materials used in new tire manufacturing. The types and quantities of potentially recoverable materials represented by scrap tires include elastomers and oils (57%), metals (15%), carbon black (26%), and sulfur compounds (2%). Since elastomers are hydrocarbon-based polymers, an alternative to recovering elastomers is to recover the monomer, or even to recover a sort of synthetic oil. Recovered elastomers (or monomers) can be re-used either within the tire sector or elsewhere. In either case, the recycled materials would substitute for virgin materials and would reduce the quantities of post-consumption tire wastes.

An alternative to elastomer recovery is energy recovery. On average, tires contain about 31.8 megajoules/kg of recoverable energy. This is mostly embodied in the elastomers, which have a thermal energy content of about 47 megajoules/kg. This makes scrap tires a more concentrated energy source than coal, which averages about 21.25 megajoules/kg.

Given that about 3 MMT of scrap tires are estimated to be available each year within the US and 2.5 MMT in the EU, the materials recovery potential this affords is considerable (Table 13.4). As indicated earlier, less than 20% of this potential is currently utilized.

Table 13.3:   Material inputs to new tire manufacturing as a percentage of all material inputs

Material	%
Polymers	
— Natural rubber	17.0
— SBR	15.2
— Poly-butadiene	7.0
— Butyl	3.7
— Reclaim/powder	0.6
Cords	
— Rayon	2.8
— Nylon	1.3
— Polyester	0.1
— Steel	13.1
Fillers	
— Carbon black	25.8
Vulcanizing agents	
— Sulfur	1.5
— Zinc oxide	2.0
— Stearic acid	1.0
— Accelerators	1.2
Protecting agents	1.8
Oils	5.0
Others	0.9
TOTAL	100.0

Table 13.4:   Materials recovery potential of scrap tires in the EU

Material	Percentage in scrap tires	Quantity available annually for recovery/reuse (kMT)
Elastomers/oil	57	1 425
Steel	13	325
Zinc oxide	2	50
Carbon black	26	650
Sulfur compounds	2	50

13.7. MATERIALS RECOVERY TECHNOLOGIES

The potential advantages of materials recovery, in terms of reduced disposal problems, energy and materials savings, environmental benefits, and increased materials self-sufficiency are considerable. A range of materials recycling technologies for scrap tires exist. The state of development of different technologies ranges from basic R&D, through pilot testing/demonstration to commercial application (past and current). Our review considers:

1. physical applications for whole tires;
2. physical applications for parts of tires (including processes for size reduction and splitting);
3. chemical processes for recovery of materials;
4. incineration processes for energy and materials recovery.

As well as describing theoretical possibilities, we draw upon case examples and experience from both the US and the EU. We have concentrated on actual or potential large-volume technologies at the same time trying to be comprehensive.

Physical Applications for Whole Tires

Carcass recovery and retreading
Retreading/remolding is currently the best method for recycling old tires. Retreading involves stripping the old tread from a worn tire and reclothing the old carcass or casing with a tread made from new materials. The tire may then be re-cured (warm retreading). High-quality standards can be achieved from both cold and warm retreading methods. The processes use only 20% of the virgin materials used in making a brand new tire. Also, when tires are retreaded, the old treads are routinely sent for materials recovery (granular rubber production). Retreading is standard practice in the commercial vehicle segment of the market. The main obstacles in the passenger car segment are that the poor condition of many used tire casings force retreaders to reject many of the scrap tires they collect. This adds to their waste-disposal costs. Labor costs in retreading operations are also high. Vulcanizers throughout the EU have been losing market share in the passenger car segment to cheap new tire imports. In Germany, poor test results on a high-speed remold are also reported to have adversely affected the reputation of all remolds (EIU 1989).

Engineering applications for whole tires
Apart from retreading, other uses for whole tires include engineering applications such as to stabilize embankments, line channels, build offshore reefs,

construct road bases and highway crash barriers, and attenuate sound. In these cases, the physical properties of tires offer specific advantages. Currently, these are all relatively minor applications.

Physical Applications for Split Tires and Ground Rubber

Many physical applications for scrap tires require that scrap tires be dismembered, split or finely ground to a crumb or powder. Also, a significant factor in the economics of scrap tire retrieval is freight cost. Significant freight cost savings can be achieved by increasing the bulk density by size reduction. For these reasons, as well as because shredding is often needed for tires going to landfill, proven size-reduction technologies already exist. Debeading of scrap tires and splitting into continuous strips (ribbons) of uniform width are automated processes. Machinery exists for shredding scrap tires (including the bead and steel reinforcements). Scrap tires can also be cooled in liquid nitrogen to below their glass transition temperature and pulverized in a hammer mill. Cryogenic fragmentation of scrap rubber is a continuous process. Shredding or chipping costs are typically about $20 per tonne (Guelorget *et al.* 1993).

Granular rubber

Granular rubber ('powder' or 'crumb') is produced by grinding scrap rubber using one of several processes; ambient grinding, cryogenic grinding (in liquid nitrogen), or solution grinding in water. Each process produces powdered rubber with different particle size. Grinding costs are estimated at $40–$60 per tonne. Crumb is the major material recovered by physical processing of scrap tires and other rubber wastes. Its size varies from 12–15 mm to submillimeter size. Powdered rubber has, to some extent, replaced reclaimed rubber in tire applications. Even so, its use in blending formulae for treads, carcasses, inner liners and other tire elements is limited because of its inferior physical and chemical properties. The major current market is in carpet and sports surface manufacturing. Some is also used to manufacture solid wheels (Burlace 1991).

The best potential large-scale re-use option would be in road-surfacing applications either as a filler for conventional asphalt or as an asphalt substitute. Following Goodyear's discovery that liquid latex (not a waste product) can improve the durability and traction of highway pavement, some interest has been shown in using powdered rubber obtained from scrap tires as an asphalt filler. At a level of only 5%, it was long since pointed out that the US could use all its scrap tires this way. The same would hold for the EU. A demonstration road surface, based on a combination of materials derived from discarded bottles (finely ground glass granules) and tire wastes, known as 'glasphalt', was tested in the US and shown to have satisfactory performance. Rubber from discarded tires, used as a binding material, can provide greater flexibility and cracking-resistance to road surfaces. Test results have shown that powdered rubber increases asphalt's overall cohesiveness so that pavements do not split when roadbeds shift slightly or sink.

However, evidence from different demonstration projects has been somewhat contradictory. In some instances, the resulting surfaces have proven to be unreliable. Further technical work is needed to improve the technology. The major obstacle is cost. Rubber asphalt is difficult to lay thinly so that the costs of using it as a road surfacing material are high compared with other materials. A recent US survey reported that the cost of rubber asphalt is up to double that of regular asphalt (Sweeney 1993).

Chemical Processes for Materials Recovery

Several processes exist for chemically recovering the materials held within scrap tires. These include: digester, heater and 'reclaimator' technologies (to produce reclaimed rubber); pyrolysis/tyrolysis/gasification and depolymerization technologies (to recover oil, steel, carbon black and sulfur); and experimental biodegradation/fermentation technologies.

Reclamation
Reclaimed rubber is produced using mechanical and chemical processes to sever the crosslinks of the vulcanized rubber; i.e., to partially reverse the vulcanization. Tires are most commonly reclaimed by digestion. Scraps of rubber are prepared by mechanical shredding. The wires and fibers are removed by mechanical separation using hammer mills.

An alternative is to use metal chlorides to reduce the tire fibre chemically during digesting. The scrap rubber is charged into a steam-heated pressurized tank (the digester) along with caustic soda, oils, and reclaiming chemicals (sulfides, mercaptan, and amino compounds). After several hours, the pressurized digester batch is forced into a blowdown tank and is washed and dried. Compounding ingredients are added to modify or maintain specific mechanical properties. As with powdered rubber, the physical properties of reclaimed rubber produced from synthetic elastomer blends (as opposed to natural rubber) are inferior to those of virgin materials. This limits the proportion of reclaimed rubber that can be used in tire applications. The market outside the tire sector is small.

Pyrolysis
Pyrolysis involves high temperature decomposition in the absence of air, so that materials are separated without oxidation. Pyrolysis of tires can be used

to regenerate basic chemicals (carbon black, zinc, sulfur, steel) and oil. Yields per tire are typically as follows:

oil	1 gallon	7 lb
char	7 lb	7 lb
gas	57 cubic feet	3 lb
steel and ash	2 lb	2 lb

Work on pyrolysis systems for tires has a long history. In the US, for example, R&D was undertaken by Firestone in cooperation with the US Bureau of Mines as early as the 1970s. The Tosco II process pyrolysis research study was conceived to develop recovery equipment to maximize quality carbon black production. A pilot plant, designed to handle 15 tonnes of tires per day, successfully recovered carbon black, oil and steel. Microwave pyrolysis is possible and has been successfully demonstrated.

Interest in pyrolysis increased at the time of the oil price shocks and the technology has been developed to the point of commercial operation in several countries, including the UK. The UK has had at least two, small-scale but commercial tire pyrolysis ('tyrolysis') plants in operation. The technical performance was high. The plants were able to deliver high-quality (low sulphur), light oil on a reliable basis. The main obstacle is cost. Such a process would be economic only if the costs of virgin materials were to increase substantially.

Recently, existing coal gasification technologies have been applied to tires. The cost of recovered materials is higher than that of virgin materials, however. If recovered materials are to be used to recover heat energy (rather than as feedstocks), neither pyrolysis nor gasification can be justified over direct incineration on direct cost grounds.

Another very recent and surprising development of considerable interest is microwave depolymerization. Although this technology was not being considered at all by the large government programs, it has apparently been developed privately. Details are lacking, but there is a report that rubber tires are now being depolymerized by microwaves, to recover oil, char, steel and even sulfur, at a commercial plant in British Columbia, Canada by the so-called EWMC system. It is claimed that, after startup, the energy released by the depolymerization (captured by heat exchangers) is sufficient to power the microwave generator (WRF 1994). The system is apparently about to be applied in the UK for the disposal of hospital wastes.

Biodegradation/fermentation

A study at Rutgers University's Institute of Microbiology (Nickerson 1969) found that tires could be used as a substrate for growing a yeast-based food product by fermentation with bacteria. The food was found to be nutritious and suitable for animal consumption. Scrap rubbers, reduced to powder by a fungus, can also be used to condition poor quality soil. Another suggested use is in water purification, since degraded rubber powder has ion-exchange properties (Nickerson and Faber 1972). None of these techniques is seriously suggested, although one twist to this past work is that it shows the plausibility of using organisms (perhaps genetically engineered) to transform scrap tires into reusable materials.

Incineration for energy/materials recovery

There are two main specialized forms of scrap tire incineration for dedicated energy and materials recovery, other than heat recovery when tires are burned in municipal incinerators. One is to use tires as fuel within specialized facilities to raise steam for electricity generation. The other is to use tires as fuel for cement plants using specially-built or modified kilns.

Electricity generation

The direct combustion of tires to produce heat has been widely and successfully practiced in the US by Oxford Energy Co. in Modesto, California and Sterling, Connecticut (with two other plants coming on line in Buffalo, NY and Las Vegas, Nevada) and in several European countries; e.g. Germany and Italy. The first two Oxford plants burn 5 million and 10 million scrap tires per year, respectively and generate 15 MW and 30 MW of electric power. A tires-to-energy electricity generating plant has recently been commissioned at Wolverhampton in the UK by Elm Energy and Recycling (EER). The plant is designed to burn 94 kMT of waste tires (21% of annual UK scrap tire generation) and generate 175 000 MWh (144 000 MWh net of internal consumption) of electricity annually.

The EER plant comprises five tire furnace units, each with steam boilers and flue-gas treatment systems. The steam raised is drawn off and fed into a single turbogenerator. Tires are to be burned whole. To ensure complete hydrocarbon combustion and to minimize formation and release of pollutants, combustion occurs in stages with a gradually increasing air supply. The first stage ensures complete burnout of the solid residues. The second and third stages ensure complete burnout of the organic matter. The final stage moderates the gas temperatures to increase ash recovery. Spent gases from the boiler unit first pass through a bag filter house to remove and recover particulate material, primarily zinc oxide. The gases are then cleaned to remove acid-forming compounds. Gas cleaning is by injection of a lime/water mixture. Byproducts are captured by a bag filter house. Byproducts from the overall plant, including steel wire, zinc oxide, calcine and calcium salts, are expected to total 27 kMT annually.

Firing cement kilns

Another possibility is for tires to be used to fuel portland-cement kilns since the cement neutralizes and contains the sulfur released during combustion and encapsulates the other potential pollutants (including the steel). This method for using waste tires was pioneered in Japan and is now widely used in Germany. In France, the method is in its infancy. In Britain, limited experience by one producer with tire burning identified technical problems and was not economic at a time when high demand for cement called for maximizing kiln output. The French plant, the Lafarge plant of La Malle (Marseille), has been operating since mid-1992.

Entire tires are introduced with the other raw materials into the furnace. This avoids shredder costs. There is no waste: tire combustion residues including metal parts are incorporated in the clinker. The effluent gas emissions are reported to be the same as from a conventionally-fueled plant. It is planned to extend this technology to other cement plants in France, providing capacity to burn 200 kMT of used tires/yr. However, there are some problems still to be overcome. Although the existing plant has capacity to burn 20 kMT/yr of used tires, it has been burning only 10 kMT/yr. The higher capital costs of the plant are offset by charging a fee for accepting tire deliveries, and this has led to a supply shortfall.

13.8. DISCUSSION AND CONCLUSIONS

Scrap tires can be considered either as 'wastes', whose disposal is problematic, or as a 'resource' from which useful raw materials and/or energy can be recovered. In recent years, the tendency has been to regard scrap tires as wastes and their disposal as problematic. Yet, the materials present in tires were once routinely recovered for re-use by the rubber industry. Whether scrap tires are waste or raw material, is mostly a function of the price and performance of recovered materials relative to virgin materials.

The Current Situation

The bulk of the estimated 2.5 MMT of scrap tires generated annually within the EU is considered and treated as a waste. Evidence is incomplete but, based on data that are available, we estimate that less than 20% (0.5 MMT) has been exploited as a raw material source. This leaves more than 2.0 MMT of materials as wastes.

Although information on the fate of this material is incomplete (and this would warrant further inquiry) evidence from those EU countries for which we have data suggests that perhaps only one-quarter is incinerated. We can reasonably estimate that the bulk is currently either landfilled or stockpiled. Disposal of these wastes presents potential environmental and human health problems. It also constitutes a loss of potentially reusable materials and recoverable energy which, if used, would reduce the draw on virgin resources (including non-renewable raw materials such as oil, iron, and zinc) and decrease the EU's dependence on raw material imports.

The longstanding (postwar) trend away from tire materials recovery/re-use is attributable in part to the abundance, high quality and low price of virgin raw materials, and in part to the rising technical standards required of tires. It is also partly due to greater use of synthetic rubber and blends of natural/synthetic rubbers in tire making and the near-total shift to steel-belted radial designs for passenger car tires. These trends in tire making have made basic materials recovery more difficult and the recovered materials less suitable for re-use in high-specification applications.

While the driving force behind these trends is primarily technological and economic, they have been facilitated by the legal and regulatory context. This sees responsibility for the tire and the materials contained therein transferred, together with ownership, at the point of sale. In this regulatory context, manufacturers have had no incentive to factor 'recyclability' into tire design or to encourage patterns of use that would favor greater recyclability. Indeed, to the contrary, they have had every incentive not to do so since longer life and/or greater recycling would cut into sales and profits.

Designing a 'Green' Tire Life Cycle

Decisions that currently determine materials use and end fate in the tire sector are made on the basis of economic motivations and rationality. These result in a tire life cycle that falls short of maximizing material productivities and minimizing environmental disturbance. A 'green' life cycle would be fundamentally different in the following respects:

1. Manufacturers would factor tire longevity and materials recovery/re-use potential into the choice of materials and product design.
2. Patterns of ownership/usage would facilitate materials return, recovery and re-use.
3. Materials would be 'cascaded' down a hierarchy of economic uses; i.e., re-used several times, each time maximizing the materials efficiency of recycling and optimizing the materials/application match.
4. At the end of the cascade, there would be a 'final' destructive/reconstructive stage (incineration) for energy and basic materials recovery with minimum environmental disturbance.

5. R&D in the tire sector would be prioritized on a life-cycle materials productivity improvement and environmental impact reduction basis.

Even absent new R&D (item 5 above), a 'greener' tire life cycle is possible. We have already demonstrated many physical and chemical materials recovery/re-use possibilities with today's technologies. There are also some promising trends that could be encouraged.

Retreading is by far the most important physical re-use option both now and most probably also for the future. Retreading is a standard aspect of materials re-use within the commercial vehicle tire sector and is facilitated by tire leasing arrangements between manufacturers and haulage operators. Its greater use in the passenger car sector depends upon overcoming perceptual barriers. The poor image of retreaded tires is generally unwarranted. EU regulations to increase the minimum tread depth from 1.0 to 1.6 mm should result in an improvement in the quality of scrap tire casings. The trend towards low-rolling-resistance passenger car tires is seen as a positive move to increasing tire longevity and an alternative or complement to higher levels of retreading.

To illustrate the potential effectiveness of increasing the retreading rate and/or tire longevity we cite data based upon a French tire life-cycle study (Guelorget *et al.* 1993). Table 13.5 gives the material and energy requirements for different combinations of retreading (measured as percentage of retreaded tires by weight of total production) and different tire service lives (measured in kilometers) for a hypothetical tire intended to reflect the average of French tire production.

To manufacture 679 kMT of tires in 1991, the French tire industry used 656 kMT of non-carcass materials (of which 99% were virgin). The current

Table 13.5:   Virgin materials used (tonnes) per 100 000 km of tire service, France

% of retreads in total production	Average tire life (1000 km)			
	50	100	150	200
0	1.88	0.94	0.63	0.47
10	1.73	0.86	0.57	0.43
20	1.58	0.79	0.52	0.40
30	1.42	0.71	0.47	0.35
40	1.28	0.64	0.42	0.32
50	1.12	0.56	0.37	0.28

materials intensity — the draw on non-carcass materials for each tonne of tires produced — was therefore 0.965 tonnes per tonne of tires produced. The overall energy intensity of French tire production was estimated to be 2.59 tonnes of 'oil equivalent' per tonne of tires produced. Given the split between passenger car and truck tires (a ratio of approximately 4:1) and the current average kilometrage of each (50 000 km for passenger car tires and 250 000 km for commercial vehicle tires), the current service life of the average French tire was estimated to be 90 000 km.

If the current level of commercial vehicle tire retreading in France (over 50%) was matched within the passenger car sector, the overall materials requirement of the French tire industry would reduce by 35%. The energy requirement would drop by an equivalent percentage. If the average retreading rate was to remain at the current (10%) level, but the average service life of tires was increased to 180 000 km, the materials and energy requirement would be halved. A combination of more modest changes (say, a 40% retreading level and a 150 000 km average tire life), would yield materials and energy productivity gains of 230%.

Apart from retreading, which is the optimum re-use option for scrap tire materials within the tire sector, there is some potential scope outside the tire sector. This includes uses for whole tires, split or punched tires, shredded tires and ground rubber. Applications were discussed above. The total of such applications currently accounts for about 7% of US scrap tires.

The application most likely to grow is in paving material. There are two types. One is called rubber modified asphalt concrete (RUMAC), which uses ground rubber in place of some of the aggregate in concrete. The other type is called asphalt rubber (AR) and blends ground rubber with asphalt. Costs are up to twice as high as conventional asphalt paving, but roadway life is also up to twice as long, with less paving material required. Legislation passed in 1991 called for possible use of AR on 5% of new paving in the US starting in 1994, increasing to 20% by 1997, subject to the results of continuing evaluation. The development of a market for crumb rubber would also begin to reduce the cost. This, in turn, could open wider markets. There is a need to improve rubber-crumbing technology and to identify the most cost-effective methods of doing so.

Burning of scrap tires for energy recovery has been mentioned. There is substantial potential for expansion in this area. The trend towards incineration in cement kilns (US Germany, France, etc.), pulp and paper plants (US) and the new tires-to-energy generating facilities in the US and UK are positive steps. The economic recovery of zinc from incinerator ash has already been demonstrated by the Oxford Energy Co. in the US (see Chapter 6, Zinc). The materials/energy recovery performance and environmental compatibility of alternative dedicated tire incineration methods needs to be assessed and the quality (i.e., further reusability) of the materials burned monitored. The potential for burning non-tire rubber waste, including wastes from non-tire uses of materials formerly embodied within tires (e.g., rubber mats, rubber-backed carpets, and even asphalt waste) needs to be assessed.

A range of chemical processes can be applied to decompose tires and recover basic raw materials. The principal disadvantage in chemical recovery is that the recovered materials are generally inferior to the virgin counterparts and not directly substitutable in all applications. This is the case for re-claimed rubber and for carbon black. In the latter case, inferiority is a particu-lar disadvantage since the market for carbon black is almost exclusively back in the tire sector (Gerstle *et al.* 1977). In the case of oils, valuable mostly for their energy content, the heating value could more easily be recovered by direct tire incineration. This reduces the value of a chemical recovery process under usual circumstances. An unlikely exception might be if liquid fuels or oil feedstocks were in particularly short supply. Although pyrolysis is techni-cally feasible, a UK study was unable to identify any commercially success-ful system (Burlace 1991). However, Conrad Industries is reported to be operating a pyrolysis unit in Centralia, Washington (Noyes 1993, p. 34). Several other firms are also currently working in this field.

In general, physical methods of re-use are to be preferred if there is a high economic value and a re-use possibility for the structural properties of tires, which represent a value that was added to the raw materials through the tire fabrication process. The 'structural information' content of scrap tires is achieved at an economic and environmental cost. The best possible economic return on this investment should be secured. Increasing tire longevity is the simplest route, and should be encouraged as the complement to recycling. The re-use of whole or part tires (e.g., by retreading) should be the preferred (first-order) recycling option. Chemical processes for recovering raw materi-als, which involve both the loss of existing structural information and further investment to create new structural information (implicit both in the breaking down and rebuilding phases of materials recovery and refabrication), should then be considered as second-order options. Incineration can be considered among these second-order options as a chemical process with potential to exchange structural information of organic materials for heat energy.

Implementing a 'Green' Tire Life Cycle

The chief obstacles to implementing a green tire life cycle are economic, institutional, and perceptual rather than technological. Economic factors in-clude, especially, the relative price/performance ratios of virgin and recov-ered materials and the intensely competitive nature of the tire industry. The industry has high fixed costs and low margins and is one where producers' operating strategies therefore emphasize volume sales. Market share is critical. A high percentage of production (c. 40%) is for new vehicles. But margins in this 'original equipment' market are low and sometimes even negative. Tire manufacturers usually enter into limited term supplier contracts with vehicle manufacturers. A large OE volume reduces average production costs. Profits are then made in the replacement market.

However, competition here has intensified recently because of freer international trade, which has brought Far Eastern and East European products into EU markets. Tire 'performance' is used to differentiate the market. At the upper end of the market, market share and price premiums depend heavily upon brand name and reputation. The industry is, therefore, generally risk averse, especially if risk threatens potential loss of customer confidence or the product's image. Tire safety is a priority. At the lower end of the market, cheap new tire imports have tended to displace locally made retreads and remolds.

At both ends of the market, these trends conflict with the idea of greater materials recycling and re-use within the tire sector. To 'green' the tire life cycle would therefore depend upon establishing a different — an 'enabling' — economic, regulatory and market context. Conditions would need to be created to favor materials recycling/re-use, stimulate collaboration between those concerned with different parts of the tire life cycle, and facilitate R&D to improve the available range of materials recovery/re-use options.

Fiscal measures could include taxes on virgin materials or subsidies (direct or indirect) on the recovery and re-use of materials. R&D could be targeted to receive subsidies. Following past practice in some US states, R&D might be partly financed through taxes on new tire sales. Non-fiscal measures might include 'take-back' legislation to make manufacturers liable for final disposal. Coupled with increased charges for scrap tire disposal, this would have a powerful influence over tire design, choice of materials, and marketing strategy. It would be a strong incentive to increase tire longevity.

In turn, this would encourage a shift towards tire-leasing arrangements whereby manufacturers would sell 'tire service' rather than tires. In the case of continuing with present tire-marketing arrangements (i.e., selling rather than leasing), enforcing the newly increased minimum tread depth requirement would result in more tires being returned in a condition suitable for retreading. More generally, a system of mandated refundable deposits on purchases would discourage fly-tipping and ensure responsible decision making about further use or final disposal. Deposits could also be used to subsidize the costs of scrap tire collection and delivery to materials/energy recovery facilities.

NOTE(13)

1. Based on calculations presented later. Noyes puts the heating value of tires somewhat lower, at 'slightly higher than coal' (Noyes 1993, p. 33).

14. Coal ash: sources and possible uses

14.1. SUMMARY

Coal is the second most important source of energy in the world (after petroleum), and it is the one with by far the largest reserves. But it is not a 'clean' fuel.

Coal is a carbonaceous material of variable composition. It contains, on average, 1–3% sulfur and 10–40% ash. Since coal is consumed in very large quantities (billions of tonnes), ash is also generated in very large quantities. No detailed census exists. In the industrialized countries, coal is used primarily to generate electric power, and secondarily as a source of coke for steel production and a fuel for cement manufacturing. Ash recovery from these activities, by means of electrostatic precipitators (ESPs) is quite high, typically 95–99%. However, even the small amount of unrecovered fly ash is a significant source of toxic heavy metals such as arsenic, cadmium and mercury. Coal ash is one of the major sources of each of these metals — if not the largest source — in the environment.

In Eastern Europe and the former Soviet Union, not to mention China and India, large amounts of coal are consumed with very little ash recovery. Thus, disposal is less of a problem but the toxic effects of ash are much more widespread.

Ash that is captured and recovered must either be put to use, or disposed of. At present, only a small fraction is utilized beneficially. Most of it is currently used as landfill. Thus, uncontrolled coal ash is both a health hazard and a wasted resource, particularly rich in aluminum, iron and silicon. As an industrial feedstock it has three important qualities: (i) it is already finely divided (i.e. powder), (ii) the material is homogeneous, at least in a given location, and (iii) it is anhydrous. The latter is a particularly useful characteristic for many potential industrial uses of the material.

From an economic point of view, the key to successful use of ash as a resource — either for cement manufacturing or metals recovery — is physical integration with the electric power generating plant and ash supply. Integration is essential to assure reliable availability of the ash and its intermediate products, on the one hand, and reliable utilization on the other hand. In the absence of existing established markets for intermediates (like high/low

iron ash) the entire complex of related activities must be designed and operated *as a unit*.

Under normal conditions, private firms from different industries would
specialize in each of the component elements of the system. Electric and gas
utilities want to sell electricity, not sulfuric acid or cement; certainly not
alumina or ferrosilicon. Aluminum companies tend to be more interested in
high-value aluminum products than in alumina production or smelting. Similarly with steel companies. Yet the viability of each component of the system
depends on byproduct credits. Integration on this scale in the US is normally
discouraged by anti-trust laws. Fortunately, there is some history of successful — if partial — integration along such lines in Europe (see Chapter 15).
Integration of coal-burning with waste recovery, metal recovery and even
metal processing may well evolve in future industrial ecosystems. It is probably the key to ultimate success.

Goals of public policy: reduce the uncontrolled dispersal of fly ash; maximize the recovery of use-values from this material.

14.2.   PRODUCTION OF COAL ASH

Coal is mined and consumed in staggering quantities. Total world production
(and consumption) of hard coal in 1988 was 3.45 MMT; in 1992 production
was 3.471 MMT. International trade amounted to 405 MMT. Western Europe
(12 countries) produced 211.4 MMT in 1988 and 183.4 MMT and imported
(net) 135 MMT in addition.

Brown coal and lignite are produced in larger quantities in Europe. In 1988
Western Europe accounted for 179.7 MMT, two-thirds from (West) Germany.
East Germany added another 310.3 MMT and the rest of Eastern Europe
contributed 269.0 MMT.

Ash is a mineral component of all coals. There is a wide variation in ash
content, however. German bituminous coals range from 6% to 40% ash.
British bituminous coal averages 16.5% ash. Sub-bituminous coals in West-
ern Europe range from 27% (France) to 50% (Spain). As regards lignite, West
Germany is low (6.5%) but otherwise the range is high (27–45%). Most
Eastern European coals and lignite have ash contents in the 15–40% range.
An overall average for Europe would probably be close to 1% for sulfur and
at least 15–20% for ash.

Table 14.1 contains data compiled by the World Energy Council on the
average composition, including sulfur and ash contents, of coal from most
major countries. It will be noted that the figures usually sum to more than
unity. This suggests that the carbon content refers to the combustible fraction
only; however, it is not clear whether the moisture content is counted as

Table 14.1:   *Sulfur and ash content of coal*

Steam Coal		
Country	*Sulfur rate (% gross)*	*Ash rate (% gross)*
Australia	0.6–1.0	9–14
China	0.9–1.1	13–14
Columbia	0.7	6–8
Poland	0.6–0.8	14
Russia	0.3–0.5	12–16
South Africa	0.5–0.8	10–15
US	0.8–1.0	12–14
Venezuela	0.5–0.7	8
Sub-bituminous Coal		
Country	*Sulfur rate (% dry)*	*Ash rate (% dry)*
Australia	0.5–0.7	6.5–9.5
Canada	0.4–0.5	9.5
Norway	1.4	8.0
Poland	0.6–0.9	5.0–8.0
US	0.6–1.2	4.5–8.0

Source: Adapted from WEC 1992.

Table 14.2:   *Composition of fly ash*

Constituent	*Weight %*	*Standard deviation %*
SiO_2	45.6	4.8
Al_2O_3	21.9	5.4
Fe_2O_3	17.4	4.7
CaO	3.8	1.8
SO_3	2.5	3.7
K_2O	1.6	0.7
MgO	1.0	0.2
TiO_2	0.9	0.5
Na_2O	0.7	0.6
P_2O_5	0.3	0.1

Source: ˙ Roy *et al.* 1979.

Industrial ecology

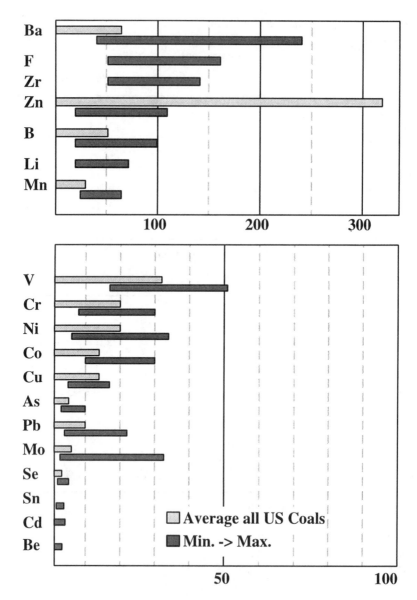

Note: 'All coals' data from Torrey, 1978; all other data compiled by author (Bolch). Note inconsistency in the case of Zn.

Source: Bolch 1980.

Figure 14.1: Trace elements in coal (ppm)

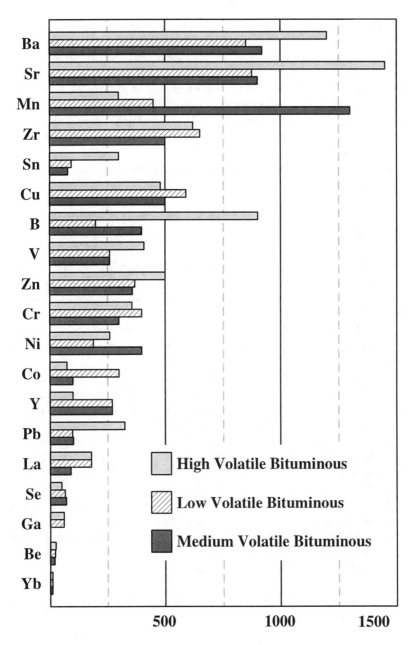

Source: Bolch 1980.

Figure 14.2: *Trace elements in coal (ppm)*

'volatile' or not. Nor is it clear whether the reported sulfur content refers to the combustible fraction or the total mass. However, these uncertainties make little difference to the analysis of potential uses of ash, which follows.

Coal ash is a mixture of light metal oxides (Table 14.2) together with trace quantities of many heavier metals, as illustrated in Figures 14.1 and 14.2. Coals from different locations vary considerably in mineral and trace element content, and it is usually possible to find some example where a given trace element, such as arsenic or mercury, is present in concentrations as much as ten times the average.

Sulfur recovery from coal is discussed in some detail in Chapter 7, Sulfur. That discussion need not be repeated here.

14.3.   COAL ASH RECOVERY AND USE

From 10% to as much as 40% or more (in a few cases) of the mass of coal consists of ash, of which 70% to 90% escapes via the stack (depending on the degree of pulverization of the coal feed) (see Table 14.1). At present, much of the fly ash is not even collected, although in the advanced industrial societies recovery by means of electrostatics precipitators is generally quite high (up to 99% from coal-burning power plants). But, after recovery, utilization is very low.

A detailed study of the use and storage of fly ash in the US was carried out in 1988 (USDOC 1988). The key highlights were as follows: in the year 1986 US utilities generated 61 million tonnes of coal ash, of which 74% was fly ash, 20% was bottom ash and 6% was boiler slag. Of this ash, about 22% (13.6 million tonnes) was used in some fashion. The utilities themselves used about 3.6 million tonnes. Usage rates varied by the type of ash: 52% for boiler slag, 27% for bottom ash and 18% for fly ash. Usage rates in 1986 were significantly lower than in 1985 for unexplained reasons.

Major uses of boiler slag (clinker) were as follows: blasting grit, roofing granules, and snow and ice control. Fly ash and bottom ash were used mainly as additives for cement and concrete products, road bases and structural fills. There were also many minor uses, some of which we discuss hereafter.

Potential uses for ash include the following:

- as an additive or substitute for Portland cement or other cements; also as grout;
- aggregate for concrete;
- for ice control on roads in winter, as 'fill', e.g. for road ballast, structural fill or in bituminous mixtures (asphalt);
- as a soil conditioner for acid soils;

- as a sorbent for sulfur dioxide in flue-gas desulfurization (FGD),
- as a component of drilling mud for oil or gas wells;
- as metal ores, especially for silicon, iron and aluminum, but potentially for titanium and minor metals.

Some uses are only appropriate for fly ash, others for bottom ash (clinker), some for either.

The first use noted above (in concrete) is well known but somewhat limited by the fact that ash can only be used in small quantities (order of magnitude 5%) without adversely affecting the time required for the cement to harden. It is useable as a substitute, primarily in applications where hardening time is not an important competitive factor. The use of ash-concrete as a way of fixing and stabilizing hazardous chemical or mildly radioactive wastes would appear to be a significant use, for instance.

Use of ash as a lightweight aggregate for concrete is promising. However, a manufacturing process is involved: the ash must be sintered or melted and then blown into a suitable gravel-like consistency. This requires energy, of course, but (in principle) such a process could be integrated with the combustion process itself. In some countries (indeed, much of Central Europe) the traditional aggregates — sand and gravel — are becoming scarce and costly. Moreover, mines and quarries are environmentally damaging. Thus, the use of ash as a raw material for concrete aggregate is likely to grow rapidly in Central Europe.

In many of the 'fill' applications, the only impediment to wider use is marketing, packaging and distribution. All of these applications already exist somewhere. Use for soil conditioner is, of course, limited to areas with acidified soils, but fly ash could be used as a substitute for, or in a mixture with, lime. This would depend, however, on having fairly good knowledge both of the trace metals profile of the particular ash, but also the soil where it is to be used.

The use of fly ash as a sorbent for FGD has the considerable attraction of using a locally available waste to solve a local emissions problem. One method of doing this ('Trimex') was mentioned previously in connection with sulfur. Use of fly ash as a component of drilling mud is obviously location dependent. Unfortunately, this use is not likely to be appropriate for Eastern Europe where a lot of the ash is being generated.

The final possibility is to use ash (especially fly ash) as a metal 'ore', especially for aluminum. This possibility is considered next.

14.4.   METALS RECOVERY FROM COAL ASH

Use of coal ash as a source of iron ore (magnetite) is a possibility (see Table 14.3). Magnetic separation is quite straightforward, and has been demonstrated in several places (Nowak 1978; Roy *et al.* 1979). The hematite content of the magnetic fraction ranges between 60% and 70%. The magnetic fraction itself varied between one-quarter and one-third. Let us assume that Western Europe consumes coal with an ash content of 15%. Given an annual coal consumption of 700 MMT, the ash output would be 100 MMT, and the iron 'ore' content of the ash would be of the order of 3% or 3 MMT. While this could hardly displace all of the virgin iron ore needed in the steel industry of the region, it is not quite insignificant.

Ferrosilicon is another possible product of ash smelting. Fly ash can be smelted in an electric arc furnace (even without magnetic separation) to produce ferrosilicon (Morton 1978). All of the aluminum remains in the slag (see Table 14.4). Thus, in effect, this process would recover the iron and about half of the silicon in a very marketable form, while upgrading the slag as a potential aluminum source. (See also Chapter 3, Aluminum, where a

Table 14.3:   *Composition of sample fly ash and fractions obtained by magnetic separation*

| | | Chemical composition, weight percent | | | |
| | | Dry separation | | Wet separation | |
Constituent	Whole fly ash 100 parts	Magnetics 23.6 parts	Non-magnetics 76.4 parts	Magnetics 26.1 parts	Non-magnetics 73.9 parts
SiO_2	42.36	20.31	47.89	20.83	53.0
Al_2O_3	17.91	10.21	20.04	9.95	22.83
Fe_2O_3	19.29	60.08	6.56	65.00	5.24
CaO	4.49	1.87	4.88	13.20	5.82
MgO	0.71	0.40	0.76	0.42	0.99
Na_2O	0.35	0.18	0.35	0.14	0.31
K_2O	1.72	0.81	1.85	0.71	1.91
SO_3	2.13	0.79	2.04	c	c
LOD[a]	0.58	0.13	0.45	0.12	0.56
LOI[b]	10.39	2.13	12.40	1.70	8.46

Notes:
a.   LOD is loss on drying at 100°C.
b.   LOI is loss on ignition from 110–800°C.
c.   Not detected.

Source: Chou *et al.* 1978.

Table 14.4: Composition of products of fly ash without magnetic separation

Ferro silicon		Slag	
Iron	61.00%	Aluminum oxide	35.00%
Silicon	33.00%	Silica	26.40%
Chromium	1.89%	Calcium oxide	11.68%
Carbon	1.88%	Magnesium oxide	10.63%
Vanadium	1.07%	Iron oxide	7.80%
Magnesium	0.09%	Sulfur	2.17%
Copper	0.04%	Chromic oxide	0.50%
Sulfur	0.01%	Copper	0.08%
Phosphorus and other trace elements	1.02%	Phosphorus	0.03%
		Vanadium and other trace elements	5.71%
	100.00%		100.00%

Source: Morton 1978.

process to produce aluminum-silicon and ferrosilicon from clay and bauxite was discussed briefly.) In principle, virtually the same process would be applicable to coal ash smelting, with the further virtue that the process would be very easy to integrate into a 'coalplex', using coal as the fuel and ash as feedstock.

Basically the process would start with an oxygen-blown blast furnace using ash as a feedstock. The molten Al-Fe-Si alloy would then pass to a fractional crystallizer where the Fe-Si (ferrosilicon) phase separates from the Al-Si (alumino-silicon) phase. The latter could then be used as an alloying agent, or electrolytically reduced to pure Al and pure Si in a diaphragm cell (Bruno 1982). (See Figure 15.5 in Chapter 15, Industrial ecosystems).

In the early 1970s there was widespread concern about an impending producers' cartel of bauxite exporters, leading to higher prices. This concern led the US Bureau of Mines to undertake a major program of research into potential alternative sources. In the course of this research a large number of potential processes were studied, and some of them were tested at the bench level. The US Bureau of Mines studied at least 18 alternative processes for extracting alumina from domestic resources such as clay or anorthosite in the early 1970s (Peters and Johnson 1974). None appeared to be immediately competitive with the Bayer process (alumina from bauxite), at then current prices (Table 14.5). By the end of the decade, the producers' cartel had collapsed and worries about shortages subsided.

Table 14.5: Summary of published Bureau of Mines estimates of alumina process costs (1973 basis)

Raw material Bureau of Mines Reference # Input Process	Energy (utility) cost $ per ton Al_2O_3	Total operating cost $ per ton Al_2O_3	Fixed capital cost 1000 tpd plant million $
Clay (cost, $1/ton)			
RI6431 Nitric Acid ($83/ton)	32.04	93.47	110
RI6133 Hydrochloric Acid; isopropyl ether extraction	31.76	98.94	116
gas precipitation	59.76	135.80	156
gas precipitation – isopropyl ether extraction	98.65	187.67	195
caustic purification	24.74	13.53	143
sinter purification	35.45	121.76	151
RI5997 Sulfurous Acid; caustic purification	27.33	103.23	130
RI6229 Sulfuric Acid; electrolytic iron removal	50.59	133.84	152
chemical iron removal	51.34	131.89	135
ethanol purification	58.35	136.97	126
RI7758 Sulfurous Acid/Sulfuric Acid	92.14	142.67	97
RI6290 Potassium Alum	40.48	148.17	166
RI6573 Ammonium Alum; ammonium bisulfate leaching	82.06	187.40	243
ammonium sulfate baking	62.89	168.18	224
RI6927 Lime-Soda Sinter; dry-grinding option	34.55	13.12	104
wet-grinding option	32.19	104.88	96
RI7299 Lime Sinter; double leach	44.23	122.77	122
single leach	59.33	138.60	124
Anorthosite (costs: anorthosite, $2.50/ton; limestone, $1/ton)			
RI7068 Lime-Soda Sinter; dry-grinding option	33.94	111.15	110
wet-grinding option	38.49	111.26	101
Bauxite (cost, $8/ton)			
RI6730 Bayer process	10.48	63.15	67

Source: Peters and Johnson 1974.

However, fly ash is inherently a more attractive raw material than clay, since the most energy-intensive step in clay processing is dehydration, and this is unnecessary when fly ash is the starting material (e.g. Yun *et al.* 1980). Also, the magnetic fraction has some value, as noted above. Based on 1981 prices several of these processes appeared to be promising. Later, the Electric Power Research Institute (EPRI) reconsidered a number of the processes considered by the Bureau of Mines. However, only two were studied in detail. One, the direct acid leach (DAL) process is described as a 'minimum treatment' process for removing those metals that might otherwise leach out of ash in a landfill. The other process, known as pressure digestion-acid leach (PDAL), is described as a 'maximum recovery process' that would extract all of the metals in the ash.

The DAL process begins with an acid leach (metal removal) at slightly elevated temperature (about 105°C). The choice of acid (HCl, H_2SO_4 or HNO_3) is a matter of process economics. The scheme works, in principle, with any strong acid. Laboratory work indicates that only stoichiometric amounts of acid are needed. In other words, enough acid is needed to combine with the aluminum, iron and other heavy metals, and no more. There is little or no acid waste. The metal recovery rate from the acid leach depends on concentration and temperature. However, among the process conditions that were investigated, the best choice seems to lead to recovery rates of about 45% for Al, 76% for Fe, 64% for Mn and 29% for Ti. Under these conditions the leach residue accounts for 88% of the initial weight. It is innocuous and can be disposed of in landfills, if not used as fertilizer.

The leachate, with 10% free acid content, would then go to an anion exchange unit where iron and the other heavy metals (Co, Cu, Mo, Zn, Pb, U, Hg, Cd and As) form negatively charged complexes and mostly remain with the anion exchange medium. The effluent retains the aluminum and trace quantities of other metals. Aluminum chloride hexahydrate ($AlCl_3 \cdot 6H_2O$) is separated by fractional crystallization. The chloride is subsequently calcined to yield the marketable oxide form (alumina). A process flow sheet for the DAL process is diagrammed schematically in Figure 14.3.

The DAL process appeared to be economically favorable even in comparison with the established Bayer process. EPRI estimated a return on investment of 40% per annum — repayment of capital in 2.8 years — for an industrial scale 1 MMT/yr unit (Canon *et al.* 1981). It would be worthwhile to investigate the current economics in European conditions. At the time of the study, the more complex PDAL process was uneconomic and would have had to be operated at a loss. However, the main reasons for this appear to be physical losses of caustic soda and chlorides. It appears that further development of DAL would also reduce these losses. Moreover, if properly designed

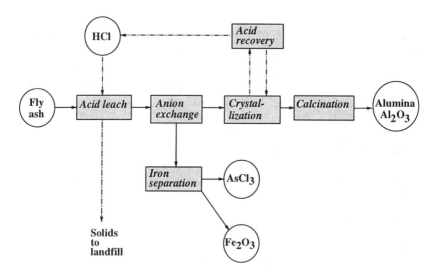

Figure 14.3:   Hydrochloric acid leach process

from the outset with this in mind, it should be possible to upgrade a DAL ash-treatment plant into a PDAL plant at some later time.

It should be noted, here, that if the ALCOA process for aluminum smelting (see Chapter 3, Aluminum) could be revived — perhaps with the help of some new materials and/or inert anode technology (see below) — it would fit very well with the DAL process described above. Recall that the ALCOA smelting process starts by chlorinating alumina from the Bayer process, whereas the DAL process ends by calcining aluminum chloride to produce salable alumina. At first sight, it appears that a combination of the two would make these two steps unnecessary, thus enabling major savings in both. Since each process appears to be potentially economically attractive on its own (assuming the necessary R&D is completed) the combination could cut aluminum production costs 'from cradle to grave' very significantly indeed.

Unfortunately, there is a serious snag: the aluminum chloride produced by the DAL process is both wet and hygroscopic (water-loving). It would have to be dehydrated prior to use in the ALCOA process, and that would be tricky, probably involving a combination of heat and vacuum. Fortunately, the heat (at least) would be readily available in a 'coalplex'. A feasibility study for European conditions, and taking into account recent technological progress in materials, would be highly desirable.

A somewhat more speculative (hence longer-range) possibility was conceived as a way to extract metals from lunar soil (Jarrett *et al.* 1980). The scheme in question is electrolytic separation of fly ash (plus slag from the smelting of iron) into all of its metallic components. Conceptually the problem is fairly simple, and closely analogous to the current Hall process for aluminum reduction.[1] The fly ash would first be dissolved in molten cryolite (Na_3AlF_6) at a temperature of 970°C. Iron, silicon and aluminum oxides can be reduced electrolytically, in a sequence of three bipolar cells at different voltages. Iron is extracted first at 1 volt; silicon follows at 1.8 volts. Finally, aluminum is extracted at 2.2 volts. Calcium, magnesium, sodium and potassium oxides actually react by ion-exchange with the cryolite, exchanging their oxygen for fluorine from the aluminum, and yielding the corresponding fluorides plus alumina. These contaminants gradually build up over time, and the cryolite must be purged and recycled at intervals. The product of this step is an alloy of the four light metals (Ca-Mg-Na-K) that can be used as a reductant. The fluorine gas is recycled back to the cryolite as AlF_3.

An inert anode (not carbon, as in the Hall cell) would be needed for this process. Cells of this type have been under development for a number of years, for eventual use in the aluminum industry itself. Indeed, the ALCOA process would be an ideal application of inert anodes, since the reactivity of carbon anodes appears to have been a problem — if not the 'Achilles' heel' — of the first ALCOA process pilot plant in Palestine, Texas. While several aluminum companies have started and later abandoned work along these lines, there is no reason to doubt that eventual success is possible. This, too, appears to be a promising area for further research support.

A rather different idea, also conceived in relation to the problem of extracting metals from lunar soil, was patented by Criswell and Waldron for Cis-Lunar Inc. in 1980 (Criswell and Waldron 1980). It is a hydrofluoric acid leach process, applicable most likely after magnetic separation. Fluorine decomposes siliceous minerals much more efficiently than chlorine. HF acid leach would substitute F_2 for O in all of the metallic elements in the fly ash, at moderate temperatures. The silica would be converted to fluosilicic acid (H_2SiF_6) in which the other fluorides are dissolved. The end result would be a mixture of fluorides, fluorosilicates, sulfite-bisulfites and sulfates.

The problem would then be to separate the various fluorides, and so on, and to recover the HF for recycling. The first step is hydrolysis of the silicon and titanium fluorides (SiF_4 and TiF_4), yielding the corresponding hydroxides and HF. This occurs at low temperatures in an aqueous solution if the input F:Si (or Ti) ratio is not much above 4:1. Hydrolysis of the other metals requires higher temperatures and pressures, in the order Fe, Al, Mg, Ca. Hence, the next step is to convert the other metallic fluorides and fluorosilicates into sulfite/bisulfites, hydroxides or carbonates, using SO_2, NH_3 or $(NH_4)_2CO_3$ respectively. There are established methods of recovering AL_2O_3 from sulfites.

But there are also commercial markets for aluminum fluoride, aluminum sulfate and other possible products.

A considerable amount of research would be needed, even to reach the pilot stage. Areas needing further investigation include: (i) solubility relations in mixtures of hydrofluoric, fluosilicic and sulfurous acids; (ii) volatile recovery of SiF_4, HF and H_2O from SO_2 carrier streams in equilibrium with leach solutions, and (iii) methods of recovery of iron hydroxide from fluoride, fluorosilicate and bisulfite solutions, and/or salts, hydroxides and HF.

NOTE(14)

1.　The idea is primarily due to Noel Jarrett, of ALCOA Research Center.

15. On industrial ecosystems

15.1. SUMMARY

Industrial ecosystems, designed 'from scratch' to imitate nature by utilizing the waste products of each component firm as raw materials (or 'food') for another, are an attractive theoretical idea, but as yet mostly at the proposal stage. It is important to stress that process changes to take advantage of returns to closing the materials cycle are very definitely *not* another version of 'end-of-pipe' treatment of wastes. Is this an idea whose time has come?

This chapter examines a number of such proposals and considers the prerequisites for success. It appears that there are several. First, a fairly large scale of operation is required. This means that at least one first-tier exporter must be present to achieve the necessary scale. Second, at least one other major firm (or industrial sector) must be present locally to utilize the major waste of the exporter, after conversion to useful form. Third, one or more specialized 'satellite' firms will be required to convert the wastes of the first-tier exporter into useful raw materials for the consumer, and to convert the latter's wastes into marketable commodities, secondary inputs to other local firms, or final wastes for disposal.

A final condition, of great importance (and difficult to achieve in practice) is that a reliable mechanism be established to ensure close and long-term cooperation — i.e. information sharing — at the technical level among the participating firms. The guarantor of this cooperation must be either the first-tier exporter itself, a major bank, a major marketing organization, or a public agency. The detailed mechanisms by which it can be achieved in practice remain to be worked out.

15.2. INTRODUCTION: RETURNS TO SCALE AND SCOPE

The notion of returns to scale — and the related notion of division of labor — are among the oldest and most familiar insights in economics, going back at least to Adam Smith. It is not necessary to expound them in detail again. However, it is helpful (for what follows) to remind the reader that the classic 'supply–demand' intersection presupposes a rising supply curve, for the economy as a whole, or for a particular good or service. This implies that the *marginal* cost of production (of the good or service) rises monotonically with output. This reflects short-term rigidities, namely, a fixed workforce, a fixed physical capital and a fixed technology.

At first sight this equilibrium picture seems incompatible with economies of scale — a point that properly bothers many thoughtful first-year economics students. However, economies of scale become meaningful when we relax the assumption of a fixed set of factors of production at a static point in time. Absent the (implied) condition of short-term rigidity, it is easier to see that alternative technologies of production can, and do, exist, *in principle*, at different scales of operation. They are likely to differ in many ways, especially in terms of capital/labor ratio. At larger scales of operation, and especially with longer production runs, more operations can be carried out by machines or other equipment than at small scales. The physical reasons why this is true range from the obvious (longer runs = less setup time) to the arcane (decreasing surface/volume ratios) and need not be considered further here. The important consequence is that the number of workers (or manhours) per unit output tends to decline with increasing scale, *ceteris paribus*.

This fact, in turn, has had a major impact on economic growth in the past. Passing from a static to a dynamic framework, consider what happens when existing productive capacity in an industry is augmented by a new and more efficient plant. The new plant can produce cheaper. Potential supply in the industry has increased. Demand will absorb the larger supply only at a lower price. If competing suppliers cut prices, demand will continue to rise. This will stimulate further investment in supply, and so on. The cycle of price cuts (permitted by economies of scale) leading to increasing demand (thanks to price elasticity of demand) has been called the 'Salter cycle'.

To maximize economies of scale, manufacturers in the late 19th and early 20th centuries adopted a strategy of product standardization and mass production. These were basically American innovations. Successful exemplars ranged from Waltham watches, Colt 45 revolvers, Remington rifles, Yale locks, and Singer sewing machines, to Ford's successful 'Model T' (which was produced continuously from 1908 to 1926). At that time, the keys to success in manufacturing were product standardization, division of labor and volume (Ayres 1991). Frederick Taylor incorporated these elements, together with some others, into a formal theory of 'scientific management' which strongly influenced (and was influenced by) Henry Ford.

The benefits of scale are diluted in the case of mechanical or electrical products which are evolving and improving over time. Mechanical automation requires large investments in specialized machinery and equipment, which must be depreciated. This tends to discourage technological change, since new models require new and costly production lines to be designed and custombuilt (e.g. Abernathy 1978). The benefits of scale are most obvious (and easiest to analyze econometrically) in the case of homogeneous commodities such as steel, petrochemicals, or electric power. Economies of scale tend to encourage industrial gigantism, and oligopolies, at the expense of competition. Economists have argued the relative benefits to consumers of scale economies vs. competition in regulated utilities, such as telecommunications, electric power, water and gas distribution, railroads, or airlines (e.g. Christensen and Greene 1976). Evidently oligopolistic pricing inhibits growth. But, it appears that economies of scale were still an important engine of economic growth even for the US, and much more so for Europe and Japan, in the post-war decades (e.g., Denison 1962, 1974, 1979). Scale economies were perhaps the *only* significant growth factor for the Soviet Union and Eastern Europe during that period.

Recently, there have been indications that economies of scale are no longer as important as they once were. Markets for many standardized products have become saturated, at least in the West. Quantity of supply (of final goods and services) is less and less important relative to quality and variety. From the classical Taylorist–Fordist point of view, variety (diversity) of output is incompatible with maximum efficiency. Yet, there are other, hitherto neglected, dimensions of production technology and other strategies for cost reduction that are more appropriate for meeting demand in markets where diversity — even 'customization' — is inherently valuable.[1] Another hitherto neglected dimension of strategy (with a few exceptions) is to maximize *systems integration*. We consider this strategy in more detail next.

15.3. RETURNS TO SYSTEMS INTEGRATION

Having emphasized that viable production strategies today no longer depend exclusively on standardization and economies of scale, one can look more systematically for other sources of competitive advantage. In particular, we wish to consider 'returns to integration', which or (equivalently) 'returns to internalization' (or 'closure') of the materials cycle.

The classical illustration of this strategy was the Chicago meat packers who prided themselves on recovering and finding markets for 'everything but the squeal' of the slaughtered animals.[2] The link between scale and integration is obvious: only a large-scale operator could invest in the various specialized facilities needed to produce various meat products from steak to sausage, lard (some of which was saponified to produce soap), pet-food, bone-meal, blood-meal, gelatin (from hooves) and even hormones from animal parts. Pig bristles became shaving brushes and hairbrushes, while the hides were tanned to make leather.

Coke, used in blast furnaces, offers another historical example. The earliest 'beehive' coke ovens were terrible polluters. However, the 'byproduct' coking process, first introduced by Koppers, in Germany, changed this situation significantly by capturing both the combustible gas and other byproducts of the coking operation.[3] High-quality coke oven gas became available near the Ruhr steelworks in the late 19th century. Its availability encouraged a local inventor, Nicolaus Otto, to commercialize a new type of compact 'internal combustion' engine — to replace the bulky steam engine (and its associated furnace, boiler and condenser) — to supply power for small factories.[4] Byproduct coke ovens also produced coal tar. Coal tar was the primary source of a number of important chemicals, including benzene, toluene and xylene, as well as aniline. Aniline was the raw material for most synthetic organic dyestuffs, the first important product of the German chemical industry. Coke ovens were also the source of most industrial ammonia, which was the raw material for both fertilizers (usually ammonium sulfate) and nitric acid for manufacturing explosives such as nitroglycerine.

The modern petro-chemical industry is the best current example of systems integration: it begins with a relatively heterogeneous raw material (petroleum), which consists of a mixture of literally thousands of different hydrocarbons. The first petroleum refiners of the 19th century produced only kerosene ('illuminating oil') for lighting and tar for road-surfaces and roofing materials. The lightest fractions were lost or flared; even natural gasoline had few uses (except as a solvent for paint) until the liquid-fueled internal combustion engine appeared on the scene in the 1890s. By the second decade of the 20th century the market for petroleum products had become mainly a market for automotive fuels; after 1920 this market expanded so rapidly as to create a need for 'cracking' heavier fractions, and later, recombining lighter fractions (by alkylation) to produce more and more gasoline. Heavier oils found uses in diesel engines, as lubricants, as fuel for heating homes and buildings, and as fuel for industrial boilers and electric power plants. Meanwhile, a great deal of natural gas was found in association with petroleum deposits, and a beginning was made on the long process of capturing, processing and utilizing this new resource.

By the 1930s, byproducts of petroleum and natural gas process engineering began to find other chemical uses. In particular, ammonia and methanol were derived from methane, from natural gas. Then ethylene (produced, at first, by pyrolysis of ethane separated from natural gas) became cheap, as did hydrogen. This encouraged the development of a family of synthetic polymers, starting with polyethylene and followed by polyvinyl chloride. Natural gas liquids and light fractions of petroleum refining also became the basis of most synthetic rubber production (via butadiene). Propylene, from propane, is now second only to ethylene as a chemical feedstock. Another whole family of chemicals was created from benzene, also a byproduct of petroleum refining. Phenol, the basis of polystyrene and phenolic resins, is a benzene derivative. Finally, the refining process has become a major source of sulfur.

Most of the organic chemicals and synthetic materials produced today are derived from one of these few basic feedstocks. A very sophisticated technology for converting a few simple hydrocarbon molecular structures into others of greater utility has arisen. Light fractions become chemical feedstocks. The heavier fractions, including asphalt, are the least valuable (per unit mass), but some products of the heavy fractions — like lubricants and petroleum coke — are extremely valuable indeed. It is fair to say that today there are scarcely any wastes from a petroleum refinery. There is a continuing trend towards adding value to every fraction of the raw material. While most petroleum products are still used for fuel, the fuel share is actually declining and the share of fuel for stationary power plants and space heating is declining quite fast. It is virtually certain that these 'low-value' uses of petroleum will be displaced in a few decades by higher-value uses without any intervention by governments.

To be sure there are other chemical families where byproducts have been much harder to utilize. One example is biomass. Cellulose and cellulosic chemicals (e.g. rayon) are derived from wood, but about half of the total mass of the harvested roundwood — lignins — is still wasted or burned to make process steam. There are a few chemical uses of lignins, but no more than a few percent of the available resource is used productively except as low-grade fuel for use within the pulp/paper plants.

The idea of converting wastes into useful products via systems integration has recently become a popular theme among environmentalists. The 3M Company introduced a formal program, beginning in 1975, with the catchy title: 'Pollution Prevention Pays' or PPP. Dow Chemical Co. has its own version, namely 'waste reduction always pays' or WRAP. Others have followed suit. These acronyms are not merely 'awareness raisers' to attract the attention of managers and staff; they also contain an element of generalizable truth (see Section 2.3, The economics of 'win–win'). Unquestionably, it is socially and environmentally desirable to convert waste products into saleable byproducts, even though the economics may be unfavorable at a given moment of time. However, the economic feasibility of converting wastes into useful products often depends on two factors: (1) the scale of the waste-to-byproduct conversion process and (2) the scale of demand (i.e., the size of the *local* market).

For example, low-grade sulfuric acid is not worth transporting but it can be valuable if there is a local use for it. Thus, sulfuric acid recovered from copper-smelting operations is now routinely used to leach acid-soluble oxide or chalcocite copper ores; the leachate is then collected and processed by solvent extraction (SX) technology and electrolytically reduced by the so-called electro-winning (EW) process. The combined SX–EW process was barely commercialized by 1971, but already accounts for 27% of US copper mine output, and about 12% of world output.[5] Capacity is expected to double by the year 2000.

Similarly, sulfur dioxide, carbon monoxide and carbon dioxide are all needed for certain chemical synthesis processes, but these chemicals cannot be economically transported more than a few kilometers at most. Hydrogen, produced in petroleum refineries, can be compressed and shipped but it is much better to use it locally. A hydrogen pipeline network has been built for this purpose in the Ruhr Valley of Germany. So-called blast-furnace gas can be burned as fuel, but it is not economical to transport very far. There are numerous examples in the chemicals industry, especially. Closing the materials cycle can take the form of creating internal markets (i.e., uses) for low-value byproducts by upgrading them to standard marketable commodities. (This often depends, incidentally, upon returns to scale, but only in a particular context.)

To summarize, there are significant potential returns to internalization of the materials cycle. For instance, the so-called integrated steel mill (including its own ore sintering and smelting stages) is an example. It would not pay to produce pig iron in one location and ship it to another location for conversion to steel, for two reasons: (1) there would be no way to use the heating value of the blast furnace gas and (2) the molten pig iron would cool off *en route* and it would have to be remelted again. Thus, energy conservation considerations, in this case, dictate integration. The same logic holds for petroleum refineries and petrochemical complexes. In each case there are a number of low-value intermediate products that can be utilized beneficially if, and only if, the use is local. However, these examples of integration obviously require fairly large scale for viability. This is in direct contrast to the strategy of end-of-pipe waste treatment and disposal, which is normally practiced in smaller operations.

15.4.   INTEGRATED INDUSTRIAL ECOSYSTEMS

At this point it is probably useful to introduce the notion of industrial ecology (IE) more formally. Industrial ecology (IE) is a neologism intended to call attention to a biological analogy: the fact that an ecosystem tends to recycle most essential nutrients, using only energy from the sun to 'drive' the system.[6] The analogy with ecosystems is obvious and appealing (Ayres 1989). In a 'perfect' ecosystem the only input is energy from the sun. All other materials are recycled biologically, in the sense that each species' waste products are the 'food' of another species. The carbon–oxygen cycle exemplifies this idea: plants consume carbon dioxide and produce oxygen as a waste. Animals, in turn, require oxygen for respiration, but produce carbon dioxide as a metabolic waste.[7] An ecosystem involves a 'food chain' with number of interacting niches, including primary photo-synthesizers (plants), herbivores, carnivores preying on the herbivores, saprophytes, parasites and decay organisms.

The idea of industrial ecology has taken root in the past few years, especially since the well-known article by Frosch and Gallopoulos in a special issue of *Scientific American* (Frosch and Gallopoulos 1989).

The industrial analog of an ecosystem is an industrial park (or some larger region) which captures and recycles all physical materials internally, consuming only energy from outside the system, and producing only non-material services for sale to consumers. This vision is highly idealized, of course. The notion of deliberately creating 'industrial ecosystems' of a somewhat less ambitious sort has become increasingly attractive in recent years. Author Paul Hawken has commented: 'Imagine what a team of designers could come up with if they were to start from scratch, locating and specifying industries and factories that had potentially synergistic and symbiotic relationships' (Hawken 1993, p. 63).

An industrial ecosystem, then, could be a group of firms grouped around a primary raw material processor, a refiner or convertor, and a fabricator, various suppliers, waste processors, secondary materials processors, and so forth. Or it could be a group of firms grouped around a fuel processor, or even a waste recycler. The main requirement is that there be a major 'export product' for the system as a whole, and that most of the wastes and byproducts be utilized locally.

But, as this book has pointed out, there are in fact a large number of plausible possibilities for 'internalizing' material flows in various ways. This possibility is not restricted to process wastes from industry. It also applies to final consumption wastes e.g. of packaging materials. At the industrial level, this implies that some firms must use the wastes from other firms as raw material feedstocks. Other firms must use the wastes from final consumers in a similar manner. The complex web of exchange relationships among such a set of firms can be called an 'industrial ecosystem'.[8]

At first glance, systems integration looks rather like old-style 'vertical integration', except that there is no need for all of these enterprises to have common ownership. In fact, the flexibility and innovativeness needed for long-term success is more likely to be promoted by dispersed ownership. Yet a considerable degree of inter-firm cooperation is needed as well. We will return to this point later.

The most influential — and possibly the only — prototype for such a system was, and still is, the Danish town of Kalundborg. In this town waste heat from a power plant and a petroleum refinery has been used to heat greenhouses and other wastes from several large industries have been successfully converted into useful products such as fertilizer for farmers, building materials, and so on. We discuss this example in more detail below.

15.5. THE KALUNDBORG EXAMPLE

Whether by accident or through intention, an interesting example of such a system has evolved in Denmark and has received considerable attention (e.g. Frosch and Gallopoulos 1989). The Kalundborg prototype industrial ecosystem began in the 1960s when the ASNAES electric power plant modified its operations so as to produce process heat in the form of steam that could be sent to the nearby Statoil refinery. (This is an old idea, known as 'co-production' of steam and electricity; it permits the power plant to achieve a higher overall thermal efficiency by producing a little less electricity and generating some steam instead, at a temperature high enough to be of some use to other users.) Once the idea of co-generation was taken seriously, it was found that the power plant could also sell steam to a pharmaceutical plant, greenhouses, local homes, and its own fish farm (see Figure 15.1).

The Kalundborg complex goes far beyond co-production, however. The Statoil refinery had excess high-sulfur gas. By introducing a hydro-desulfurization stage (admittedly, a rather standard procedure nowadays), it recovered sulfur for sale to a sulfuric acid producer, Kemira, and sold the cleaner gas to ASNAES — saving coal — and to a local gypsum wallboard manufacturer Gyproc. Meanwhile ASNAES also introduced a lime scrubber to remove the sulfur from its flue gases. The calcium sulfate sludge from this process is also sold directly to the wallboard manufacturer, replacing gypsum that would otherwise be needed. Ash from ASNAES is used for road building and cement manufacturing.

Finally, fish-processing waste from the fish farm, and (sterilized) waste sludge from the fermentation process in the Novo Nordisk pharmaceutical plant are sold to local farmers as fertilizer. Novo Nordisk happens to be the world's largest producer of insulin and industrial enzymes, with factories in seven countries. However, the Kalundborg facility is one of its largest. The firm has published a very detailed environmental report (Novo Nordisk company brochure 1993), which outlines the production cycle for the firm as a whole. It used 214 000 tonnes of raw material inputs in that year, along with 4 million cubic meters of water. It discharged 2.1 million cubic meters of non-hazardous treated wastewater, 26 500 tonnes of non-hazardous wastes and 1100 tonnes of hazardous wastes (oils and chemicals). But 1.6 million cubic meters of organic liquid wastes were recycled as agricultural fertilizer.

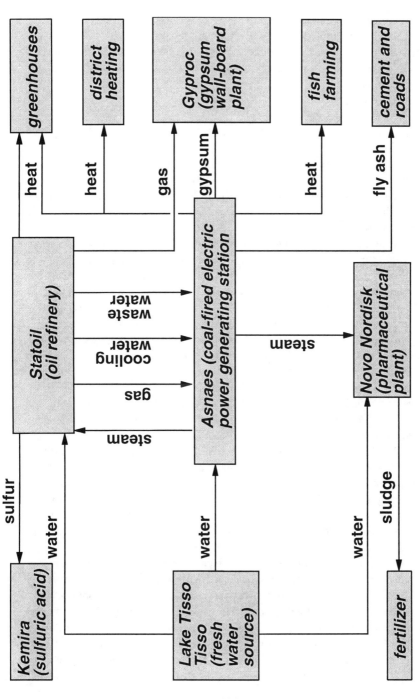

281

Source: Cornell 1994.

Figure 15.1: *Kalundborg prototype industrial ecosystem*

Obviously most of the components of an industrial ecosystem are present in Kalundborg, from the primary producers to the equivalent of the decay organisms. However, the combination of industrial activities in that location is sufficiently unusual so that it is not clear how far the Kalundborg example can be generalized.

15.6.   OTHER POSSIBLE INDUSTRIAL ECOSYSTEMS

Several proposals superficially comparable to the Kalundborg example have been made. One of the oldest is the 'nu-plex' concept, promoted vigorously by nuclear power advocates at Oak Ridge National Laboratory (US) in the 1970s. It was, however, basically an idea for an industrial park for large-scale electric power consumers.

A more interesting scheme, from our perspective, is a proposed *aluminum-kombinat* for utilizing low-grade (high ash-content) anthracite coal to recover aluminum and cement (Yun *et al.* 1980). The project was conceived at the Korean Institute of Science and Technology (KIST) as a possible answer to two problems. First, the city of Seoul needed to dispose of several million tonnes of coal ash each year. At the same time, South Korea was totally dependent on imported aluminum, and there was a strong desire to become self-sufficient. After several years of investigation, the *kombinat* scheme evolved. As of 1980, a 60 tonne per day pilot plant was in operation and process economics appeared to be favorable.

In brief, the energy from coal combustion would be used to generate the electric power for aluminum smelting. The inputs to the *kombinat* would be low-sulfur anthracite coal (1.9 MMT/yr), limestone (3.9 MMT/yr) and clay (0.48 MMT/yr). Outputs would be 100 kMT of aluminum and 3.5 MMT of Portland cement. The heart of the scheme is an alumina plant, consisting of two units: a sintering plant (coal + limestone + soda ash) yielding high temperature exhaust gases (900°C) for the steam turbine and 2 MMT/yr clinker for the leaching unit. The latter grinds the clinker and leaches the alumina with hot sodium carbonate solution. The soda combines with alumina, yielding sodium aluminate in solution, while the lime combines with silica precipitating as dicalcium silicate. The latter is sent to the cement plant. The sodium aluminate is then treated in a conventional sequence, first by adding lime to precipitate the dissolved silica and then carbonation of the solution (with CO_2 from the waste heat boiler) to reconstitute the soda ash and precipitate aluminum hydroxide. When aluminum hydroxide is dehydrated (i.e., calcined) it becomes alumina. About 40 kMT/yr of soda ash would be lost in the soda cycle, and would have to be made up. According to calculations and test results, aluminum recovery from the ash would be about 71%, while the thermal efficiency of the electric

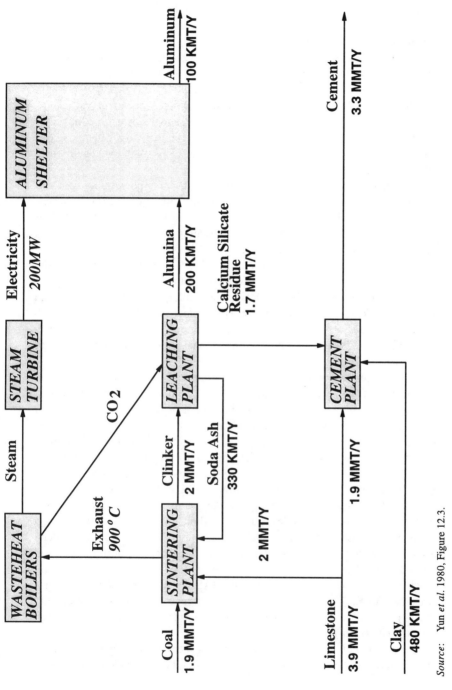

Source: Yun et al. 1980, Figure 12.3.

Figure 15.2:   Conceptual diagram of an aluminum kombinat

283

power generating unit would only be about 15% because of the considerable need for process steam by the leaching plant, mostly for calcination. The basic scheme is outlined in Figure 15.2.

A scheme similar to the *kombinat* was analyzed independently in the late 1970s by TRW Inc. for the US Environmental Protection Agency (Motley and Cosgrove 1978). The idea was motivated by the fact that flue-gas desulfurization (FGD) technology was just being introduced by coal-burning electric power plants. The technology then being adopted was lime/limestone scrubbing, which captures sulfur dioxide quite effectively but generates large quantities of calcium sulfite/sulfate wastes. The TRW study evaluated a possible use for these wastes.

The scheme was based on a conceptual coal-burning power plant generating 1000 MW, which generates 1 MMT/yr of lime/limestone scrubber wastes. The core of the scheme would be a sinter plant in which the sulfate sludges react with carbon monoxide produced by burning coal (273 kMT), clay (300 kMT/yr) and soda ash (12 kMT/yr), to yield soluble sodium aluminate, dicalcium silicate and hydrogen sulfide. These, in turn, are processed by standard means (described briefly in the description of the *kombinat* above), to yield calcined alumina (70 kMT), elemental sulfur (156 kMT) and dicalcium silicate (625 kMT). The latter, in turn, is the major ingredient to produce 850 kMT of Portland cement. At typical market prices, this scheme appeared to be viable, or nearly so. It would certainly be viable given a realistic credit for FGD waste disposal.

Another interesting proposal for an industrial ecosystem comes from Poland (Zebrowski and Rejewski 1987). It is actually a set of interrelated proposals utilizing two basic technologies that have been under development in Poland. The first is coal pyrolysis in the gas stream (PYGAS), a patented technology,[9] that has already been adopted at several Polish industrial sites. It is particularly suited to upgrading existing power plants at minimal capital cost. The basic idea is to feed powdered coal into a hot gas stream (about 800°C) where it pyrolyzes very rapidly (on the order of one second), and pyritic sulfur also decomposes at this temperature. The gas stream passes through a cyclone, where desulfurized carbon char dust is collected and removed. It is usable as a direct substitute for powdered coal in the boilers. Some of the gas is recycled. The pyrolysis gas can be desulfurized and burned or used as feedstock for chemical processing. The second building block is a technology derived from PYGAS for pyrolysis of recycled gas streams (PYREG), specialized to the case of lignite. It has been developed to the large-scale laboratory test stage at the Industrial Chemistry Research Institute (ICRI) in Warsaw.

The idea is not qualitatively different from numerous other proposals for coal gasification, but the authors have given careful consideration to the use of these technologies to integrate existing disconnected systems, especially with respect to sulfur recovery and fertilizer production. This concept is called the Energo-Chemical PYREG site, or simply ENECHEM. The base case for comparison would be a surface lignite mine (18 MMT/yr), with 0.5% sulfur content. This would feed a power station generating 2160 MW of electricity. Lignite in Poland (and Central Europe generally) contains 2–10% xylites (5% average). Xylites are potentially useful organic compounds related to xylene $(C_6H_4(CH_3)_2)$, which are not recovered when lignite is simply burned.

In the base case, annual wastage of xylites would be 900 kMT. By contrast, PYREG technology permits the direct recovery of xylites in the form of high-grade solid fuel (semicoke, 200 kMT/yr), fatty acids and ketenes (65 kMT/yr) and gaseous aromatics (benzene, toluene, xylene or BTX), which are normally derived from petroleum refineries. The proposed ENECHEM site would include a power station, but instead of burning lignite directly to generate 2160 MW as in the base case, it would gasify the lignite, via PYREG, as shown in Figure 15.3, yielding semicoke powder plus volatile hydrocarbons, tar and phenolic water. The semicoke powder would then be burned in the power station (generating 1440 MW, and emitting about 97 kMT/yr SO_2).[10]

The volatile hydrocarbon fraction of the PYREG output would be desulfurized — by conventional Claus technology — yielding about 67 kMT/yr of elemental sulfur S. The condensibles would be separated as liquid propane gas (LPG) for domestic use (150 kMT/yr). The non-condensibles, consist of methane and ethane or synthetic natural gas (SNG) would be available as a feedstock to any natural gas user, such as an ammonia synthesis plant (318 kMT/yr). The tar from the PYREG unit could be refined much as petroleum is, yielding liquid fuels and some light fractions $(C_2 – C_4)$ that would go to the gas processing unit. The yield of gasoline and diesel oil would be 430 kMT/yr, and 58 kMT/yr, respectively, plus 75 kMT/yr of heavy fuel oil. (Obviously, the tars could be a supplementary feed to a co-located conventional petroleum refinery, but the incremental outputs would be much the same). The phenolic water would be processed to recover phenols (13 kMT/yr), cresols (27 kMT/yr) and xylenols (26 kMT/yr).

Obviously, the details of ENECHEM could be varied considerably, but the scheme as outlined in the previous paragraph would reduce sulfur dioxide emissions by roughly half (from 180 kMT to 97 kMT). It would produce less electric power, but in exchange for a reduction of 720 MW, it would yield 318 kMT (400 million cubic meters) of SNG, 150 kMT LPG, 430 kMT gasoline, 480 kMT diesel fuel, 75 kMT heavy fuel oil (less than 1% S), 66 kMT of phenols, cresols and xylenols, and 67 kMT of sulfur (99.5%). This is shown in Figure 15.4.

A recent proposal by Cornell University to the US Environmental Protection Agency differs sharply from the schemes outlined above. Instead of

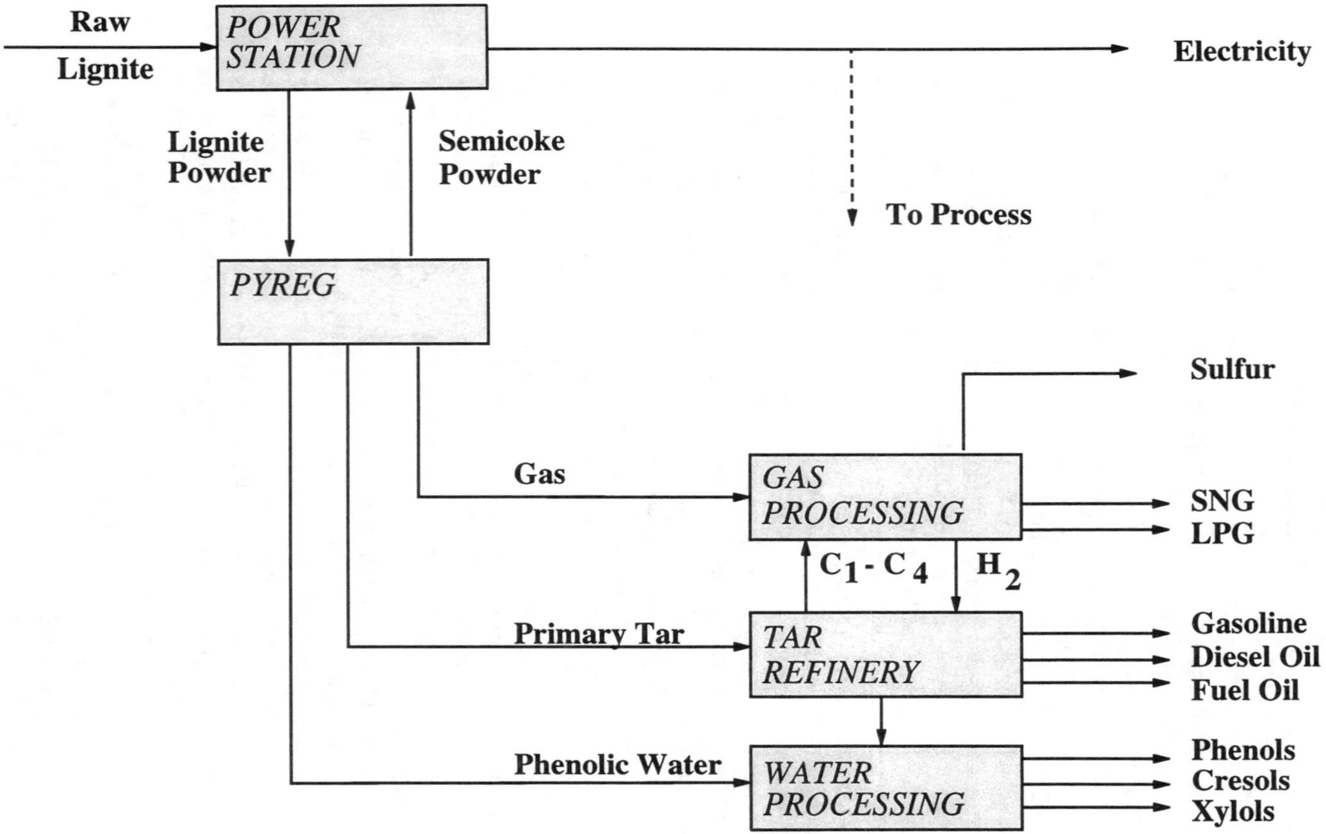

Source: Yun et al. 1980, Figure 12.4.

Figure 15.3: Lignite-burning power plant modified via PYREG

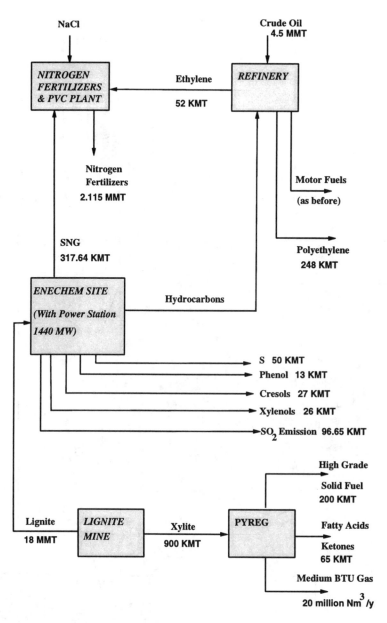

Source: Yun *et al.* 1980, Figure 12.4.

Figure 15.4: Systems integrated with ENECHEM and additional plant for xylite processing

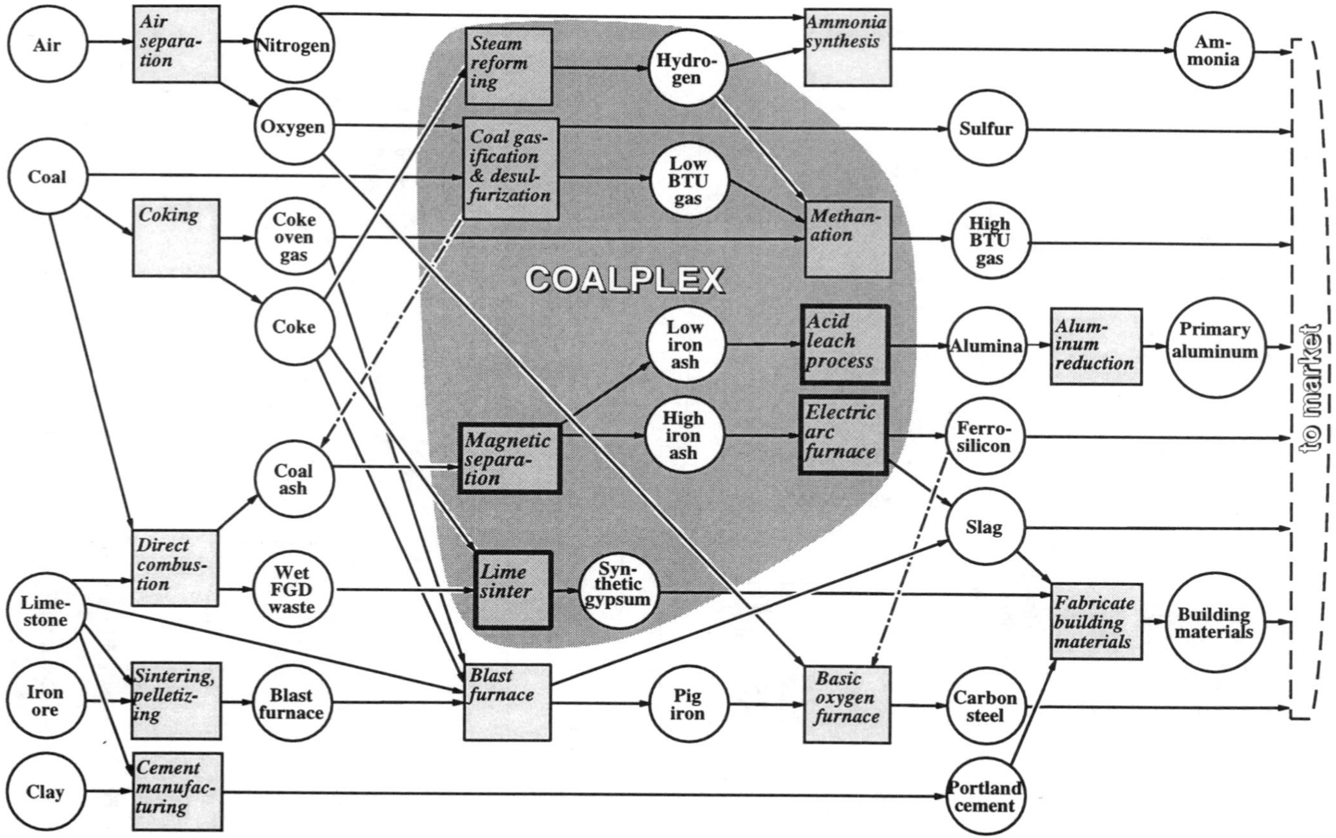

Figure 15.5: Hypothetical process-product flows for coalplex

288

focusing on utilizing an existing natural resource more efficiently, it would attempt to assemble the elements of an industrial ecosystem around a municipal waste treatment facility. In other words, it is essentially a scheme to 'mine' wastes *per se*. The proposal points out that in the 1970s a number of facilities were built with the idea of reducing landfill volumes by recovering the combustible fraction, along with ferrous metals, and converting it to a refuse-derived fuel (RDF), to be sold to a local utility to help defray the costs of operating the facility. Many of these facilities operated only briefly or not at all.

The Cornell proposal would extend the earlier waste treatment concept in two ways. First, it would include not only municipal wastes but also a variety of other industrial wastes for the whole county. Second, it would employ advanced technologies to produce a number of saleable byproducts, one of which would be flue-gas. (Nevertheless, its success would still depend on one or more utilities that would undertake to accept the gaseous fuel generated.)

Also, in contrast with other schemes outlined in this chapter, it would involve no detailed prior planning of the site or the technology, to be used, beyond the creation of an organizational structure to seek out potential participants. This approach is almost mandatory, at least in the US, where central planning is virtually anathema today. Nevertheless, the proposal (if supported) would offer some useful insights as to how a cooperative entity might be created from essentially competitive, independent production units. Or, indeed, whether this is possible.

A final example might be 'coalplex', first proposed by the author some years ago (Ayres 1982) and revised more recently (Ayres 1993, 1993a). It too would be coal-based. Like the Polish scheme it would start by gasification of the coal, recovering sulfur for sale and using the coal ash as a source of alumina (and/or aluminum), and ferrosilicon (Figure 15.5). The most attractive version — albeit somewhat theoretical — would utilize the direct (hydrochloric) acid leaching process for aluminum chloride recovery and the ALCOA process for electrolysis of the chloride. The gasified coal would be (partly) burned on site to produce electric power for the aluminum smelter and electric furnaces. A variant would also produce carbon anodes for the aluminum smelter from coke made from gasified coal (instead of petroleum coke). There are, in fact, a number of possible variants, none of which has been adequately analyzed to date.

15.7. CONCLUDING COMMENTS

The key feature of most industrial ecosystems that have been proposed is what might be termed 'economies of integration'. To be sure, large scale is also required, in most cases. But beyond that, both vertical and horizontal integration are required. All industrial ecosystems essentially depend on converting (former) waste streams into useful products. This means that some producers must be induced to accept unfamiliar inputs (i.e. converted wastes) rather than traditional raw materials. In some cases they will have to invest large sums of money to create new processing facilities, based on unproven — or semi-proven — concepts.

An industrial ecosystem must look like a single economic entity (firm) from the outside. It will have consolidated inputs and outputs (products). It will compete with other such entities (firms) in both raw material and product markets. It will also compete with other firms for capital. From the inside, however, central ownership with hierarchical management is almost certainly not the optimum solution. Too much depends on very sensitive and continuous adjustments between the different components of the system. This is much more compatible with markets — provided all parties have relatively complete information — than it is with centralized top-down management (as critics of Taylorism have been saying for a long time). Yet the modern version of a conglomerate, consisting of autonomous units linked to a corporate parent by a purely financial set of controls with each component competing for funds on the basis of profits, cannot work either.

Evidently, an industrial ecosystem based on a major primary 'exporter' with a galaxy of associated waste converters is quite unlike a traditional impersonal 'market', where goods of known and constant quality are bought and sold through intermediaries. In a traditional market there are many competing suppliers and many competing consumers. Because only high-value goods are physically shipped over distances, many suppliers need not be local. Thus, traditional industrial systems can be quite decentralized.[11]

In an industrial ecosystem, for obvious reasons, low-value materials from a first-tier exporter must be utilized locally. Assuming there is one major waste, which can be converted into a useful raw material, there must also be a local user for that raw material. This is likely to be a fairly large firm, also, to achieve the necessary scale of operation. Other satellite firms in the complex will have only one supplier for a given input, and one consumer for a given output.

The necessity for close long-term cooperation and planning between waste producers and consumers is obvious. Neither can change either processes or production levels without strongly affecting the other. Less obvious, but not less important, is the corresponding need for relatively complete disclosure of all relevant technological information on both sides. Being accustomed to a culture of secrecy, this condition will be very difficult for most firms to achieve. In general, it appears that an enforcement mechanism will be needed to ensure cooperation.

There are three existing models for a cooperative system. One is the 'common ownership' model of vertical integration, in which a single corporate entity owns all, or most, of its suppliers and manages the whole collection centrally. AT&T, GE, GM, IBM, Standard Oil (NJ) and US Steel were created by multiple mergers to dominate an industry, and mostly followed this pattern.[12] But, as the example of GM illustrates, vertical integration is no longer necessarily an advantage. In fact, GM's principal corporate disadvantage, *vis-à-vis* its competitors, is that it obtains more of its components from wholly owned subsidiaries that are forced to pay high wages negotiated with the United Auto Workers Union, than do other auto firms; the Japanese companies are the least vertically integrated of all. But perhaps the major problem with vertical integration is that it is too cumbersome. IBM has lost ground to a number of smaller, nimbler, competitors mainly because decision making is too centralized and slow.

The second model for inter-firm cooperation is most familiar in Japan, where it is known as the *keiretsu*. The *keiretsu* is a family of firms, normally controlled indirectly by a large bank, with links to a common trading company, and several major first-tier manufacturers spread over a range of industries. There is also, typically, a collection of smaller satellite suppliers for each first-tier company. Most of the larger firms in the group have interlocking stockholdings, and the smaller firms tend to be controlled by the larger ones who are their customers. Thus long-term relationships are essentially guaranteed by financial means.

The diversified portfolio conglomerate, as exemplified in the US (e.g. ITT, LTV, Textron, Berkshire–Hathaway, Seagrams) offers a superficially different scheme. In principle, it could also be a mechanism for obtaining inter-firm cooperation by means of financial controls. The diversified portfolio version rarely attempts any such thing, however. On the contrary, these entities are normally created by financiers in order to exploit 'synergies' (that often turn out to be illusory) and little or no actual cooperation at the technical level takes place. The AT&T purchase of NCR, which had a technological justification, might turn out better. But none of these examples seems ideal to fit the needs of an industrial ecosystem.

The third model for inter-firm cooperation is also top-down, usually being organized by marketing organizations. Families of (largely unrelated) suppliers with long-term contracts have been created by a number of large retail marketing firms, such as Sears, Roebuck, Wal-Mart, K-Mart and MacDonald's. Normally, however, each supplier manufactures a different product, so there is actually little need for technical cooperation among them. But, in at least one case, the supplier family evolved from a large-scale manufacturer. The traditional Italian textile industry, originally a group of large multiproduct companies in a declining industry, has radically reconstructed itself by a policy of deliberate functional spinoffs leaving many small subcontractors to a dominant marketer (Benetton). This self-induced change has been extraordinarily successful. However, it is not particularly relevant to the problem of creating industrial ecosystems.

An industrial ecosystem could theoretically be created by an actual merger of many existing firms at a single location, to promote the necessary inter-firm cooperation. But this is unlikely to make sense, except in very rare instances. More likely, the necessary cooperation could be induced by a local government or some other public body, as seems to have been the case in Kalundborg. On the other hand, no public entity in any of the major industrial countries (to our knowledge) has yet moved beyond the concept stage.

One of the most ambitious such concepts is the 'eco-park', proposed by a group at Dalhousie University, Nova Scotia (Cote *et al.* 1994). The basic idea is to convert an existing, traditional 'industrial park' — the Burnside Industrial Park in Dartmouth, Nova Scotia — into an industrial ecosystem. The Burnside Industrial Park already has a base of 1200 businesses, but the land was assembled and provided by the city, with infrastructural funds provided by the central government of Canada through the Atlantic Development Board, a regional development agency. The city still retains approximately 3000 acres. Thus, public agencies retain very significant influence over the future evolution of the area. However, it is unclear just how this potential influence can be brought to bear to create the necessary incentives *and mechanisms* to create a successful eco-park.

Each component of an industrial ecosystem has its unique role to play. Financial allocations among components cannot be made on the basis of 'profits', for the simple but compelling reason that some components will do business only with others, and there is no unique or objective way to set meaningful prices for all internal transactions. (Companies do it in a variety of ways — often to minimize taxes — but all have their disadvantages and critics.) Only by comparing different internal technology choices and transactional arrangements in terms of their impact on the external competitiveness of the system *as a whole*, can objective choices be made. Moreover, such comparisons are necessarily dynamic, rather than static, which makes the decision process very complex indeed.

To summarize, industrial ecosystems are very appealing in concept. Properly organized and structured, they exemplify a built-in incentive to minimize wastes and losses of intermediates. But much research is needed to clarify the optimum organizational and financial structure of such an entity.

NOTES(15)

1. Newer strategies maximizing 'returns to scope' (or 'economies of scope') have become increasingly important in recent years, thanks to the introduction of new computer-based technologies in manufacturing. In brief, the idea is that a manufacturer who can produce a large number of different products *efficiently* from a small number of flexible workers or programmable machines will be more able to meet variable demand than a manufacturer with inflexible machines geared to a single standardized product. It appears that advanced forms of computer-controlled production, linked with computer-assisted design and engineering — known as computer-integrated-manufacturing, or CIM — offer a feasible path away from traditional mass production (e.g. Goldhar and Jelinek 1983, 1985; also Ayres 1991a).

2. See, for example, Siegfried Giedion's *Mechanization Takes Command*, Part IV (Giedion 1948, pp. 213–40).

3. Even the most modern coke ovens are not regarded as desirable neighbors, since there are still non-negligible emissions from leaks, dust and especially from the quench-water.

4. The Otto-cycle gas engines were quickly adapted to liquid fuels, higher speeds and smaller sizes by one of Otto's associates, Gottlieb Daimler. The Daimler engine, in turn, made possible the motor vehicle and the airplane.

5. See, for instance, the chapter on copper in US Bureau of Mines *Minerals Yearbook*, 1989 (USBuMines 1989).

6. Thus, a natural ecosystem is a self-organizing system consisting of interacting individuals and species, each programmed to maximize its own utility (survival and reproduction), each receiving and providing services to others, each therefore dependent on the system as a whole. The ecosystem normally maintains itself in a balanced condition, or evolves slowly along a developmental path. But such 'dissipative systems' remain far from (thermodynamic) equilibrium.

7. In reality, the biosphere does *not* recycle all of the important nutrient elements — notably phosphorus and calcium — without help from geological processes; but this is probably a quibble.

8. The IE concept was given a considerable boost in recent years by Robert Frosch, then VP and Director of Research for General Motors and a member of both the US National Academy of Sciences (NAS) and the National Academy of Engineering (NAE). Frosch, with others, has promoted a new 'strategy for manufacturing' in an article in a special issue of *Scientific American* called 'Managing the Planet' (Frosch and Galloopoulos 1989). With others, he has also encouraged the NAE to sponsor a series of summer studies (leading to books) promoting the concept and exploring various aspects.

9. Patent no. 87904. License available from PROSYNCHEM Design Office, Gliwice, Poland.

10. Sulfur recovery in PYREG technology is only 40–60%, but since Polish lignite has a very low sulfur content (0.5%), this is not considered to be a major disadvantage.

11. Indeed, the pattern established by many multinational manufacturing firms is to build various elements of a product 'line' in several different countries, thus achieving both the benefits of scale, on the one hand, and minimizing the risk of being 'held up' by local governments or unions. Ford's 'world car' concept is a good example, although IBM was (is) perhaps the most successful practitioner of the policy of decentralized international supply.

12. ALCOA, Ethyl Corp and Xerox achieved monopoly status originally through tight control of patent rights, but both Ethyl and Xerox lost dominance when the patents expired. In ALCOA's case, as with AT&T and Standard Oil, the monopoly was broken by anti-trust action by the US government.

16. Summary and conclusions

16.1. STRATEGIC OPPORTUNITIES AND POLICY LEVERS

In the following sections we summarize the major results and conclusions drawn from our analysis, in the same order as the chapters.

Aluminum

It is important for energy reasons alone to increase the recycling rate for aluminum products. This applies especially to cans, but also to hardware, window frames, roofing, and so on. The energy required to process a tonne of aluminum from bauxite consumes 300 GJ (gigaJoules) of energy; by contrast, a tonne of secondary aluminum from average scrap requires only 18 GJ, or 6% as much (Forrest and Szekely 1991). This difference has a parallel impact on global carbon emissions, since even though aluminum smelters use only hydroelectric or nuclear power, the electricity they use could — in Europe and North America, at least — replace other electricity made by burning coal, at the margin. Energy saved in processing (and carbon dioxide not emitted into the atmosphere) is not the only benefit of recycling. Other benefits would include reduced demand for caustic soda for the Bayer process (also an energy-intensive product), reduced demand for fluorine (as aluminum fluoride) and, of course, reduced need to dispose of waste 'red mud'.

The economics of recycling are obviously favorable in the US, since the recycling rate has reached 80% without any regulatory intervention. The economics in Europe should be even more favorable, given high energy costs and logistical advantages. (Sweden actually has an even higher recycling rate.) The barriers to achieving similar results in the rest of Western Europe must be non-economic in nature, and should be relatively easy to overcome. Yet the recycling rate for aluminum in Europe is only 25% (30% in Germany), which is remarkably low.

Recycling aluminum looks like a win–win opportunity in Europe. Collection of scrap aluminum is not technically difficult, and the recycling rate for aluminum could easily be pushed up above 50% in the near term and probably to 70% in the longer term, with appropriate incentives. But such a policy will probably be strongly resisted by the primary producers with large investments in bauxite mines and alumina plants. To implement it will require government intervention or public outcry, or both.

Another possible win–win opportunity is to revive the ALCOA process for aluminum smelting, with its 20% net saving in electricity consumption, using alumina from bauxite as the raw material (as currently). The economics are favorable, provided the pollution problem can be solved satisfactorily. A significant ancillary advantage of the shift, incidentally, would be to eliminate fluoride pollution and the need for aluminum fluoride and its precursors, hydrofluoric acid and fluorspar. On the other hand, even if this were to be demonstrated on a pilot scale, the industry would be slow to replace existing capacity, unless the global demand for aluminum were to increase sharply. The most likely early adopters, therefore, would be for smelters in Asia, potentially giving Asia a long-term competitive advantage in the industry. (The analogy with the adoption of the Basic Oxygen Process in steelmaking by Japan is provocative.)

A third possible win–win opportunity — more speculative, but even more favorable in principle — would be to recover aluminum values from fly ash by direct chlorination, yielding aluminum chloride. (See also Chapter 14, Coal ash.) The latter, in turn, would become the feedstock for the ALCOA electrolytic smelting process. In effect, this would mean eliminating the need for bauxite mining and conversion to alumina via the Bayer process. Here again, the East Europeans or Chinese, with large coal-burning electric power sectors would be likely early adopters.

Copper and Cobalt

The energy argument applies with almost equal force to copper and cobalt. Copper from high-grade (1%) ore requires 100 GJ/tonne for digging, grinding, concentration, smelting and refining; in the worst case (0.3% ore) the energy requirement is over 200 GJ/tonne (Forrest and Szekely 1991). A rough average for the US might be 150 GJ/tonne, about half of that for aluminum. Yet secondary copper from high-grade scrap copper (e.g. wire) requires only 14.4 GJ and even low-grade copper-bearing scrap can be recycled for 40 GJ/tonne (ibid.). These are not the only benefits by far. Copper not mined and smelted translates into less mine waste to dump, less chemical waste from froth flotation, less SO_2 emission from refineries (not all of the sulfur is recovered) and less arsenic and other emissions from smelters. Not only that, but less arsenic will be available for recovery and subsequent dissipative use.

Yet the recycling rate for copper, even in Germany, is only 42% (BDI 1984). The problem is collection and separation. The technology can surely be developed, but again, primary producers will resist and fairly strong government intervention will be necessary. There are two ways to change this situation. The first would be to widen the scope of 'take-back' legislation to include all kinds of copper-containing small appliances and electronic goods. This, in turn, would create a more reliable supply of recyclable material, and that alone could help. However, 'take-back' legislation would also have a more profound impact on manufacturers, namely to induce them to design their products for easy recovery of the copper wire and other copper-containing elements. This is something of a challenge for designers, but it would be very surprising if major improvements in this regard could not be achieved at modest cost. Unfortunately, the design for environment (DFE) approach would not be readily applicable in the building industry, where a great deal of copper wire is used in structures.

The second way to change the rate of copper recycling would be to raise the price of virgin copper by direct taxation, or by taxation of energy (or, conceivably, by rationing and a system of tradeable permits for copper use). If this were to be done, there would be some substitution of other materials for copper, notably aluminum for some kinds of wiring and PVC for some tubing. Brass markets might shrink somewhat — especially if an alternative to brass for ammunition casings could be developed. But doubling or tripling the price of virgin copper by taxing smelter output (including imports of ores, concentrates, blister copper and copper products made from virgin copper) would undoubtedly encourage recycling and re-use.

It should be noted that restricting the production of virgin copper could also have an impact on cobalt production and silver production, since both are byproducts of copper. However, cobalt comes mainly from Zaire, which has one of the richest mines and would be one of the last to close. Thus cobalt supply is not threatened. Silver supply might be cut slightly, but not significantly. In fact silver has been declining in price because its major uses (jewelry, photography, coins) are all using less silver.

Chromium

Chromium in stainless steel, coatings, and chemicals is not being recycled effectively enough. Here the problem is to separate the stainless steel from other scrap metal, especially in the case of automobiles and consumer appliances. A technical solution is doubtless possible, but it will not be worthwhile for this very small industry to develop on its own. The difficulty of recovery is even greater for chrome plate, of course. (This last problem may be effectively insoluble.)

To increase recycling and reduce the need for virgin materials either 'take-back' legislation for automobiles and other stainless-steel-containing appliances, or a tax on virgin materials, or a combination of both would help. The potential of DFE is considerable. There is probably a win–win opportunity for recycling refractory furnace linings, since at least one firm (Cookson Group) is already doing it profitably. In the case of chromium chemicals, most if not all have substitutes and if the conversion of Cr III to Cr VI under oxidizing conditions in soils is confirmed, certain uses — such as pigments, leather tanning, wood preserving and decorative chrome-plating might have to be banned.

Zinc and Cadmium

The recycling energy advantage for zinc is much less than for aluminum or copper, but still significant. However, there is relatively little zinc scrap in pure form. In the case of zinc the problem is more complex. A very important new market has developed for zinc coating (galvanizing) of steel in the automobile industry for protection of auto bodies from the underside. Unfortunately, under present conditions, it is very difficult to recover any of this zinc, except in dust from electric arc furnaces (EAFs). Another major use of zinc is for batteries, which are also rarely recycled.

The recovery of zinc from EAF dust began in the US on a commercial basis at one plant in 1981. But the classification of zinc-rich EAF dust as hazardous waste and tighter regulation of disposal in the US has encouraged rapid growth of this type of recycling since 1989. Recovery of zinc (and possibly cadmium) from scrap tire combustion ash also appears to be economically feasible, even on a fairly small scale. Both of these look like potential win–win candidates. Tire combustion for energy recovery is a promising area for future growth, given the enormous backlog of scrap tires to be disposed of in the US and Western Europe. This will add to the secondary zinc supply (see the section on Tires, below).

It is particularly important to recycle nickel cadmium batteries, which are becoming very widely used, to prevent them from accumulating in landfills or (worse) going to incinerators. This should not be too difficult technically, if the collection problem can be solved. The latter will surely require government intervention. The recycling of nickel-cadmium (nicad) batteries is not economically feasible at present without government intervention, but the only problem is lack of a collection mechanism. A returnable deposit on such batteries would probably be an effective way to solve this problem.

Sulfur

From a global perspective, the recovery of sulfur from coal, as sulfuric acid or in some other form, is a classic win–win opportunity. On the one hand, it would have enormous benefits in reducing air pollution and acid rain, with their associated social costs. On the other hand, it would also eliminate the need to extract and recover sulfur for industrial use from natural deposits or pyrites.

Unfortunately, the potential savings to society cannot easily be converted into profit opportunities for existing industrial actors. For one thing, the current technology of flue-gas desulfurization (FGD) is not suitable for sulfur recovery in useful form. On the contrary, FGD requires large quantities of limestone (that must be mined) and generates large quantities of a messy waste material that has no industrial value in most locations. If coal were gasified before combustion it would be technically possible to recover the sulfur in elemental form, which is suitable for industrial use. At any rate, if the social costs of SO_X emissions could be internalized by means of resource taxes, emissions taxes or tradeable permits, and especially if some of the money were used to subsidize sulfur recovery, society would gain in two ways, both through reduced emissions and through more efficient use of natural resources.

Both the challenge and the opportunity, in the case of industrial sulfur metabolism, are so large that it deserves much deeper study and analysis.

Phosphorus, Fluorine and Gypsum

One, and perhaps two, possible win–win opportunities can be identified. The first is to recover fluosilicic acid from phosphate rock processing. Several possible processes exist for converting fluosilicic acid to hydrogen fluoride, aluminum fluoride or sodium fluoride, depending on downstream uses. Some of these processes need further development, but given the fact that recovery is already commercially viable in the US and Sweden, wider applicability is virtually assured. Efficient recovery of fluorine values from phosphate rock could replace much, if not all, natural fluorspar.

The other potential opportunity is to recover phospho-gypsum from phosphate rock processing and utilize it in place of natural gypsum. In this case the economics are not favorable under present circumstances, because the phospho-gypsum is wet. It must be dehydrated before it can be calcined. This suggests the possibility of integrating phosphate rock processing facilities with either blast furnace operations or petroleum refineries that generate large amounts of moderate-temperature heat. Blast furnaces generate quantities of carbon monoxide rich gas (blast furnace gas) which can be burned locally as a fuel. Petroleum refineries generally flare small non-commercial quantities of 'light ends' from cracking or reforming operations. Fuels such as these, which are otherwise wasted or used inefficiently, could be used for dehydrating wet calcium sulfate.

With regard to both opportunities, the economics would be much more favorable if extractive resources were taxed, as part of a program to shift the tax burden from labor to resources. Since phosphates are needed as fertilizers, taxes would have little impact on demand, but would increase the incentive to find markets for byproducts. However, taxes on resource extraction would reduce the current price advantage of natural fluorspar and natural gypsum as compared to byproduct recovery.

Nitrogen Chemicals

The challenge to policy is to reduce sharply the emissions of so-called 'odd nitrogen' compounds into the environment, especially N_2O, so as to minimize anthropogenic interference with the radiation balance of the atmosphere and with the natural N-cycle. Yet increasing food production and energy conversion will call for increasing amounts of ammonia-based synthetic fertilizer, and increasing use of fossil fuels resulting in NO_X emissions — barring major technological breakthroughs. We have identified no clear win–win opportunities in this area.

The best way to reduce N-emissions and encourage more conservationist use of nitrogen chemicals is to raise the costs of doing so *vis-à-vis* alternatives. Development of biotech approaches to increase the efficacy of nitrogen fixation by crop plants would be the ideal solution, so far as fertilizer nitrogen is concerned, but it is a distant prospect. Taxation of emissions based on nitrogen content would be the ideal solution, and would encourage industry to invest in the biotech approach, but it would be difficult to 'sell' to legislatures or industry, and difficult to implement in practice. It would be much easier to tax ammonia production (or natural gas used in the ammonia synthesis process). But this would leave the NO_X problem — which is probably worse — untouched. The latter problem is very difficult to deal with through prices; only regulation seems likely to be effective at all.

The entire area of industrial N-metabolism (like industrial sulfur metabolism) deserves a deeper and more detailed analysis.

Chlorine Chemicals

In the chlorine chemical industry there are essentially five existing recycling routes. These are (1) recycling sodium chloride and calcium chloride from process wastes, (2) recycling hydrochloric acid (HCl) wastes as such, or by converting waste HCl to chlorine, (3) burning chlorinated hydrocarbons (CHCs) to recover HCl, (4) recycling chlorinated solvents and CFCs and (5) recycling the plastic PVC. We consider the last possibility, which is outside the chemical industry, in Chapter 12, Packaging.

Of the other four possibilities, it appears that the second and third are already being exploited to very nearly the maximum extent possible, given the present mix of products. The basis for saying this is that virtually all hydrochloric acid that is consumed is actually recycled process waste, and has been for a number of years. Moreover, in Europe and the US at least, virtually all waste CHCs are burned to recover HCl. (Small amounts are disposed of in other ways, such as landfills.) In fact, if HCl is regarded as a chlorine carrier, it appears that 36% of all chlorine used in Europe — and probably a similar percentage in the US — is in fact recycled. In many cases the recycling of HCl was economically justified even without making any allowances for waste-disposal costs. On the other hand, HCl recovery from CHCs is a relatively recent phenomenon, probably resulting from the high and rising costs of alternative means of disposal. However, as noted, there is not much more scope for this form of recycling, at least in Europe and the US.

The recycling of sodium and calcium chloride wastes is still a technological possibility. As noted, some firms (like Dow) do recycle some sodium chloride process wastes back through the electrolytic cells to make chlorine. However, though exact figures are confidential, it is clear that only a very small percentage of total sodium chloride inputs to the chlorine industry are recycled in this manner. Moreover, economic opportunities for future increases in this area are limited — unless the price of 'virgin' salt rises sharply. Calcium chloride is not a feedstock for electrolysis, and has very limited markets, though there is a lot of scope for using calcium chloride in place of sodium chloride for snow control on roads and highways. Other inorganic chlorine process wastes, notably calcium chloride, are essentially not recycled at all, nor do we know of any short-term possibilities along these lines.

Chlorinated solvents used in industry and also for 'dry cleaning', can and should be recycled far more effectively than they are. There are already opportunities for providing profitable services in this area — a likely win–win opportunity. Similarly, CFC refrigerants can and should be recovered from discarded refrigeration and air-conditioning equipment. (A high tax on the new product would ensure this more effectively than a ban on use.)

Electronic Grade Silicon

Despite its reputation as a 'clean' industry, the semiconductor industry is in fact one of the dirtiest imaginable, in terms of waste and pollution output per unit of physical output. The Siemens process for purifying metallurgical grade polysilicon (from an electric arc furnace) has an extraordinarily low yield — only about 20% — and consumes several tons of chlorine per ton of silicon. Moreover, because of secrecy in the industry and the small number of producers, it is difficult to trace the byproducts and wastes. Thus, our analysis was necessarily more theoretical than empirical. The major waste products of the Siemens purification process are HCl and $SiCl_4$. In principle these are recyclable, either within the process or to other processes such as silicone production. Also, there are other possible purification routes.

There are probably no significant win–win opportunities at current output levels for EGS. However, the potential future growth of a new application of ultra-pure silicon, photovoltaic (PV) cells to generate electric power directly from sunlight, creates the potential of a much greater waste/pollution problem. At present, PV cells are manufactured from scrap EGS lost in the wafer production process — mainly silicon powder and fragments. If this approach to PV manufacturing technology were the only one possible, silicon PV cells would involve an unacceptable burden of environmental pollution and energy consumption. Luckily, PV technology does not require as high a degree of purity as silicon 'chips' for computers.

This fact opens the door to a much more attractive possibility, namely for the large-scale introduction of a new and much less wasteful silicon purification process that does not involve chlorine at all. If (or when) the PV market grows sufficiently, PV silicon will be made by a different and far more efficient (less-polluting) process. Market growth will, of course, bring down unit costs, stimulating further expansion of the PV market. This can be regarded as a real win–win opportunity for the near future. Government intervention could obviously help to accelerate this process in various ways. We think the best approach would be to encourage the use of PV in new building construction; however, the details of such a policy are beyond the scope of this book.

Tires

Scrap tires are the most compelling case for a recycling policy. At present most used tires are discarded on open fields or burned under uncontrolled conditions, despite the serious pollution problem thus created on the one hand, and the waste of high-quality energy on the other.

This area offers at least one clear win–win possibility, namely the use of scrap tires as fuel, either for cement plants or electric power generation. (The pulp and paper industry is also a possible consumer of tires as fuel, currently, but more efficient use of bark and lignin waste as fuel should make external sources superfluous.) Both of these applications are economically attractive now, and would be more so with minor improvements in tire-burning technology. However, proposals to use scrap tires in this way run into strong opposition from local citizens in many places, and may be discouraged by regulation. It is certainly very important to control sulfur dioxide pollution and to dispose of the zinc-rich furnace ash (in the case of electric power production, at least), preferably by recovering the zinc.

Depolymerization of tires to recover raw materials is attracting some interest from industry. Chemical and pyrolytic means do not appear to be cost competitive, however. A surprising new possibility is microwave depolymerization. It is claimed that such a process is operating commercially in Canada and, shortly, in the UK. The economics are unknown.

Another possibility attracting considerable interest in the US, but as yet unproven, is that granulated tire materials, mixed with asphalt, can produce a paving material (asphalt rubber, or AR) that lasts sufficiently longer than current materials to justify higher costs. This depends largely on the development of more efficient tire granulation technologies.

However, by far the most attractive possibility from a public standpoint would be to induce manufacturers to extend tire life and sharply increase retreading. The most plausible way to accomplish this is by means of tire 'take-back' legislation. (Ideally, tires should be provided as part of a service, not sold.) This is exactly what already happens in the case of truck and aircraft tires, which are normally leased, retreaded several times and which last several times longer than tires for private cars. If tire manufacturers could generate the same revenues they do now with significantly smaller material and fabrication costs, this approach might prove to be attractive in the long run. In fact, tire life could be extended considerably (as noted under the heading 'dematerialization') and worn tires can and should be remanufactured several times — as truck and aircraft tires are now — before being discarded. The technology exists.

As long as tires are being sold directly to consumers (or to car companies) the system will not change without government intervention. Such intervention will be resisted strongly by the tire manufacturers, since it would sharply reduce their sales (which is exactly the objective). The most effective way to achieve this outcome would be for society to shift away from direct vehicle (and tire) ownership to leasing. This could be encouraged by appropriate tax policies, such as a VAT exemption for lessors, for instance. Tire lessors would, of course, have every incentive to minimize tire wear and ensure maximum recycling. At the end of a tire's life, it should be used as fuel in a cement plant or in some other way that takes advantage of either the energy value of the material or the peculiar properties of rubber.

Packaging Materials

The virtues of recycling aluminum beverage cans have already been mentioned. This is already being done on a large scale in the US and is a true win–win opportunity for Europe. Glass bottles can be refilled and re-used as such, but the advantage of doing so in energy terms is minor (15%). Glass is heavy, and transport costs are significant, so major increases in the current recycling rate may not be particularly beneficial except to reduce the volume of waste for disposal.

Paper recycling is probably close to the economic limit at current prices for pulp. It can be increased by mandating the use of recycled paper (as in Europe) but the recycling process itself is dirty and energy intensive, so the optimal system would certainly involve continued use of significant amounts of virgin fiber. (The big problem here is to find better uses for lignin wastes.)

PVC bottles can and should be re-used, for some purposes, as such. The same is true of newly introduced PET and polycarbonate bottles. Public health authorities can help by permitting such re-use, subject to reasonable requirements for sterilization. Again, the primary producers of plastic will resist strongly. There are also many other opportunities to use recycled PVC and PET. Polystyrene foam can be recycled for some purposes. Recycling of packaging (and other) components of municipal waste can be significantly increased through the implementation of modern sorting and separation technologies that appear to be quite well developed, but not yet widely known. Modest subsidies are probably needed, at first, but such subsidies should be easily justified by the benefits of extending the life of scarce landfill sites, not to mention the sale of recyclable materials and compost.

However most plastic packaging wastes — indeed, municipal wastes in general — should probably be incinerated or (eventually) gasified for fuel recovery.

Fly Ash

Fly ash is an ideal industrial raw material, being dry and finely divided (i.e. needing no grinding or dehydration). The problem is to find uses for it and to develop significant markets. A number of such uses have already been demonstrated for fly ash in its 'raw' form. The most important of these is the use of fly ash as an additive for concrete and as a raw material for making synthetic aggregates for concrete.

More interesting in the long run is the potential use of fly ash as a source of metals. The technology for recovering metals such as aluminum, iron and silicon is known, though not fully developed. However, the economics are not favorable, at least by standard accounting rules. Given the reality of subsidies for the coal industry and unrealistically low prices, there is no immediate win–win opportunity here. The situation changes radically if the social and environmental costs of coal combustion were to be internalized. In particular, if this were done by means of a carbon tax or equivalent, and if some of that money were earmarked to subsidize the disposal of ash (and FGD wastes) — or even to subsidize R&D and demonstration projects — the economics of metals (and sulfur) recovery from coal wastes would be much more favorable.

16.2. TECHNOLOGICAL GAPS

A few areas have been identified where a powerful new technology seems to be 'on the cards' but where the missing ingredients for a breakthrough cannot be described precisely. What this means is that applied research of a rather fundamental nature may still be needed, and it is impossible to predict how long it may take or how costly it will be.

The outstanding example in this category that emerges from our study is the long-sought bipolar cell with an inert (non-consumable) electrode. Such a cell would be applicable to any sort of 'conventional' electrolytic reduction process, including aluminum smelting, copper refining, and chlorine/caustic soda production. It would also open the possibility of efficient separation of light metals from fly ash (or lunar soil) along a voltage gradient. This would be the electrolytic analog of a distillation column, which separates materials according to boiling point along a thermal gradient. In both cases, arbitrarily high levels of purification could (can) be achieved by recycling the outputs.

The problem so far encountered in developing an inert electrode is surface corrosion and the resulting variable electrical resistance, not to mention mechanical problems. Solutions might be sought in various directions (e.g. nitrides? diamond coatings?), but the answer is not yet clearly in sight.

Another well-known example of this kind is the problem of engineering ceramics for turbine blades and other components of turbo-machinery and rocket engines. If successful, ceramics could replace virtually all uses of 'superalloys' and high-speed tool steels, thus sharply reducing the industrial demand for cobalt and, to a minor extent, for chromium. Here the problems are formability and elimination of defects.

A third example of some interest is the very crude Siemens process for purifying metallurgical grade silicon to electronic grade silicon. There is no doubt that progress in photovoltaic (PV) cell technology has been held back because the only source of silicon pure enough for PV cells is scrap from semiconductor (chip) manufacturing. The latter is actually much purer than necessary and would be too expensive for large-scale use in PV. A number of alternative processes more suitable to PV have been suggested and studied on paper or to the pilot stage, but the gap remains.

The other category of technology gap applies to industrial processes. It is composed of three parts. The first is the gap between designs on paper and laboratory or bench-test models. The second part is the gap between the laboratory version and the small pilot plant. Finally, there is another gap between the pilot plant and the industrial-scale plant.

In general, 'scaling up' is a learning and optimization process. In the course of this process many design parameters must be determined empirically. The dynamic behavior of a complex non-linear system cannot be completely predicted by computer simulation; the behavior of the actual system under various perturbing influences (voltage, pressure and temperature excursions, or input contamination, for instance) can only be verified by building and operating it. Finally, of course, there may be unexpected corrosion problems, side reactions and the like. For all of these reasons, the multi-stage scale-up is necessary.

At the level of paper design, process research is relatively inexpensive and we think it would be appropriate for some governmental organization to support some exploratory research on alternative processes as noted below:

- Extract metals (especially aluminum) from coal ash; hydrochloric acid leaching processes should be investigated in particular.
- Extract fluorine from phosphate rock process waste. Explore the ammonia route, in particular.
- Dehydrate, purify and utilize contaminated calcium sulfite/sulfate sludges in place of natural gypsum.
- Explore depolymerization processes for rubber (in particular) and plastics. The microwave process appears promising.
- Gasify mixed plastics (and other organic materials) at low temperatures, remove metals, hydrogen chloride and sulfur from the gas stream.

At the next two levels, bench testing and pilot plants, it would also be appropriate for the public sector to provide significant support. It is important in this regard to distinguish between areas where established industries have a positive incentive to contribute because a successful outcome would be of direct benefit to them in international competition, *vis-à-vis* those areas where established industries currently have major investments in older technologies that might be devalued and supplanted. It is basically unreasonable to expect a primary producer with large investments in mines and smelters to invest willingly in recycling technology, or even in alternative processes that compete with profitable existing ones.

However, despite the potentially critical role of the public sector, it is clear that pilot plants can only serve a useful purpose when built and operated by a firm that is seriously interested in, and capable of taking the next and final step. Thus, government support at this stage should only be on a cost-sharing basis.

It is worth noting, once again, that many of the opportunities for increasing resource productivity — especially in the area of recycling — do not require any new technology. They are apparently being held back by other barriers, especially resistance by established (and politically influential) primary producers who would lose market share. This issue is discussed at length in Section 2.3, The economics of 'win–win'.

Appendix A: Production and consumption data

Table A.1: *European and world production of bauxite, alumina and aluminum, 1991 (kMT)*

Country	Bauxite	Alumina	Aluminum
Austria			80
France	193	150	286
Germany		1 165	690
Greece		520	152
Iceland	2 130		89
Ireland		900	
Italy		760	218
Netherlands	9		264
Norway			833
Spain		950	355
Sweden	3		97
Switzerland			66
United Kingdom		110	294
W. Europe	**2 335**	**4 545**	**3 414**
Albania	8		
Czechoslovakia		150	68
Hungary	2 204	546	64
Poland			45
Romania	200	400	158
Yugoslavia	2 700	900	
E. Europe	**5 112**	**1 996**	**315**
Turkey	530	159	57
USSR	3 800	3 000	2 400
US	na	5 230	4 030
Australia	40 503	11 713	1 235
World	**107 920**	**39 827**	**19 575**

Source: USBuMines 1991, Table 35, p. 224 (bauxite), Table 37, p. 226 (alumina), Table 20, p. 215 (aluminum).

Table A.2:   European and world copper mine, smelter, and refinery output,
              1991 (kMT)

	Mine	Smelter		Refinery	
		Primary	*Secondary*	*Primary*	*Secondary*
Austria				8.4	44.4
Belgium		0.2	100	185	102
Finland	11.7	90.1	12	56.5	8
France	0.3		9	16	30
Germany	9	191.2	82	306.5	216
Italy					82.5
Norway	17.4	38.4		38.5	
Portugal	165	1	2	6	
Spain	16	115	34	115	50
Sweden	80.5	84	24	66.1	30.5
United Kingdom	0.2			17.1	53
Western Europe	**300.1**	**490.9**	**263**	**815.1**	**615.4**
Albania	6.1	6		8	
Bulgaria	30	29	1	14	10
Czechoslovakia	2.5	2.5	15.5	2.5	15.5
Hungary			0.1		
Poland	390	360	20	378	19
Romania	20	25	1	20	2
Yugoslavia	138	95	30	100	22.2
Eastern Europe	**586.6**	**517.5**	**67.6**	**522.5**	**68.7**
Turkey	38.4	19.7	2	85	
USSR	550	700	120	750	120
US	1631	1123	364.3	1577.4	417.8
Chile	1814.3	1296.1		1237.8	
World Total	**8819.5**	**8007.8**	**1044.0**	**8410.4**	**1495.3**

Source: USBuMines 1991, Table 30 (mine), Table 32 (smelter), Table 31 (refinery).

Table A.3:   *European and world chromium materials production, 1991 (kMT)*

	Chromite ore	*Ferro chromium*	*Chromium metal, 92*	*Sodium dichromate*	*Chromic acid*
Finland	458	190			
France		23	1.2		
Germany		50	0.5		
Greece	22	11			
Italy		47			
Norway		90			
Spain		6			
Sweden		122			
United Kingdom			3.0		
W. Europe	**480**	**539**	**4.7**	**23.5**	**0**
Albania	587	25			
Czechoslovakia		37			
Poland		12		19.2	2
Romania		20			
Yugoslavia	9	60			
W. Europe	**596**	**154**	**0**	**19.2**	**2**
Turkey	870	85			
USSR	3 800	925			
US		68	3	146.9 (UN)	
World Total	**13 245**				

Source: Roskill Cr 1993; and UNSO 1988.

Table A.4: European and world zinc and cadmium production, 1991 (kMT)

| Country | Zinc | | | | | |
	Mine ore[a]	Primary	Smelter Secondary	Total	1989 Zinc oxide[a]	Cadmium refinery
Austria	14.8			16.3		
Belgium				297.6		1.807
Finland	55.5	170.4		170.4	1.8	0.593
France	27.1			299.6	41.0	0.271
Germany (W)	54.0	305.5	39.0	346.5	44.6	1.060
Germany (E)				2.0	20.0	
Greece	30.0					
Ireland	187.5					
Italy	37.5			265.0		0.207
Netherlands				201.0		0.549
Norway	18.9	124.6		124.6		0.227
Portugal		5.0		5.0	4.0	
Spain	260.0			273.4	8.8[b]	0.300
Sweden	155.0				2.5[b]	
UK	1.0			100.7	16.1[c]	0.449
W. Europe	**841.3**	**605.5**	**39.0**	**2102.1**	**121.8**	**6.538**
Bulgaria	31.0		1.7	600		0.200
Czechoslovakia	7.0		1.3	1.7		
Hungary				1.3		
Poland	144.0			125.4		0.370
Romania	15.0			10.0		0.010
Yugoslavia	75.0			87.4	8.7	0.280
E. Europe	**272**		**3.0**	**285.8**	**8.7**	**0.990**
Canada	1148.2	660.6		660.6		1.829
Japan	131.8	640.6	90.2	730.8		2.889
Turkey	39.4	17.4		17.4		0.050
USSR	810.0	700	100	800	NA	2.500
US	288.3	253.3	124.1	377.4	93.5	1.676
World	**7282.4**	**4442.8[d]**	**370.3**	**7081.7**	**417**	**20.463**

Notes:
a. Zn content.
b. 1987.
c. 1984.
d. 2268.6 = 'undifferentiated'. We split this in the same ratio as primary/secondary.

Sources: Zn (USBuMines 1991); ZnO (UNIS 1989); Cd (USBuMines 1994).

Table A.5: European and world sulfur and gypsum production, 1989 (kMT)

Country	Mined	Gas	By-product Oil	By-product Metal	Unspec	Total	Gypsum mined
Austria			36[c]	12		48	625
Belgium					320	320	
Denmark			20			20	
Finland	300		45	240		585	
France		636	235		180	1 051	5 569
Germany (W)		1 050	210	315	310	1 885	1 850
Germany (E)					290	290	1 850
Greece	70	105	5			180	500
Ireland							314
Italy	330	330			500	820	1 250
Netherlands			310[d]			310	
Norway	170		10		80	260	
Portugal	120				5	125	300
Spain	1 000		8	225	2[c]	1 235	5 500
Sweden	225		50	125		400	
Switzerland			4			4	218
UK			130	55		185	3 990
W. Europe	**2 215**	**1 791**	**1 063**	**1 052**	**1 607**	**7 728**	**19 426**
Bulgaria	70				60	130	400
Czechoslovakia	60				11	77	775
Hungary	1				10	11	115
Poland	4 920[a]		20	150		5 090	1 090
Romania	150				120	270	1 595
Yugoslavia	255		3	170		428	550
E. Europe	**5 462**		**23**	**320**	**201**	**6 006**	**4 515**
Turkey	45				80	125	250
USSR	5 050[b]	2 500	450	1 350	4	9 350	4 800
US	3 888	2 537	3 973	1 190		11 592	16 000
World	**24 788**	**12 191**	**7 176**	**7 521**	**6 872**	**58 348**	**100 000**

Notes:
a. Frasch 4400, native 500, gypsum 20.
b. Gas and oil.
c. Frasch 1100, native 1800, pyrites 2150.
d. Includes 60 from Curaçao.
e. From coal gasification.

Source: USBuMines 1991.

Table A.6:   *European and world sulfuric acid production and consumption,*
             1989 (kMT)

Country	Production	Consumption Fertilizer	Other
Belgium	1 957	2 070	2 704
Finland	1 375	706	1 286
France	4 064	1 689	4 009
Germany (W)	3 725	460	3 342
Germany (E)	1 070[a]	368[a]	1 068[a]
Greece	1 025	957	1 016
Italy	2 212	722	1 972
Netherlands	1 387	1 234	2 004
Norway	636		
Portugal	267	213	300
Spain	3 146	2 184	3 014
Sweden	905	339	899
UK	2 148	56	2 404
Others	783[b]	261[d]	1 030[c]
W. Europe	**23 629[e]**	**6 492[e]**	**23 893**
Albania[b]	65	53	65
Bulgaria[b]	522	216	576
Czechoslovakia[b]	1 090	402	1 152
Hungary[b]	244	115	250
Poland[b]	2 000	1 515	1 815
Romania[b]	1 170	510	1 170
Yugoslavia[b]	1 350	566	1 337
E. Europe[b]	**6 441**	**3 377**	**6 365**
Turkey		704	869
USSR[b]	645	16 644	27 144
US[b]	27 300	28 999	41 999
World	**158 201**	**99 879[b]**	**161 431**

Notes
a.   1990.
b.   Ireland, Denmark, Luxembourg and Switzerland.
c.   Ireland, Denmark, Luxembourg, Norway and Switzerland.
d.   Austria, Ireland, Denmark, Luxembourg, Norway and Switzerland.
e.   Does not include East Germany.

Source: Kemira.

Table A.7:   *European and world consumption of sulfuric acid, 1990*

	Fertilizer				Non-fertilizer	Total
	N $(NH_4)_2SO_4$	P_2O_5	*Other fertilizer*	*Total*		
W. Europe	2 312 (10%)	6 295 (27.3%)	953 (4.1%)	9 560 (41.5%)	13 454 (58.5%)	23 014 (100%)
E. Europe	873 (13.6%)	2 504 (39.4%)	—	3 377 (53%)	2 988 (47%)	6 365 (100%)
USSR	2 579 (9.9%)	14 065 (51.6%)	—	16 644 (61.5%)	10 500 (38.5%)	27 144 (100%)
US	1 653 (3.9%)	27 347 (66%)	—	28 999 (69.9%)	12 500 (30.1%)	41 999 (100%)
World				97 787 (61.7)	60 696 (38.3%)	158 482 (100%)

Source: Kemira.

Table A.8: European and world production and consumption of phosphoric acid and processed phosphates (kMT P_2O_5 content)

Country	1988 Prod	1988 Cons	1991 Prod	1991 Cons	1992 Production P_2O_5	DAP	MAP	TSP	1992 Home deliveries DAP	MAP	TSP	P_2O_5	1992 Exports DAP	MAP	TSP
Austria	44	50	24	11	29.6			9.3			2.5	7.0			6.9
Belgium	320[a]	135[a]	320[a]	120[a]	355.0			20.0			19.7	235.3	34.0	38.5	12.9
Denmark	0	59	0	38											
Finland	209	185	157	121	189.0							92.3			
France	684	687	430	451	430.6							112.0	0.8	1.1	0.7
Germany (W)	110	313	75	242								15.7	4.2	0.7	
Germany (E)		1		0											
Greece	166	176	168	199	120.3			0.6			0.6				
Italy	214	405	101	201	48.6							1.2			
Netherlands	320	390	330	320	256.2	50.0	15.0		3.5	0.3		111.1	37.5	17.2	115.3
Portugal	24	28		6											
Spain	580	409	470	375	415.0	51.1	60.8	11.5	54.7	60.8	12.6	33.0			
Sweden	165	131	90	100											
UK	215	325	40	180	60.0							2.8	0.8	0.8	
Others	42[b]	42[b]											0.8	0.8	
W. Europe	3093	3336	2205	2364	1904.3	101.1	75.8	41.4	58.2	61.1	35.4	610.4	77.6	58.3	135.8
Bulgaria					43.8			31.8			13.0				
Czechoslovakia					6.5							1.8	0.2		19.0
Poland					306.1	60.6		60.3	25.6		12.5	4.7	40.8	2.5	48.4
Romania					267.0			20.1			16.8		34.8		3.5
E. Europe					623.4	60.6		112.2	25.6		42.3	6.5	75.8	2.5	70.9
Turkey	230	589	180	325				865.5							
US	10 071	9 262	10 591	10 151	11 154.4	6164.7	1104.8		2231.3	625.6	363.5	478.8	3895.6	423.7	484.3
World	28 660	27 724	26 509	25 930	24 892.0				4856.7	2456.7	1760.9	3741.0	5743.0	1663.0	1627.0

Notes:
a. Luxembourg included. b. Cyprus. DAP = Diammonium phosphate. MAP = Mono-ammonium phosphate. TSP = Triple superphosphate.

Source: Kemira, USBuMines, various years.

Table A.9:   Western European production and consumption of AlF$_3$, HF and Acid Spar, 1991 (kMT)

Country	AlF$_3$ 1991 Production	AlF$_3$ 1991 Consumption	HF 1991 Production	Acid Spar 1991 Production	Acid Spar 1991 Consumption
Austria		1.6			
Belgium			5.0[a]		
France	40.0	7.5	34.4	64	72.2
Germany (W)		11.0	72.9		153.1
Germany (E)					
Greece		3.0	8.8		18.5
Iceland					
Ireland					
Italy	10.0	6.0	54.4	16	114.2
Netherlands		5.7	7.2	16	15.1
Norway	16.3	16.0		18	
Spain	11.0	9.0	25.2	[b]	52.9
Sweden	17.7	1.9			
Switzerland		1.2			
United Kingdom		6.7	57.6		121
W. Europe	**95.0**	**69.6**	**265.5**	**124[b]**	**547**

Notes:
a.   From fluosilicic acid.
b.   +16 kMT fluosilicic acid.

315

Table A.10: Western European production, consumption and exports of ammonia (MMT)

Country	Production			Consumption		Home deliveries		Exports	
	1988	1990	1992	1988	1990	1990	1992	1990	1992
Austria	408.0	410.0	410.0	411.0	413.0	406.2	393.4	3.8	16.6
Belgium-Lux	365.1ª	264.7	500.0	868.0	85.0	264.0	500.0		
Denmark				261.7	294.0				
Finland	41.9	23.3	10.0	311.3	324.0	23.3	10.0	14.1	53.2
France	1 831.7	1 588.0	1 407.0	1 980.0	2 032.0	1 571.7	1 353.8		
Germany	1 824.4	1 671.4	2 135.8	1 649.3	1 475.7	1 332.4	1 917.8	301.7	218.0
Greece	263.4	258.8	139.5	408.5	385.6	257.3	139.5		
Ireland	413.5	395.4	384.3	350.0	308.0	310.7	380.0	84.7	
Italy	1 436.5	1 197.0	1 097.9	1 635.0	1 254.0	1 048.8	1 112.2	148.1	7.2
Netherlands	2 955.6	3 162.5	2 666.6	2 046.0	2 268.0	2 262.2	2 103.5	955.8	558.7
Norway	411.0	408.2	342.5	494.4	570.0	430.8	342.5		
Portugal	190.1	198.3	100.3	212.4	181.2	177.7	71.0	27.2	9.6
Spain	484.6	469.1	479.2	1 082.2	1 086.2	479.6	465.3		10.7
Sweden	7.6			180.6	210.1				
Switzerland	31.2	32.0	31.2	47.5	42.0	10.9	31.2		
UK	1 137.2	1 148.0	760.0	1 424.8	1 370.0	1 018.8	760.0	143.0	108.5
Others (Iceland)	7.6	32		22.6	9.2				
Total W. Europe	**11 801.8**	**11 258.8**	**10 573.6**			**9 594.4**	**9 580.2**	**1 678.4**	**982.5**
Turkey	282.5	347.5		880.0		868.2			

Source: Kemira.

Table A.11: *Production and consumption of N-fertilizers: Western Europe, 1990–1991: kMT (N)*

PRODUCTION

Country	Straight N fertilizers						Composite fertilizers			Total N
	NH3	AS	U	AN	CAN	Total N	APN	NPK	Total	
Austria					150	150		64	68	218
Belgium/Lux.		192	18		348	558	4	198	212	770
Denmark					51.2	57.4		119	127.5	184.9
Finland					17.6	17.6		240.7	250.4	268.0
France	34.0	4.0	104.0	650.0		984.0		431.0	497.0	1481.0
Germany	17.0	188.0	90.0		625.0	1080.0		75.0	85.0	1165.0
Greece				115.8	70.8	186.6		58.2	232.8	419.4
Ireland			135.0		144.0	279.0				279.0
Italy	1.0	64.0	266.0		256.0	603.0		153.0	188.0	791.0
Netherlands	2.0	109.0	448.0		966.0	1693.0	21.0	214.0	235.0	1928.0
Norway				0.3		127.6		359.0	389.8	517.4
Portugal		8.9	18.3	5.4	89.0	126.7		31.6	31.6	158.3
Spain	9.1	92.6	224.4	135.2	253.9	773.6	44.7	143.1	187.8	961.4
Sweden		1.2			104.7	111.1		41.9	64.9	176.0
Switzerland					24.6	24.6		2.1	2.1	26.7
UK	4.0	10.0		650.0		680.0			300.0	980.0
Others (Iceland)				1.1	0.5	1.6		8.3	8.5	10.1
Total W. Europe	**67.1**	**669.7**	**1303.7**	**1557.8**	**3101.3**	**7453.8**	**69.7**	**2138.9**	**2880.4**	**10334.2**

Table A.11: continued

CONSUMPTION

Country	NH3	Straight N fertilizers					Composite fertilizers			Total N
		AS	U	AN	CAN	Total N	APN	NPK	Total	
Austria		0.3	2.1		80.5	84.2	3.6	47.9	52.6	136.7
Belgium/Lux.		2.0	1.0		135.0	143.0	2.0	41.0	43.0	186.0
Denmark	62.5	1.3	7.4		132.7	213.2	3.5	157.0	181.7	394.9
Finland			2.4		18.4	20.8		180.4	185.6	206.4
France	33.9	44.2	254.3	1058.8		1942.6		441.8	550.2	2492.8
Germany	17.0	23.0	194.7	115.1	1207.6	1530.0		185.0	257.6	1787.6
Greece		39.5	7.4		54.4	216.4		41.3	211.1	427.5
Ireland	1.0	2.0	63.0		134.0	202.0		168.0	168.0	370.0
Italy		52.0	343.0		203.0	622.0	59.0	133.0	235.0	857.0
Netherlands	2.0	1.0	2.0		315.0	326.0	1.0	65.0	66.0	392.0
Norway			0.6	0.4	16.8	24.6		82.7	86.2	110.8
Portugal	13.9	13.9	20.6	1.7	68.1	109.7	4.2	36.3	40.5	150.2
Spain	13.9	98.3	248.0	112.3	234.1	797.7	66.9	193.6	265.8	1063.5
Sweden	0.2	0.1	2.2	10.0	66.4	144.7		52.1	66.8	211.5
Switzerland		2.3	12.5	3.1	32.6	51.0	2.1	10.3	12.4	63.4
UK	4.0		146.0	722.0	50.0	1005.0		520.0	520.0	1525.0
Others (Iceland)				1.3	0.9	2.2		9.1	10.3	12.5
Total W. Europe	**134.5**	**279.9**	**1307.2**	**2024.7**	**2749.5**	**7435.1**	**142.3**	**2364.5**	**2952.8**	**10387.8**

Notes:
NH3: anhydrous ammonia. AS: ammonium sulfate. U: urea. AN: ammonium nitrate. CAN: calcium ammonium nitrate. APN: ammonium phosphate. NPK: nitrogen-phosphorus-potassium.

Source: IFA.

Table A.12:   *Western European production of nitric acid, 1989 (MMT)*

Country	MMT
Austria	0.47
Belgium/Luxembourg	1.35
Denmark	0.36
Finland	0.51
France	3.18
Germany	2.31
Greece	0.45
Ireland	0.28
Italy	1.19
Netherlands	2.40
Norway	1.08
Portugal	0.20
Spain	1.25
Sweden	0.42
Switzerland	0.09
UK	2.80
Total W. Europe	18.33

Source: Kemira.

Table A.13:   *US and Western European mercury consumption in chlorine*
             production, 1970–1992

Year	Hg for Cl mfg US tonnes	Cl from Hg cell US %	Cl production US kMT	Cl production W. Europe kMT	Cl from Hg cell W. Europe %
1970		25%[b]	8 858	5 008	
1973	450.6		9 437		
1974	582.5		9 755		
1975	524.8		8 316	6 734	
1976	553.4		9 415		
1977	370.4		9 592		
1978	384.9		10 026		
1979	419.9		11 150		
1980	326.5		10 361	8 272	
1981	252.4		9 764	8 050	
1982	215.2		8 324	7 881	62%
1983	277.6		8 948	8 715	
1984	253.0	20%[c]	9 707	9 421	
1985	235.0		9 437	9 564	
1986	259.0		9 473	9 422	
1987	311.0		10 050	9 807	
1988	445.0		10 212	9 800	63%
1989	381.0	17%[c]	10 354	9 750	
1990	247.0	16.25%[c]	10 713	9 250	
1991	184.0		10 361	8 800	
1992			10 107	8 560	
	a		d	e	e

Sources:
a. USBuMines *Minerals Yearbooks*, various years.
b. Tellus Institute 1992.
c. US Bureau of Mines preliminary estimates.
d. US Department of Commerce, *Business Statistics, 1961–1991 and Current Industrial Reports: Inorganic Chemicals*, 4th quarter 1992.
e. SRI, unpublished, various years.

Table A.14:   *Western European production and consumption of chlorine,*
 caustic soda and hydrochloric acid, 1988 (kMT)

Country	Chlorine 1988 Prod	Cons	Caustic soda 1988 Prod	Cons	HCl[a] Prod	Year
Austria	87	40	82	205		
Belgium	685	693	685	130		
Denmark	25	30	28	149	8	1987
Finland	240	240	269	480	14.4	1987
France	1418.5	1415	1480.5	1427	237.8	1989
Germany	3452	3496	3625	2228	957.6	1989
Greece	20	20	22	77	53.4	1985
Ireland	3	5	3	111		
Italy	1050	994	1176	993	500	1986
Netherlands	550	504	616	914	81.2	1989
Norway	230	237	258	112		
Portugal	70	70	78	100	53.6	1986
Spain	578	563	625	466	147.3	1988
Sweden	360	318	403	508	82.4	1987
Switzerland	70	67	78	57		
United Kingdom	1050	1055	1176	1367	166.5	1989
W. Europe	**9888.5**	**9747**	**10604.5**	**9324**	**2302.2**	

Note: a.   Consumption of HCl is almost entirely captive.

Source: EcoPlan.

Table A.15:   *Western European production and consumption of EDC, 1990*
 (kMT)

Country	Production	Consumption
Benelux	2200 (22%)	2307 (24%)
France	1630 (16%)	1650 (17%)
Germany	2592 (26%)	2598 (27%)
Other	3472 (36%)	3127 (32%)
Total	**9894**	**9682**

Source: Eurochlor.

Table A.16: Western European production and sales of chlorinated solvents, 1986–1992 (kMT)

Year	Trichloro-ethylene Prod.	Trichloro-ethylene Sales	Perchloro-ethylene Prod.	Perchloro-ethylene Sales	Methyl chloride Prod.	Methyl chloride Sales	1-1-1-tri-chloroethane Prod.	1-1-1-tri-chloroethane Sales
1986	182.7	138.7	340.6	161.6	331.5	197.0	204.6	137.8
1987	165.7	134.3	322.8	151.8	305.2	181.2	203.2	129.6
1988	168.9	133.9	342.9	144.1	309.8	182.4	218.1	128.5
1989	153.6	118.4	317.1	131.3	293.4	175.4	222.3	129.3
1990	130.9	107.8	279.8	122.6	293.3	169.6	228.5	122.4
1991	113.3	96.1	218.5	113.4	244.0	157.1	202.1	109.0
1992	125.2	83.0	210.6	88.6	234.1	153.9	198.3	92.7

Source: European Chlorinated Solvents Association undated.

Table A.17:   *Materials consumed in chip production in Japan, 1988*

Category	kMT	Million $US
Acids (as etchants)		
Sulfuric acid (H_2SO_4)	6	14
Ammonia (NH_3)	7	17
Nitric acid (HNO_3)	8	25
Hydrochloric acid (HCl)	3	8
Acetic acid (CH_3COOH)	3	7
Hydrogen peroxide (H_2O_2)	5	16
Other (includes HF, CrO_3, P_2O_5)	na	8
	>32	95
Solvents		
Xylene ($C_6H_4(CH_3)_2$)	3	8
Isopropanol ($CH_3CHOHCH_3$)	2	6
Trichloroethylene (ClHC=CCl$_2$)	5	20
Acetone (CH_3COCH_3)	4	12
Methanol (CH_3OH)	9	22
CFCs (mainly 113)	2	8
Other	2	5
	27	176
Silicon source gases		
Silane (SiH_4)	60	47
Dichlorosilane (SiH_2Cl_2)	50	18
Tetrachlorosilane ($SiCl_4$)	45	4
	155	69
Carrier gases, inert(N_2, O_2, H_2, He, Ar)		157
Specialty etchants (CF_4, HF, SiF_4)		18
Dopants (AsH_3, BCl_3, BF_3, B_2H_6, PH_3)		11
Aluminum+alloys (95% Al, 1% Si, 3–4% Cu)		37
Chrome, nickel, tin, etc.		45
Precious metals(Au, Pt, Pd)		51

Source: Various authors.

Table A.18: *Western European paper production, consumption, recovery and recycle, 1992*

Country	Production (kMT)	Consumption (kMT)	Used paper cons. (kMT)	Recovery (%)	Recycling (%)
Belgium	1 125	2 180	286	31.4	13.1
Denmark	356	1 105	307	39.1	27.8
France	7 132	8 870	3 367	34.3	38.0
Germany	12 132	15 221	6 109	47.2	40.1
Netherlands	2 862	3 273	1 895	53.2	57.9
Portugal	865	778	339	40.4	43.5
Spain	3 426	4 582	2 222	37.8	48.5
UK	4 951	9 393	2 953	33.0	31.4
TOTAL	**32 849**	**45 402**	**17 478**	**39.6**	**37.5**

Source: Confederation of European Paper Industries, CEPI.

Table A.19: *French tire production by type, 1991 (tonnes)*

	All tires	Retreaded tires
Car tires	355 811	6 999
Van tires	40 741	1 546
Truck/bus tires	102 171	57 059
Tractor tires	62 214	1 484
Others	118 039	0
TOTAL	**678 977**	**67 087**

Source: SESSI 1993, cited in Guelorget *et al.* 1993.

Appendix B: Data sources for the study

B.1. PUBLIC SECTOR DATA SOURCES

It is an unfortunate fact that it would have been impossible to carry out this study based on data from public sector sources in Europe. Indeed, the best source for Europe, in a number of cases, turned out to be the US Bureau of Mines (Department of the Interior), which collects and compiles international data on about 80 minerals and metals, including non-renewable (petroleum-based) organics. These are published annually in *Minerals Yearbook* (USBuMines annual) as well as numerous special studies. The US data include production, both primary and secondary, reported and apparent consumption (by use and/or sector), exports (by country), imports for consumption (by country of origin), prices, reserves, discoveries, technological developments, and a variety of other useful information.

The US Bureau of Mines also maintains an International Division, which compiles and publishes occasional summaries of international production, consumption and trade in mineral commodities, and metals, by country. The latest version of this report *Mineral Industries of Europe and Central Asia* (1991) (USBuMines 1991a) was of considerable value in preparing this study.

There is no European source of chemical industry production statistics comparable to the two standard US sources. The US Bureau of the Census (Department of Commerce) *Current Industrial Reports* publishes quarterly statistics on production, imports and exports of all the major inorganic chemicals (about 50) for which there are at least 4 domestic producers. The US International Trade Commission (USITC) publishes US production and shipments data for all synthetic organic chemicals. The title of this annual report is *Synthetic Organic Chemicals*. The ITC publication lists tens of thousands of chemicals produced in significant quantities. Production and shipments data are given for only a small subset (perhaps 200) for which there are several different domestic producers. However, the chemicals are grouped by major category (e.g. feedstocks, cyclic intermediates, rubber chemicals, pharmaceuticals, surface active agents, pesticides, miscellaneous n.e.c. etc.) and again, within each category there are further subdivisions by structure (e.g. C_2 hydrocarbons, C_3 hydrocarbons, amines, alcohols, ketones, cyclics, etc.). Thus, while many data are withheld because 'publication might tend to reveal operations of individual firms', subtotals by category are available in many cases.

The UN Statistical Office collects and publishes production statistics for several hundred major industrial commodities, by country, in *Industrial Statistics Yearbook*. However, imports, exports and consumption are not given, and UN data not infrequently disagrees with national data. Since the UN obtains its data from national sources, we cannot account for the discrepancies in general. However, in a number of particular instances we have found that the UN has misclassified US data, probably because the US industrial classification system (SIC) does not correspond exactly to the international systems (ISIC, SITC). The UNSO does not attempt to correct even the most obvious errors in national inputs, which is also a problem with regard to data from many countries.

Other UN agencies also produce data. For example, the UN Lead and Zinc Study Group produces extensive and detailed statistics on production, processing and trade in these two metals. A newly created Copper Study Group (approved in 1991) will probably do the same for copper. The UN Commission on Trade and Development (UNCTAD) collects and publishes trade statistics (available on computer tapes), but makes no effort to reconcile gross discrepancies. In fact, there is little or no correlation between reported imports by country X from country Y *vis-à-vis* reported exports from Y to X. This makes the UN trade data almost useless, except perhaps to full-time trade specialists who are able to fill in the gaps and correct the errors. For our purposes, the UNCTAD data were essentially useless.

The International Energy Agency (IEA), which is a component of the Organization for Economic Cooperation and Development (OECD) compiles and publishes detailed data on fuel and energy production and consumption (by category), for all the OECD countries. These data are carefully balanced and reliable. We had relatively little use for them in our study, however, because for our purposes energy consumption was only relevant in the context or production of specific metals or other materials. The OECD does not publish quantitative data on other commodities, except in monetary terms.

The Statistical Office of the European Union (EUROSTAT), in Luxembourg, publishes aggregate production/consumption data for major industrial commodities, by country. This is a better source for Europe than the UN, but barely. EUROSTAT also publishes an annual report on the state of major industrial sectors. However, the level of aggregation is so high, and the coverage is so minimal, that the EUROSTAT materials proved to be of little value to us.

National government agencies in France, Germany, the Netherlands and Sweden can provide some detailed information about particular materials in those countries. For instance, the Landesgewerbeanstalt Bayern (LGA) in

Nürnberg, carried out special studies of cadmium, lead, mercury and PVC, for Germany, in the early 1980s. But in general national sources such as LGA are not a satisfactory way of gathering data for Europe as a whole.

B.2.   OTHER PUBLICATIONS

One publication with a long history is the annual *Metalstatistik*, published by Metallgesellschaft AG (Reuterweg 14, Postfach 101501, 60323 Frankfurt-am-Main, Germany). This publication gives time series for production of a dozen major metals from primary ores (including tin, but not chromium), but otherwise contains much less data than *Minerals Yearbook*. It is more readily available in Europe, however.

The best source of data on major commodity chemical producers and production capacities, worldwide, is the magazine *Informations Chimie*, published in Paris (SETE-4, rue de Sèze, 75009). Several times a year the magazine publishes a special section on one such commodity (e.g. methanol, ethylene, chlorine) which lists all significant producers, worldwide and their capacities. In some cases, production capacity is differentiated by major process. For example, in the chlorine case, mercury cell, diaphragm cell and membrane cell. However capacity utilization is not given.

A better source, as regards actual production, consumption and usage, for the US only, is the *Chemical Marketing Reporter* (Schnell Publishing Co., New York) which records and publishes sales transactions and prices on a regular basis. It, too, publishes 'profiles' at regular intervals. These are much less detailed as regards producers and capacities, but information is included on demand, growth rates, and uses. However, except for the use data, the coverage of CMR is roughly the same as that of the Commerce Department and the ITC.

A more widely available source that gives time-series production data (US only) for roughly the top 50 organic and the top 25 inorganic chemicals, as well as some aggregated data on plastics, synthetic rubbers, and synthetic fibers is the *Chemical and Engineering News* (C&EN). This list is updated each year in its mid-summer edition.

Among the most useful published sources on materials production and use we have found is *Modern Plastics International* (McGraw-Hill International, Lausanne, Switzerland). The January issue, each year, summarizes production by country, in the previous year, for all major plastics, elastomers and synthetic fibers. This source also provides some data on markets, also by country. For instance, it subdivides plastic markets by major category (e.g. automotive, structural, agricultural, packaging). It further subdivides packaging markets by type.

Technical data from recent patents and US government sponsored studies are published on a regular basis at reasonable prices by Noyes Data Corp (120 Mill Rd., Park Ridge, NJ 07656). A number of recent titles in NDC's most recent catalog are relevant to our study, including the following:

- *Recovery of Metals from Sludges and Wastewater* ($45);
- *Recycling Equipment and Technology for Municipal Solid Waste* ($45);
- *Scrap Tire Technology and Markets* ($54);
- *Solvent Substitution for Pollution Prevention* ($48).

None of these were actually used, however, because we were unaware of them.

B.3.   INDUSTRY ASSOCIATIONS

Unfortunately, industrial associations seem to be the only source of published (i.e. available to the general public) data for Europe in a number of areas.

One of the major examples is the World Energy Council, which publishes an annual *Survey of Energy Resources*. It contains a great deal of useful data on production levels of raw and processed fuels, including reserves and coal quality data, by country.

The International Institute of Synthetic Rubber Producers publishes annual yearbooks which give synthetic rubber production capacities, by producer, country and type of rubber.

For the European chemical industry, the sole source and guardian of production statistics seems to be the industry association of chemical manufacturers (CEFIC), together with numerous subgroups, such as the association of chlorine producers (Eurochlor), the European chlorine solvents association (ECSA), the association of plastics manufacturers (APME) together with its subsidiary, the European Center for Plastics in the Environment (PWMI). All of these organizations are headquartered in Brussels (Avenue E. Van Nieuwenhuyse 4, B-1160, Brussels). However the various associations do not publish any catalog of production/trade/consumption statistics for chemical products. Their annual reports give aggregate data in monetary units only. Other quantitative data are published only in the context of specific reports written by committees or consultants of CEFIC or its subsidiaries. We did find some of these reports useful, mainly in regard to plastics waste recycling and chlorine-related topics.

The German chemical industry has produced a series of interesting special reports on special topics of interest, under the general heading *Fonds der Chemischen Industrie*, published in Frankfurt-am-Main. These range from 'catalysts' to 'noble metals'. However, one topic of special interest for our purposes was the report 'Chlorine' (FondsChem 1992).

The Chlorine Institute (2001 L St. NW, Washington DC 20036) is the US counterpart of Eurochlor. It publishes directories and provides some annual production data, but nothing that cannot be found more easily elsewhere. However, there are European counterparts at the national level, e.g. Syndicat des Halogenes et Derives (Cedex 99, 92909 Paris-La Defense).

B.4. CONSULTANTS

Apart from the sources noted above, and perhaps a few others we have not found, it was necessary to rely on market data from market research and consulting organizations. There are a great many such organizations, and we cannot undertake to evaluate them in terms of quality. Sources used in the study, in alphabetical order, are listed as follows:

Economist Intelligence Unit/Business International (40 Duke St. London SW1 A1LD). Information on packaging markets, by country.

EcoPlan (8, Rue Joseph Bara, F-75006 Paris). Special studies of technological opportunities in chemical markets; also tires. Thanks to Eric Britton (managing director) and Albert Hahn (senior partner) for giving us limited access.

Ecotec. Environmental consultants, located in Munich. Special studies. Ecotec did a major study of the European chlorine industry for Eurochlor, which in turn provided us with the executive summary (Ecotec 1995).

IFA. Specialists on fertilizer production and consumption data, by type and by country.

Kemira is a large Scandinavian chemical producer that also sells consulting services and data; provided data on sulfuric acid production and use, by country.

PCI-Fibers and Raw Materials (Worth Corner, Turner's Hill Rd., Crawley West Sussex, RH10 7SL). Information on fibers and raw materials.

Roskill Information Services Ltd. (2 Clapham Rd., London SW9 OJA). Roskill publishes market studies containing extensive data on metals producers, supply, demand, markets and prices. This data is more extensive than that of the US Bureau of Mines for countries other than the US. (It is also occasionally cited by USBM.)

Stanford Research Institute (SRI International) *Chemical Economics Handbook*; *World Petrochemicals*, etc. Proprietary multi-client studies on chemical production, costs, capacity (by process), demand (by use), by country. This is the most complete chemical industry data base in the world.

Unfortunately, it is so expensive that only a few large organizations can afford it. One of them (anon) gave us access to some SRI data from a few years ago.

Tecnon Ltd. A UK consulting firm, publishes market studies. In 1991 they published a worldwide chlorine study which is currently being updated. They kindly provided two summary tables and discussed their methodology with us on the telephone.

Costs of the above consulting services are variable. They range from $100 for a computer printout to $10 000 for a multi-client market report or even $100 000 for the wide-ranging SRI service. We were fortunately able to negotiate some discounts and to extract some information from these sources for lesser amounts; however, the cost of purchased information for this study *in toto* amounted to over $15 000.

The point of mentioning costs here is to point out that it would be in the interests of making better public policy to make data of the kind presented here more readily available to researchers and analysts. There is no good reason why governments should collect information from industry, only to suppress much of it as 'proprietary' on the grounds that it might help competitors. In particular, there is no good reason why production and use data for toxic chemicals and toxic metals (like arsenic, cadmium and mercury) should be kept secret.

The 'competitive advantage' argument for secrecy is weak enough even for current-year data, but it makes no sense at all as an argument to suppress previous-year production/sales data. It makes equally little sense to allow private consultants to have an effective monopoly in this domain. (There really are no industrial secrets, except arguably the formula for Coca Cola.) Firms do not have much trouble finding out what their competitors are doing, at least in terms of sales. The only ones kept in ignorance are members of the public and the public sector. The public interest should far outweigh the private interest in this case.

B.5. OTHER

It should be acknowledged that some of our best sources were information provided without cost by colleagues. We particularly wish to acknowledge help from Stefan Anderberg of IIASA, who provided us with his data on arsenic and cadmium flows in Europe (even though we found and cited the original sources). Similarly, Donald Rogich, of the US Bureau of Mines sent us copies of a number of USBM reports (some in draft form) that we might not have found for ourselves, or not until too late. He also persuaded several of the specialists at USBM to review our early drafts and suggest improvements. Philippe Feron, Executive Director of Eurochlor, also went to some trouble to obtain documents for us.

One rather remarkable document that does not fit any other category deserves specific mention here. It is a 1992 study by Geneviève Renaux, entitled *Packaging in the Single European Market,* under the auspices of the Club de Bruxelles. We do not know what the 'Club de Bruxelles' is, or how the work was financed, but we found the report extraordinarily rich in data.

References

Abernathy, William J. (1978), *The Productivity Dilemma*, Johns Hopkins University Press, Baltimore.

Abramovitz, Moses (1956), 'Resources and Output Trends in the United States Since 1870', *American Economic Review* **46**, May.

Altenpohl, Dieter (1982), *Aluminum Viewed from Within*, Aluminium-Verlag, Düsseldorf.

ANRED (1985), *Le Recyclage du Caoutchouc et des Matières Plastiques*, Rapport de Journées Techniques, ANRED, Angers, France.

ANRED (1986), *Les Dechets de Caoutchouc*, Rapport de Journées Techniques, ANRED, Angers, France.

Arthur, W. Brian (1988), 'Self-Reinforcing Mechanisms in Economics', in: Anderson, Philip W., Kenneth J. Arrow and David Pines (eds), *The Economy as an Evolving Complex System*:9–32 [Series: Santa Fe Institute Studies in the Sciences of Complexity], Addison-Wesley, Redwood City CA.

Arthur, W. Brian (1988a), 'Competing Technologies: An Overview', in: Dosi, Giovanni, Christopher Freeman, Richard Nelson, Gerald Silverberg and Luc Soete (eds), *Technical Change and Economic Theory*:590–607, Pinter, London, 1988.

Association of Plastics Manufacturers in Europe (APME 1993), *Plastics Recovery in Perspective: Plastics Consumption and Recovery in Western Europe 1989–91*, Association of Plastics Manufacturers in Europe, Brussels.

Axtell, Robert (1993), *Unpublished Calculations*, Brookings Institution, Washington DC, 1993.

Ayres, Robert U. (1982), *Coalplex: An Integrated Energy/Resources System Concept*, UNEP Seminar on Environmental Aspects of Technology Assessment, United Nations, November/December 1982.

Ayres, Robert U. (1989), 'Industrial Metabolism', in: Ausubel, J. and H. Sladovich (eds), *Technology and Environment*, National Academy Press, Washington DC.

Ayres, Robert U. (1991), *Computer Integrated Manufacturing: Revolution in Progress* [Series: IIASA CIM Project] **I**, Chapman & Hall, London.

Ayres, Robert U. (1991a), 'History of Mechanization', in: Ayres, Robert U., William Haywood, M. Eugene Merchant, Jukka-P. Ranta and H.-J. Warnecke (eds), *Computer Integrated Manufacturing: The Past, the Present and the Future*, Chapter 1 [Series: IIASA CIM Project] **II**, Chapman & Hall, London.

Ayres, Robert U. (1993), *Transboundary Air Pollution: An Opportunity for Innovation*, Working Paper (93/41/EPS), INSEAD, Fontainebleau, France, June 8.

Ayres, Robert U. (1993a), *Industrial Metabolic Systems Integration: The Black Triangle*, Working Paper (93/44/EPS), INSEAD, Fontainebleau, France, June 28.

Ayres, Robert U. (1994), 'On Economic Disequilibrium and Free Lunch', *Environmental and Resource Economics* **4**:435–54.

Ayres, Robert U., Leslie W. Ayres *et al.* (1988), *An Historical Reconstruction of Major Pollutant Levels in the Hudson–Raritan Basin 1800–1980*, Technical Memorandum (NOS OMA 43), National Oceanic and Atmospheric Administration, Rockville MD, October, (3 Vols).

Ayres, Robert U., Vicki Norberg-Bohm, Jackie Prince, William M. Stigliani and Janet Yanowitz (1989), *Industrial Metabolism, the Environment, and Application of Materials-Balance Principles for Selected Chemicals*, Research Report (RR–89–11), International Institute for Applied Systems Analysis, Laxenburg, Austria, October.

Ayres, Robert U. and Vicki Norberg-Bohm (1993), *Industrial Metabolism of Sulfur*, Working Paper (93/23/EPS), INSEAD, Fontainebleau, France, September 8.

Ayres, Robert U., Vicki Norberg-Bohm and Leslie W. Ayres (1993), *Industrial Metabolism of Nitrogen*, Working Paper (93/11/EPS/TM), INSEAD, Fontainebleau, France, October 1.

Ayres, Robert U., William H. Schlesinger and Robert H. Socolow (1994), 'Human Impacts on the Carbon and Nitrogen Cycles', in: Socolow, Robert H., C.J. Andrews, F.G. Berkhout and V.M. Thomas (eds), *Industrial Ecology and Global Change*, Cambridge University Press, Cambridge, UK.

Ayres, Robert U., Leslie W. Ayres, Paolo Frankl, Howard Lee, Nichole Wolfgang and Paul M. Weaver (1995), *Materials-Optimization in the Production of Major Finished Materials*, Final Report (Contract BRE2–CT93–0894), Center for the Management of Environmental Resources of INSEAD, Fontainebleau, France, January 25 [prepared for the European Commission DGXII, Science Research and Development].

Balzer, D. and Arnold Rauhut (1987), *DEHP/DOP-Bericht*, Landesgewerbeanstalt Bayern (LGA), Nürnberg, Germany, September.

Barnett, Harold J. and Chandler Morse (1962), *Scarcity and Growth: The Economics of Resource Scarcity*, Johns Hopkins University Press, Baltimore.

Barney, Gerald (Study Director) (1980), *The Global 2000 Report to the*

President, Technical Report (Volume 2), Council on Environmental Quality/US Department of State, Washington DC.

Barney, C. (1985), 'Untitled', *Electronics Week*, February 25.

Bartlett, R. and B. James (1979), Title missing, *Journal of Environmental Quality* **8**(31).

Battelle Columbus Laboratories (BCL 1977), *Multimedia Levels: Cadmium*, (EPA–560/6–77–032), Battelle Columbus Laboratories, Columbus, OH, September (for USEPA).

Bennett, James T. and Walter E. Williams (1981), *Strategic Minerals: The Economic Impact of Supply Disruptions* [Series: Critical Issues] (ISSN 0194–1909), The Heritage Foundation, Washington DC.

Bergbäck, Bo, Stefan Anderberg and Ulrik Lohm (1989), 'A Reconstruction of Emission, Flow and Accumulation of Chromium in Sweden 1920–1980', *Water, Air and Soil Pollution* **48**:391–407.

Bolch, William E. Jr. (1980), 'Solid Waste and Trace Element Impacts', in: Green, Alex E.S. (ed), *Coal Burning Issues*, Chapter 12:231–48, University Presses of Florida, Gainesville FL.

Braudel, Fernand (1981), *Civilization and Capitalism (15th–18th Century)*, Harper & Row, New York, English edition (3 Volumes).

Brenneman, R.K., A. Schei, R. Kaiser and Y. Lee (1992), 'Issues in Solar-Grade Silicon Feedstock Development', in: *Proceedings of the 11th European Photovoltaic Solar Energy Conference and Exhibition*, Montreux, Switzerland, October 12–16.

Briant, Yvette (1990), *Packaging in Europe: France*, Special Report (EIU 2046), The Economist Intelligence Unit, London, August.

Brimblecombe, P., C. Hammer, H. Rodhe, A. Ryoboshapko and C.F. Boutron (1989), 'Human Influence on the Sulfur Cycle', in: Brimblecombe, P. and A.Y. Lein (eds), *Evolution of the Global Biogeochemical Sulfur Cycle*:77–121, Wiley, New York.

Brown, Andrew C. (1983), 'Alcan Shakes the Aluminum Market', *Fortune*, February 21.

Bruno, Marshall J. (1982), *Production of Aluminum-Silicon Alloy and Ferrosilicon and Commercial Purity Aluminum by the Direct Reduction Process*, Final Technical Report (CONS–5089–16 UC95f), Aluminum Company of America Alcoa Laboratories, Alcoa Center PA, March (prepared for the United States Department of Energy).

Bundesverband der Deutschen Industrie e. V. (BDI 1984), *Industrie und Öcologie*, BDI–Drucksache (172), Bundesverband der Deutschen Industrie e. V., Koln, Germany, November.

Burlace, C.J. (1991), *Scrap Tires and Recycling Opportunities*, Report (LR834/MR), Warren Springs Laboratory, Warren Springs, UK.

Canon, R.M., T.M. Gilliam and J.S. Watson (1981), *Evaluating Potential*

Processes for Recovery of Metals from Coal Ash (CS–1992), Electric Power Research Institute, November.

Chapman, Duane (1989), *Environmental Standards and International Trade in Automobiles and Copper: The Case for a Social Tariff*, Department of Agricultural Economics, Cornell University, Ithaca NY, February.

Chemical and Engineering News (CEN 1990), 'Production by the US Chemical Industry', *Chemical and Engineering News*, June 27.

Chemical and Engineering News (CEN 1992), 'Production by the US Chemical Industry', *Chemical and Engineering News*, June 29:39ff.

Christensen Laurits and Wm. It. Greene (1976), 'Economies of Scale in U.S. Electric Power Generation' *J. Political Economy* Vol. *84*(4): 655–676.

Communication from the Commission to the European Parliament and Council (1994). 'Economic Growth and the Environment: Some Implications for Economic Policy Making'.

Cornell University (1994), Work and Environment Initiative, *Ecological Industrial Park Proposal to Monroe County, New York*, Center for the Environment and School of Industrial and Labor Relations, Cornell University, Ithaca NY.

Corradini, Roland (1990), *Packaging in Europe: Belgium, the Netherlands and Luxembourg*, Special Report (EIU 2048), The Economist Intelligence Unit, London, November.

Cote, Raymond P., Robert Ellison, Jill Grant, Jeremy Hall, Peter Klynstra, Michael Martin and Peter Wade (1994), *Designing and Operating Industrial Parks as Ecosystems*, School for Resource and Environmental Studies, Faculty of Management, Dalhousie University, Nova Scotia, Canada.

Criswell, David R. and Robert D. Waldron (1980), *HF-Acid Leaching Process for the Recovery of Major Separated Compounds from Fly Ash*, Proprietary, Houston TX, May 27 (Presentation to the Houston Power and Light Company).

Crutzen, Paul J. (1976), *The Nitrogen Cycle and Stratospheric Ozone*, Nitrogen Research Review Conference, United States National Academy of Sciences, Fort Collins CO, October 12–13.

Denison, Edward F. (1962), *The Sources of Economic Growth in the United States and the Alternatives Before Us*, Supplementary Paper (13), Committee for Economic Development, New York.

Denison, Edward F. (1974), *Accounting for US Economic Growth, 1929–1969*, Brookings Institution, Washington DC.

Denison, Edward F. (1979), *Accounting for Slower Growth*, Brookings Institution, Washington DC.

Detournay, Jean-Paul (1993), *Tendences Actuelles et Futures de la Production du Chlore, de la Soude Caustique et des Derives Chlores*, GEST (93/184), Troisième Seminaire Technique EURO CHLOR, December 2–3.

Donaldson, J.D. (1986), 'Cobalt in the Environment', in: *Proceedings of the First Congress on Cobalt and the Environment*:1–21, Cobalt Development Institute, Toronto, April 2–3.

DRI, DHV, TME, IVM, ERM, ECOTEC, Travers Morgan and M+R (DRI *et al.* 1994), *The Potential Benefits of Integration of Environmental and Economic Policies: An Incentive-Based Approach to Policy Integration*, Draft Final Report (X1/814/94), Prepared for the Commission of the European Communities Directorate-General for the Environment, Nuclear Safety and Civil Protection (DGXI), Brussels.

Duchin, Faye (1994), *Household Use and Disposal of Plastics; an Input–Output Case Study for New York City*, Report to the AT&T Industrial Ecology Faculty Fellowship Program, Institute for Economic Analysis, New York University, New York, June.

Economic Intelligence Unit (EIU 1989), *Rubber Trends*, The Economist, London, 1989.

Economic Intelligence Unit (EIU 1991), *Rubber Trends*, The Economist, London, 1991.

EcoPlan (1993), *New Developments in Tire Technology*, Multi-client study, EcoPlan International, Paris.

Ecotec (1995), *Chlorine Flow in Europe, 1992; Based on 61 Companies*, Executive Summary, Ecotec, Munich, July.

Electronic Industries Association of Japan (EIAJ 1990), *Annual Data Book*.

Ellison, W.L. and L.M. Luckevich (1984), 'FGD Waste: Long-Term Liability or Short-Term Asset?', *Power* **128**(6):71–83.

Elm Energy and Recycling (EER 1994), *Scrap Tires as Fuel: The Elm Energy and Recycling Approach*, EER UK Ltd., London.

Engdahl, Richard B. (1968), 'Stationary Combustion Sources', in: Stern (ed.), *Air Pollution: Sources of Air Pollution and Their Control*, Chapter 32:4–54 (Series: Environmental Sciences) **III**, Academic Press, New York, 2nd edition.

Enquete Commission of the German Bundestag on the Protection of Humanity and the Environment (1994), *Responsibility for the Future: Options for Sustainable Management of Substance Chains and Material Flows; Interim Report* (ISBN 3–87081–044–4), Economica Verlag, Bonn, Germany (translated from the German).

Eriksson, E. (1960), 'The Yearly Circulation of Chloride and Sulfur in Nature', *Tellus* **12**:63–109.

European Commission (1994), 'Growth, Competitiveness, Employment — The Challenges and Ways Forward Into the 21st Century', White Paper.

Eurostat (1990), *Panorama de l'Industrie Communautaire, 1990*, EEC, Luxembourg.

Fonds der Chemischen Industrie (1992), *Die Chemie des Chlors und seiner*

Verbindungen, Folienserie des Fonds der Chemischen Industrie (24), Fonds der Chemischen Industrie, Frankfurt am Main.

Forrest, David and Julian Szekely (1991), 'Global Warming and the Primary Metals Industry', *Journal of Metallurgy* **43** (ISSN 1047–4838), December:23–30.

Fraser, J.L and K.R. Lum (1983), Title missing, *Environmental Science and Technology* (17):52–4.

Friend, J.P. (1973), 'The Global Sulfur Cycle', in: Rasool, S.I. (ed.), *Chemistry of the Lower Atmosphere*:177–201, Plenum Press, New York.

Frosch, Robert A. and Nicholas E. Gallopoulos (1989), 'Strategies for Manufacturing', *Scientific American* **261**(3), September:94–102.

Gaines, Linda L. (1981), *Energy and Materials Use in the Production and Recycling of Consumer-Goods Packaging*, Technical Memo (ANL/CNSV–TM–58), Argonne National Laboratory, Argonne IL, February (prepared for the US Department of Energy).

Gaines, L.L. and S.Y. Shen (1980), *Energy and Materials Flows in the Production of Olefins and Their Derivatives* (ANL/CNSV–9), Argonne National Laboratory, Argonne IL, August (for US Department of Energy, Washington, DC).

Gaines, L.L. and A.M. Wolsky (1981), *Energy and Materials Flows in Petroleum Refining*, Technical Report (ANL/CNSV–10), Argonne National Laboratory, Argonne IL, February.

Galloway, James N. *et al.* (1982), 'Trace Metals in Atmospheric Deposition: A Review and Assessment', *Atmospheric Environment* **16**(7).

GCA Corporation (1973), *National Emissions Inventory of Sources and Emissions of Chromium* (EPA–450/3–74–012), GCA Corporation, Bedford, MA, May [for USEPA].

Gerstle, R.W., J.R. Richards, T.B. Parsons and C.E. Hudak (1977), *Industrial Process Profiles for Environmental Use: The Carbon Black Industry*, Report (EPA–600/2–77–023d), United States Environmental Protection Agency, Cincinnati OH.

Giedion, Siegfried (1969), *Mechanization Takes Command*, W.W. Norton & Company, New York, 2nd edition [1st Edition: Oxford University Press 1948].

Goldhar, Joel D. and M. Jelinek (1983), 'Plan for Economies of Scope', *Harvard Business Review*:141–8.

Goldhar, J.D. and M. Jelinek (1985), 'Computer Integrated Flexible Manufacturing: Organizational, Economic and Strategic Implications', *Interfaces* **15**(3):94–105.

Gough, Michael (1988), 'The Most Potent Carcinogen?', *Resources* (92), Summer:2–5 [ISSN 0048–7376].

Granat, L., H. Rodhe, and R.O. Hallberg (1976), 'The Global Sulfur Cycle', in: Svensson, B.H. and R. Soederlund (eds), *Nitrogen, Phosphorus and Sulfur: Global Cycles*:89–134 **22** (SCOPE Report 7), Ecology Bulletin, Stockholm.

Guelorget, Yves, V. Julien and Paul M. Weaver (1993), *A Life Cycle Analysis of Automobile Tires in France*, Working Paper (93/67/EPS), INSEAD, Fontainebleau, France, September.

Habersatter, K. and F. Widmer, *Ecobalance of Packaging Materials State of 1990*, Environmental Series (132), Swiss Federal Office of Environment, Forest and Landscape, Zurich, February.

Hagedorn, G. and E. Hellriegel (1992), *Environmentally Relevant Mass Inputs for Solar Cell Production: A Comparative Analysis of Conventional and Selected New Processes, Taking into Account Both Input Materials, Process Chains and Decommissioning and Recycling Options Final Report,* Forschungsstelle für Energiewirtschaft, Munich, February [Part I: Conventional Processes].

Hall, E.H., W.H. Hanna, L.D. Reed, J. Varga Jr., D.N. Williams, K.E. Wilkes, B.E. Johnson, W.J. Mueller, E.J. Bradbury and W.J. Frederick (1975), *Evaluation of the Theoretical Potential for Energy Conservation in Seven Basic Industries*, Final Report (PB-244, 722), Battelle Columbus Laboratories, Columbus, Ohio, July 11 (For United States Federal Agency Administration).

Harrison, R.M., D.P.H. Laxen and S.J. Wilson (1981), Title missing, *Environmental Science and Technology* (15):1378–83.

Hawken, Paul (1993), *Ecology of Commerce*, Harper Brothers, New York.

Hotelling, H. (1931), 'The Economics of Exhaustible Resource', *Journal of Political Economy* **39**:137–75.

Huntzicker, James J., Sheldon K. Friedlander and Cliff I. Davidson (1975), 'Material Balance for Automobile-Emitted Lead in Los Angeles Basin', *Environmental Science and Technology* **9**(5), May:448–57.

Husar, Rudolf B. and Janja D. Husar (1985), 'Regional River Sulfur Runoff', *Journal of Geophysical Research* **90**(C.1), January 20:1115–25.

Industrial Economics, Incorporated (IEI 1991), 'Materials Balance Profiles for 33/50 Chemicals', Draft Report (EPA Contract 68–W1–0009), Industrial Economics, Incorporated, Cambridge MA, September.

Ivanov, M.V.O. and J.R. Freney (1983), *The Global Biogeochemical Sulfur Cycle*, Wiley, Chichester, UK.

Jackson, M.W. (1968), Cited in R.W. Hurn 'Mobile Combustion Sources' Chap. 33 in: Stern A.C. (ed.), *Air Pollution: Sources of Air Pollution and Their Control* [Series: Environmental Sciences] **III**, Academic Press, New York, 2nd edition.

Jarrett, Noel (1982), Personal Communication, Alcoa Corporation, Pittsburgh PA.

Jarrett, Noel (1994), Personal Communication, Alcoa Corporation, Pittsburgh PA.

Jarrett, Noel, S.K. Das and W.E. Haupin (1980), 'Extraction of Oxygen and Metals from Lunar Ores', *Space Solar Power Review* **1**:281–7.

Johnston, P. and S. Troendel (1993), *PVC – An Environmental Perspective*, Greenpeace Exeter Laboratory, Earth Resources Center, University of Exeter, Exeter UK, May.

Junge, C.E. (1963), *Air Chemistry and Radioactivity*, Academic Press, New York.

Kellogg, W.W., R.D. Cadle, E.R. Allen, A.L. Lazrus and E.A. Martell (1972), 'The Sulfur Cycle', *Science* **175**:587–96.

Kirchner, Christian (1988), *Study of the European Aluminum Industry*.

Kostick, Dennis (1994), Personal Communication, Washington DC.

Kramer, D.A. (1994), Personal Communication, November 14.

Kuo, Benjamin P., 'Polystyrene Recycling: A Step Away from Disposable', Industrial Metabolism Course Paper, Carnegie Mellon University, Pittsburgh PA, December.

Laboratory for Energy Systems (LES/ETH 1994), Frischknecht, R., P. Hofstetter, I. Knoepfel, R. Dones and E. Zollinger, *Ökobilanzen für Energiesyteme (Ecobalances for Energy Systems)*, Laboratory for Energy Systems, Swiss Federal Institute of Technology (LES/ETH), Zurich, 1994.

Landsberg, H.E. (1961), 'City Air – Better or Worse', in: *Air Over Cities*, SEC Technical Report A62–5, New York, A United States Public Health Service Symposium.

Larson, Eric D. and Stefano Consonni (1994), *Biomass-Gasifier/Aeroderivative Gas Turbine Combined Cycle Power Generation*, Biomass Resources: A Means to Sustainable Development, BioResources 94, Bangalore, India, October 3–7.

Lim K.J., R.J. Milligan, H.I. Lips, C.Castaldini, R.S. Merrill and H.B. Mason (1981), 'NO$_x$ Combustion Modification', in: A.E. Martin (ed.), *Emission Control for Industrial Boilers*, Chapter 3:222–79, Noyes Publications, Park Ridge NJ. (Reprinted from *Technology Assessment Report for Industrial Boiler Applications: NO$_x$ Combustion Mod.* EPA 600/7-79-178f for EPA 1979.)

Lotka, Alfred J. (1956), *Elements of Mathematical Biology*, Dover Publications, New York, 2nd reprint edition (original title: Elements of Physical Biology, 1924).

Lowenheim, Frederick A. and Marguerite K. Moran (1975), *Faith, Keyes, and Clark's 'Industrial Chemicals'*, Wiley-Interscience, New York, 4th edition.

Lübkert, Barbara, Y. Virtanen, M. Muhlberger, I. Ingham, B. Vallance and S. Alber (1991), *Life Cycle Analysis: International Database for Ecoprofile*

Analysis (IDEA), Working paper (WP–91–30), International Institute for Applied Systems Analysis, Laxenburg, Austria.

Lum, K.R., J.S. Betteridge and R.R. MacDonald (1982), Title missing, *Environmental Technology Letters* (**3**):57–62.

Lushington, Roger (1990), *Packaging in Europe: West Germany*, Special Report (EIU 2047), The Economist Intelligence Unit, London, August.

Lushington, Roger (1991), *Packaging in Europe: The United Kingdom*, Special Report (EIU 2157), The Economist Intelligence Unit, London, November.

Lushington, Roger and Rowena Mills (1987), *The European Market for Rigid Packaging*, Special Report (EIU 1100), The Economist Intelligence Unit, London, May.

Lynn, Leonard H. (1982), *How Japan Innovates*, Westview Press, Boulder CO.

Manzone, R. (1993), *PVC: Life Cycle and Perspectives*, Commett Advanced Course, Urbino, Italy.

Martin, E.E. (1974), *Development Document for Effluent Limitations Guidelines and New Source Performance Standards for the Major Inorganic Product Segment of the Inorganic Chemicals Manufacturing Point Source Category*, Report (EPA/440/1–74–007–A), United States Environmental Protection Agency, Washington DC, March.

Massachusetts Institute of Technology (MIT 1993), Technology Business and Environment Program, Center for Technology Policy and Industrial Development, *Dimensions of Managing Chlorine in the Environment: Report of the MIT/Norwegian Chlorine Policy Study*, Massachusetts Institute of Technology, Cambridge MA, March.

Matthews, Vincent (undated), *Markets for Recovered Post-User Plastics Materials in Europe*, European Center for Plastics in the Environment (PWMI), Brussels.

Mauerhofer, Fritz (1993), *Personal Communication of letter from D. Factor*, November 24.

Meadows, Donella H, Dennis L. Meadows, Jorgen Randers and William W. Behrens III (1972), *The Limits to Growth: A Report for the Club of Rome's Project on the Predicament of Mankind*, Universe Books, New York.

Meister Publishing Company (1994), *Farm Chemicals Handbook*, Meister Publishing Company, Willoughby, OH.

Metallgesellschaft AG (1993), *Metal Statistics 1982–1992* (ISSN 0076–6682), Metallgesellschaft AG, Frankfurt am Main, Germany [in German and English].

Meyer, B. (1977), *Sulfur, Energy and Environment*, Elsevier Science Publishers, Amsterdam.

Michelin (1993), 'Michelin and the Environment', *Scientific American*, March:FR16 [Special Advertising Supplement].

Midwest Research Institute (MRI 1980), *Source Category Survey: Secondary Zinc Smelting and Refining Industry*, EPA–450/3–80–012 (PB 80–191604) (PB 80–191604), Midwest Research Institute, 1980.

Morrison, G.F. (1986), *Control of Sulfur Oxides from Coal Combustion*, Technical Report (ICTIS/TR21), IEA Coal Research, London, November.

Morton, W.E. (1978), 'Direct Reduction of Fly Ash into Ferrosilicon', in: Torrey, S. (ed.), *Coal Ash Utilization: Fly Ash, Bottom Ash and Slag*, Noyes Data Corporation, Park Ridge NJ.

Motley, E.P. and T.H. Cosgrove (1978), *Utilization of Lime/Limestone Waste in a New Alumina Extraction Process* (EPA–600/7–78–225), TRW Inc for United States Environmental Protection Agency, Washington DC, November.

Muehlberg, P.T., J.T. Reding, B.P. Shepherd, T. Parsons and G.E. Wilkins (1977), 'Phosphate Rock and Basic Fertilizer Industry', in: *Industrial Process Profiles for Environmental Use*, Chapter 22 (EPA–600/2–77 023v), Government Printing Office, Washington DC, Dow Chemical Company and Radian Corporation, February.

National Academy of Sciences (NAS/NRC) (NAS 1978), *Nitrates: An Environmental Assessment*, Washington DC.

National Academy of Sciences (NAS/NRC 1992). 'Human Causes of Global Change', in: *Global Environmental Change; Understanding the Human Dimension*, Chapter 3:44ff., National Academy Press, Washington DC.

National Materials Advisory Board (NMAB 1979), *Trends in Usage of Cadmium*, Report (NMAB–255), National Materials Advisory Board, Washington DC, November.

Nectoux, François (1991), *Report on the French Nuclear Industry*, cited in Young, 1992.

Nickerson, W.J. (1969), 'Fermentation Advances', in: Perdman, D. (ed.), *Papers of the Third International Fermentation Symposium 1968*:631ff., Academic Press, New York, 1969.

Nickerson, W.J. and M.D. Faber (1972), 'Microbial Degradation and Transformation of Scrap Tire Mesh', 164th Annual Meeting, American Chemical Society, New York, August 1972.

Nowak, Z. (1978), 'Recovery of Minerals and Elements from Ash', in: Torrey, S. (ed.), *Coal Ash Utilization: Fly Ash, Bottom Ash and Slag*, Noyes Data Corporation, Park Ridge NJ.

Noyes, Robert (1993), *Pollution Prevention Technology Handbook*, Noyes Publications, Park Ridge NJ.

Nriagu, Jerome O. (1990), 'Global Metal Pollution', *Environment* **32**(7):7–32.

O'Mara, W.C., R.B. Herring and L.P. Hunt (eds) (1990), *Handbook of Semiconductor Silicon Technology*, Noyes Publications, Park Ridge NJ.

Organization for Economic Cooperation and Development (1991), *The State of the Environment*, OECD, Paris.

Organization for Economic Cooperation and Development, Environmental Directorate (OECD/ED 1974), *Cadmium and the Environment*, OECD, Paris, 1974.

Ottinger, R.S. *et al.*, (1983) *Recommended Methods of Reduction Neutralization, Recovery, or Disposal of Hazardous Waste: Volume XIV; Summary of Waste Origins, Forms and Quantities*, NTIS (PB 224 593/4), TRW Systems, Washington DC, 1983.

Pacyna, Jozef M. (1986), 'Atmospheric Trace Elements from Naturalized Anthropogenic Sources', in: Nriagu, J.O. and C.I. Davidson (eds), *Toxic Metals in the Atmosphere*, John Wiley & Sons, New York.

Papp, John F. (1991), *Chromium, Nickel, and Other Alloying Elements in US-Produced Stainless and Heat-Resisting Steel*, Information Circular (9275), United States Bureau of Mines, Washington DC.

Papp, John F. (1994), 'Chromium Life Cycle Study', Information Circular (9411), United States Bureau of Mines, Washington DC (draft in progress).

Papp, John F. (annual, 1991), *Chromium Annual Report 1991*, United States Government Printing Office, Washington DC.

Papp, John F. (annual 1993), *Chromium Annual Report 1993*, United States Government Printing Office, Washington DC.

Patterson, Sam H. (1977), 'Aluminum from Bauxite: Are There Alternatives?', *American Scientist* **65**, May–June:345–51.

Peacey, J.G. and W.G. Davenport (1974), 'Evaluation of Alternative Methods of Aluminum Production', *Journal of Metals*, July:28.

Peters, Frank A. and Paul W. Johnson (1974), *Revised and Updated Cost Estimates for Producing Alumina from Domestic Raw Materials*, Information Circular (8648), United States Department of the Interior, Washington DC.

Pichat, Philippe (1982), 'Utilization of Gypsum and Phosphogypsum', Internal Report, Azote et Produits Chimiques, Groupe CdF Chimie, Paris, February.

Porter, Michael (1991), 'America's Competitiveness Strategy', *Scientific American*, April.

PWMI (undated), *Weighing Up the Environmental Balance*, PWMI (European Center for Plastics in the Environment), Brussels.

Rathje, William and Cullen Murphy (1992), *Rubbish: The Archaeology of Garbage*, Harper-Collins, New York.

Reeves, Teresa (1990), *Packaging in Europe: Italy*, Special Report (EIU 2049), The Economist Intelligence Unit, London, August.

Renaux, Geneviève (1992), *Packaging in the Single European Market*, Club de Bruxelles, Brussels.

Robinson, E. and R.C. Robbins (1970), 'Gaseous Sulfur Pollutants From Urban and Natural Sources', *Journal of the Air Pollution Control Association*:233–5.

Roskill Information Services Ltd. (Roskill As 1992), *The Economics of Arsenic 1992* (ISBN 0–86214 377–2), Roskill Information Services Ltd., 2 Clapham Rd., London SW9 0JA, 8th edition.

Roskill Information Services Ltd. (Roskill Cd 1990), *The Economics of Cadmium 1990* (ISBN 0–86214 330–6), Roskill Information Services Ltd., 2 Clapham Rd., London SW9 0JA, 7th edition.

Roskill Information Services Ltd. (Roskill Cr 1993), *The Economics of Chromium 1993* (ISBN 0–86214 400–0), Roskill Information Services Ltd., 2 Clapham Rd., London SW9 0JA, 8th edition.

Roskill Information Services Ltd. (Roskill Ga 1990), *The Economics of Gallium 1990* (ISBN 0–86214 328–4), Roskill Information Services Ltd., 2 Clapham Rd., London SW9 0JA, 1990, 5th edition.

Roskill Information Services Ltd. (Roskill Si 1991), *The Economics of Silicon and Ferrosilicon* (ISBN 0–86214), Roskill Information Services Ltd., 2 Clapham Rd., London SW9 0JA, 7th edition.

Roy, R., M.J. Murtha and G. Burnet (1979), 'Industrial Applications of Magnetic Separation', *IEEE*.

Russell, Clifford S. and William J. Vaughan (1976), *Steel Production: Processes, Products and Residuals*, Johns Hopkins University Press, Baltimore MD.

Schlesinger, William H. (1991), *Biogeochemistry; An Analysis of Global Change*, Academic Press, New York.

Schlesinger, William H. and Anne E. Hartley (1992), 'A Global Budget for Atmospheric NH_3', *Biogeochemistry* **15**:191–211.

Semiconductor Industry Association (SIA 1987), *Waste Generation and Disposition Practices and Currently Applied Minimization Techniques Used Within the Semiconductor Industry*, Final Report, Semiconductor Industry Association, Washington DC, August.

Service des Statistiques Industrielles (SESSI 1991), *Production Industrielle: Industrie du Caoutchouc*, Centre D'Enquetes Statistiques, Caen, France.

Shedd, Kim B. (1993), *The Materials Flow of Cobalt in the United States*, Information Circular (IC 9350), United States Bureau of Mines, Washington DC.

Shreve, R. Norris (1956), *The Chemical Process Industries*, McGraw-Hill Book Company, New York.

Smith, V. Kerry (ed.) (1979), *Scarcity and Growth Revisited*, Johns Hopkins University Press, Baltimore.

Solar Energy Research Institute (SERI 1990), *The Potential of Renewable Energy*, Interlaboratory White Paper, Solar Energy Research Institute (SERI),

Golden CO, March (prepared for the Office of Policy Planning and Analysis, United States Department of Energy).

Solow, Robert M. (1956), 'A Contribution to the Theory of Economic Growth', *Quarterly Journal of Economics* **70**:65–94.

Solow, Robert M. (1957), 'Technical Change and the Aggregate Production Function', *Review of Economics and Statistics*, August.

Solow, Robert M. (1974), 'The Economics of Resources and the Resources of Economics', Richard T. Ely Lecture.

Stanford Research Institute (SRI 1989), Chemical Economics Program, 'Special Report on Semiconductor Markets', Palo Alto, Cal.

Starreveld, P. Folkert and Ekko C. van Ierland (c.1994), 'Recycling of Plastics: A Materials Balance Optimization Model', *European Association of Resource Economists* (327).

Stigliani, William D. (1988), 'Changes in Valued "Capacities" of Soils and Sediments as Indicators of Non-Linear and Time-Delayed Environmental Effects', *Environmental Monitoring and Assessment* **10**:245–307.

Stigliani, William M. (undated, c.1988), 'Chemical Emissions from the Processing and Use of Materials: the Need for an Integrated Emissions Accounting System', draft, International Institute for Applied Systems Analysis, Laxenburg, Austria.

Stigliani, William M. (undated c.1989), 'Toxic Materials: Europe 1975–2050', draft, International Institute for Applied Systems Analysis, Laxenburg, Austria.

Sweeney, J.W. (1993), 'Tire Business Keeps Recycling On', *The Earth Times*, March 21.

Taylor, S.R. and S.M. McLennan (1985), *The Continental Crust: Its Composition and Evolution*, Blackwell Scientific Publications, New York.

Tellus Institute (1992), *CSG/Tellus Packaging Study: Inventory of Material and Energy Use and Air and Water Emissions from the Production of Packaging Materials*, Technical Report (89–024/2), Tellus Institute, Boston MA, May (prepared for the Council of State Governments and the United States Environmental Protection Agency).

Thiemens, Mark H. and William C. Trogler (1991), 'Nylon Production: An Unknown Source of Atmospheric Nitrous Oxide', *Science* **251**:932–4.

Towle, Stewart W. (1993), *World Copper Smelter Sulfur Balance 1988*, Information Circular (IC 9349), United States Bureau of Mines, Washington DC.

United Nations Statistical Office (UNSO 1988), 'Industrial Statistics', Vol 2 N.Y.

United States Bureau of Mines (USBuMines 1975), *Mineral Facts and Problems*, United States Government Printing Office, Washington DC.

United States Bureau of Mines (USBuMines 1977), *Minerals Yearbook*, United States Government Printing Office, Washington DC.

United States Bureau of Mines (USBuMines 1985), *Mineral Facts and Problems*, United States Government Printing Office, Washington DC.

United States Bureau of Mines (USBuMines 1989), *Minerals Yearbook*, United States Government Printing Office, Washington DC.

United States Bureau of Mines (USBuMines 1991), *Minerals Yearbook; Volume I: Metals and Minerals* (ISBN 0–16–041842–9), United States Government Printing Office, Washington DC.

United States Bureau of Mines (USBuMines 1991a), 'Mineral Industries of Europe and Central Asia', United States Government Printing Office, Washington D.C.

United States Bureau of Mines (USBuMines 1992), *Gallium*, USBM Information Circular (IC9208), United States Bureau of Mines, Washington DC.

United States Bureau of Mines, (USBuMines 1993) 'Chromium Life Cycle Study', United States Bureau of Mines, Washington DC, August 12 (Draft).

United States Bureau of Mines (USBuMines 1994), *Mineral Commodity Summaries*, United States Bureau of Mines, Washington DC.

United States Bureau of Mines (USBuMines 1994a), *Cadmium in 1993*, Mineral Industry Surveys, United States Bureau of Mines, Washington DC, November.

United States Bureau of Mines (USBuMines annual), *Minerals Yearbook*, United States Government Printing Office, Washington DC, annual.

United States Department of Commerce (USDOC 1988), International Trade Administration, *Overview on the Use and Storage of Coal Combustion Ash in the United States*, Discussion Paper, United States Department of Commerce, Washington DC, November.

United States Environmental Protection Agency (USEPA 1978), *Mobile Source Emission Factors*, Technical Report (EPA–400/9–78–005), United States Environmental Protection Agency, Washington DC, September.

United States Environmental Protection Agency (USEPA 1979), *Methods of Controlling NO_X in Combustion*, Technical Report (EPA 600/7–79–178 e,f,g), United States Environmental Protection Agency, Cincinnati OH.

United States Environmental Protection Agency (USEPA 1984), *Annual Hazardous Waste Generator Report 1984*, United States Environmental Protection Agency, Washington DC.

United States Environmental Protection Agency (USEPA 1987), *Annual Hazardous Waste Generator Report 1987*, United States Environmental Protection Agency, Washington DC.

United States Environmental Protection Agency (USEPA undated), *Compilation of Air Pollutant Emission Factors*, Technical Report (AP–42), United States Environmental Protection Agency, Research Triangle Park NC (Supplements 1–13).

United States International Trade Commission (USITC 1991), *Synthetic Organic Chemicals 1991*, United States Government Printing Office, Washington DC.

Voigt, Claus (1982), 'The Materials Cycle of Cobalt in Magnets', in: *Materials and Society*, Chapter 4:465–8 **6**, Pergamon Press, New York.

von Weizsäcker, Ernst Ulrich (1991), *Erdpolitik* (ISBN 3–534–10998–8), Darmstadt, Germany.

von Weizsäcker, Ernst Ulrich and Jochen Jesinghaus (1992), *Ecological Tax Reform: A Policy Proposal for Sustained Development* (ISBN 1–85649–096–3), Zed Books, London.

Waldichuk, M. (1977), *Global Marine Pollution: An Overview*, UNESCO, Paris.

Walley, Noah and B. Whitehead (1994), 'It's Not Easy Being "Green"', *Harvard Business Review*, May–June:46.

World Energy Council (1992), *1992 Survey of Energy Resources*, World Energy Council.

World Health Organization (1982), *Rapid Assessment of Sources of Air, Water and Land Pollution*, World Health Organization, Geneva, Switzerland.

Williams, Robert H. and Eric D. Larson (1993), 'Advanced Gasification-based Biomass Power Generation', in: Johansson, T.B., H. Kelly, A.K. Reddy and R.H. Williams (eds), *Renewable Energy: Sources for Fuels and Electricity*, Chapter 17, Island Press, Washington DC.

Williams, Robert H., Eric D. Larson, Ryan E. Katofsky and Jeff Chen (1994), *Methanol and Hydrogen from Biomass for Transportation*, Biomass Resources: A Means to Sustainable Development, BioResources 94, Bangalore, India, October 3–7.

Windom, H.L. and R.A. Duce (1977), *Marine Pollutant Transfer*, Lexington Books, New York.

Wood, J.M. (1974), 'Biological Cycles for Toxic Elements in the Environment', *Science* **183**:1049–52.

World Resources Foundation (WRF 1994), *Warmer*, Information Bulletin, World Resources Foundation, London.

World Resources Institute (WRI 1994), *World Resources 1994–1995*, Oxford University Press, New York.

Wormgoor, J.W. (1994), *Sources of Dioxin Emissions into the Air in Western Europe*, Report, TNO Institute of Environmental and Energy Technology, Apeldoorn, Netherlands, November.

Worrell, E., B. Meuleman and K. Blok (1994), 'Energy Savings by Efficient Application of Fertilizers', unpublished report, Utrecht University, Utrecht, Netherlands.

Young, John E. (1992), 'Aluminum's Real Tab', *Worldwatch* **5**(2), March–April.

Yun, C.K., S.B. Park and W.H. Park (1980), *Aluminum Kombinat; An Integral Utilization of Low Grade Anthracites for Simultaneous Recovery of Aluminum and Energy*, Fourth Joint Meeting, MMIJ–AIME, Tokyo.

Zebrowski, M. and Pawel Rejewski (1987), 'Technological Innovations for Ecologically Sustainable Development: The Case of the Chemical and Energy Industries in the Context of National Economic Development', draft, Industrial Chemistry Research Institute, Warsaw, Poland, January.

Index of individual chemicals and chemical compounds

(see general index for occurrences in context; e.g. smelting, aluminum)

Index of organizations

General Index